Contents

C000181773

At Nottingham's Victoria Baths, where Rebecca Adlington did much of her early training, and as at so many historic baths around Britain over the last few decades, swimmers rally in support of their local pool, following closure threats in February 2008. At the last count there were some 20 active campaign groups in Britain fighting to save their local pools.

Foreword

by Rebecca Adlington

I suppose I must have swum in at least 40 or 50 swimming pools around the country since I started, and like most swimmers there are some that I like and some that I don't. But if you have swum in one particular pool all your life then it does mean something to you.

You always have a connection to that place.

For me, Sherwood Baths in Mansfield Woodhouse is my special pool. It's only a two minute walk from where we lived. It isn't necessarily the best pool, but it's not just about that.

I was four when my mum first took me, and both my sisters and I learnt to swim there. We sort of grew up there too, wearing the yellow and black colours of the Sherwood Swimming Club.

I hadn't realised until Ian Gordon told me that it was built as long as ago as 1934 and that it was paid for by the local coal miners' welfare fund. I don't think there any miners in our family but I'm grateful for what those men did.

When I was thirteen I made the step up to the Nova Centurion Swimming Club, which meant a

completely new regime for me and for my mum Kay, who gave up her job to help me, getting up at five every morning so that I could train with the club at the Nottingham Victoria Baths before the public were allowed in.

I always knew the pool there was old. Sometimes it had to close so they could repair the roof or something like that, and there are really strong pumps at the end of the outside lanes that would just blow you right back so you couldn't come in to turn properly. So naturally I tried to avoid those.

Of course when you're a competitive swimmer you don't take much notice of a pool's history, but I quite understand why people feel so strongly about saving their particular pool. After I'd been swimming with the club for around five or six years we found out that the Victoria Baths might be closing, so our coach decided to move us to Beechdale.

My main concern, whether a pool is brand new or a hundred years old is that a pool itself must be clean. Light is also important. If there's a lot of glass around the

pool you can tell whether its day or night time outside, and if you're up before the dawn or training on winter evenings that really makes a difference, because if it's not really well lit inside then even before you go in you can feel tired and a bit lethargic. Also, at some pools, I can't explain it, you feel like you're swimming through treacle.

So every pool does have its own character, and even though we competition swimmers need to have the best possible facilities, it is just as important that children have a pool near to them where they can learn and feel part of something, like I did.

For me to be part of Olympic history after my two gold medals in Beijing is amazing, and now that they are going to name Sherwood Baths after me I will be even more part of history. It's such an honour, which is why I am also delighted to be linked with this book. So many lovely pools to look at and enjoy.

It makes me realise that all us swimmers are part of a very long and proud tradition.

Long may it continue.

Just what the doctor ordered – Dr Ian Gordon, lifelong chronicler of swimming pools but also Chief Medical Officer for British Swimming and doctor to the GB swimming team at the 2008 Beijing Olympics, meets up with Rebecca Adlington at the Water Cube just after she had won the first of two gold medals, in the 400m freestyle. The last British swimmer to have won more than a single Olympic gold medal was Henry Taylor of Chadderton, a century before in 1908.

Tadley Pool, by S & P Architects – opened at a cost of just £2.8m in 1999 – offers a modern take on a classic layout, with a deck level 25m pool, a moveable floor, timber and brick cladding and roof lights that provide natural lighting but minimal glare. It is a design that would be instantly familiar to Victorian architects, yet one filled with technological wonders.

Introduction

by Keith Ashton, S & P Architects

In common with most people my first experience of visiting a public indoor swimming pool – 'the baths' as they were more commonly known – was at an early age. Urmston Baths, just outside Manchester, was my local, and even now I can still conjure up how I felt as a toddler, staring up into its wonderful glass dome and the Art Deco curves and angles of its soaring vaults and staircases, and of being inspired by the neatly inscribed honours boards, listing champions and swimming club captains of the past.

I shall never forget the cold floors either.

Going to the baths then, as now, was a real rite of passage, and for me an unforgettable introduction to the architectural order and formality that distinguishes so many of our historic baths.

S & P Architects began designing aquatic facilities in the late 1970s, and have since become leaders in this most specialist of areas, having successfully completed hundreds of projects.

Throughout the last four decades, whether working on a small community pool (such as Tadley, *opposite*), a regional centre of excellence, or, as recently, on international aquatic centres, our key design drivers have remained unchanged; that is, to promote increased user participation, to encourage pool users to return regularly, and to provide, for those who can exceed performance expectations, unrivalled world class facilities.

As architects frequently called upon both to refurbish old pools, and to design new facilities, ever changing social and economic patterns require us to continually refine the swimming experience.

We also have to recognise that in these more financially constrained times, the civic pride that was so clearly articulated in many of the ornate structures featured within *Great Lengths* can seem a distant aspiration for local authorities.

Yet time and time again we have been able to show, like many of the baths designers of the past, that proper investment in these assets can reap rewards not only in terms of the revenues generated but more importantly in the improved health and wellbeing of the community itself.

It is often said that a building is never finished, and this is especially true of swimming pools. Changes in technology, in legislation and in fashion mean that we must continually update and improve our pools to ensure their popularity and viability.

But pools designers of today can no longer assume that it is better to demolish and rebuild rather than to preserve and upgrade existing pools. At one of S & P's current regeneration projects, for example – the Grade A listed Royal Commonwealth Pool in Edinburgh – the introduction of modern sustainable technology has resulted in a saving of 400 tonnes of CO_2 emissions per year.

Schemes like this show that the re-use of historic pools can

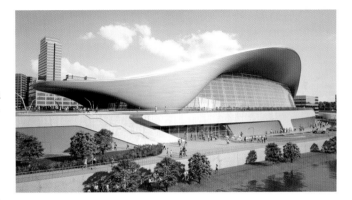

and do deliver economic and social sustainability, not only by investing in the fabric of buildings but also by ensuring that their core activities are more directly targeted to the needs and demands of the community.

Unfortunately it is too late for my beloved Urmston Baths. It was demolished in 1987.

But my hope is that this unique overview of our surviving historic baths will, in addition to serving as an invaluable record of Britain's swimming heritage, also serve to raise awareness of the need to retain and improve buildings that are not just historic places to swim, but great community and national assets too.

At S & P we are therefore proud to support this important work by Dr Ian Gordon and Simon Inglis under the auspices of English Heritage.

In completing this study they and their team of researchers have clearly gone to great lengths.

So please, dip in and enjoy!

'Only rarely do pool architects gain the opportunity to build a pool of genuine national and international significance, such as the Empire Pool at Wembley and Crystal Palace,' writes Keith Ashton. 'We hope that the London Aquatic Centre being designed by Zaha Hadid and S&P, which will be used for the 2012 Olympic and Paralympic Games, and by local and national swimmers for many years after, will in time be celebrated with equal enthusiasm. Pool design is always a huge challenge. But in a nation of swimmers, a great honour too.'

'Public baths reflect honour on the town, bestow abundant credit on the council, are model sanitary purifiers, and are hourly bestowing blessings, cheap, pure, and healthful, on the toiling masses of this great community.'
Quote by Hugh Shimmin from the *Liverpool Mercury,* 1856. Spittoon, vintage 1904, at Manningham Baths, Bradford, 2008.

Chapter One

Great Lengths

Swimming, or more accurately the provision of facilities for swimming, has become in recent years one of the most contentious areas of public policy; its waters rippling with claims and counter-claims, and muddied by a daunting array of statistics, reports and strategy documents.

On one hand we are told that the first decade of the 21st century has witnessed a significant rise in the number of indoor pools in Britain – probably the largest increase since the boom years of the 1960s and 1970s – that more pools are opening than closing, and that more National Lottery funding has been expended on swimming than on any other sport or recreation.

Most recently, in June 2008 the Government announced a £140 million package of grants for local authorities wishing to extend free swimming to all 60 year olds and over and all 16s and under from April 2009.

But for every good news story, it seems, there is so often a caveat.

Swimmers, as *Played in Britain* discovered whilst compiling *Liquid Assets* – Janet Smith's 2005 study

of open air pools (*see* Links) – tend to be both passionate about their sport and highly protective of their local facilities.

As many a politician would attest, as a lobbying group they are difficult to ignore.

Firstly, there are so many of them. According to the Amateur Swimming Association (ASA) – the sport's governing body in England, founded in 1869 – nearly one in ten of us swims weekly, and between 12–16 per cent of the adult population across England, Scotland and Wales swim monthly.

In 2001, the Local Government Association estimated that 80 million visits a year are made to pools in the public sector alone.

Amongst the over 60s swimming is the most popular form of participation activity, with seven per cent taking a dip once a week, while amongst 11–16 year olds, 38 per cent swim at least once a month.

In survey after survey, only walking emerges as a more popular form of recreation.

Secondly, unlike most sports, swimming is no longer a man's

world. Swimming is now the most popular sport for girls, and a high proportion of swimmers at every level are female (which may explain why so many pool campaign groups have been led by women who have established close ties with a particular pool or swimming club through years of social and family activities).

Thirdly, swimmers are great believers in the positive benefits that swimming brings to the health (physical and mental), welfare and social cohesion of a community, a belief that appears to be backed by teachers, social researchers, health professionals and a mass of evidence, academic and anecdotal.

But if the benefits of swimming are nowadays uncontested, the resolution of how many pools we should have, and of which variety, and where, and how they can be afforded, remains as elusive and as divisive an issue as ever.

In 2002 Sport England calculated that merely to modernise the country's existing stock of pools, 60 per cent of which were 20–40 years old, would cost £2 billion. »

A post war school badge reminds us that the experience of going to a public swimming pool is one shared by the vast majority of people in Britain. Perhaps you too earned one of these, or a similar life saving badge? Every swimmer has his or her own motivation. Some choose to swim for fitness, some for sport, some for fun or to accompany family members. As a result every swimmer has his or her own notion as to what makes the ideal pool. But in one respect swimmers are united. All swimmers believe that swimming enhances life, and that no-one should be denied its benefits.

The majority of pools featured in *Great Lengths* fall within the following categories:

The **public** sector, including baths funded by philanthropists for use in the public sector (such as Hereford's former baths, *above*, located, of course, on Bath Street) The **private and commercial** sectors, including members-only clubs, staff association clubs, spas, hotels and holiday camps **Educational** institutions, such as schools, colleges and universities **Military** establishments

Note that no residential pools are featured, and that although our emphasis is on public provision, because so few pre–1945 indoor pools survive from other sectors, these are included where deemed to be of historical or architectural significance.

Post 1945 our focus rests solely upon the public sector.

» According to a 2001 report portentously titled *The Ticking Time Bomb*, the equivalent sum for Scottish pools was estimated at £544 million over 20 years.

Various tools exist to aid decision makers as to how these resources should be invested.

For example, the Facilities Planning Model, first evolved during the 1980s at the University of Edinburgh, seeks to establish supply and demand in any one area based upon such factors as population, participation rates and catchment areas.

Another method, called the Comprehensive Performance Assessment, evaluates not only the population within a 20 minute travel time but also the quality of facilities on offer.

That quality, as numerous observers have stressed, varies a great deal.

For example, the ASA considers that many of the new indoor pools counted in government statistics are not 'fit for purpose' because they are too small or too shallow, or because they are irregularly shaped leisure or 'splash' pools, unsuited to swimming or learning.

Competition swimmers protest further that there are not enough 50m, or Olympic-sized pools. In late 2008 the whole of Britain had only 23 indoor pools measuring 50m, compared with, say, 18 in Paris alone and 19 in Berlin.

The Great Britain Diving Federation, meanwhile, cites the loss of 78 per cent of diving facilities since 1977, the majority owing to health and safety issues.

The ASA and other critics also point out that most of the new pools are in the private sector and are unaffordable for the majority.

And while the number of indoor pools has undoubtedly

risen overall, in certain cities, such as London, Manchester and Birmingham, the number of public pools has actually dropped, or their redistribution has left some districts without facilities that were once taken for granted.

As to school facilities, according to the Central Council of Physical Recreation in 2006, the loss of 2–3,000 school pools since 1972 has been a major factor in one in six eleven year olds being unable to swim 25m, as required by the National Curriculum, and only three in ten knowing basic survival techniques in water. Each year, say the statistics, around 50 under 16 year olds drown.

To those readers who have participated in any one of the many lobby groups to have emerged since the 1990s, statistics of the sort cited here are all too familiar.

They crop up again and again; in *Testing the Waters*, a House of Commons Select Committee Report of 2002; in ASA and Sport England documents, in regular campaign reports in the *Daily Telegraph*, on numerous websites and on the airwaves generally.

Readers may find plenty more within the sources and forums listed in our *Links* section.

But, in this context we mention these statistics primarily as background, to set the scene.

For vital and important though the swimming debate undoubtedly is in contemporary Britain, it is not the purpose of *Great Lengths* to pass comment on the modern day provision of swimming facilities, or to argue for the construction of more pools.

Nor is it our aim to consider the future of aquatic sports.

Our prime concern is for historic indoor pools, and for the heritage of swimming.

Historic pools – a definition

Amid all the complexities that inform and influence the operation, funding and planning of Britain's swimming facilities lies one important truth.

Britain has a stock of historic pools that is unrivalled by any other nation.

For the purpose of this study an historic pool is defined as one that opened prior to 1970 and that retains a significant number of original features.

The term 'historic' does not automatically ascribe to a building any architectural merit.

Nor does it mean that the building is listed. For example, the oldest operational indoor pool our research has discovered – the 1864 Boys' Pool at Crossley Heath School, Halifax (see page 49) – is, and always has been, a building of modest pretensions and, as of late 2008, was not listed.

The cut-off year of 1970 has been adopted because that is the date of Britain's most modern listed pool, the Royal Commonwealth Pool in Edinburgh, listed Grade A by Historic Scotland.

Historic pools and heritage

Historic pools, and particularly those built in the public sector, are not only important local resources, but also form an intrinsic part of our national heritage.

Along with schools, libraries, hospitals, town halls, museums, art galleries and parks, historic public pools offer tangible evidence of the civic ideals upon which our communities were moulded in previous centuries; built not for private gain but for the public good.

That more historic pools survive in Britain than in other countries is owing to a number of factors.

Partly it is because, as a result of the industrial revolution and rapid urbanisation during the 19th century, we started to build public baths – of which swimming pools formed originally only one element – earlier than other developed nations.

Britain's first publicly funded baths appeared in Liverpool in 1829 (see page 24). A national movement in England then started in earnest with the passing of the Baths and Wash Houses Act in 1846, spreading to Wales in the 1860s and to Scotland in the 1870s.

As shown in Table 1 (right), since 1846 the overall trend in the number of public baths which feature one or more swimming pools has always been upward, even if the rate of construction has varied considerably.

But this still does not explain why so many of our older baths have survived.

One reason is that, particularly during the late 19th and early 20th centuries, baths were built so robustly and using such high quality materials that – interludes of inadequate maintenance and under-funding notwithstanding – they have endured extremely well and in some cases much better than many of their modern counterparts.

Also significant is the fact that in certain towns and cities, and at certain periods in history (most notably after the Second World War and again during the 1980s), a lack of investment in modern facilities meant that older buildings had to be patched up and kept in service longer than might otherwise have been the case. They have survived, in other words, by default.

There is one other reason, however, why so many of Britain's historic pools have survived, and that is because they are so highly treasured by their users, and have been so carefully nursed by generations of dedicated pool managers and attendants.

The expression that crops up most often when discussing historic pools is 'much-loved'.

And of course buildings that are much loved are also fiercely defended.

Granted, not all defenders of old pools are motivated by the historic or architectural value of the building. They may simply be fighting to retain a local facility that is otherwise not due to be replaced.

We must also concede that not all historic pools are attractive, convenient or well equipped.

Yet somehow, when factoring in all the diverse motives that inspire swimmers and local residents to campaign on behalf of a threatened pool, it is safe to assert that historic pools retain qualities and inspire loyalties that modern pools are seldom able to match.

But are such loyalties enough?

Britain may indeed possess an impressive stock of historic indoor swimming pools.

But it is a stock whose numbers are dwindling rapidly.

Historic pools – statistics
All statistics relating to swimming pools, historic or modern, need to be cited with great caution.

Only figures for the public sector are reasonably reliable, and across all sectors, overall numbers tell only one part of the story.

For example, Table 3 (overleaf) shows there to be 144 surviving historic baths from all sectors dating from before 1945, where at least one original pool remains operational as of late 2008, or »

Table 1: Public pools in use, by year		
		sites
1880	England	83
	Scotland	2
	Wales	1
	Total	**86**
		sites-pools
1918	England	327-544
	Scotland	35-50
	Wales	6-10
	Total	**368-604**
		sites
1967	England	666
	Scotland	119
	Wales	19
	Total	**804**
		sites
1978	England	898
	Scotland	103
	Wales	75
	Total	**1,076**
		sites-pools
2008	England	876-1587
	Scotland	165-259
	Wales	126-176
	Total	**1,167-2,022**

Table 2: Indoor pool totals for England, Scotland and Wales by sector		
		sites-pools
1918	Public	368-604
	Private	58-69
	Education	95-96
	Other*	10-10
	Total	**531-779**
		sites-pools
2008	Public	1167-2022
	Private	1438-1585
	Education	981-1048
	Other*	52-62
	Total	**3,638-4,717**

* includes health authorities, police and fire services, MOD and charitable trusts

◄ Apart from the periods 1914–25 and 1939–60, the national trend in the provision of public baths has been steadily upwards, as shown in **Table 1**, although this trend masks a reduction in several urban areas since the 1990s.

The figures for 1880 and 1918 are based on the Carnegie UK Trust's *Report on Public Baths and Wash Houses in the United Kingdom* (see *Links*), supplemented by the authors' own researches. The 1967 and 1978 figures derive from reports by the Sports Council.

Detailed, reliable data beyond the public sector cannot be sourced for most periods, hence **Table 2** compares only the 1918 figures with those of 2008.

The 2008 figures are based on databases maintained by Sport England, sportscotland and the Sports Council for Wales, supplemented by *Played in Britain* researches.

Note that in Table 2 a margin of error of ten per cent should be allowed for the private sector, where, it can be seen, numbers have risen the most.

What these figures do not show is that there was also a rapid rise in the number of school pools built after 1950, to an estimated total of 5,000 by 1969.

Thus the 2008 figures for the education sector reflect a recent decline, not a rise.

Table 3 records the number of pre-1945 sites where at least one pool remains in use, such as Glasgow's Arlington Baths Club (*above*), one of seven survivors from the 1870s.

| Table 3: Pre-1945 sites still in use for swimming, or in the process of being refurbished for swimming, in England, Scotland and Wales, as of late 2008, by decade of construction |

p public *c* commercial/private
n navy *e* educational

	total sites	by sector
1860s	1	1*e*
1870s	7	3*p* 3*c* 1*e*
1880s	12	8*p* 4*e*
1890s	26	20*p* 1*c* 5*e*
1900s	30	23*p* 2*c* 4*e* 1*n*
1910s	12	8*p* 1*c* 3*e*
1920s	19	18*p* 1*e*
1930s	36	36*p*
1940s	1	1*p*
Total	144	117*p* 7*c* 19*e* 1*n*

» where pools are currently being refurbished.

Of these 144 sites, it will be noted, 117 are in the public sector.

Further analysis of public sector pools built during the post war period shows there to be 142 sites dating from 1945–70 that have at least one swimming pool in use as of late 2008.

In the public sector as a whole therefore, there are 259 operational sites dating from 1970 or before, which constitutes 22 per cent of the nation's stock.

Those numbers and percentages are destined to fall steadily over the next decade, however.

Of course there has always been a steady turnover of public baths, ever since the first generation of buildings – erected during the 1840s and 1850s – were replaced in the later decades of the 19th century. Thus a number of the historic baths we now treasure were themselves built to replace existing buildings that had historic or architectural merit of their own.

However, it was only in the 1970s that widespread closures of baths dating from before 1939 started in earnest. In Chapter Seven we touch briefly on some of the earliest campaigns set up to counter this trend.

Ironically, and for reasons discussed in Chapter Six, one of the highest rates of closures during the late 20th century related to public baths built as recently as the 1960s.

Of an estimated 197 built during that difficult decade for baths design, 55 had been demolished by late 2008.

By comparison, a far greater proportion of Victorian and Edwardian baths enjoyed much longer lifespans, typically varying between 70–100 years.

That said, the rate of closures of sites dating from before 1945 shows no sign of easing.

Between 2000 and late 2008 at least 20 sites from pre-1945 shut down, at an average of 2–3 per year, the highest toll being six closures in 2005.

A further five more sites at least are scheduled to close by 2010, and for a further eleven at least the short term future must be regarded as extremely uncertain.

It is also reasonable to assume that the closure rate will continue at existing levels during the period 2010–20, after which it will almost certainly accelerate, given that by 2020, half the nation's surviving pre-1970 baths will be over a century old.

But as stated earlier, numbers alone are only part of the story.

What counts more is that we do not lose buildings of genuine quality or importance.

In identifying those baths that should be saved, it is equally crucial that we take into account the wider social and cultural history of bathing, and acknowledge the heritage of aquatic sport too.

To aid in this process, a list of all 288 known surviving sites dating from before 1945 can be found in the Directory on page 278.

Of these 288 sites, 144 were operational as of late 2008 for swimming, wholly or partially (that is, several also have pools that have been either closed, mothballed or boarded over for other uses).

The remaining 144 are those sites where all or part of the original structures survive, but where swimming no longer takes place. Several of these are featured in Chapter Eight, which focuses on the adaptive re-use of historic baths buildings.

Listed baths

Of 288 wholly or partially surviving structures in the Directory, 116 are listed as being of architectural or historical importance.

These include 84 in England, 29 in Scotland and three in Wales.

(Note that the Directory includes only baths which have, at one time or another, featured swimming pools. Buildings such as 'cottage baths' that housed only baths for washing, are not included.)

Of the 84 listed baths in England, six are Grade II*, although one of these is the Royal Automobile Club, whose pool forms only a small part of the overall listed structure. Only three of the six still have operational pools, or will have once current refurbishment work has been completed.

The remaining 78 in England are listed Grade II, of which only 31 have operational pools, or will have after current refurbishment.

Of the 29 listed structures in Scotland, two are Category A, both currently open; 25 are Category B, of which 16 have operational pools, or will have after current refurbishment; and two are Category C(S), both closed.

All three listed structures in Wales are Grade II, but none remains in use for swimming.

Design and management issues

Architectural or historical significance alone offers no guarantee that an historic pool will remain open for swimming. By their very nature, indoor pools are complex buildings, expensive to operate and reliant upon a finely tuned matrix of building services.

The reason for this, need it be stated, is that unlike other buildings they accommodate large bodies of water in an enclosed environment.

Because that water, and the air around that water, has also to be heated, an indoor pool is uniquely exposed to those two fearsome enemies of the built environment, humidity and condensation. (Think of your own bathroom writ large.)

Add to this punishing levels of usage by the public, plus the potentially corrosive influence of chlorine containing compounds in the atmosphere (resulting from the use of chlorine-based disinfectants in pool water), and it can be appreciated just how important good design, high quality materials and regular maintenance is, particularly if the building in question is an old one.

In recent years, as highlighted on the right, historic baths have had to meet a further challenge to their constitution, in that they must now cope with far higher water and air temperatures than those for which they were originally designed.

It does not necessarily follow that older buildings are less able to withstand these conditions than modern ones, however. Indeed tests have shown that with their thick, loadbearing masonry and brick walls, and their smaller areas of glazing, properly maintained Victorian and Edwardian baths can actually be more thermally efficient than many modern counterparts.

Their original surfaces, such as glazed bricks and tiles, are also well able to cope with more aggressive atmospheres.

Nor are there any reasons why, other than an initial capital outlay, older baths cannot be fitted with modern heat recovery systems, or have their exposed metalwork treated with modern protective paints, or be fitted with any one of a number of technical innovations

that make 21st century pools so much more energy efficient than their predecessors.

Nevertheless, there are certain design and management issues that need always to be taken into account when considering the viability and future usage of historic baths.

Poolside cubicles, which were phased out in new baths after the late 1920s, but which survive in several earlier examples, present particular challenges to pool managers in terms of hygiene, security and the number of bathers able to use the pool at any one time.

Many historic pools from before the 1930s are characterised by their intricate and often vulnerable roof systems, which require regular attention. Examples of this can be seen at Kentish Town, London (*see page 104*) and Victoria Baths, Manchester (*page 143*).

Awkward access to gutters, pipes, air ducts, cabling and drains can also be problematic and expensive to work around, while there exists a whole raft of health and safety issues, and issues of accessibility, that were simply not factored into the design of older baths, and which frequently require attention and expensive remedial work.

Historic pools are rarely suitable for competitive swimming, for which organisers require pools of a standard 25m or 50m length, or for competition diving.

They are also less attractive to teenagers or family groups who may be seeking a more varied aquatic experience with flumes, slides and sundry other amenities (such as car parking areas).

Given these drawbacks, it is little surprise that when faced with the option of refurbishment

or replacement, many a local authority has opted for the latter, particularly if the old pool occupies a valuable site, or if there are grants or tranches of private investment on offer for new facilities tied up with other leisure or sporting developments.

Why, therefore, persist with an historic pool?

Indoor pools – the power of place
Swimmers, readers will hardly need reminding, often develop strong emotional bonds with pools, be they historic or modern, not only as buildings but as key points of reference within their own personal histories.

This is particularly true of public pools, where perhaps one's forebears, one's children and one's friends have swum over the course of several generations.

And because virtually every British person has, at one time or another in their lives, had the experience of swimming in a public pool, almost everyone has a view to express or a memory to share, be it warming or chilling, happy or (often) humiliating.

Britain's collective pool of memories, as is evident from our researches, is both deep and abiding.

Why so? Perhaps it is because a visit to an indoor pool can be such an intensely physical experience, 》

▲ Down in the boiler room of **Moseley Road Baths, Birmingham**, the temperature gauges tell their own story. When the baths opened in 1907 water was commonly heated to around 68°F (or 20°C). By the 1930s this had risen to 69°F in summer and 72°F in winter.

Government advice in 1962 then set a higher recommended range of 72–76° (22.2–24.5°C). Yet today's norms are 26–27°C for training and competition pools and, as seen above, 28°C for standard pools and at least 30°C for teaching pools.

In short, modern swimmers are a cosseted bunch, for which we are now paying the price, in terms of energy costs and in the added strain which higher temperatures impose upon the fabric of our pools, old and new.

Since this image was taken in 2003, for example, the main pool at Moseley Road has been mothballed. Hotter temperatures are only part of the problem, but they hardly help.

▲ For Britain's aquatic sportsmen and women, indoor pools are not merely places to swim or dive but places to watch events, to train and to socialise. As Rebecca Adlington wrote, her home pool in Mansfield was like a second home as a child.

The multi-functional **Billingham Forum**, **Stockton-on-Tees**, opened in 1967 and with a sports hall, ice rink, indoor bowls hall and a Grade II listed theatre on the same site,

is home to the Billingham Amateur Swimming Club, the Hartlepool Triathletes Club, four sub-aqua clubs and a life saving club.

In 2008, 1,176 such clubs were affiliated to the ASA, plus a further 167 in Scotland and 103 in Wales. Some 237 of these clubs are over a century old, of which Brighton SC, formed in 1860, is the oldest.

Given swimming's history and its popularity it is thus unfortunate that it has no museum or central archive, and that it is largely left to private collectors to safeguard so much of the sport's proud heritage. This Edwardian souvenir card for the **Leeds Swimming Club**, formed in 1866, for example, is just one of hundreds of items assiduously gathered by Joan Gurney of Essex, who has amassed at her own expense Britain's largest collection of historic swimming costumes.

An historic baths building would surely make a fine museum setting for such an important collection.

and one that therefore leaves a lasting impression.

All the transitional states that going for a swim entails – from outdoors to indoors, from clothed to unclothed to costumed, from dry to wet, hot to cold, and back again – ensure that swimmers interact with the essence of an indoor pool to a degree that is rare in other buildings.

As we move from one part of the building to another we feel on our exposed skins and in our lungs the changes in temperature and humidity of our surrounds.

Swimming pools are supremely tactile locations. We touch, we grab, we brush against a range of surfaces with our bare feet and hands. We hear sounds, muffled and echoing, soft and hard. We detect odours, natural and man-made. The quality of the light changes at each turn.

Space and water, intimacy and anonymity we share with complete strangers; at once both part of a communal experience, yet locked within our own private worlds.

And because each and every one of our senses is so powerfully assailed – whether we swim with vigour or simply splash for fun – our reactions to the qualities and faults of the building are that much more intensely felt.

As a result, to swim in an indoor pool is, in effect, to subconsciously test and to evaluate the building at every level; its design, its services, its upkeep, its very functionality.

Hence, it follows that the experience of swimming in an historic pool is palpably different from swimming in a modern pool.

Not necessarily better. But indubitably different.

An historic pool looks different. It sounds different. It smells different. It feels different.

Perhaps, ultimately, this 'power of place' is why so many swimmers have campaigned so vigorously to save their local historic pool.

For here are buildings that are not only much loved, but much used.

Sources and approach
Research for this study has been assisted by five main sources.

These have been the records of English Heritage, the archive of co-author Dr Ian Gordon, the pioneering work undertaken in the early 1980s by SAVE Britain's Heritage (which resulted in an exhibition and booklet called *Taking the Plunge*), numerous historical reports on individual baths drawn up by such companies as Alan Baxter Associates and the Architectural History Practice (to name but two), and finally the unpublished dissertations of several individuals.

Among these mention must be made of Michael Copeman (on pre-1914 London baths), Simon Ramsden (on the north west) and Douglas Campbell (on Scotland).

There also exists a wealth of fascinating published material on the subject.

Since the mid 19th century a number of architectural, engineering and trade journals have reported faithfully on the progress and development of baths, starting with their creation as buildings for sanitary purposes, before evolving into the fitness and leisure centres that we know today.

Indeed it is fair to say that no other branch of sporting or recreational architecture has been more comprehensively written about than swimming baths.

Yet the vast bulk of this reporting, supplemented by a succession of excellent design guides, manuals and reference works – some as early as the 1850s – has been written from a technical point of view, addressed to a specialist audience.

Great Lengths is therefore an attempt to distill all these sources into a single volume directed at lay readers, while in addition, for the first time ever, to record, describe and illustrate the best and most interesting of the hundred or more surviving buildings that form the legacy of that single piece of enlightened legislation, the 1846 Baths and Wash House Act.

Having undertaken that task, the authors are acutely aware that some readers will feel aggrieved that their own much loved pool has not received sufficient attention. But had we included all the wonderful material we had to hand, the book would have expanded to twice its current size.

At the same time *Great Lengths* is not intended to be either an encyclopedia or a gazetteer.

We have also eschewed delving too deeply into technical issues, on the assumption that readers interested in such matters as water filtration, sterilisation, boiler technology and the like will find plenty of references to follow up in our Links section.

Instead, in support of the brief narratives that focus mainly on the years 1846–1970, we have selected a number of case studies based on the following criteria.

Firstly, the building in question must still stand, whether in use for swimming or not.

Secondly, it must either be of architectural significance or of historical significance, as a building *per se*, or within the wider context of British aquatic sports.

Thirdly, at least one element of its development, or of its structure

or fittings or decorative features, must enhance in one way or another our sum of knowledge, so that we may gain a clearer and more comprehensive overview of the current state and future fate of all historic baths.

For each case study there is an information box.

This gives opening dates, which, it should be noted, can differ from the dates displayed on the buildings. The date on Ripon Spa Baths, for example (*above*) is 1904, the date the foundation stone was laid, whereas the actual opening took place a year later.

Building costs are those cited at the time of opening. But, as is often said, a building is only started, and rarely finished.

All baths from all periods require continual investment and periodic upgrading, so that the lifetime costs of any one building will always far exceed the initial outlay.

Great Lengths

The title of this book is, we hope, self explanatory.

This is a study of buildings that are functional, that are robust, that bring great pleasure and health benefits (physical and mental) to our communities, that are part of our social and cultural heritage, and that, above all, are often quite stunning in appearance.

They are buildings for which, quite literally, local authorities, architects and engineers, builders and craftsmen, manufacturers and designers, and most importantly of all, the ratepayers of Britain, have gone to great lengths to procure, and which generations of superintendents and matrons, attendants, engineers and maintenance crew have nurtured with skill and dedication, often against the odds.

It now rests with the current generation to ensure that their efforts are matched by our own.

At the time of going to press in late 2008 – a caveat that appears all too frequently within the pages of *Great Lengths* – the splendid Ripon Spa Baths, opened in 1905, was one of at least sixteen historic public baths whose fate hung in the balance. Its swimming pool, added at the rear of the spa in 1936, seemed unlikely to survive, while its magnificent porte-cochere, seen here, could find itself as the entrance to a much contested residential development on the site.

Once covered by a vaulted roof, the Great Bath at Bath, fed by hot spring water at 45-46° C, was developed between 70AD and the 2nd Century as a place for healing, mingling but only gentle swimming at most. Its rectangular, colonnaded form (substantially rebuilt in the late 19th century) would nevertheless form a useful template for much later pools.

Chapter Two

Before 1846

Whether for survival or for recreation, it is fairly safe to assume that man has always possessed the potential to swim.

We also know that around 3,000 BC, ancient civilisations in both Egypt and India created the earliest known man-made pools. Whether for bathing or swimming, these pools were in the open air, fed by rivers and streams.

However the desire and ability to build an artificially enclosed body of water under cover, large enough and deep enough to cater specifically for swimming, is a more recent phenomenon.

Both the Greeks and Romans started the process, but only in the past two centuries has the indoor swimming pool become a recognisable building type *per se*.

Its evolution in Britain falls into several distinct periods, governed mainly by changing social patterns and by advances in technology.

But by far the most significant date is that of 1846.

Before the passing of the 1846 Baths and Wash-houses Act (of which more in Chapter Three), and with only one exception in

Liverpool, the few indoor pools that existed in Britain were in private hands, and were mostly small plunge pools, attached to bath houses. Entry was either by subscription or by an admission fee, typically a minimum of one shilling; that is, beyond the pocket of the ordinary man or woman.

After 1846, local authorities were empowered to borrow or raise money in order to construct public baths affordable to all.

As will be noted, the 1846 Act concerned itself with three key areas of activity. Firstly, the provision of individual baths (usually called 'slipper baths'), designed for personal ablutions.

Secondly, the provision of wash-houses, for the laundering of clothes and linen, and thirdly, the provision of 'open bathing places'.

By 'open' the Act did not mean open air. Rather, it meant bathing places, indoor or outdoor, 'where several persons bathe in the same water'. Thus, although the main thrust of the legislation aimed at promoting cleanliness amongst the poor, and not once in the Act is the word swimming mentioned,

clearly Parliament recognised that 'open' or communal bathing places – effectively plunge pools – had their place in the proposed new breed of public baths.

What few people envisaged in 1846 is that, as the century wore on and more homes became connected to a mains water supply, more people would visit public baths to swim than to wash or to use the laundry facilities.

This gradual shift in emphasis, from bathing to swimming, from small plunge pools to large swimming pools, and in more recent years from pools to leisure centres, forms the underlying theme of *Great Lengths*.

Before 1846, the waters appear much less clear, as it were.

In British history, the earliest known reference to swimming appears in Plutarch's account of a riverside battle during Caesar's expedition of 55 BC. A soldier distinguishes himself in action against the 'barbarians' before returning to his comrades 'partly swimming and partly wading' (though he is mortified to have lost his shield in the process). »

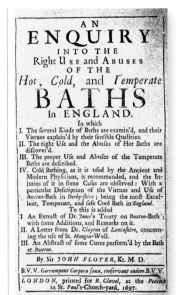

Sir John Floyer of Lichfield was one of the first doctors to advocate the use of cold baths, and apparently remained hale and hearty, despite his asthma, right up until he died aged 84. His 1697 treatise on bathing, and on the baths at Buxton and Matlock, was one of earliest works on hydrotherapy.

» Caesar himself was said to have been a strong swimmer, whilst in Greek society, as we learn from both Plato and Aristophanes, the common definition of an idiot was someone who could neither read nor swim.

But if the value of swimming was commonly recognised, the notion of a man-made swimming pool had its architectural and cultural roots in the Greek *gymnasium*, and more specifically in the bath house.

In the male-only *gymnasium* the bath served mainly as a place to wash after the exertions of the *palaestra*, or exercise yard. Then gradually, from the first century BC onwards, and especially in Rome, the bath house evolved more into a communal amenity for both sexes and all ages, until, by the first century AD, afternoon bathing became a widely observed part of the daily social routine.

To satisfy this trend, the number of known baths in Rome alone grew from 170 in 33BC to 856 by the late 4th century AD. At the same time, as the leading engineers of the Empire applied their skills to a whole range of innovative building materials and techniques, the bath houses themselves – their furnaces, boilers and heating systems (or hypocausts) – became ever more sophisticated. Not least, the use of concrete allowed

for larger and more ambitious structures, while improvements to bronze taps and lead piping revolutionised the management of water and drainage. (It is from the Latin *plumbum*, for lead, that we derive the term plumbing).

The introduction of aquaducts also obviated the need to site baths close to natural water sources.

There were three temperature zones in the standard Roman bath: the cold *frigidarium*, the warm *tepidarium* and the extra hot *caldarium*.

But again, as Rome's wealth and technical nous increased, an additional element started to appear at the larger bath houses.

This was the *piscina* (literally fish pond) or *natatio* (from *natare*, to swim).

The *natatio* at the Thermae of Caracalla, completed in 217AD, for example, measured 52 x 23m, and was said to have accommodated 1,600 bathers. Even larger was the Thermae of Diocletian, completed a century later, described in one account as holding 3,000.

In Britain the remains of baths have been identified at some 40-50 archaeological sites associated with the Roman period, of which six had pools apparently large enough to have facilitated swimming. These are at Bath (*see page 18*), Chester, Exeter, Wroxeter, Caerleon and Gadebridge.

These pools, and others of their ilk around the Empire, were mostly unheated and either partially or entirely open to the elements. At Whitley Grange in Shropshire, however, there was a covered plunge bath 15' square.

But although theoretically large enough to swim in, most historians doubt that that was a Roman *piscina's* actual function.

Firstly all were of an even depth (that is with no deep or shallow end), varying from site to site between 0.5m–1.2m. True, the latter depth is just sufficient for swimming, but what seems equally likely, based on what we know of bathers' habits, and from the design of the pool surrounds – which encouraged people to sit – is that the pools were more suited to wading and mingling, with perhaps a few strokes here and there in between.

Secondly, there are no evidence of any pools being used for competitions or training.

But whether the Romans swam, floated, waded or simply soaked in their lavish surrounds, in the same way that Roman amphitheatres were to provide a model for modern stadiums, so too did Roman baths provide the inspiration for the bath houses that emerged in Britain from the 17th century onwards, and from which the modern pool evolved.

Before we turn our attention to those baths, however, what of the 1200 years or more that followed the Romans' departure from Britain in the early 5th century?

As has been widely recorded elsewhere, for centuries Christian doctrine remained hostile towards any activity that might promote licentiousness or sloth. Bathing or indeed any immersion in water constituted just such an activity.

This attitude, so alien to today's ultra-clean sensibilities – and in contrast to the Romans' obsession with personal grooming – persisted well into the early 19th century. Not only the poor, but even the great were essentially unwashed, claiming that it was far better to change one's clothes and dab on more perfume than to use soap and water. Even doctors reinforced this prejudice, arguing that by opening up the pores, washing actually increased the risk of infection.

But what of swimming, with all its associations of immersion, nakedness and physicality?

If various references in medieval literature are to be believed, man's natural urge to swim could never be totally suppressed by the Church. The 11th century poem *Beowulf*, for example, includes an admiring account of an epic swimming race between Beowulf and Breca in the 7th century.

Located in the Fellows Garden at Emmanuel College, Cambridge, the 17th century Fellows Pool is almost certainly Britain's oldest known operational swimming pool – albeit an outdoor one whose thatched changing hut dates from a mid Victorian refurbishment.

Early 14th century literature equally praises swimming as an essential skill for knights.

In 1315 Edward II is described as taking a holiday in the Fens with his 'silly company of swimmers,' while so many students were drowning at Cambridge that in 1571 the University's Vice-Chancellor, John Whitgift, banned swimming altogether. Any undergraduate caught in the act was to be flogged. A Bachelor of Arts faced a day in the stocks and a ten shilling fine.

Perhaps the ban had little effect, because in 1587 Britain's earliest known manual on swimming was published, also in Cambridge, by Everard Digby, a Fellow of St John's College. Illustrated with 43 woodcuts, *De Arte Natandi* described in Latin various techniques, including forms of both breaststroke and backstroke.

Further signs that doctrinal disapproval of immersion was easing followed in the 17th century. Again in Cambridge, between 1630 and 1690 a small open air pool (*opposite*) was built at Emmanuel College.

In 1658 *De Arte Natandi* was translated into English as *The Compleat Swimmer*.

During the 1690s Scarborough took steps towards becoming Britain's first seaside resort, while in Bath, renewed interest in the restorative powers of thermal waters launched a new era of respectability for spas in general.

In Restoration London, meanwhile, another form of bathing establishment emerged, the 'bagnio' (from the Italian *bagno*, for bath). Closer in style to what would later be styled Turkish baths, or *hammams*, the earliest of these were the Royal Bagnio in Newgate Street (opened c.1679) and the King's Bagnio in Long

Acre (1682), both designed by a man described as an Italian, John Valentine.

Each had a small circular plunge pool surrounded by a colonnade under a domed roof. One account adds that men and women were admitted by tokens on alternative days.

Yet despite this, and their royal appellations, London's bagnios soon earned a dubious reputation, the word bagnio itself becoming synonymous with brothel. (The Long Acre one had been financed by Sir William Jennens, a feckless naval captain described by Pepys as 'a proud, idle fellow'.)

But whether this reputation was earned or not – and the Long Acre bagnio did remain open well into the Victorian era, until 1876 – it was at another London bagnio, on Lemon Street (now Leman Street), that we find the first indoor plunge pool specifically advertised as a place to swim.

A notice in *The Advertiser* of May 28 1742 stated:

'This day is opened... The Pleasure or Swimming Bath which is more than 43ft in length. It will be kept warm and fresh every day and is convenient to swim or learn to swim in. There are waiters who attend daily to teach or assist Gentlemen in the said Swimming Bath if required. There is also a good Cold bath.'

No images of this indoor Pleasure Bath survive, but it may well have been similar in style to another, much better documented indoor pool that opened the following year, a mile to the north.

Financed by a jeweller, William Kemp, the Peerless Pool Baths, off Old Street, were fed by springs that had once formed a pond referred to in John Stow's 1603 *Survey of London* as the 'Perrillous pond,

because diverse youths swimming therein have been drowned'.

Having rediscovered the springs over a century later, Kemp claimed that bathing in the water had cured him of 'a violent pain of the head.'

Thus 'generously' and 'for public benefit' he created an entire resort, consisting of a bowling green, saloon, library, two fish ponds (one used also for sailing model boats and for ice skating), and two swimming pools, all set amid a secluded grove.

The larger pool, referred to as the Pleasure Bath, was outdoor and measured 170' long x 100' wide – roughly equivalent to a modern Olympic pool – and was 4' 6" deep, with, according to one prospectus, 'a fine gravel bottom'.

As at Leman Street, a year's subscription to this pool and to the grounds in general cost one guinea. For an extra 9s subscribers could also gain access to a small indoor Cold Bath (*above*).

Stated dimensions for the Cold Bath vary between 36' x 18' and 40' x 20', invariably accompanied by the claim that it was the »

The Cold Bath at the Peerless Pool, in Finsbury, London, from a prospectus of c.1840, nearly a century after its opening. Note the dressing rooms and central oculus over the water. Apparently the marble surrounds were executed by a young mason, William Staines, who despite his illiteracy later became Lord Mayor and always regarded the bath as 'amongst his best work'. Peerless Pool closed in 1850 and the site is now occupied by a housing estate, bordered by Peerless Street and Bath Street. In 1999 the pool was the focal point of a Georgian mystery novel, *Death at Peerless Pool*, by Deryn Lake.

LONDON BOROUGH OF ISLINGTON
PEERLESS STREET E.C.1

NOTTINGHAM
BATHING ESTABLISHMENT,
No. 34, Pelham Street.

PETER MYERS respectfully solicits the attention of the Public to the above Baths, which are now open,, and which he trusts will be found to give universal satisfaction.

TERMS:

	S.	D.
Swimming Bath	1	0
Hot Bath	2	0
Large Hot Bath	3	0
Shower Bath	1	6
Vapour Bath	2	6
Salt Bath	2	6
Eau de Cologne Bath	4	6
Artificial Source-Royal at Bareges, Bath	5	0
Artificial Sea-Water Bath	4	0

OPEN FROM SIX IN THE MORNING, UNTIL EIGHT IN THE EVENING.

Pelham Street baths, Nottingham – opened in the early 19th century by Peter Myers, and carried on after his death in 1838 by his wife Miriam, until c.1848 – lists a swimming bath as one of its amenities. Another advert suggests that there may also have been a women's swimming bath (possibly a Jewish ritual bath) that was heated during the winter.

largest of its type in England. (Presumably the Leman Street pool was narrower.)

In depth it was 4' 6", and was fed by a 'very cold spring' that could be seen 'constantly rising through the latticed bottom'.

Not so salubrious was the looming proximity of 'the madhouse of St Luke's' and of an adjoining vinegar manufactory.

Nevertheless, the Peerless Pool stayed in business under various owners for over a century, from 1743 to 1850, during which time, it is worth noting, its prices remained remarkably stable. As already stated, in 1743 an annual subscription cost one guinea for the use of all the facilities except the Cold Bath. A single visit to either pool cost 1s.

Astonishingly, that figure had not altered by 1840, meaning that allowing for inflation, the cost had effectively halved over the years, thereby bringing use of the pool within reach of a much wider sector of society (if still beyond the range of the poor).

Outside London possibly the largest bathing establishment was the Ladywell Baths, Birmingham, located where Bath Passage stands today, off Ladywell Walk.

Known in the early 18th century as the Cold Bath, by the time Samuel Lewis visited in 1831 the premises had been expanded to accommodate ten individual bath houses or pools of varying sizes.

Situated in a well planted garden surrounded by high walls, the facilities ranged from a small ritual bath for local Jewish women, up to an outdoor swimming pool measuring 110' x 52' and 'supplied with a constant influx of water, at the rate of 1,000 hogsheads per hour'. A swim there cost 6d, half the fee at the Peerless Pool.

There were also swimming facilities at Thomas Rennison's baths, in Montpelier, Bristol, open from 1765 until 1916. This was part of a larger pleasure garden, of which the only surviving remnant is the Old England pub.

In Bath, the splendid Grade II listed Cleveland Pools (featured in *Liquid Assets*), opened in 1815. It still stands today, albeit derelict since the 1990s.

But in common with the Peerless Pool and the Ladywell Baths, these establishments were still the exception rather than the rule, and their swimming facilities were still predominantly outdoors and with unheated water, viable during the summer months only.

In his seminal work of 1801, *The Sports and Pastimes of the People of England*, Joseph Strutt concluded that swimming 'was by no means so generally practiced with us in the present day as it used to be in former times'.

And although by 1840 subscription baths had opened all over the country, other than those mentioned above, and also possibly in Nottingham (*see left*), few offered more than a small plunge pool for swimming.

At the majority of other baths built between 1800–40 (such as at Edinburgh, Newcastle, Harrogate, Lancaster, Northampton, Oxford, Leamington, Exeter and Plymouth), the accent was on hot and cold baths and on treatments, rather than on swimming.

Fine buildings they may have been, their Greek Revival and Regency façades betokening a new era of bathing splendour, at a time when few middle class households had running water, let alone bathing facilities.

Yet none can be regarded as a true template for the public »

▲ London's Regency terraces nowadays offer prestigious office and residential accommodation. But for all its apparent grandeur, **York Terrace East**, built c.1820 by James Burton, was intended as mere service accommodation for the larger apartments and villas of John Nash's adjoining Regent's Park. Note however the central portico. This was, until the First World War, the entrance to the **Royal York Baths** (and later Turkish baths); an example of how smaller Georgian baths were often slotted discreetly into street frontages.

There were two plunge pools; one for gentlemen measuring 66' x 21' at a depth of 3-5', with a springboard at each end and 20 narrow dressing cubicles, and one for ladies, measuring 30' x 14', 4'6" deep, with six changing boxes.

According to Dr RE Dudgeon's survey of London baths in 1870, the latter pool, barely large enough in which to learn to swim, was still the only one in the capital reserved solely for women.

Otherwise he was not impressed. 'The plaster was peeling off the walls in patches, and green mould was creeping up the walls. This, with the low ceiling (and) the dim illumination... gave a gloomy and uninviting aspect to the place. Still, I am bound to say, the water was clear and pleasant.'

No trace of either pool, or a Turkish bath added c.1865 survives, and the Grade II listed building is now occupied by the Royal Academy of Music.

From the same period, the **Montpellier Baths, Cheltenham** (*top left, centre and bottom*), has also long ceased to function.

Built by Henry Thompson in 1806 – and still bearing the spa town's crest and motto, *Salubritas et Eruditio* (Health and Education) over one doorway (topped by Neptune's bearded visage) – the building was converted into a public swimming pool in 1898, and again into the Playhouse Theatre in 1945 (*see page 270*).

Apparently the Duke of Wellington took the waters here in 1823 and enjoyed idling in one of the warm baths, at 3s a session, whilst reading the newspapers.

›› baths that would follow in the wake of the 1846 Act.

Except one, that is, in Liverpool.

As previously recounted in *Played in Liverpool (see Links)*, before the industrial revolution Liverpool was considered Lancashire's premier sea bathing resort (hence Brighton-le-Sands in Crosby, and New Brighton, on the opposite bank of the Wirral peninsula).

Perhaps to encourage this trade, as early as 1701 the Liverpool Common Council had considered building a small bath on shoreland near the old Pool inlet. Instead, the area was developed as Liverpool's first dock. But the idea persisted and in 1756 John Naylor Wright established Liverpool's first baths at the end of the New Quay, later renamed Bath Street.

Wright's establishment was unusual in that it offered both sexes equal access to private baths, and steps down, either to the Mersey, or to a plunge pool fed by the river, enclosed by high walls and measuring 33' x 30'.

But what made these baths even more noteworthy was that in 1794 the Common Council bought the leasehold. This cost £4,000, and was followed by a further £1,000 spent on improvements. Almost certainly this was the first time (at least since the Roman era) that a public authority had involved itself in baths management.

Not only that, but when these baths – which were admittedly modest – had to be demolished in 1817 in order to make way for the Prince's Dock, Liverpool's Corporation Surveyor, John Foster Junior, was asked to design a modern replacement.

As the architect of several diverse public buildings in the city – an infirmary, a parish church and cemetery, a market hall, the Custom House, and the first grand stand at Aintree Racecourse – and as someone who had travelled extensively in Greece as a youth, Foster was a practised exponent of the then popular Greek Revival style, which lent itself well to the lofty and publicly-spirited notion of a bathing establishment.

Opened on June 6 1829, the St George's Baths (*below*) did not disappoint. Indeed it represented a considerable leap forward.

Here was a highly visible, simply articulated and almost austere working building, one that championed classical notions of cleanliness and physical culture, whilst also using modern engineering techniques.

Foster even made a classical feature of the chimney stack, an idea borrowed from factory and mill buildings of the period and one that would characterise baths for the next century or more.

Almost like a church spire, this tapering chimney rose up above the central service block of the building, either side of which were sections for men and women. Although the space allocated to each was the same, the men's swimming pool was larger, at 45' x 27', compared with 39' x 27' for the ladies. Also provided were warm and cold private baths.

Water was conveyed from the river into a reservoir under the building, from which it was pumped up by a steam engine into pans, where it could be heated.

Before being channelled to the baths, it was then pumped again through a filter consisting of sand and charcoal, a system attributed to a Mr Sylvester.

Such sophistication did not come cheap, however.

Britain's first baths to have been built and funded entirely by a municipality, St George's cost a colossal £24,481 initially, plus a further £6,000 or so when the foundations were found wanting. This was roughly the same as it would cost the Corporation to build the much larger Cornwallis Street Baths, their first under the 1846 Act, some 22 years later.

On the other hand, St George's Baths was not intended for the working classes.

Publicly funded it might have been, but it was still essentially a subscription baths, operated by a private manager and with charges that either matched those we have featured previously – such as 1s per

St George's Baths, Liverpool, enjoyed a prime location on the Pierhead. As an 1829 poster declared, 'The structure viewed as a whole is chaste and unique, and forms a striking, tasteful addition to the architectural beauties of the town'.

swim – or were much higher. For example a six month subscription at Liverpool in 1829 cost £1 10s, twice the rate at the Peerless Pool.

This was no philanthropic institution therefore.

But it would not be long before the Corporation was forced to take heed of the needs of Liverpool's poor and under-privileged.

The story has been told many times before, but in essence, in 1832, three years after St George's opening, a cholera outbreak in the densely populated working class districts around the port killed at least 1,500 people.

The authorities did little, and appeared to understand even less. But one woman, Kitty Wilkinson, and her husband Tom, set up a laundry in the kitchen of their terraced house in Denison Street, so that neighbours could at least wash clothes and bed linen and thereby help to stave off infection. (The couple also set up a school for orphans in their bedroom.)

Before long the Wilkinsons gained support from a local Provident Society, while a wealthy merchant, William Rathbone, and his wife Elizabeth, did what they could to persuade the Corporation to fund other similar efforts.

It was not easy, but in the end the pressure told, and on May 28 1842 Liverpool opened Britain's first combined public baths and wash house, on Frederick Street.

In recognition of their work, Kitty and Tom Wilkinson were appointed as Superintendents, with prices set at a level that most working class people could afford.

Cold baths cost from one penny up to 6d, a shower cost 4d, and a warm bath from 2d up to one shilling. A vapour bath was priced at one shilling. Compared with subscription baths, such as at

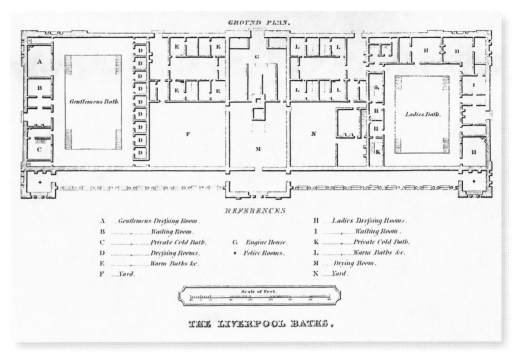

GROUND PLAN.

Gentlemens Bath.

Ladies Bath.

REFERENCES

A .... Gentlemens Dressing Room.
B .... Waiting Room.
C .... Private Cold Bath.
D .... Dressing Rooms.
E .... Warm Baths &c.
F .... Yard.

G ..... Engine House.
✦ ..... Police Rooms.

H .... Ladies Dressing Rooms.
I .... Waiting Room.
K .... Private Cold Bath.
L .... Warm Baths &c.
M .... Drying Room.
N .... Yard.

Scale of Feet.

THE LIVERPOOL BATHS.

Nottingham (*see page 22*), these prices were exceptionally low.

No figures are known for the useage of the wash-house, located in the basement (but with a section for 'infected clothes' in an outside yard), other than that the 26 tubs were almost always in use. But in the slipper bath section's first year, 11,661 baths were taken, 90 per cent of which were at the cheapest end of the price scale. This rose to 16,323 in the second year, despite an increase in the price from 1d to 2d for cold baths, and from 2d to 3d for warm.

Less propitiously, in both years the income, of £118 and £229 respectively, fell short of the average running costs of £287.

For the architect, City Surveyor Joseph Franklin, Frederick Street offered a useful prototype before embarking on a second, much larger plan for Paul Street. »

▲ **St George's Baths** in Liverpool. Note the ladies' dressing rooms were larger than the men's but fewer in number, suggesting that women either shared or were accompanied by a servant.

Neither of the swimming baths was fully covered, at least not in the early years. Instead, only their surrounds were sheltered by a projecting roof on iron columns.

After the 1846 Act management of the baths fully reverted to the

local authority, by which time it had fallen into serious disrepair, described in 1850 by the City Surveyor, James Newlands, as scarcely deserving of the title 'public baths'. Yet with further patching up it remained open until October 1906.

Today the site is a piazza next to the Pierhead Ferry Terminal, in front of the Port of Liverpool building and directly over the Queensway Mersey tunnel.

›› Opened in 1846, Paul Street Baths was the first publicly funded building in Britain to house under one roof all three elements provided for in the Baths and Wash-houses Act of that same year: that is, slipper baths, a wash-house and two 'open baths' (or plunge pools).

As such, it has rightly been celebrated as a pioneering building.

But what is rather less well known is that the private sector had already come up with a much larger building of this nature, two years earlier, in London.

Like Liverpool, London's poorest districts had been hard hit by cholera, leading to a series of initiatives that – backed up by the work done in Liverpool – would finally lead to the formulation of the 1846 Act.

But in the preceding years, private companies had continued to invest in the development of subscription baths.

Two in particular are of great significance: the Metropolitan Baths in Hoxton, opened c.1842, and the National Baths in Holborn, which followed a year later.

Not only did both house indoor swimming pools of a scale yet unseen in Britain, but they also catered for first and second class users, offered a full array of private baths, and in the latter case at Holborn, a laundry.

Frustratingly few records survive of either building. We do not know, for instance, the identity of their architects, or their backers. But from what we can see of their internal layouts from various bills and posters, they appear much closer in form to the public baths that would emerge after 1846 than any of the subscription baths that preceded them up until the 1830s.

In that sense they appear to represent a sort of missing architectural link between the two.

In 1841 the *Penny Encyclopaedia* reported that there were no more than eight swimming baths in London, all of whose facilities compared unfavourably to those in other countries.

Alas it does not identify the eight (or the other countries), but the eight must have included the Royal York Baths, the Peerless Pool, the bagnio in Long Acre, a Tepid Bath in Stamford Street (known to have existed in 1831), and perhaps the open air Serpentine in Hyde Park, where the newly formed

National Swimming Society of England staged its first national championships in August 1837.

The article concluded, 'the English are not much inclined to swimming'.

But even if that were true, they did like to take a dip.

According to a Royal Humane Society report the number of bathers at the Serpentine rose to at least 8,000 a day during the hot summer of 1844, and other lakes around the capital were similarly packed (such as at Brockwell Park and Plumstead Common).

Certainly the main selling point of the Metropolitan Baths was the swimming pools; open 5.00am to 10.00pm on weekdays, and on Sunday and Monday mornings.

Its other claims were the usual stuff of baths advertisements of the period; gas lighting, the purity of its spring water and its suitability for swimming lessons.

But in the context of this brief overview of pre-1846 baths architecture, several other features stand out.

Firstly, it was entered via a normal terraced house on Ashley Crescent, where the manager lived, with only a neo-classical porch to distinguish it from its neighbours. The actual baths were on land behind the terrace.

Secondly, it is one of several baths of the period advertising itself as a Tepid Bath, to ensure that the public would know that the water was heated.

Thirdly, as illustrated opposite, it had no walkway around the water's edge on three sides. Instead, bathers entered their changing box from an external corridor, and from the box stepped down directly into the water (as also at Bath, *see below left*).

Even though mixed bathing was out of the question, this was designed to guard bathers' modesty (particularly as most men still swam naked at this time).

But perhaps the most significant aspect of the Metropolitan Baths was the dimensions of its main pool, and the fact that an even larger one for second class bathers existed alongside.

Known as the Wenlock Baths, this was accessed separately from Wenlock Road.

Pool sizes had been growing steadily since St George's Baths opened in Liverpool in 1829.

In 1839, for example, Newcastle's newest subscription baths, in Ridley Place, designed by John Dobson, had pools measuring 90' x 45' and 54' x 17'.

But the tepid bath at the Metropolitan Baths measured 110' x 48', (with the depth ranging from 3'10" to 5'), while the Wenlock Bath was even larger at 180' x 30'. (In fact until the Empire Pool was built at Wembley in 1934 this would be the longest pool in London.) ››

Opened in 1832, the oval-shaped Tepid Bath on Beau Street, Bath, was designed by the prolific Greek Revivalist, Decimus Burton, son of James (architect of the Royal York East baths in Regent's Park). Note how bathers accessed the water directly from the dressing rooms. The building made way for new baths in 1922.

INTERIOR VIEW OF THE TEPID PLUNGING & SWIMMING BATH.
BATH.

METROPOLITAN
Tepid and Cold Swimming Baths
Ashley Crescent,

NEAR THE   EAGLE TAVERN

TEPID BATH.

COLD BATH

PRIVATE TEPID & HOT BATH

CITY   Length 110 feet width 48 feet   ROAD.

The increasing patronage afforded to this Establishment by the Medical Profession in London and its Environs, and the beneficial effects of

TEPID BATHING

Now universally admitted, induce the Proprietor earnestly to invite an inspection! The Baths possess advantages strikingly novel, containing a superficial extent of **5000 FEET** of the

PUREST SPRING WATER,

which is constantly flowing and changing at the rate of

15,000 Gallons per Hour!

They thus allow the Swimmer the lengthened enjoyment of his art, and enable the Learner to practice in Summer or Winter, as the temperature may be varied at pleasure!

THE BATHS ARE BRILLIANTLY LIGHTED WITH GAS,

And all means which capital or science could insure, have been adopted to render the arrangement complete!

Attached is a Private Bath the Temperature of which can be varied from 34 to 100 Degrees

Open from Five o'Clock in the Morning till Ten in the Evening, & on Sunday Mornings from Five till Ten

SINGLE BATHE, ONE SHILLING!   1 MONTH 9s.   3 MONTHS 14s.   6 MONTHS 21s.   1 YEAR 30s.

Medicated Vapor, Shower and Slipper Baths

▲ Despite its discreet entrance on Ashley Crescent, on what is now Shepherdess Walk, Hoxton (portrayed here by IJ Borgnis c.1843), London's **Metropolitan Baths** was a highly sophisticated bathing complex.

As the proprietor's florid notice from c.1844 clearly infers (*left*), the moderrn day swimming bath was the direct descendant of the Roman *tepidarium* – that is, a midway point between the cold and the hot baths.

Since the baths closed in c.1905 the site has become an open play area bound by Shepherdess Walk, Sturt Street and Wenlock Road.

In Borgnis's painting, the famous Eagle Tavern on City Road lies just behind the trees in the distance.

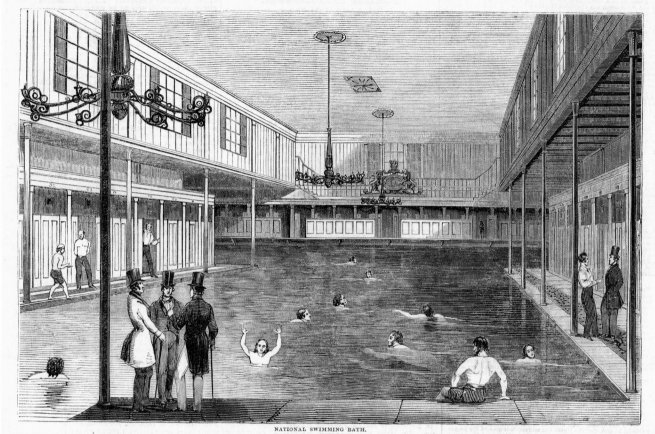

NATIONAL SWIMMING BATH.

▲ From the *Pictorial Times* of May 18 1844, this engraving of the **National Baths, Little Queen Street, High Holborn** shows how, following on from the Metropolitan Baths in Hoxton, swimming pool design was already evolving rapidly in advance of the 1846 Act.

Reckoned to have cost at least £20,000, the baths' main feature was its T-shaped tepid pool, 135' long x 70' at its widest. As always, water was supplied from an underground spring (mains water was still not available), pumped up a 280' deep shaft by a 15 horse power engine and then

passed twice through filters before being heated to 80° F, or 26.6° C (compared to today's norm of 29°).

Unlike the tepid bath at the Metropolitan Baths there was a walkway between the changing boxes and the water, plus a viewing gallery at the far end.

Indeed the National Baths was the first indoor pool in Britain to stage an official championship, on July 18 1843. Organised by the National Swimming Society, the event was open to 'young swimmers who have never before received a prize'. There were six heats over 4 x 100' and the final

was won by a Master Webb.

Another early event, also in 1843, saw two North American Indians, Flying Gull and Tobacco, demonstrate a wild, crawl-like stroke which was then considered quite uncivilised by those more used to a sedate breaststroke.

Adjoining the tepid bath were the usual private baths and showers for men and women. But the National Baths was not solely for the middle classes. After all, it was located only a few hundred yards from some of the worst slums in London. There was therefore a laundry on the premises, and a separate

second class tepid bath, entered from Prince's Street, for which the cost was 4d.

Whether it was competition from cheaper public baths after the 1846 Act, or possibly problems with the water supply – nearby Soho was the epicentre of yet another cholera outbreak in 1854 – the National Baths had closed by 1855. The building was then converted to a dance hall called the Casino de Venise, then into the Holborn Restaurant, before being demolished during the 1870s.

The site today is occupied by Holborn tube station.

» In his survey of London baths in 1870 (*see Links*), RE Dudgeon wrote that the water in the Wenlock Baths was 'very far from clear', was rather cooler than in the Metropolitan next door, and that the arrangements were 'altogether very second class'.

But he conceded that a 'vast number of bathers' could be accommodated, and that the pool's length and the existence of a gallery made it popular as a venue for swimming matches.

Unfortunately no images of the Wenlock Baths survive. But, as shown by an engraving published to mark the opening of the National Baths in High Holborn in 1843 (*see opposite*), the basic elements of swimming pool design were clearly already in place by the time the 1846 Act was passed.

Of course those who were campaigning for public baths at that time were motivated not by a love of swimming but by their concern for the health, hygiene and morality of the poor.

As the *Pictorial Times* commented alongside its engraving of Holborn in 1844, 'It is on all hands admitted that health is a primary blessing of life; but the poor man's health is his all. To him, sickness brings poverty; poverty is soon aggravated into destitution; and destitution brings that worst and most enervating consequence – filth...

'London is worse off for baths than any other European capital, and therefore it is incumbent upon all who seek the improvement either of the "Great Metropolis" or of its inhabitants, to aid in the support of public bathing places.'

Truly, the world had come full circle.

When it came to the building of baths, the Victorians were about to become the new Romans.

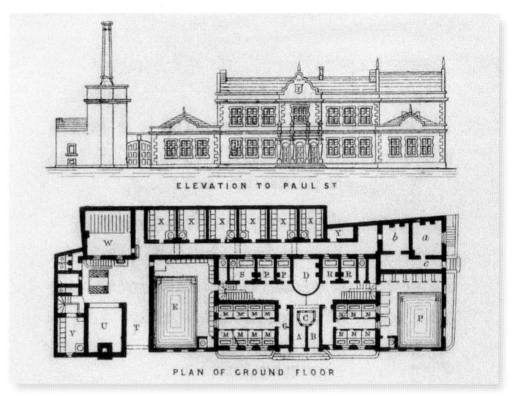

ELEVATION TO PAUL ST

PLAN OF GROUND FLOOR

Opened in 1846, Liverpool's Paul Street Baths (*above*) survived only until 1879, partly because its two pools were too small. By contrast, Bolton's Lower Bridgeman Street Baths (*left*), opened in 1847 but planned and privately financed in advance of the 1846 Act, operated until 1976. The Grade II listed building is now a business centre.

Chapter Three

Early Victorian 1846–1870

In the overall sweep of 19th century British history – a period of such momentous political reform, urban and social change, economic growth and scientific progress – the government's sanction of public baths and wash houses in 1846 rarely merits more than a passing reference.

Moreover, if mentioned at all, it is invariably in the context of, as the Act itself put it, 'the Health, Comfort, and Welfare of the Inhabitants of Towns and populous Districts'.

As stated earlier, the Act's mainly middle class promoters almost certainly had no concern at all for swimming.

Their crusade was one against dirt, which was itself the product of ignorance and immorality, and which led inexorably to disease and poverty.

And while not a sin itself, poverty acted as a drain on the economy, and especially on those of the middle and upper classes who were expected to subsidise the construction and operation of workhouses through payment of the poor rate.

Nor did dirt and unhealthy conditions make for an efficient workforce.

As Edwin Chadwick attested in his *Inquiry into the Sanitary Conditions of the Labouring Population of Great Britain* in 1842, a lethal cocktail of damp, filth, bad air, poor water and overcrowding had produced 'an adult population short-lived, improvident, reckless, and intemperate, and with habitual avidity for sensual gratifications.'

In 1854 George Cape, secretary of the Lambeth Baths Company, wrote that before the availability of public wash houses, if a working man came home 'in the middle of a November fog or a January frost,' and found that his wife had filled their confined quarters with 'damp and dripping garments', he was much more likely to resort to 'the gin palace or skittle ground'.

As to his taking a bath, that was quite impossible without an affordable water supply, even if he wished. But in truth many people had no such wish, preferring in the words of one man, cited by Chadwick, to wear their dirt like 'a great coat'.

In 1844 the Commissioner of a further report noted that the only time a poor man was 'really well washed' was at his birth, and at his death. Plus, the Commissioner might have added, when he was admitted to the work house and given a thorough scrub.

Attempts to provide affordable public baths (as opposed to private subscription baths) predated the 1840s. Around 1810 William Harley set up a small suite of baths in Glasgow (on what is now Bath Street). A surgeon, William Strutt, installed baths in Derbyshire General Infirmary. At the Quarry Bank Mill in Styal, Cheshire, Samuel Greg laid on baths for his workforce, using water heated by steam engines during the manufacturing process.

In Bath, where it was reported that some 5,000 hogsheads of hot water from the various spa baths went to waste every week, in 1841 a scheme was set up whereby the poor could gain a free bath providing they could supply a doctor's note.

The efforts made in Liverpool we have already noted in the »

As of 2008 twelve baths buildings from the period 1846–70, public and private, remained standing in Britain, wholly or partially (*see Directory*). Of the public baths the oldest survivor is the now derelict Greengate Baths, on Collier Street, Salford (*see page 46*), opened in 1856. This entrance, marked Womens Baths, leads not to a swimming pool but to slipper baths. Any woman wishing to swim had to attend at certain times when one of the men's pools was made available. Not until the 1870s were separate ladies pools considered, and even then, they were always smaller than those for men.

Park Road Public Baths, Halifax (*left*), was opened in 1859 thanks to a £6,000 donation from Francis Crossley. Perhaps appropriately, given that the head of John the Baptist forms the centre of the town's coat of arms, the building is now a church. Also in Halifax and gifted by the Crossley family, in 1864, is the oldest operational indoor pool in Britain (*see page 49*).

▲ The name most associated with the 1846 Act is that of **Sir Henry Dukinfield**, the vicar of St Martins-in-the-Fields, London. Despite his background as a baronet and Old Etonian, Dukinfield earned a reputation for piety and hard work as a young rector in Reading during the 1832 cholera outbreak. Two years later he was sent to the troublesome parish of St Martin's, where his diplomacy and weekly 'cottage lectures' won him a loyal following amongst rich and poor.

In promoting the Act Sir Henry always dismissed attempts to show how baths could be self-supporting or even profitable. They should be built for their benefits alone, he argued, not for financial motives.

Ill health forced him to quit St Martin's in 1849, but he remained active in public life, in particular helping to sort out the Model Baths at Whitechapel (see *opposite*).

He died in 1858, aged 67, and is buried at Kensal Green.

» previous chapter. But in political terms, the decisive breakthrough on baths provision occurred in London.

Unlike in provincial towns, the capital's unwieldy system of local government – still organised along parish lines in the form of vestries – militated against co-ordinated action at a public level.

On October 16 1844, therefore, a 'Committee for Erecting and Promoting the Establishment of Baths and Wash Houses for the Labouring Classes' was formed at the Mansion House.

Note its twin aims, to erect and promote.

Chaired by William Cotton, Governor of the Bank of England and supported wholeheartedly by the Bishop of London, and with 230 members signed up by 1846, this alliance of businessmen, philanthropists and churchmen sought to achieve its first aim by erecting four 'model baths' in poor neighbourhoods, three north of the Thames, one south, each expected to cost £7-10,000.

There is a suggestion that none of the Committee at that stage had much knowledge of the progress already made in Liverpool.

But certainly they struggled. Only £6,500 was raised during the early months of the campaign, and as landowners sensed an opportunity to profit in otherwise poor areas of the city, affordable sites proved difficult to find.

Designers were nevertheless invited to submit plans for these model baths. Twenty two entries were submitted, the winner in February 1845 being a 26 year old engineer, Price Prichard Baly.

Inevitably his appointment led to barbed comments from architects. But Baly had powerful friends, one of whom was Charles

Barry, architect of the most talked-about building of the decade, the new Houses of Parliament (then nearing completion). He had also worked for Brunel on both the Clifton and Hungerford suspension bridges.

Baly's first commission for the Committee was essentially a trial conversion of an existing building in Glasshouse Yard, Clerkenwell, in May 1845.

So popular was this that up to 200 people had to be turned away in one week. But then it did reportedly have only two baths and two wash tubs.

Baly next focused on what was intended to be the first of the Committee's model baths, on Goulston Square, Whitechapel, where the foundation stone was laid in December 1845.

As it transpired, six difficult years passed before Whitechapel entered full service, by which time, embarrassingly for the Committee, three of Baly's later designs, independently commissioned by various London vestries, were already in operation or nearly complete.

But that was for the future. While work proceeded slowly at Whitechapel, the Committee now embarked on the second of its aims, to promote baths and wash houses at a national level.

Several leading members of the Committee took on this challenge, led by chairman William Cotton, his deputy chairman William Hawes, Sir John Pirie and John Bullar. But the one man whose name would be forever associated with the campaign was Sir Henry Dukinfield, vicar of St Martin's-in-the Fields, a parish in which extremes of wealth and poverty were to be found within a small corner of what we now think of as

the West End. A liberally minded Tory, Dukinfield was well versed in the art of raising subscriptions for good causes. But he soon concluded that public baths were too important to be dependent on charity and philanthropy.

With support from the Bishop of London and two Parliamentarians, Benjamin Hawes, MP for Lambeth, and Lord Courtenay (later known as 'the good earl'), Dukinfield therefore promoted a Bill that would allow corporations and vestries to raise money for baths and wash houses, either through local rates or by borrowing.

At the same time, armed with statistical accounts of how well Liverpool's Frederick Street establishment, and the Glasshouse Yard building in Clerkenwell were both doing – the number of warm and cold baths taken, the number of women using the laundries, the income, the expenditure, the likely rate of return on investment, and so on – the Committee set about orchestrating an ambitious nationwide campaign.

The timing was not ideal. Most politicians' minds were fixated on repeal of the Corn Laws. But still, according to *The Builder* – the weekly journal, founded in 1842, that did most to report the baths movement – the Committee wrote letters to every mayor, alderman, town councillor and town clerk in England and Wales, and to the editors of almost every newspaper.

They also distributed an estimated 70,000 circulars – including in Aberdeen, even though the Act would not extend to Scotland – and helped orchestrate various petitions, including one that was signed by the heads of over 100 companies, and another drawn up on behalf of London dockers.

So successful was this publicity, it was later reported, that in the hustings that followed Prime Minister Robert Peel's resignation in June 1846, hardly a politician did not have some view to impart on the desirability of public baths.

If there was any opposition, it appeared to be limited to the owners of subscription baths, those who argued that laundries were speculative ventures best left to the free market, and old school patricians who opposed any institution that might pamper working people. Also aired (for example in a session of the City of London's Common Council) were misogynistic fears that innocent wives risked being corrupted at the wash house by gin soaked professional washerwomen.

These objections apart, the Dukinfield Act, as it was often referred to, sailed through with relative ease on August 26 1846.

But before we turn to the Act's provisions, it is important to consider what factors other than 'health, comfort and welfare' were at play during this period.

Firstly there were growing concerns for water safety.

In the mid 19th century, just as Joseph Strutt had lamented in 1801, the vast majority of Britons were unable to swim. One report even found that only one in 100 seamen knew how to swim.

As a result, as urban populations rose sharply in both numbers and in density, more people were drowning, in urban rivers, ponds and increasingly in canals that were either unsafe or polluted.

As the *Manchester Guardian* argued in 1845, the deaths of 33 local people from drowning that year alone made the provision of

swimming pools as necessary as baths and wash houses.

Allied to this was the question of public indecency.

No working class man or boy owned a swimming costume, and the majority were quite happy to swim naked, whoever might be passing by.

In Birmingham this led to the proprietors of certain canals banning all swimmers to avoid offending any women who might be walking along the towpaths.

In London, swimming at the Serpentine in Hyde Park and at Victoria Park in Hackney was restricted to the early hours of the morning (before 'ladies' were assumed to be about).

Similar concerns were voiced at a public meeting in Hull in ⟫

◀ Now forming an entrance to **The Women's Library** on **Old Castle Street**, **Whitechapel,** this is the surviving remnant of Price Prichard Baly's **Model Baths**, whose main entrance had originally been on Goulston Square (now Street).

Far from being a model, after its foundations sank into an old cesspool the building opened a year late in 1847 (despite the date plaque). It then suffered a fire, and was not fully operational until 1851. Worse, it ended up costing £30,000, nearly triple the original estimate. *The Builder* derided it as 'downright ugly' with 'no architectural merit'.

It then closed c.1865 and had to be rebuilt by the Vestry, after which, with a swimming pool replacing the small original plunge pool, it stayed in use until 1989.

No trace remains of the **Frederick Street Wash House, Liverpool,** seen left in 1914. One of the earliest recommendations concerning wash houses, not in place here, was for tall divisions between the tubs, to cut chatter and to prevent women from judging their neighbour's 'articles'.

The legendary Kitty Wilkinson was superintendent at Frederick Street until her dismissal in 1852. Later rehired as a 'mender and hemmer', she died in 1860, and is commemorated by a stained glass window in Liverpool Cathedral.

▶ As its title suggests, the **1846 Act to Encourage the Establishment of Public Baths and Wash-Houses** was a permissive piece of legislation. That is, local authorities could vote on whether to adopt it or not.

Those that did were permitted to raise money from their rates, or borrow funds secured against their rates, provided that they appoint between three and seven commissioners to oversee and manage the baths and wash house's construction and operation; all income to be set against expenses, and to be independently audited. If necessary, two or more local authorities could combine.

The Act also sanctioned the purchase of existing private baths, while water and gas companies were encouraged to supply without charge or at favourable rates.

In wash houses, the cost of hiring one tub or trough, or a pair, was one penny for one hour and threepence for a maximum of two hours, not including drying time.

Regarding individual, or slipper baths, there had to be *at least* twice as many baths provided for 'the labouring classes' as for any higher class, to be charged at the following maximum rates:

For an individual over eight years old, supplied with fresh water and a clean towel: one penny for a cold bath, twopence for warm. (This compared with a typical charge of one or two shillings per warm bath at a subscription baths).

For up to four children to share – if male, no older than eight years old – each receiving a clean towel: two pence for a cold bath, four pence for warm.

An amendment to the Act in July 1847 added into that band of charges provision also for cold and warm shower baths, and for warm

ANNO NONO & DECIMO

VICTORIÆ REGINÆ.

•••

C A P. LXXIV.

An Act to encourage the Establishment of public Baths and Wash-houses. [26th *August* 1846.]

WHEREAS it is desirable for the Health, Comfort, and Welfare of the Inhabitants of Towns and populous Districts to encourage the Establishment therein of public Baths and Wash-houses and open Bathing Places: Be it enacted by the Queen's most Excellent Majesty, by and with the Advice and Consent of the Lords Spiritual and Temporal, and Commons, in this present Parliament assembled, and by the Authority of the same, That this Act may be adopted in any incorporated Borough in *England* which is regulated under an Act passed in the Sixth Year of the Reign of His late Majesty, to provide for the Regulation of Municipal Corporations, or any Charter granted in pursuance of the said Act, or any Act passed for the Amendment thereof, and also, with the Approval of One of Her Majesty's Principal Secretaries of State, for any Parish in *England* not within any such incorporated Borough.

vapour baths. The amendment also stipulated that slipper baths of a higher class could not be charged at more than threepence for a cold bath or shower, and sixpence for a warm bath, shower or vapour bath.

Although three times the rate for the labouring classes, this was still comfortably below the typical rates at subscription baths.

But in the context of *Great Lengths*, undoubtedly the most significant charge set by the Act concerned 'open bathing places', or plunge baths, 'where several persons bathe in the same water'.

These were to be charged at the cheapest rate of all, at one halfpenny per person (compared with usual charges of sixpence or a shilling at subscription baths).

Unsurprisingly, a dip in a plunge bath soon became the most popular means for the poor, and particulary boys over eight, to get clean (albeit without soap).

In the days before mechanisms existed for water in such baths to be continually changed and filtered – as would not be the case until the Edwardian era – the quality of the water after a few days' use can readily be imagined.

April 1847, where, according to the *Hull Packet*, the provision of public baths was supported partly because it promised to 'put an end to those indecent exhibitions which the lack of bathing conveniences in Hull has rendered of daily occurrence…'

That more people, especially the middle classes, were now swimming in the sea was yet another factor in raising support for public baths.

This was particulary so after Queen Victoria took her first, well publicised dip in July 1847, on the Isle of Wight.

Meanwhile further impetus for the cause of public baths came from those who sought to promote the new craze for hydrotherapy.

But finally, one of the key reasons why the Victorians started to build ever larger and more sophisticated baths, featuring ever larger indoor pools, was simply that they could.

Lest we forget, the Victorians were terrific innovators and builders.

In common with the Romans, they had acquired the knowledge (or at least the confidence to experiment); they had the incentive (both in social and commercial terms); and crucially, they had increasing access to all the basic building materials required, particularly after a second rapid expansion of the railway network during the 1840s.

As a result of this network there was now also an abundance of affordable coal, the fuel on which the great Lancashire and Yorkshire boilers of every baths establishment, private or public, would depend for its tepid pools, hot baths and laundries.

Water itself was also in more plentiful supply.

By the 1840s private water companies were established in every town and city (although piped water to every home was still some way off – in 1876 it was estimated that 47 per cent of London homes still had no constant feed).

The quality of water was another matter, as was the cost. In the early 1850s Birmingham Corporation was charged nine pence per 1,000 gallons at its baths, whereas in Lambeth the charge was only two and a quarter pence.

In some areas water was piped to baths without charge, as an act of charity.

But the ideal was still, as the Romans found, to site baths in areas where a free and natural source existed, either from a river or the sea, or from underground springs, thereby limiting costs to the creation of pipelines or the digging of shafts and the installation of pumps.

So it was, taking all these factors and the 1846 Act together, that a new era in baths construction now beckoned.

Dukinfield and his fellow campaigners had done their bit. Architects and engineers were keen to enter this new market, as were a host of companies in the business of manufacturing and supplying materials and products: stoves and drying machines, water closets and zinc tubs; slate screens, fire bricks and tiling; pipes, cocks, valves and cisterns; towels, cocoa nut fibre matting, brushes and soaps.

Then there were all the employment opportunities; for swimming instructors, insurance agents, plumbers, engineers and gas fitters, not to mention all the staff needed to run the new baths. Price Prichard Baly reckoned a typical establishment required a dozen people of varying skills, from superintendent and matrons down to cleaners and stokers.

Now, it was up to the local authorities.

Appropriately, the first one to adopt the 1846 Act was the Vestry of St Martins-in-the-Fields, Sir Henry Dukinfield's parish, which had clearly drawn up plans in advance and was therefore able to open its Orange Street Baths relatively soon after the Act, in 1847. Designed by Baly, the final cost was over £19,000, far in excess of the Committee's original estimates, even though, unlike all those that followed, it did not have a plunge pool.

Two further baths by Baly, both opened in 1851, were on Great Smith Street, Westminster, costing £14,686 (and in operation until it was replaced in 1893), and Poplar Baths, which cost £12,480 (and was replaced in 1934).

Baly also worked on baths at Marshall Street, opened 1852 (replaced 1931); Endell Street, 1853 (*see right*) and Spa Road, Bermondsey, 1854 (demolished in 1926).

Other London baths built in the years following the Act were on Marylebone Road, designed by Christopher Eales in 1849 (where remnants of the two original plunge baths still exist under the frontage of a later building on Marylebone Road); on London Street, Greenwich, in 1850, designed by Robert Ritchie and similar in external treatment to Paul Street in Liverpool; and on Davies Street, Hanover Square, 1852 (architect unknown).

That made nine public baths altogether in London, built under the terms of the Act in its first ten years.

There were of course several other baths in existence, such as those in Regent's Park, Hoxton and Holborn mentioned in the previous chapter, plus the Model Baths at Whitechapel, and another baths built by a private society in 1846 around three sides of the New River Company's reservoir by Euston Square.

This was a large undertaking, but alas, the society chose not to employ an architect, with the result that both its plunge pools leaked and were rendered useless.

Such 'penny-wise and pound foolish' cost-cutting, warned *The Builder*, was a major mistake. Or, as a member of the Mansion House Committee wrote to *The Times* in October 1846, 'A mere shed, which may be run up for a small sum may, in a few years, be found a source of constant expense.'

Nevertheless, the Euston Square Baths did go on to be profitable, until in 1856 the reservoir was sold for housing (on what is now Tolmers Square). »

▲ As an engineer Price Prichard Baly was more concerned with such issues as drying, heating and ventilation, which may explain why he teamed up with an architect (either George Pownall or Frederick Hyde Pownall) to design the **St Giles and St George Bloomsbury Baths and Wash Houses**, the first establishment to be built under the 1846 Act jointly by two vestries.

This view of the **Endell Street** frontage shows an early example of what would become standard layout. That is, with an entrance and administration block masking the more utilitarian baths and laundries behind (an echo of railway station architecture).

Note the prominent lettering on the upper frieze, a deliberate attempt to draw public attention.

Note also there are six doors, each serving different classes and specific parts of the establishment. In total the building housed 73 baths, 56 wash tubs and, at the rear, first and second class plunge pools, 36' x 24' and 40' x 24'.

Those pools were merged into one in the 1890s, before the building was demolished in the 1930s. The site is now occupied by The **Oasis Sports Centre**.

▲ Designed by Borough Engineer James Newlands, **Cornwallis Street Baths, Liverpool** was opened on May 5 1851 (four days after the Great Exhibition in London).

Like Baly in London, Newlands kept external detail to a minimum, in order to concentrate resources on internal details. Also to save money, the plunge pools were built at basement level.

Most significant of all, however, is that when originally planned there were going to be two plunge pools, as there were at Paul Street (see page 29), though a little larger at 57' x 40' and 42' x 27'.

Yet once the building opened, so popular were these two that an area set aside for a wash house was hastily converted into a third pool (see opposite).

Even then, four years later

the two original pools had to be enlarged to cope with demand.

No other public baths of the 1850s was so well equipped, at least for swimming. As a result Cornwallis Street was the natural choice for hosting Liverpool's first ever swimming gala, in 1860 (a male-only affair – women were not allowed their own until 1887).

Including the installation of an engine to pump river water up the hill from the Mersey via an underground pipe – hence the pool's distinct taste and odour – the building cost £28,000.

Yet judging by Baths Committee records, it was the only baths in Liverpool to make a regular, if modest, profit. In one year, it was calculated, users of its First Class baths – just twelve per cent of the total – contributed 50 per cent of

the overall income (an equation similar to the one which dictates that executive boxes are installed at modern football stadiums).

In short, here was a model for the future; one that put more emphasis on swimming and, crucially, on facilities likely to attract middle class users.

Changing demographics and the depopulation of that part of the city after the Second World War put an end to the baths' prominence, and by the time it closed in 1967 it was in a sad state. Nevertheless, over 116 years, its total admissions topped 16 million.

Today the site is occupied by the Liverpool Community College. But its neighbour (above, far right), the Workshops for the Outdoor Blind, by George Redmayne, opened in 1870, still stands.

» Outside the capital, it took five years until the first baths built under the 1846 Act started to welcome the public.

Opened in 1850 were establishments at Trippett Street, Hull; Broad Weir, Bristol (though with no pool until 1878); Davenport Street, Macclesfield, and Gedling Street, Nottingham.

These were followed in 1851 by Bath Street, Bilston; Kent Street, Birmingham; Saul Street, Preston, and Cornwallis Street, Liverpool (see left and opposite), and in 1852 by Fairmeadow, Maidstone, and Hale Street, Coventry.

As in London, however, the 1846 Act by no means signalled the end of private investment.

Both in Birmingham and Macclesfield, although the new baths were run by the local authorities, they were still partially funded by subscriptions, while in Manchester and Salford, a private company was formed specifically by local worthies because neither of the borough councils were willing to adopt the Act.

Other privately funded baths (among several from this period) were in Bolton (1847, see page 29), Hereford (1850, page 12), Miles Platting, Manchester (gifted by Sir Benjamin Heywood in 1850), Wolverhampton and Walsall (both 1851).

This growing network of baths soon drew the attention of foreign visitors, no doubt including some who had come to gaze in wonder at Joseph Paxton's iron and glass Crystal Palace, built for the 1851 Great Exhibition and itself an inspirational model for Britain's first generation of specialist baths designers.

Among a number of official delegations in the late 1840s, Sir Henry Dukinfield met with representatives from the French and Belgian governments, each interested in establishing similar networks of public baths. He also met with private interests from New York. And it is no coincidence that movements for public baths in Germany and Austria both emerged in the 1850s and 1860s.

Interest in baths design and history was also spurred by the publication of various pamphlets and books (*see Links*).

Price Prichard Baly was first off the mark in 1852, with *A Statement of the Proceedings of the Committee Appointed to Promote the Establishment of Baths and Wash-houses*.

(Occasionally the butt of criticism in *The Builder*, Baly himself seems to have ended his involvement with baths around 1854, and in the 1860s headed off to work in Russia on the Trans-Siberian Railway. He died in 1875.)

But the most detailed book of the period, simply called *Baths and Wash Houses* and published in 1853, was by Arthur Hurst Ashpitel (1807-69) and John Whichcord (1823–85). This London-based duo had designed two public baths, the aforementioned ones at Bilston and Maidstone, and the privately-funded Lambeth Baths in south London.

Its first chapter reprised an earlier historical treatise written by Ashpitel called, *Public Baths of the Ancients*, c.1850, which had run to three editions and was a considerable work of scholarship. (Both Ashpitel and Whichchord were also Fellows of the Society of Antiquarians.)

The Secretary of the Lambeth Baths Company, George Cape, then adapted their work and added his own observations in an 1854 edition of *Baths and Wash Houses*, subtitled 'the history of their rise and progress, showing their utility and their effect upon the moral and physical condition of the people.'

In common with Ashpitel and Whichcord, Thomas Worthington in Manchester also designed a trio of baths, the first of which, in Collier Street, Salford, is the only building from this decade where the actual swimming pools survive, albeit in a ruinous state.

Collier Street is therefore the first of three case studies ending this chapter (*see page 14*), all three of which – ironically, in view of our focus on the 1846 Act – were built by private interests.

No public baths from this period have survived.

Was this because they were of a a lower standard?

Not necessarily. It is rather that public baths have always been subject to regular upgrading, and so, by the 1880s, improved technology and increasing demand rendered obsolete most of those built in the 1840s and 1850s. (It should be added, however, that although the original buildings have not survived, a few of the sites on which they were built continue to be occupied by baths built during later periods; for example, Kent Street in Birmingham, and Endell Street, Holborn.)

As for the social and welfare benefits of the early public baths, these are rather harder to analyse.

Beyond doubt, they represented a huge leap forward in civic life.

But we must not think of them as agents of democratisation, at least not in this period.

Certainly men like Dukinfield did not envisage all classes of people – or as Disraeli expressed it in his novel of 1845, Britain's *Two Nations* – sharing the same water, let alone the same waiting »

▲ Few photographs of early plunge pools have survived, but this one from 1967 shows the Ladies Pool at **Cornwallis Street Baths, Liverpool**, and is probably typical. Measuring 40' x 27', originally this was the men's third class pool.

By modern standards the facilities were extremely basic.

Above the changing boxes were galleries housing slipper baths, supported on iron columns that doubled as waste pipes. Natural lighting was limited, and the water was changed no more than once a week. The tank was tiled only above water level, and lined with plain cement below.

In 1856 journalist Hugh Shimmin provided a vivid account of a Saturday night in the third class pool in the *Liverpool Mercury*. Despite a rise in the price from one halfpenny (as per the 1846 Act) to 2d (compared with 6d in the more luxurious first class pool), 'upwards of a hundred boys, most of them in a state of nudity,' wrote Shimmin, could be seen 'ducking, diving, floundering, plunging, dousing, rolling, sprawling and tossing in the water'.

He also noted that there were 24 changing boxes, none with a door, in some of which as many as 12 boys at a time had deposited their 'habitments.'

In Lambeth, George Cape saw similar scenes. 'Were it not for enjoying the pleasure of a swim more than the wash, these lads would seldom come'.

▶ Writing in their 1853 book, architects **Arthur Ashpitel** and **John Whichcord** asserted that 'baths and washhouses should be erected in a substantial manner; all superfluous ornament, and the adaptation of Gothic or other masks, ought to be forbidden; a character of cheerfulness should be given to them, which the architect will well know how to stamp with an expression of its purpose.'

Shown here from *The Builder*, with its unusually shaped pool but little discernible cheerfulness, is Ashpitel and Whichcord's design for **Bilston Baths**, opened in 1852.

By contrast, **Kent Street Baths** in nearby **Birmingham** (architect John Cresswell), opened in May 1851 (*opposite top*), was a curious blend of Queen Anne styling with an Italianate colonnade and chimney.

In a similarly eclectic mode but with more pronounced Jacobean leanings was **Greenwich Baths** (*opposite centre*), opened in September 1851, on the corner of Greenwich High Road and Royal Hill. Its design was by civil engineer Robert Ritchie, an authority on heating and ventilation.

None of these buildings survives. Despite its roof collapsing in 1892, Bilston soldiered on until being converted into a factory in 1948. It was demolished in the 1980s. Kent Street was rebuilt in the 1930s and Greenwich demolished in 1928.

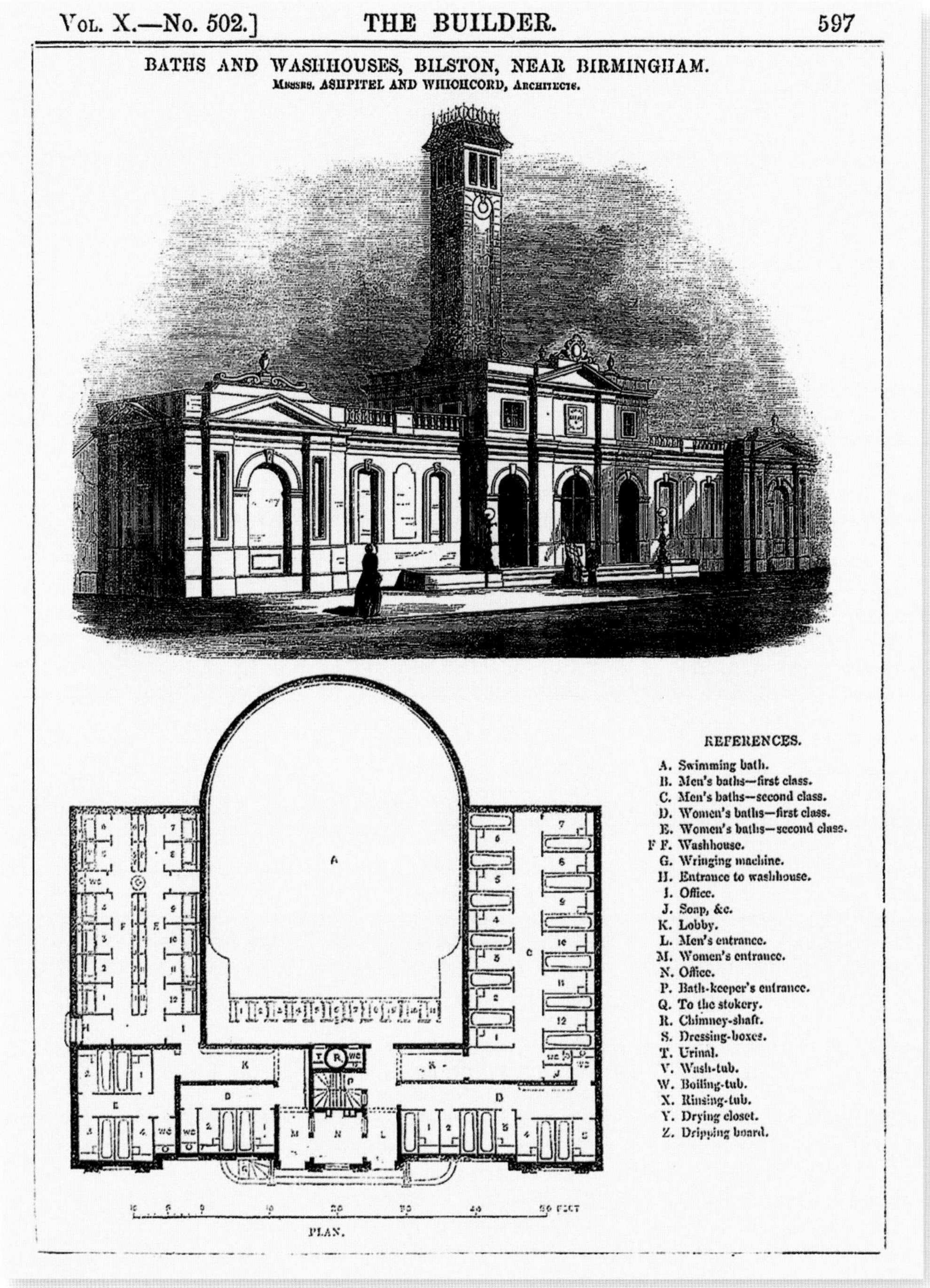

VOL. X.—No. 502.]   THE BUILDER.   597

BATHS AND WASHHOUSES, BILSTON, NEAR BIRMINGHAM.
Messrs. ASHPITEL AND WHICHCORD, Architects.

REFERENCES.

A. Swimming bath.
B. Men's baths—first class.
C. Men's baths—second class.
D. Women's baths—first class.
E. Women's baths—second class.
F F. Washhouse.
G. Wringing machine.
H. Entrance to washhouse.
I. Office.
J. Soap, &c.
K. Lobby.
L. Men's entrance.
M. Women's entrance.
N. Office.
P. Bath-keeper's entrance.
Q. To the stokery.
R. Chimney-shaft.
S. Dressing-boxes.
T. Urinal.
V. Wash-tub.
W. Boiling-tub.
X. Rinsing-tub.
Y. Drying closet.
Z. Dripping board.

PLAN.

» rooms or even entrances. Strict segregation of First and Second, and in some cases Third Class bathers, made sure of that.

And of course in every case women, of whatever social standing, were still treated as second class citizens, either not allowed to swim at all, or at best granted access to the mens' baths only at certain times of the week (usually during working hours).

At the same time, the oft-quoted Victorian ideal of 'a healthy mind in a healthy body' – taken from Juvenal's expression *mens sana in corpore sano*, and espoused by muscular Christian thinkers such as Thomas Hughes and Charles Kingsley – led to more middle class men organising themselves for swimming, just as they already had done for bowls, cricket, archery, and most recently, for croquet.

In the previous chapter we noted the first organised swimming events at the Serpentine in 1837, and the first indoor gala at Holborn in 1843. Among the earliest known swimming clubs were those formed in Maidstone, in 1834, Brighton 1860, Durham 1861, both Huddersfield and Birmingham in 1862, and Halifax in 1864.

But these pioneer clubs were not simply interested in racing. They also clearly saw themselves as ambassadors for swimming. Hence the London Swimming Club, formed at Lambeth Baths in 1859, expressed its aim as the 'raising the art of swimming from its comparative disuse, and placing it amongst the first of our national recreations.'

According to the *Penny Illustrated Paper* in September 1866, the London SC set out to achieve this by 'the holding of periodical races, in which the elite of the club should show us as to what perfection the art could be brought and amateurs of all ages might strive for prizes graduated as to their efficiency'.

The club also set out to entertain.

An account of one of its early 'water fêtes' at Lambeth describes 'a number of aquatic amusements of a strikingly novel and amusing character'. There was a hurdle-race, using poles floating on the surface, contested by youths under sixteen who had never previously won a prize. Next came an egg diving contest and an extraordinary 'pole-walking' competition amongst members of the club.

But the 'great feature' of the programme was the final race of the night for the captaincy of the London Swimming Club, covering 400 yards, or ten lengths of the pool.   »

The Italianate Woodcock Street Baths and Wash House, Birmingham, designed by Edmund Jones and opened in August 1860, was clearly influenced by Liverpool's Cornwallis Street. The building was remodelled in 1902 and then almost entirely replaced by the current sports centre in 1926.

THE LAMBETH BATHS.——Messrs. Ashpitel and Whichcord, Architects.

▲ Designed by Ashpitel and Whichcord on a long, irregular site, accessed through a gap in houses on Westminster Bridge Road, **Lambeth Baths and Wash Houses** opened in July 1853.

Partly because the building was funded by a mix of donations and private capital (rather than via the 1846 Act), its first and second class pools were unusually large, at 122' and 133' respectively.

This, combined with the baths' proximity to Waterloo Station, and the efforts of the company secretary George Cape, helped make

Lambeth one of the most important competition baths in the capital. In November 1861 it was also the first baths in Britain to admit women to a 'water fête' (or gala).

As noted earlier, Cape penned one of the earliest books on baths architecture, in 1854, following on from Ashpitel and Whichcord's own treatise the year before. But for all this trio's avowed expertise, certain features at Lambeth would not catch on.

As seen here, in the centre of the first class pool stood a terracotta fountain, through which warm

water was channelled, apparently to enhance circulation and reduce scum. Either it failed in this, or was simply removed to allow competitive swimming.

Another quirk not repeated elsewhere was the provision of an aquarium at the shallow end (presumably not in the water itself).

However one feature which did become standard was the use of glazing in the central roof section.

The pool itself, comparatively shallow at 3-5' in depth, was lined by tiles of 'a dusky colour' with white porcelain tiles around the

edge. The timber roof was also white, with vermillion details.

Note the stairs at the far end. Made from slate, a material often used in baths of this period, these led to 16 first class slipper baths raised above the changing boxes.

Entry to this pool cost 6d, and 3d to the adjoining second class pool. There were a further 55 slipper baths at the rear, next to the wash house.

Closed c.1902, the site of Lambeth Baths was between Lower Marsh and what is now Baylis Road.

》 Even though all competitors were amateurs, as in the world of athletics there would soon be a distinction made between those who swam for honour and those who competed for prizes.

For example from the oldest known surviving poster issued for a swimming gala, staged by the Leeds Swimming Club at the newly opened Cookridge Street Baths on July 28 1866, we learn that prizes were offered to both 'working men' and 'gentlemen amateurs', and that the top prize was the Mayor's gold watch.

Small wonder that galas started to attract serious swimmers, and regular audiences, and that in turn, this offered a further incentive to local authorities not only to provide larger pools but also to incorporate spectator galleries into their design.

But it also required swimmers to dress for the occasion.

As noted earlier, until the mid 19th century most men swam naked. Indeed most boys continued to do so until the early 20th century, even at public baths.

However, according to Archibald Sinclair's Badminton Library edition of Swimming (see Links), 'the wearing of drawers' for men was first recorded in certain London baths around 1850.

Presumably the admission of female spectators to galas, first recorded at Lambeth in 1861 (see left), hastened this trend.

Sinclair also reported that Endell Street Baths in Holborn was one of the last establishments to enforce the practice

At first it charged bathers one penny to hire the standard-issue drawers, but then fell into line with other baths by issuing them free with the price of admission, along with a fresh towel.

But the practice also meant that baths now had to contend with larger volumes of laundry.

Or, as would become common on busy days, bathers had to put up with donning a pair of damp drawers only recently discarded (though it must have been worse for women, whose costumes remained absurdly voluminous until at least the 1880s).

The hygiene implications of this system, combined with the baths' general lack of adequate sterilisation and of systems for water circulation were, in retrospect, potentially lethal.

But then the 1846 Act was only one of several measures enacted for the health of the nation; for example the Metropolitan Buildings Act (1844), the Towns Improvement Act (1847) and the Public Health Act (1848).

It was also contemporaneous with such enlightened legislation as the Museums of Art Act of 1845 and the Public Library Act of 1850, both equally significant cornerstones of Britain's burgeoning civic ethos.

Between 1846 and 1870 at least 49 public baths and wash houses were completed under the terms of the Dukinfield Act.

Experimental they may have been in design, and crude by the standards of later years.

Yet each provided a gateway into an idealised world of cleanliness, modernity and good health, a gateway that was now within reach of anyone with at least a halfpenny to spare for a dip in a plunge pool.

And because there were so many halfpennies spent in this fashion, the baths that followed in the next phase of development after 1870 would see pools, and swimming, come to the fore as public baths' main source of income.

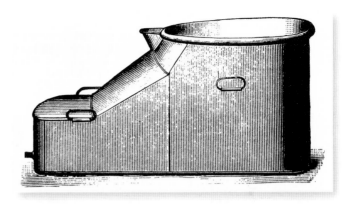

▲ One feature of Britain's early public baths that foreign visitors found hard to fathom was the belief that the best way to wash was to soak for 20-30 minutes ('like a potato' wrote architect Robert Alsop in 1894) in one's own soiled water.

Certainly by 1900 most European and American baths establishments had installed showers (also referred to as spray baths, lavatory baths, rain baths or Lassar Baths, after a Berlin skin doctor).

That said, it is unlikely any of Britain's early public baths featured contraptions such as this, illustrated in a catalogue issued by Ewart & Son of Euston Road, London.

Designed for use in a home with no running water, it served both to retain heat and maintain modesty, and for good reason was known as a **slipper bath** (or *baignoire sabot* in French, meaning boot bath).

The individual baths installed at Britain's early public baths were like this one only in the sense that they had hinged lids. Otherwise they were fairly similar in design to modern baths, or at least were once zinc tubs were superceded in the 1850s by more durable and hygienic glazed porcelain models.

Yet oddly the name slipper bath never died out.

In 1899 a trial at Cheltenham found that six showers could service the same number of bathers as 25 slipper baths, and use a quarter of the water. Consequently several local authorities started to install showers.

But only ever as a supplement to slipper baths, which in most locations remained in use right up until the baths departments finally started closing in the mid to late 20th century.

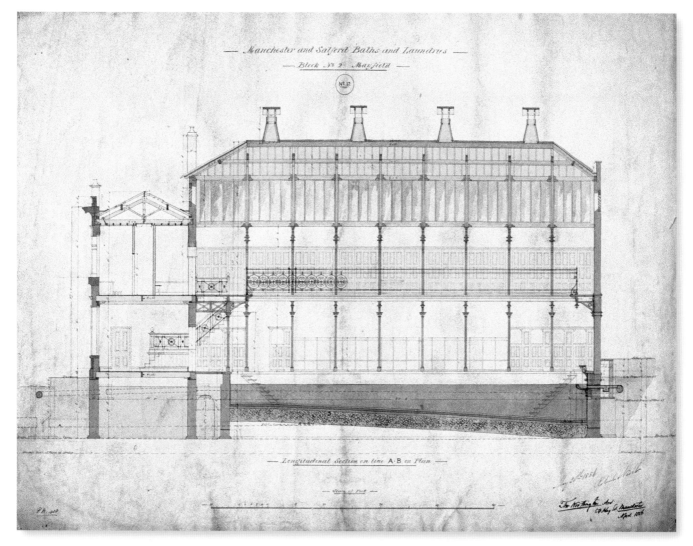

— Manchester and Salford Baths and Laundries —
— Block N° 2 Mayfield —
— Longitudinal Section on line A·B on Plan —

▲ Drawn on canvas and dated April 1856, this is one of three surviving plans of **Mayfield Baths, New Store Street, Ardwick**, young architect Thomas Worthington's second commission from the Manchester and Salford Baths and Laundries Company.

The four prominent vents in the roof are significant, because only a few months later, in August 1856,

Worthington's first commission for the company – Greengate Baths on Collier Street, Salford – opened, only to suffer almost immediately from condensation. This drawing suggests that the problem had already become evident.

Partly as a result, Collier Street remained operational only for about 25 years (although the building still stands, having spent most of

its life since as a warehouse, *see page 46*), whereas Mayfield Baths stayed in business from 1857 until an air raid in 1941.

Worthington's third and final commission for the company (whose baths were eventually taken over by Manchester and Salford Corporations in the late 1870s) was Leaf Street, Hulme. Opened in 1860, this survived until 1976.

▶ Thomas Worthington's **Mayfield Baths** in **Ardwick, Manchester**, as illustrated in *The Builder* in 1858, appeared to ape the lofty pretensions of a Gothic church. Yet it was a thoroughly modern building.

Worthington (1826-1909) had recently set up office in King Street and went on to design *inter alia* Manchester's Albert Memorial, the Crown Court and a number of churches and hospitals.

As noted opposite, his first baths commission had its faults. But Worthington learnt from them, and his designs for Mayfield Baths are subtly different. Apart from the addition of vents, instead of a glazed roof, a glazed clerestory was added above the gallery. The two pools were also larger, at 63' x 24' and 55' x 30'. But he kept to the same roof structure as at Collier Street, using iron columns that doubled as drainpipes for the first floor bathrooms, and laminated timber for the arch-braced trusses.

Mayfield Baths cost £24,660, over twice the cost of Collier Street, but it lasted much longer, as did his next effort, on Leaf Street, Hulme. This had three pools, two of them 75 feet in length. Leaf Street was also the first public bath, albeit run by a private company, to have a Turkish bath. (Britain's first private Turkish bath had opened a short distance away on Broughton Lane, in 1857.)

Another innovation by the company, built close to Mayfield, was a boys-only Penny Bath.

Recalling the scenes described by Hugh Shimmin in Liverpool (*see page 37*) it probably seemed a good idea to segregate boys from other users. However, the Penny Bath was soon converted to slipper baths, following complaints that boys were forever hanging around outside, begging for entry money.

MAYFIELD BATHS AND LAUNDRIES, MANCHESTER.——Mr. Thomas Worthington, Architect.

▲ Considering the Victorians' love of all things Oriental, and, after 1857, the growing popularity of Turkish baths, relatively few public baths were built in either the Byzantine or Moorish styles.

In **Leeds**, however, where four Turkish baths opened between 1858–63, a private company commissioned the town's leading architect, Cuthbert Brodrick, to design the **Oriental and General Baths,** on **Cookridge Street**, to combine all the public's bathing needs under one roof, or rather, under a series of domes, topped by a minaret-style tower.

Costing £13,000 and opened in July 1866, this exotic building (albeit in a rather more urban setting than depicted in this water colour), housed two pools, 75' x 36' (oval shaped) and 50' x 24'.

Alas Brodrick's domes proved impracticable and were replaced during a Gothic-style refit in 1882 (although the tower was retained).

The baths was then taken over by the Corporation in 1889, and remained open until 1965. It was then demolished in 1969, since when the site has been remodelled as the Millennium Square.

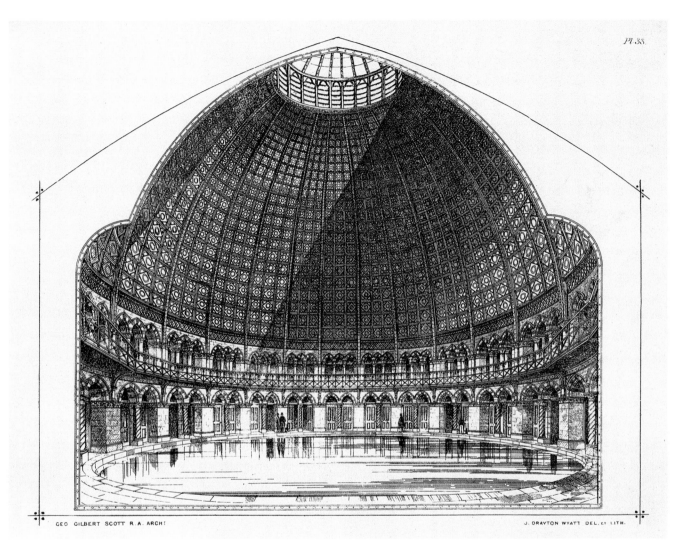

GEO GILBERT SCOTT R.A. ARCH!   J. DRAYTON WYATT DEL. ET LITH.

▲ With the exception of a few oval pools (as at Leeds, opposite), and of various, irregularly shaped leisure pools since the 1980s, the rectangular pool has remained the standard. This apparently unique Victorian oddity – **Brill's Gentlemen's Baths** on **East Street, Brighton** – was billed as the largest seawater baths in Europe, at 65' in diameter, when it opened in 1869.

Certainly it was the most expensive. Built to replace an earlier circular bath (known as 'the onion', that had stood on the site since 1823), this Pantheon-like wonder cost Charles Brill's Baths Company a colossal £90,000. And Brill had already spent heavily on a more conventional Ladies Bath, opened across the road on Pool Valley in 1862.

For all Brighton's popularity as a resort, Brill must have had huge faith in swimming as an attraction, not least because the architect he hired was George Gilbert Scott, the high priest of Gothic Revival, who had just completed the Albert Memorial. On the other hand, Scott's practice was so prolific that the great man himself may not have had much involvement in it.

Alas only one photograph of the baths is known, taken four years before its demolition in 1929, by which time it appeared shabby, and rather smaller than on this lithograph. Signs in English and Greek proclaim the water to be as fresh as seawater, but safer.

The site is now occupied by the former Savoy Cinema. Nearby is Brills Lane.

Case Study

Greengate Baths, Collier Street, Salford

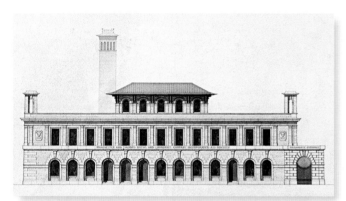

Opened August 27 1856
Closed c.1880
Address Collier St M3 7DW
Architect Thomas Worthington
Cost £9,913
Pool sizes 1st & 2nd both 53' x 25'
Owner Ask Developments
Listed Grade II* (1980) and on
Buildings at Risk Register since
1998

Tucked away in a forgotten
back street, yet only a short
stroll from Manchester's busy
Deansgate, our first case study is
of a genuinely unique building.

Boarded up and virtually
derelict, Greengate Baths is the
oldest surviving public baths in
Britain, and one of only five public
baths to be listed Grade II*.

That it operated as a baths for
barely 25 years, and spent the
following hundred years or so as a
warehouse cannot be denied.

But as the sole surviving
example of the earliest generation
of public baths in the mid 19th

**Viewed in 2003, the boarded-up
façade of Greengate Baths retains
its original crest on the upper
storey (*nearest the camera*). Just
legible, it states 'Manchester &
Salford Baths & Laundries Erected
Anno Domini MDCCCLV' (although
it opened the following year). The
central attic storey provided living
accommodation for the baths
superintendent and his family.**

century it is of immense historical
and architectural importance.

Today, surrounded as it is by
a dual carriageway, industrial
units and new developments
forming part of the Greengate
Embankment regeneration area,
it is hard to picture how deprived
and densely populated this part
of the city was in the 1850s. And
yet unlike their counterparts in
London, Birmingham, Liverpool
or Preston, neither of the local
authorities in Manchester or
Salford were prepared to adopt the
1846 Act. Instead, in 1854 local
philanthropists and businessmen
stepped into the void by forming
the Manchester and Salford Baths
and Laundries Company, with
7,000 shares of £5 each.

As mentioned earlier in this
chapter, Greengate Baths was
its first venture, for which the
company hired an untested but
promising local architect, Thomas
Worthington (1826-1909), whose
front elevation and chimney
design (*see left*) clearly shows the
influence of his recent tour of Italy.

Unusually, the first and
second class pools were of equal
dimensions, at 53' long (to suit
the site rather than any stipulated
minimum), but as was the norm,
no provision was made for
women, other than in a separate
slipper bath section at the side.

The baths was undoubtedly
popular. In its first five months it
was used by 16,000 people, and
as it had cost barely a third of

Cornwallis Street in Liverpool or Kent Street in Birmingham, the company was delighted. One of its leading shareholders, an engineer, declared that Greengate would be an example across the kingdom, and was much superior to any of the baths he had visited in London.

But he was mistaken.

Problems with ventilation in particular – remedied by Worthington in his two other baths for the company (*see page 42*) – persuaded Salford Corporation, who took the baths over in 1877, to build new baths on nearby Blackfriars Road instead. (These opened in 1880, and in 2001 were converted into offices).

Until recently it was hoped that a similar fate might save Greengate Baths. Having served from 1880 until around 1990 as a warehouse, it then stood empty and unguarded. Its chimney had already been demolished in the 1980s, and in 1998 it was placed on English Heritage's Buildings at Risk Register.

Three years later it was bought by Ask Developments. They spent £400,000 on securing the fabric against further deterioration, but after considering various options to convert the shell into offices or residential units, a collapse in the propety market in 2008 left its future as uncertain as ever – a relic in desperate need of deliverance.

Apart from the remains of the warehouse floor, the First Class pool is remarkably intact, as are Worthington's roof trusses. Springing from cantilevered iron consoles, these were arch-braced using an early form of laminated timber, with cross bracing in the spandrels. After being superceded by steel for many years, timber is now back in vogue for pool design.

Case Study

Park Road Baths, Halifax

Opened July 23 1859
Closed 1990
Address Park Road, HX1 2TS
Architect poss. Paxton & Stokes
Engineer George Wilson Stevens
Cost £6,839
Pools (before 1924) 1st 53' x 19', 2nd 57' x 19, Ladies 24' x 16'
Owner The King's Church
Listed Grade II (1994)

Park Road was the first of two baths in Halifax to have been gifted by Sir Francis Crossley, whose Dean Clough carpet mills, less than a mile to the north, were once the largest and most profitable on the planet.

Also a long serving local MP, Crossley lavished his wealth on the improvement of Halifax. For the construction of the baths, by the Waterworks Committee, he donated £6,000.

It was located, moreover, in a corner of the People's Park, for which Crossley had donated a further £30,000, and hired for its layout the great Joseph Paxton (who by that time was also an MP and near the end of his long career). Opened in 1857, the park is now listed Grade II★.

Paxton may also have had a hand in designing the baths, otherwise credited to the borough engineer, George Wilson Stevens.

However, although finely dressed in coursed stone and ashlar on a rusticated base, and with a splendid crest celebrating its opening in 1859 (*see page 30*), the Greek Revival building lacks real presence compared with other baths of the period, suggesting that Paxton may not have had that much of an influence. It also lacks balance. Closest to the park, the two storey entrance block housed the superintendent on the upper floor, while at the southern end the upper floor is windowless.

But at least, thanks to Crossley's benevolence, it was one of the few baths of its time (since Liverpool

in 1829) to feature a plunge pool for ladies, albeit a small one with only five changing boxes.

Also unusually, as the baths was fed directly from Ogden Reservoir, its water was changed every other day, when once a week was the norm elsewhere.

(Incidentally its opening also spelt the end for Halifax's original open air pool, a members only establishment called Greece Fields Baths, that a plumber called Rawlinson had opened in 1793 and which had 'the most expensive suite of baths in Yorkshire'.)

Between 1921–24 a series of internal changes saw Park Road's two main original pools re-roofed with reinforced concrete and the ladies' pool replaced by extra slipper baths.

Fifty years later the baths survived a road widening scheme. But in 1990 they were finally closed by Calderdale Council, despite protests from the Halifax Swimming Club, which had formed at the baths in 1864 (and is still one of the oldest clubs in Britain).

For a while the building served as offices, until the King's Church bought it for £61,000 and transformed the interior into a church, complete with baptism pool, café, meeting rooms and a prayer hall in the former second class pool. The scheme, designed by John Watson Hardy architects, won a Civic Trust Award in 2001.

A Congregationalist himself, Sir Francis would no doubt be content that both this building, and his park, are still serving Halifax.

Boys' Pool, Crossley Heath School, Halifax

Not content with financing a park and public baths, in 1860 the ever generous Sir Francis Crossley and his brothers John and Joseph combined to endow an orphanage on Delph Hill, at a cost of £56,000 initially, plus a further £50,000 to cover its running costs.

Large enough to accommodate up to 400 children, it was designed in a solid Northern Renaissance style by local architect John Hogg, (who also designed the villas lining Park Road).

But it is not Hogg's orphanage, with its gables, finials and towers that concerns us. Instead, at its rear stands a range of single storey buildings. They are of no architectural merit. But in one of them is a small swimming pool with a remarkable claim to fame.

Originally designated for boys, this modest building is thought to be the oldest operational indoor pool in Britain, having been built at the same time as the Crossley Orphanage, in 1864.

Not only that but it has a twin, for across the yard is an almost identical building which once housed a pool reserved for girls.

This pool, with its original tiling, is still extant, but has been boarded over since 1918.

Also noteable, if equally anonymous in the same range of buildings, is the orphanage's original gymnasium from 1864; still in use in 2008 and believed to be oldest of its type also.

By the turn of the 20th century school pools would be common, the majority being outdoor. After one of its scholars drowned in 1839, Eton College set the trend by making swimming lessons compulsory for any boy wanting to take a boat on the river.

The first educational institution to build an indoor pool is believed to have been the Royal Medical Benevolent College, at Epsom. That was in 1861, shortly before Crossley Heath. (The building still stands, but having closed as a pool in 1977 is now Epsom College's design and technology centre.)

Elsewhere, the indoor pool at Ipswich School, similar in scale and style to Crossley's, has been in use since 1884, while a mile to the west of Crossley Heath, Warley Road Primary School has one that

dates from 1897. Only in recent years have pools at other Halifax schools closed; at Moorside (b. 1879) and Mount Pellon (b. 1903).

The survival of Crossley Heath's pool is partly owing to the school's status. In 1985 it merged with Heath Grammar and is now a co-educational foundation school and a Specialist Language College.

Rugby is apparently its forté. But swimming is definitely part of its heritage.

Well done the Boys' Pool!

Opened 1864
Address Scircoat Moor Road HX3 0HG
Architect John Hogg
Pool 38' x 15'
Owner Crossley Heath School
Listed pool building unlisted, main school Grade II (1973)

An interior view in 1899 (*above*) shows the Boys' Pool (before the late 20th century addition of a suspended ceiling and a graffiti-style mural painted by pupils along one wall). Note the individual bath behind the column. The building's plain exterior is virtually identical to the neighbouring Girls' Pool (*left*), which also dates from 1864.

Captured at the time of its opening in 1898, Alloa Baths illustrates the greater refinement of pools in the late Victorian period. Note the decorative use of ferns, coloured tiles and carved dragons' heads on the projecting hammer beams, and the now standard range of accessories; that is, diving board, trapezes and hanging rings. For a view of this pool today see page 97.

Chapter Four

Late Victorian 1870–1901

By the 1870s it was evident that where properly designed and managed, public baths and wash houses were yielding the health and welfare benefits that had been promised, even if, in the absence of any detailed studies, those benefits were measured mainly in terms of user statistics and anecdotal evidence.

But equally clear to local authorities was that in order to keep their debt repayments to within the oft-quoted 'penny in the pound' limit they had promised ratepayers, the income derived from swimming was critical.

After a relative lull in the construction of baths during the 1860s, the remaining years of Queen Victoria's reign were therefore characterised by three main trends.

Firstly, there was a great leap forward in the number of baths around the nation generally. In 1865 there were around 50 public baths in England. By 1885 this figure had doubled, and by 1901 it had doubled again to some 210 establishments.

Secondly, this building boom included a surge in the number of baths that featured larger and more sophisticated swimming pools, and also Turkish baths, vapour baths, showers and the like, all designed to raise standards and attract more middle class and female users.

Thirdly, by tapping into the public's seemingly insatiable appetite for entertainment and sporting activity, baths of the late 19th century evolved into multi-purpose event venues.

Numerous factors underpinned these developments.

Not least, the population of England, Scotland and Wales rose from 26 million in 1871 to 37 million in 1901, ensuring that civic provision in all areas of the public realm – whether for schools, libraries, parks or cemeteries – had to keep pace with demand.

Meanwhile rising living standards created an increase in the number of ratepayers who harboured demands of their own, above and beyond any consideration for the needs of the poor.

Inevitably, the late 19th century building boom still left large areas of Britain underprovided. Even in London, where 24 new baths were built during this period, poorer parishes were often the last to be able to raise the money, depending instead on a neighbouring vestry to cater for its constituents.

Wales was behind too, with only four baths before 1900 (Cardiff being the first, in 1862), while Scotland, omitted from the terms of the 1846 Act, had to await other pieces of legislation before its local authorities were brought into line with England and Wales. These included local Police Acts for Glasgow and Dundee in 1866 and 1871 respectively, the Burgh Police (Scotland) Act of 1892, and finally the Local Government (Scotland) Act of 1894.

As a consequence Dundee opened Scotland's first public baths, in 1871, followed by Glasgow at Greenhead in 1878. There then followed a surge similar to the one in England, so that by 1901 the Scottish total had reached 32, of which 22 had one or more pools.

Philanthropy continued to play a pivotal role during this period. The buildings featured on these facing pages, for example, Alloa and Glossop, were both built courtesy of gifts from mill owners.

In fact, roughly ten per cent of public baths built between 1870 and 1901 benefitted wholly or in part from philanthropic gifts.

Most gifts were concentrated in Scotland and in the north of England, for example at Ashton-under-Lyne and Stalybridge (both 1870), Manchester's Whitworth Baths (1890), Bacup (1893) and Lochee, Dundee (1894).

In some cases gifts consisted of grants of land, or of a donation to kickstart a public appeal, as at Perth (*see next page*). Most donations also still left local authorities with the responsibility of maintenance and day to day management.

But there is no doubt that wealthy individuals, families and trusts played a crucial role in plugging the gaps that public funding could not fill.

The private sector remained active throughout this period too.

Indeed as case studies in this chapter demonstrate, Glasgow's private baths clubs at Arlington (1871) and Western (1878), plus Edinburgh's Drumsheugh Baths (1882), have survived until the present day seemingly against ⟫

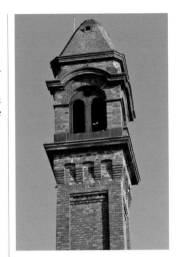

Glossop's 100 foot tall chimney on a nine foot square base is one of the Derbyshire town's most distinctive landmarks. Whenever the budget allowed, Victorian and Edwardian architects seemed to revel in the decorative opportunities presented by a baths' chimney, often taking as their influence the medieval *campanile* of Italy. Such chimneys were as much a symbol of their age as they were functional.

▼ Foundation stones on public buildings are so familiar – and therefore so easily ignored – that we forget the great sense of occasion that accompanied their laying.

Here on **Dunkeld Road, Perth**, in 1887, a temporary grandstand has been erected in front of where the stone itself hangs in mid air like a sacred object, from ropes attached to a timber hoist. In the best seats were those who had subscribed to the bath's construction.

Perth Baths served for almost exactly one hundred years before a new leisure centre opened elsewhere in the town. The site is now a bank, and the foundation stone has not been preserved.

» all the odds, whereas all but a handful of private baths south of the border either went out of business by 1918 or were taken over by the local authority.

Among those in the former category were four built in London during the 1870s.

In 1874, William Higgs, a building contractor (later of Higgs & Hill), opened the Crown Baths in Kennington (page 61), hoping to appeal to a select clientele.

Others followed in Ferndale Road, Brixton (1875), Martins Road, Peckham (1876) and King's Road, Chelsea, where in 1877 the Chelsea Swimming Bath Company built a three pool complex that, significantly, included a pool set aside specifically for women.

But as architect Robert Alsop wrote in 1894, 'Proprietors of private swimming baths cannot keep high class concerns going at the low prices of the public baths.'

On the other hand, private baths companies, free of legislative control, did lead the way when it came to maximising their earnings during the winter, by the simple expedient of draining their largest and therefore costliest pool and hiring out the space for other activities, as at Lambeth (opposite).

Pressure for public baths to be able to do likewise culminated in three key amendments to the 1846 Act, in May 1878.

Firstly, a new clause allowed for the provision of 'covered swimming baths'. (It will be recalled that no mention of swimming was made in 1846.)

In truth this made no practical difference. Local authorities had been building indoor pools under the Act for over 30 years. But it did at least bring the legislation into line with existing practice.

Secondly, the amendment allowed public swimming baths to be drained and boarded over for up to five months a year, between November and March, and used instead as gymnasiums, or for 'other means of healthful recreation', or 'for vestry meetings or other parochial purposes'.

Not that these activities proved especially profitable, since the 1878 amendment also made it clear that events involving 'music or dancing' were specifically excluded, a condition that would hold for a further two decades.

Nevertheless, the concession did reduce outgoings, for although at baths where there were two or more pools it was usually only the largest that was boarded over for the winter – while the smaller pools remained open – the savings on fuel were considerable, and on staffing too, as the amendment allowed local authorities to lay off staff during the winter period.

(Winter closures, it should be added, were rare in Scotland.)

A third part of the amendment worth noting related to charges.

In an earlier, minor amendment to the Act in 1847, charges for 'higher classes' had been set at no more than three times the level for 'the labouring classes'. But that pertained only to slipper baths.

Now that swimming was factored into the Act, maximum charges were set at four times the lowest level; that is, at 8d for first class swimming, 4d for second class, and 2d for third.

Small though this concession might seem to modern eyes, it gave authorities in more affluent areas much more leeway to plan for broader levels of provision.

Four years earlier, for example, St Marylebone had become the first local authority to build a 'premium' public bath. Opened in 1874, the 'Pompeiian Bath' »

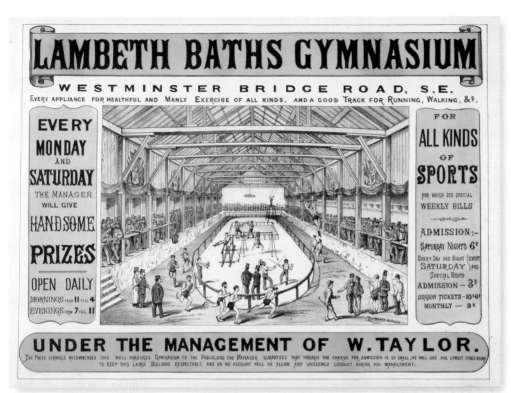

LAMBETH BATHS GYMNASIUM

WESTMINSTER BRIDGE ROAD, S.E.

EVERY APPLIANCE FOR HEALTHFUL AND MANLY EXERCISE OF ALL KINDS, AND A GOOD TRACK FOR RUNNING, WALKING, &c.

EVERY MONDAY AND SATURDAY
THE MANAGER WILL GIVE
HANDSOME PRIZES

OPEN DAILY
MORNINGS FROM 11 TILL 4
EVENINGS FROM 7 TILL 11

FOR ALL KINDS OF SPORTS
FOR WHICH SEE SPECIAL WEEKLY BILLS

ADMISSION:—
SATURDAY NIGHTS 6ᵈ
EVERY DAY AND NIGHT (EXCEPT SATURDAY) AND SPECIAL NIGHTS
ADMISSION — 3ᵈ
SEASON TICKETS - 10ˢ6ᵈ
MONTHLY — 3ˢ

UNDER THE MANAGEMENT OF W. TAYLOR.

THE PRESS STRONGLY RECOMMENDED THIS WELL ARRANGED GYMNASIUM TO THE PUBLIC, AND THE MANAGER GUARANTEES THAT THOUGH THE CHARGE FOR ADMISSION IS SO SMALL, HE WILL USE HIS UTMOST ENDEAVOURS TO KEEP THIS LARGE BUILDING RESPECTABLE, AND ON NO ACCOUNT WILL HE ALLOW ANY UNSEEMLY CONDUCT DURING HIS MANAGEMENT.

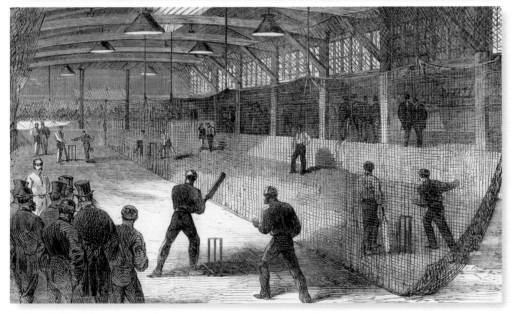

◀ As acknowledged by the 1878 amendment to the 1846 Act, early public baths struggled most during the winter, when heating costs were highest and user numbers lowest.

In the private sector, **Lambeth Baths** in London set an example of how this issue could be addressed.

As these images from 1881 (*top*) and 1868 (*below*) illustrate, the largest pool was drained in winter and transformed into a veritable multi-purpose venue.

During warmer months Lambeth was already a hive of activity, staging well attended competitions (in which ropes to separate lanes were first seen), and opening its doors to both female spectators and swimmers. In 1879 the celebrated Matthew Webb (who had trained at Lambeth for his epic channel swim of 1875), won a six day marathon, completing 74 miles in 145 hours – great lengths indeed!

But as competition from public baths increased, so too did the management's enterprise.

In 1889 Herbert Fry noted that Lambeth Baths was 'more famous for its Temperance Meetings and social assemblies of working people than even for its sanitary appliances. Here all kinds of simple amusement, in the way of songs chorused by the people, newspaper readings, social discussion and temperance meetings, are held regularly through the winter.'

▶ Designed by Lewis Isaacs and opened on Queen's Road (now Queensway) in 1874, **Paddington Baths, London,** was a forerunner of the larger complexes of the Edwardian era, featuring four pools (including one for women), 96 slipper baths and a wash house.

Its ground floor plan, reproduced in *The Builder* of January 31 1874, illustrates just how complicated circulation routes had to be, and also how much space was taken up by duplicated services, purely to ensure that bathers of different classes, and sexes (and the staff who serviced them) were kept apart.

Paddington's costs of just over £50,000 – extremely high for the period – reflected this complexity.

Note that space was allocated for Turkish baths, pending an appeal to see whether they could be financed under the 1846 Act.

They answer was that they could be, the local government board having deciding to consider them as 'vapour baths'. But they appear not to have been installed at Paddington, which was in any case no great success and was eventually replaced in the mid 1920s by the present day baths at Porchester Place (see page 186).

The original site was then sold to Whiteley's department store.

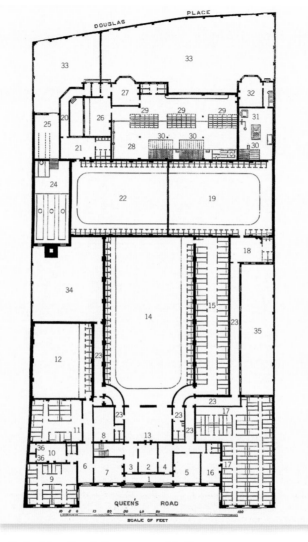

1. Vestibule
2. Ticket office
3. First class entrance
4. Second class entrance
5. Superintendent's office
6. Women's entrance
7. Shampooing room
8. Women's 2nd class waiting room
9. Women's 2nd class slipper baths
10. Women's 1st class waiting room
11. Women's 1st class slipper baths
12. Women's swimming bath
13. Men's 1st class waiting room
14. Men's 1st class swimming bath
15. Men's 1st class slipper baths
16. Men's 2nd class waiting room
17. Men's 2nd class slipper baths
18. Men's 2nd class waiting room
19. Men's 2nd class swimming bath
20. Men's Third class entrance
21. Men's 3rd class waiting room
22. Men's 3rd class swimming bath
23. Corridor
24. Boiler house
25. Engineer's workshop
26. Lobby
27. Waiting room for wash house
28. Wash house
29. Washing trays
30. Drying closets
31. House laundry (towels and costumes)
32. Engineer's living room
33. Yard
34. Space available for Turkish baths
35. Space available for gymnasium
36. Closets

» featured ornate ironwork and tilework, deliberately appealing to Victorian notions of classical indulgence and luxury.

The same year, also in London, Paddington raised expectations further by completing a four pool complex (see left), while the sea water baths at Southport, opened in 1871, featured no fewer than six pools in total (page 68).

Not surprisingly, Marylebone and Paddington were amongst the first to charge first class swimmers the maximum 8d entry, whereas at other less well appointed public baths, first class charges were typically held at 6d, or even 4d.

But compared with private baths, the 8d maximum was still competitive; it was, for example, 3d cheaper than the equivalent private pool at Kensington, and a penny less than at Chelsea.

Paddington, Southport and Chelsea offer examples of another important trend to emerge during the 1870s. When the Princess Alice pleasure boat sank in the Thames in September 1878, with the loss of 640 lives, it was reckoned that of 350 women on board, only one had been able to swim.

True, the earliest ladies-only pools were much smaller than the men's. At Ashton-under-Lyne – opened in 1870 and the oldest baths from this period to still stand (page 64) – the ladies' pool was a mere ninth of the men's in area. At Paddington the ladies' pool was one fifth the area of the three men's pools combined.

And by 1898 there would still be just fourteen public baths in the whole country with ladies-only pools. Elsewhere women were restricted to using the men's pools at set times, usually during a weekday, thereby excluding working women.

Small wonder therefore that in an address to the Royal Institute of British Architects in February 1899 (*see* Links), one of leading baths architects of the period, Alfred Hessell Tiltman reckoned that male swimmers outnumbered females by 10:1.

But, he added, the number of female swimmers was 'daily increasing, partly no doubt due to the encouragement of swimming at the Board Schools'.

The situation was hardly better in the slipper baths department, where male:female ratios could be as imbalanced as 6:1, and even 2:1 was rare. Only in Lancashire, at Chadderton and Bacup for example, did women achieve parity, and only then in the 1890s.

But it was at least a start, and one that, for female swimmers at least, went furthest in London.

In 1888 Hampstead Baths on Finchley Road, a fairly affluent area, became Britain's first public baths to offer first and second class pools for women. Nearby Hornsey Road (1892) and Kentish Town (1901) did the same.

Also significantly no wash house was provided at Hampstead, nor indeed at two baths opened four years earlier in south London, at Forest Hill and Ladywell.

The most obvious explanation is that wash houses were now known to be the least remunerative section of a baths' operation.

But it may also have simply reflected the fact that more and more households in the areas in question owned one of the new generation of washing machines, or least could afford a servant to perform the household's laundry duties (whereas the wash house at Kentish Town, later converted into a launderette, remained in operation until 2005). »

▲ After Cookridge Street in Leeds (*see page 44*), the Victorians' prediliction for all things Middle Eastern and Oriental led to this Moorish extravaganza, designed by Horace Gundry for the London vestry of **St Pancras** and opened in May 1878 on **Whitfield Street**, just behind Tottenham Court Road.

In an area known for its large stores, theatres and clubs, but also for its tenements and artists' quarter (later to be rebranded as Fitzrovia), no doubt the baths appeared as startlingly modern as the penny farthing depicted in this engraving from *The Builder*.

But although apparently lavishly detailed in red brick with stone dressings, with an interior finished in Portland cement and encaustic tiles, Whitfield Street was quite compact and cost only £39,500.

It had two pools, 90' x 30' and 57' x 21', 109 baths (only 18 for women), a 78 stall wash house, and, ironically, no Turkish baths.

From one of only two interior views known to exist (*below*), Whitfield Street's main pool hall and grand central dome appeared to conform exactly with one's image of a grand, Byzantine bath.

Yet Whitfield Street was no folly. Compared with its sister site in Camden Town, on King Street (now Plender Street) – co-designed a decade earlier by Gundry and Joseph Messenger – it was highly popular, described in 1900 as 'one of the best paying establishments in London'.

But alas there would be no more of the Moorish, at least not on this scale. For although St Pancras went on to commission even more elaborate baths in Kentish Town (*page 102*), only in the decor of Turkish baths was the Moorish style ever reprised in Britain, and even then almost tokenistically.

As for Whitfield Street, alas Gundry's marvel was destroyed during the Blitz in World War Two, leaving a void that has since been turned into a play area, called The Warren.

▲ As a teenager in 1875, **Agnes Beckwith** swam from London Bridge to Greenwich, a distance of four miles, in a dress, petticoats, pantaloons and stockings. But it took years for her and others to persuade the male dominated swimming authorities to drop their insistence on voluminous costumes, a debate which carried over onto the letters pages of *The Times*. Finally in 1890 the Amateur Swimming Association agreed to compromise, as long as ladies wore a straight neckline, sleeves that extended at least three inches from the shoulder, and legs that went within three inches of the knee.

▲ A rate card from **Central Baths, Dundee**, illustrates the range of baths typically available at larger establishments during the late Victorian period.

Douche or needle baths, (effectively showers), usually cold water only, started to appear poolside in the 1870s, and by 1890 were supposedly obligatory before entry to most first class swimming baths.

Sitz baths, as the name suggests, were for sitting in, while somewhat confusingly Turkish Baths (first introduced to Britain during the 1850s) offered dry heat in the Roman tradition, and vapour baths offered steamy, wet heat in the Russian tradition.

For detailed descriptions and a history of the Turkish baths movement in Britain generally, readers are directed to Malcolm Shifrin's informative website, at www.victorianturkishbath.org.

For more background on all the different varieties of baths on offer, the work of Lawrence Wright is recommended (see *Links*).

≫ But whatever their social status, girls and women of this generation certainly had a role model when it came to swimming.

Agnes Beckwith was the daughter of 'Professor' Fred Beckwith, master of swimming at Lambeth, who together with his wife, Agnes' brother Willie, and a veritable 'merman' called Thomas Attwood, formed a troupe of 'marine acrobats' referred to in adverts as the 'Beckwith Frogs'.

Often hired as the aquatic entertainment at baths' openings, they equally performed in theatres, where part of their act was to eat, drink and even smoke underwater in a large glass tank. At the Westminster Aquarium in 1880 Agnes drew huge crowds to see her tread water for 30 hours, a record previously held by the other great swimming celebrity of the age.

Captain Matthew Webb, a Shropshire merchant seaman achieved national renown by becoming the first man to swim the English Channel, in August 1875. After that he joined the Beckwiths and others to perform in a series of endurance tests and celebrity appearances, before an attempt to swim under Niagara Falls killed him eight years later.

Inspired by Webb and the Beckwiths, young Britons flocked to join the growing ranks of swimming clubs. In 1879 Charles Dickens Junior identified 16 such clubs in the capital. By 1890 there were at least 134 across England, Scotland and Wales, increasing dramatically thereafter to over 1,500 by 1914.

Offering free lessons to the public in 1881, the Leander club of Birmingham stated haughtily, 'After this, to those who cannot swim, be it to their everlasting shame.'

National associations for swimming, meanwhile, formed in England in 1869 (becoming the ASA), in Scotland in 1888, and in Wales in 1897.

For baths operators, swimming clubs were good for business.

So too was the emergence of water polo in the 1880s (*see page 61*), and the formation of the Royal Life Saving Society in 1891.

Even London's social elite caught the bug, leading in 1894 to two members of the Carlton Club setting up the exclusive Bath Club, at 34 Dover Street, the former residence of Lord Abergavenny.

The club's pool, created in what had been the ballroom, quickly became a popular haunt, particularly among women who, radically, were invited to dine with the men, and who enjoyed exclusive access to the pool on three days a week.

Ladies Nights at the Bath Club were said by *Sporting Life* in December 1899 to have been attended by 'some of England's prettiest daughters'.

Among the entertainments described was a 'plunging' contest, the aim of which was to dive in and then glide, face down on the water's surface, for as far as possible in 60 seconds without taking a breath. Two contestants managed the full 73' length.

There followed 'an interesting display of diving from a trapeze' and 'gymnastic work on the rings', before the evening concluded, as did many a gala of the period, with a men's water polo match.

(Incidentally, of all the private clubs, the Bath Club was the most enduring, surviving until an air raid in 1941. A few years before this the Princesses Elizabeth and Margaret were said to have learnt to swim there.) ≫

Situated between **Harrogate** and **Knaresborough**, the delightful **Starbeck Baths** is Britain's oldest operational public baths.

Admittedly, when opened in 1870 it was a private spa bath, fed by a sulphurous spring, and not until 1900 was it taken over by Harrogate Borough Council. They in turn converted it to a standard swimming pool in 1939, a process which led to many of the original features being removed. But the exterior is little altered.

Inside is a modernised 18m pool with rounded ends and heated to 86° F (4-6° higher than the norm), in order to suit both younger and older swimmers in the community.

When Starbeck's survival was threatened in 2004 a local action group formed, culminating in October 2007 with the injection of £760,000 from Council funds to secure its immediate future.

Another survivor from the 1870s is **Steble Street Baths**, **Toxteth, Liverpool** (*below left*) opened in 1874 at a cost of £20,000. More recently rebranded as Lifestyles Park Road and with a modern extension, both its original pools, each c.52' x 38', have been modernised, while the former wash house is now a gymnasium.

Furthest from the camera, the two storey end block (on whose wall the above sign is displayed) was the superintendent's house.

Also built with accommodation for the 'poolkeeper' but in a parkland setting, was **Cheltenham College Baths** (*below*).

This opened in 1880 with a pool measuring 80' x 40', and was designed by WH Knight, the architect of several equally poised buildings nearby (including the Library, Museum and Art Gallery on Clarence Street, and the 1839 synagogue, off St James' Square).

Of note is that the College principal who proposed that the baths be built was Alfred Barry, son of the architect Charles Barry, who, as previously mentioned, was a great friend of Price Prichard Baly.

Now listed Grade II (as is the poolkeeper's cottage) the baths closed in 1989 and has since been converted into a record office for the NHS (*see Chapter Nine*).

▶ Opened in April 1898 at a cost of £48,695, including drilling for an Artesian well, Thomas Dinwoody's baths for the vestry of St Paul's, Deptford, on **Laurie Grove, Lewisham,** illustrate how, on a constrained site with a limited street frontage, elaborate detailing was used to attract attention, express civic pride, and demarcate the various departmental entrances.

Yet despite the identical 'his and hers' entrances (*centre*), the facilities were still heavily weighted in favour of males. They were allocated four times more hours of swimming, and had three times as many slipper baths.

Grade II listed, the baths closed in 1991 and since 1994 have been used as art studios and as an urban and community research centre by Goldsmiths College.

Also opened in 1898 on a site hemmed in on both flanks, **East Hull Baths** on **Holderness Road** (*below right*), cost a mere £15,000, had two pools, but yet again, one was reserved for boys, and there were 27 slipper baths allocated for men compared with eight for women.

Still in use following a major refurbishment in 1986, East Hull's red brick and terracotta façade, and its internal tiles and faience work (*see page 4*) are typical of the period. It also has a unusually exposed water tower (*below*).

》 Also to appear during this period were timed swimming records, the earliest of which is attributed to Winston Cole, who swam three separate 100 yard races in 75 seconds in 1871, probably at Lambeth.

Swimming's first recognised world record was also achieved in Britain, at New Islington Baths in Manchester, in 1889, when ET 'Stivie' Jones won the ASA's 200 yard 'freestyle' event. His time, incidentally, was two minutes and 57.5 seconds (whereas the most recent record for this distance, recorded in the USA in 2008, was one minute and 31 seconds, almost twice as fast).

Three years later, the first competitive 'great length' for ladies in a British pool, and indeed the world, was recorded in Scotland at the Townhead Baths, Glasgow, in 1891. A Miss E Dobbie won a ladies 200 yards freestyle in a time of 4 minutes 42 seconds.

As the following case studies will show, the popularisation of swimming, and of swimming and of water polo as spectator sports, had a marked effect on the design and accessorisation of pools.

Just as important were advances in the range, durability and ease of cleaning of new, mass produced materials such as ceramic tiles, glazed brickwork, terrazzo flooring and porcelain-coated slipper baths.

During the 1890s, electric lighting started to supercede gas. In many baths iron lattice roof girders took the place of timber, before being superceded by steel in the 1890s. Even the design of spittoons, embedded within the pool surrounds, improved as designers and manufacturers sought to learn from the mistakes of their predecessors. 》

▶ As at all Victorian baths, the 26 staff at the **Essex Road Baths, Islington** – seen here around the time of the baths' opening in April 1895 – were organised along strictly hierarchical lines.

Known also as Greenman Street Baths or 'The Tibby' (as it backed onto Tibberton Square and a large Peabody Estate), the baths were designed by Alfred Hessell Tiltman and were of average size, with first and second class pools for men (90' x 30' and 94' x 30'), one for women (50' x 20'), plus 91 slipper baths and 65 wash house stations.

It stayed open for 89 hours a week from May–September, and 80 hours a week from October–April, with the wash house open 72 hours a week all year round.

In 1913-14 it was used by a total of 227,709 individuals (an average of 600-700 per day).

Of its total staff it is thought that 16-17 would have been full time.

Unfortunately no documentation accompanies this photograph.

But assuming that the stern looking woman seated in the centre was the matron, the man either to her right or left must have been the superintendent, and therefore almost certainly her husband, as these two key positions, which came with free accommodation, were usually filled by couples. Their rank was similar to that of head butler and housekeeper at a stately home.

Often ex military, constabulary or civil service, the superintendent was accountable to the Baths Committee. Every two months or so in the baths' board room he would set out all income and expenditure as recorded in his Day Book, and report on all matters pertaining to the operation.

His was therefore a respected role, requiring discipline, a range of business and practical skills, and

an ability to deal with the public. In the 1890s he would receive 40-46 shillings a week, plus rent free accommodation, coal and gas, for himself, his wife and children.

Competent superintendents might expect promotion to the larger and more prestigious baths. But it was also known for fathers to hand on the role to their sons, and for the same people to stay in post for much of their working lives. Between 1849 and 1914, for example, St Marylebone Baths in London had only two superintendents and three matrons.

While the superintendent took overall charge of the operation, the matron oversaw the women's departments (that is, the ladies' pool, slipper baths and wash house). She worked the same 62.5 hours a week as her husband, but for a third of his rate of pay.

Just below the superintendent was the engineer (perhaps the other man next to the matron). He

earned around 40s a week for a 55 hour week, and had charge of at least three or four maintenance men (such as a plumber, carpenter, gas fitter and electrician), and two or three stokers, whose main job was to feed the boilers with coal. Burns and injuries were not uncommon in this area, and there are several instances of boilers exploding.

In the white coats are the baths attendants. Their role was to service the pools and slipper baths, and to maintain order. Although attendants were expected to be able to swim, it was not actually a legal requirement until 1900.

A typical attendant would work 68-72 hours a week, with an upper age limit of 35-40 for those starting the job. Once hired, however, they might remain in post for life. Older, more experienced attendants tended to work in the first class pool, and some taught swimming.

Other staff included clerks, money takers, towel and costume

washers and a needlewoman. The role of the uniformed man on the far right is unclear. He may have been the porter, a commissionaire, or a driver, employed to ferry towels and costumes to baths without their own establishment laundries.

Finally, there was the 'pool professional' or swimming instructor, whose identity on this photograph we can only guess.

Unlike modern instructors he would not enter the water but use poles, ropes, or even elaborate winches, wires or moving belts designed to aid buoyancy.

Although paid for his time, some baths also staged annual galas or 'entertainments' as a reward for the instructor's services.

As to the paper bags lined up at the front, these appear to contain seedlings, perhaps for the new bath's garden, which seems appropriate given that after the baths closed in 1984 the site became a park.

Cossington Road Baths, Leicester, opened in 1898, still has its original teak gallery seats and a line of now very rare demountable cubicles (*right*), designed to be easily removed on gala nights.

» As a result, by 1900 virtually every one of the baths built in the 1840s and 1850s had been either modernised or completely rebuilt.

Then, as now, a flawed design soon revealed itself.

Yet this did not stop the majority of local authorities continuing to depend on their borough engineer or surveyor to take on the design of new baths.

This led, as AH Tiltman warned in his 1899 RIBA lecture, to a constant repetition of old faults and the introduction of new ones.

Other authorities opted for design competitions, thereby at least allowing professionals to build up a specialisation. To entice the judges architects would gives names to their proposals, such as 'Progress', 'Sweetness and Light' and 'Simplicity and Utility'.

In London in particular the competition process led to three architects coming to the fore.

Henry Spalding (1839-1910) first entered the field by designing the baths in Hampstead and on Buckingham Palace Road in 1888.

Spalding then went into partnership with Alfred Cross (1858-1932). Together this pair worked on eight baths (seven in London and one in Coventry).

After 1900 Cross would go on to design two more in London, and write the first definitive design guide to baths architecture (of which more in the next chapter).

Also active was the previously mentioned AH Tiltman (1854–1910), who designed four baths in London and two in Bradford, as well as advising on several others.

Tiltman was an advocate of the principle, already established in Birmingham and Liverpool, of having one large central baths complex, with smaller 'branch' establishments, with or without swimming pools, in the suburbs.

Contrary to the spirit of the 1846 Act, argued Tiltman, the poor actually shied away from larger establishments, and needed cheap 'ablutionary baths' more than they needed to be able to swim.

Tiltman also made it quite clear that, particularly when it came to washing arrangements, Britain's 'somewhat blundering system' fell some way behind those of Germany and Austria.

There, he stated in his 1899 RIBA lecture, 'No bather, be he rich or poor, is permitted to enter a swimming pond until he has carefully washed himself, from head to foot, under the warm douches, and if necessary, used the foot bath.'

And yet such practices would not become obligatory in Britain until the late 1920s.

As the 19th century came to a close, two further amendments to the 1846 Act were to have an impact on baths design.

The first, passed in August 1896 and applying only in London, repealed the 1878 limitation by allowing public baths to stage 'music or dancing' during the winter. A second amendment in August 1899 extended this to the whole of England and Wales.

In order to stage such events, pools had to meet the same regulations for ingress, egress and fire safety, as public halls or theatres. As we shall see in the next chapter, the concession also prompted designers to add proscenium arches, temporary stages and even dressing rooms.

Thus the public bath evolved one stage further, from being a place solely devoted to health and welfare, to one geared towards recreation, sport, and now entertainment.

▲ Water polo at the **Crown Baths, Kennington**, as depicted in *The Graphic* in August 1890, a month after the sport's first international had been played a few miles away at Kensington Baths. In that encounter England had been beaten 4-0 by Scotland, where the game as we know it today first came about.

The story goes that early forms of water polo had been played in the sea at Portsmouth and Bournemouth during the 1870s, while, independently, members of the Bon Accord Swimming Club in Scotland devised a similar game on the River Dee, based on football.

As noted by Peter Bilsborough (*see Links*), it cannot have been easy to play this game, using only feet to pass or shoot in the water, and so not surprisingly the game failed to catch on.

In 1877 Bon Accord's president then wrote to William Wilson, manager of the Victoria Baths Club in Glasgow, to ask if he knew of any other team game that might entertain spectators who were otherwise bored by the diet of races at a typical gala of the day.

Not knowing of such a game, Wilson set about inventing one.

He called it aquatic football, but it was actually closer to handball,

with goals scored like tries in rugby, by touching the ball down on opposite banks of the river.

Bon Accord's first trial proved that Wilson's game could work, but moreso in the still waters of an indoor pool. The second trial thus took place at the Victoria Baths Club, with further refinements tried out at Paisley Baths in October 1877. Goalposts, as in football, were introduced in 1879.

Meanwhile experimentation took place also in Birmingham, leading to the Amateur Swimming Association formally recognising the sport south of the border in 1885.

Strangely, no one can explain

why this new game became known as water polo, although in 1880, using extreme artistic licence, an illustrator in *The Graphic* concocted an image showing players mounted in the water on barrels fitted with horses' heads. Unlikely indeed.

As to the Crown Baths, it hosted the first ever Varsity water polo match in 1891 (as there were then no adequate indoor pools in Oxford or Cambridge), before it went out of business in 1903 and the fixture moved to the more upmarket Bath Club in Dover Street.

Note the absence of goal nets. These followed after they had been introduced in soccer, in 1891.

◄ One of the most intriguing forms of baths design to emerge during the 19th century was the floating bath, of which the most advanced, in Britain at least, was moored on the River Thames by Hungerford Bridge. Featured in the *Illustrated London News* in August 1875, the **Charing Cross Floating Bath** was one of the great curiosities of Victorian London, a structure that was to spawn a host of imitators.

Essentially a water-filled barge covered by a standard glasshouse roof, its swimming area measured a generous 135' x 25', with a sloping floor creating depths from 3' to 7'. There were dressing rooms along one side and, instead of diving boards, two arched bridges spanned the width (which perhaps also helped to brace the structure).

Designed by E Perrett (engineer also to the Chelsea Swimming Baths Company), and constructed by the Thames Iron Works & Shipbuilding Company, its backers, the Floating Swimming Baths Co Ltd., hoped it would be the first of several similar baths to be stationed along the Thames.

After all, similar enterprises of a far more basic nature had enjoyed a measure of success elsewhere.

The earliest records of boats or pontoons being converted into floating baths are from Frankfurt and Vienna in the 1760s.

Subsequently Paris had six such baths in various forms during the 19th century, of which the best known was *Les Bains Deligny*.

First moored by the Quai d'Orsay in 1796, this was reconstructed several times over the next two centuries, bobbing in and out of fashion until it sank in 1993.

Meanwhile Britain's earliest known floating bath was launched on the River Mersey in Liverpool in June 1816, followed by a similar venture by Waterloo Bridge in London in 1819. Both were housed within the timber hull of a ship, and were aimed mainly at gentlemen about town seeking novelty, indulgence and a safe, if bracing dip.

According to Samuel Cornish's *Stranger's Guide to Liverpool*, the Mersey floating bath had a swimming pool 80' x 27', with a continual flow of river water passing through the vessel via an iron trellis at each end. A door at the side allowed users to swim freely in the river, while for those who preferred to soak in privacy, there was a small plunge bath inside the hull, screened so that individuals could pass from the dressing rooms into the water 'unobserved'.

Following the Parisian models, two further cabins were provided for relaxation, offering newspapers and refreshments, while on the upper deck were seats and tables affording 'a most pleasing and ever-varying prospect'.

Neither the Liverpool or the Waterloo Bridge baths appear to have stayed in business beyond 1830, but further floating baths followed in 1831 at Gravesend, and in August 1860 at Ironbridge. There the pool measured 50' x 16', and attracted 345 men and 58 women in its first week.

Floating baths were vulnerable, however. One in Paris was destroyed by ice. Ironbridge's fell victim to a storm after only one season in use. But that did not stop other companies following suit once they saw the Charing Cross bath.

On the River Severn alone, six floating baths would start trading: at Worcester in 1878, at Stourport, Bridgnorth and Ironbridge again a year later, and at Evesham in 1889. Apparently Bridgnorth's baths, owned by the local rowing club, was 'noted for its tendency to capsize'. But the one at Stourport, formed by two oak hulls, remained in service until 1907, while its successor lasted until 1933.

There are also records of floating baths on the River Clyde in Scotland in 1878, featuring a swimming area 120' x 45', at Ramsden's Dock in Barrow-on-Furness (twice destroyed in gales) and at Chester (*see right*).

But despite setting the trend, Charing Cross was not a success, and despite attempts to turn it into an ice rink during the winter, by 1884 the bath had closed.

Whether this was for technical reasons or from lack of custom we cannot be sure. Although the proprietors installed 'apparatus' for heating and filtering the river water, certainly the water quality must be doubted. Filtering techniques had yet to reach the levels of efficiency that would lead to public baths eventually adopting such systems during the Edwardian period.

At one shilling per swim the floating bath was also expensive, compared with 6d or 8d for the typical first class public bath.

London saw two further floating baths before the end of the century.

Of one, at Pimlico Pier, close to St George's Square, little is known other than it featured a 200' long pool. Another, called the Cleopatra, moored off the Victoria Embankment, ended up being towed to Southend in 1894 where it briefly became the Palace Baths before being scrapped.

Today, Britain's nearest floating bath is in Paris, in the form of the *Piscine Joséphine Baker*, launched in 2006 and with a retractable roof. But if history is any guide, it is surely only a matter of time before someone in London revisits the idea.

▲ The floating bath at **Chester** opened for business in 1883 on the banks of the River Dee, at The Groves, just east of Bridgegate.

Designed by William McKaigg and built by Wainwright Bros., unlike Charing Cross it was square shaped in plan, and had a canvas awning over the 70'x 30' pool area, with covered changing boxes on four sides. A series of holes in the hull allowed river water to pass through, although apparently these had to be enlarged when they clogged up with mud and silt.

A strong tide in January 1899 broke its moorings, causing it to run aground on the nearby weir. But it was repaired, only to be scrapped shortly after the City Baths (*page 100*) opened in 1901.

Case Study

Henry Square, Ashton-under-Lyne

Opened September 6 1870
Closed 1975
Address Henry Square
Architects Paull & Robinson
Cost £16,000 (gifted by Hugh Mason, mill owner)
Pools 100' x 40' and 25' x 18'
Current owner Ask Developments
Listed Grade II* (1975)

When a statue of the mill owner and philanthropist Hugh Mason was unveiled in Ashton-under-Lyne in 1887, a year after his death, 15,000 people, almost half the town's population, were reported to have attended.

Even by the standards of the day, Mason was a remarkable man, as a benefactor, as a civic leader, Cobdenite and Liberal MP, and as a progressive employer who broke ranks with other mill owners by raising wages and building a workers' colony complete with library, lecture hall, gallery and recreation ground.

But of all Mason's legacies, none remains more conspicuous today than the public baths he endowed in 1870. In use for over a century before its replacement by Ashton Pools in 1975, Hugh Mason House (as the baths was often called), remains, even in its semi-derelict state, an imposing, almost heroic statement of Victorian paternalistic values.

In fact Ashton was one of a pair of similar baths designed by the partnership of Henry Paull, who was based in London, and George Robinson, of Wolverhampton. The other, opened four months earlier and also gifted by a local mill owner, was at nearby Stalybridge, but was demolished in the 1970s.

As may be deduced from the images, Paull and Robinson specialised in church architecture. Indeed Nikolaus Pevsner called Robinson 'a rogue architect' after

From *The Builder* in July 1870, Paull & Robinson's nave-like pool hall at Ashton combined Italian Romanesque semi-circular arches and paired columns with a decidedly English hammerbeam and slate roof with no glazed sections. Note the absence of individual changing cubicles

JULY 2, 1870.]   THE BUILDER.   527

CORPORATION PUBLIC BATHS, ASHTON-UNDER-LYNE.——Messrs. Paull & Robinson, Architects.

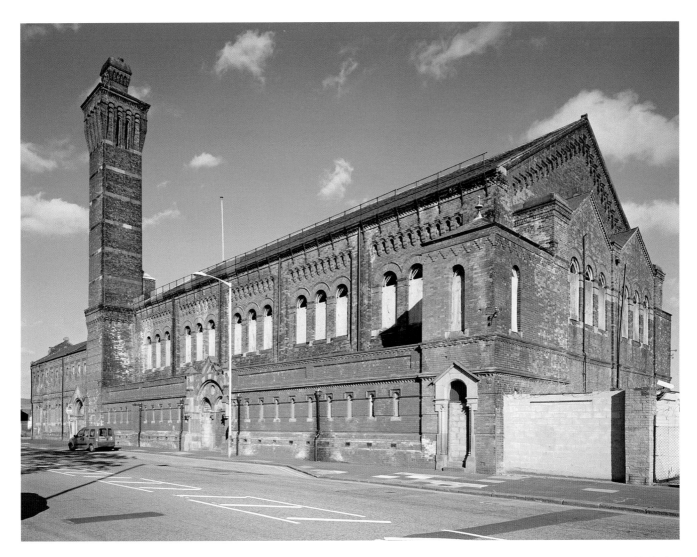

seeing the exuberance of his work at St Luke's in Blakenhall. But Robinson's bravado has endured, for both St Luke's, and the baths at Henry Square are listed Grade II*, making Ashton one of only five public baths in this rare category.

Certainly the building is of epic proportions. In the heart of what is now called the St Petersfield development area, the baths' 210'

long flank fills the southern side of Henry Square (facing a modern magistrates court), with three stone dressed entrances (*above*), and a further entrance block at the east end (*opposite, far left*), capped by a tower similar in style but much squatter than the baths' magnificent main chimney.

Two thirds of the building was taken up by the main pool which,

at 100' x 40', was claimed to have been the second largest indoor pool in Europe (although in London both the private baths at Lambeth and Hoxton were larger, as was the pool at Rossall School in Fleetwood). But it was definitely Britain's largest public pool.

Ashton was also one of the first public pools to have a separate, albeit much smaller pool for »

Clearly modelled on the 13–14th century campaniles at Siena and Florence, Ashton's 120' chimney, viewed here from Henry Square, has vents concealed between the machicolations; just one trick of many used by Victorian architects in their quest to marry centuries old styling with modern industrial processes.

▲ Viewed in 1972, three years before the baths closed, the main pool at **Ashton-under-Lyne** illustrates how the challenge of meeting 20th century standards was met in the days before conservation became an issue.

Unsightly partitions barred entry to the poolside so bathers could not bring in dirt on their shoes before going to change, while cubicles were added to the gallery, requiring access to the pool via stairs.

The baths' conversion from gas lighting to electricity, effected in 1902, resulted in a web of unsightly wires across the ceiling, while no doubt the installation of a water filtration system in 1915 and of a chlorination plant in 1937 necessitated other awkward alterations to the building's fabric.

Least altered of all was the tank, still only 5' 6" at the deep end – shallow even by later Victorian standards – with steps protruding into the water, as was common before recessed steps or ladders.

Modernising historic pools has never been easy. Yet how differently and more sensitively might Ashton have been upgraded had it hung on until the present day.

>> women. This was perhaps at the insistence of Hugh Mason, who as an MP fought for women's voting rights. (He also apparently discouraged mothers from working in his mills, and sacked any man found to have been unfaithful in marriage.)

For ladies who desired a more strenuous swim the main pool was allocated to them for three hours a week, every Thursday, except in winter when, from November to March, the smaller pool alternated between men and women and the main pool was boarded over for roller skating, concerts and public meetings (some of them no doubt addressed by Mason, who was an inveterate speech maker).

During the Second World War the women's pool was converted into a government-operated British Restaurant, before it became a laundry in the 1950s.

The original Turkish Baths – which had been amongst the earliest at a municipal level – were also converted; first into a Zotofoam bath in the 1930s, then into a sauna in 1967.

Apart from the usual slipper baths Ashton also included an area set aside originally as a fire station and later as a police station.

Here then is a building of considerable quality, interest and with a history of multiple useage.

The question is, what next?

After closing in 1975 it was used for a decade or more as industrial units, but suffered badly from vandalism and neglect, until in the late 1990s Ask Developments (who also own Collier Street baths in Salford), took it on as part of the St Petersfield regeneration scheme.

Since then the company has spent up to £700,000 on waterproofing and remedial work, so that at least the fabric is now

secure. Meanwhile modern offices and flats have sprung up alongside the new magistrates courts, helping to enclose Henry Square and bring new life and investment to what was otherwise a forgotten part of the town.

But still no long term, viable uses have emerged for the baths.

Hugh Mason's gift is now Ashton's great challenge.

Ashton Baths – its fittings stripped, its main pool infilled, but its basic structure intact and its hammerbeam roof still inspiring. As a concert hall it used to hold audiences of 4,000. Now it craves a new audience.

Case Study

Victoria Salt Water Baths, Southport

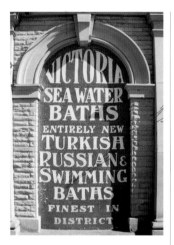

Opened July 6 1871
Address The Promenade PR9 0DS
Architects Horton & Bridgford
Cost £20,000
Pools Men's 1st, 76' x 30' (now
18m adults and 4m learner); 2nd
class, 60' x 27' (closed); Men's
cold, 48' x 26' (now 14m family).
Ladies 1st, 65' x 28' and 2nd, 30'
x 26'; Ladies cold, 26' x 15' (all
converted to other uses)
Owner Sefton MBC
Operator Victoria Leisure Club
Listed Grade II (1976)

Having emerged as a genteel seaside resort during the 1790s, Southport opened its first subscription baths in May 1839. It was named the Royal Victoria Baths, the first of several around Britain to honour the queen (the last of which, as we shall see in Manchester, was opened in 1906, five years after her death).

Unusually, this first Southport establishment had three pools – one more than Liverpool's, opened eleven years earlier – of which two (the first and second class) were of relatively generous dimensions, 76' x 30'. Each was filled daily with sea water, pumped up at 50 tons per hour by a six horsepower engine from a circular reservoir on the shore. The proprietors claimed that by 11.00am this water would be heated to 88° F.

Whether they managed this or not, by the 1860s the business was ripe for development. The railway had arrived in 1848, while Lord Street, which ran behind the bath, was developing into an impressive boulevard. A pier opened in 1860.

Adopting the 1846 Act was, at that time, out of the question.

The town was too small, and in any case there were enough local businessmen willing to invest in what they saw as a tourist attraction rather than a baths and wash house serving the poor.

Thus was formed the Southport Baths and Assembly Rooms Co Ltd., with capital of £20,000.

Of this, £6,500 was spent on purchasing the existing baths, supplemented by a further share issue worth £15,000 to finance a complete reconstruction.

The end result was a handsome edifice, French Classical in style and dressed in the warm, sandstone ashlar that would also be favoured for a series of even grander buildings on Lord Street; Cambridge Hall, the Atkinson Art Gallery and the public library, all completed during the 1870s.

But the most remarkable aspect of the new Southport Salt Water Baths – opened by

Lord Skelmersdale with a Grand Festival Gala in July 1871 – was that it contained on a single storey no fewer than six individual pools, more than any other baths establishment before or since.

This, moreover, on a site just 200' at its widest and 175' at its deepest. With private slipper and medication baths occupying much of the remaining space, this required virtually every part of the building to depend on glazed roofing for natural light.

As shown by plans reproduced in *Building News* (opposite), none of the six pools was large, and two were cold plunge pools. But in total they required 250,000 gallons, a considerable amount of water to pump in and out.

The building was divided into distinct sections for men and women, served by a central entrance, above which was a boardroom-cum-reading room.

The Southport Swimming Club formed there in 1878. Turkish baths were added in 1890.

But in common with most private establishments, the 'Viccy', as the baths continued to be

Southport's former men's first class pool retains its original ironwork roof structure (*seen also in the etching opposite*), but the pool below is now split into two modern pools at ground level, with a gymnasium on a mezzanine level in between.

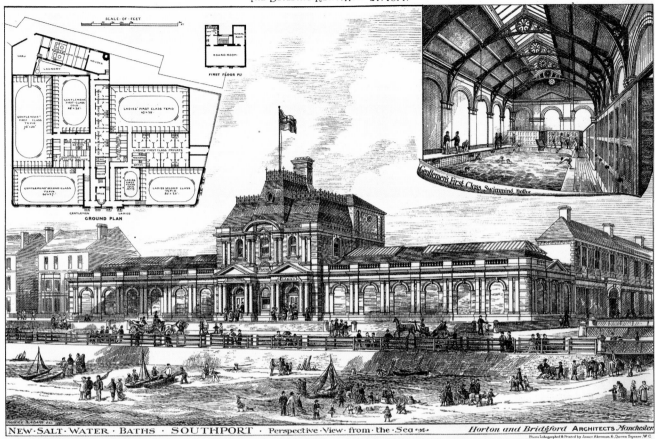

SCALE·OF·FEET

FIRST FLOOR PLAN

GROUND PLAN

Gentlemen's First Class Swimming Baths

NEW·SALT·WATER·BATHS·SOUTHPORT · Perspective·View·from·the·Sea   Horton and Bridgford ARCHITECTS Manchester

called, struggled after the turn of the century, and in 1919 was taken over by the town council. A major refurbishment followed in 1927.

Little of this can be seen today. With the opening of a new 33.3m public pool on the Esplanade (since replaced in 2007 by the Dunes Splashworld), one half of the Viccy (the men's side) was let out by Sefton Council to the Victoria Leisure and Fitness Club, which has run it as a private members' club since 1999. The ladies' side is now subdivided into bars and restaurants.

Three mains-fed pools remain, two formed from the men's former first class pool. But as all three have suspended ceilings, one must visit the mezzanine floor above, where a gym and fitness studio have been added, to gain from the surviving roof structures a sense of the original layout

What space remains is occupied by squash courts, steam rooms, saunas, bars and function rooms.

Multum in parvo, as the Victorians might have remarked, before repairing to Lord Street for tea.

Although its exterior has changed little since 1877, the interior of the Victoria Salt Water Baths is now subdivided into two sections. Bars and restaurants occupy the former ladies' side (*right, on the plan above*), while occupying the former men's side, to the left of the central pavilion, is the Victoria Leisure Club, The pavilion itself (*left*), is now a night club. The architects, Horton and Bridgford of Manchester, are known to have designed only one other baths, at Woolton (now in Liverpool), in 1893.

Case Study

Arlington Baths Club, Glasgow

Opened August 1 1871
Address Arlington Street, G3 6DT
Architect John Burnet, plus
extensions by Andrew Myles, 1893,
and Benjamin Conner, 1902
Pool 69' x 36'
Owner Arlington Baths Club
Listed Category B (1986)

Hidden away down a back street in Glasgow's Charing Cross area, with only a plate on the door to reveal its identity, the Arlington Baths Club could hardly be more discreet. Yet here stands the oldest private baths club in Britain, and perhaps even the world.

Public baths, as noted earlier, were late to appear in Scotland, the first to open being in Dundee in 1871. Glasgow followed suit at Greenhead seven years later.

But Glasgow's professional and merchant classes were not waiting upon the burgh to build them a pool. What they demanded was somewhere to swim, but without having to mix with the lower orders. Not just a subscription baths, open to anyone who could afford entry, but a gentlemen's club.

At first the Arlington Baths Company offered its members simply a swimming pool and a suite of private baths. These were, and still are housed in that part of the club – originally a single storey block flanked by two pedimented gables – which lies at the north, or far end of the Arlington Street frontage (*as seen left*).

To this was added in 1875 a Turkish Room, at the rear of the south end, to which a single storey extension with a third gable was added in 1893, to house a reading room and billiard room. (This extension can be distinguished by the higher level of its eaves.)

Added soon after was the current two storey entrance hall, with its three arched openings.

Finally, in 1902, upper storeys to both the south and north of the entrance block were built, to achieve the continuous two storey terrace we see today.

So successful was Arlington – by 1875 membership topped 600 – that similar clubs soon formed elsewhere in Glasgow. These were the Western at Hillhead (*page 72*), the Victoria on West Nile Street, plus others at Govanhill, Pollokshields and Dennistoun, joined by Drumsheugh in Edinburgh in 1882 (*page 90*).

Only in 1894 did London society catch up, when the Bath Club opened in Piccadilly.

But for any private enterprise, in any age, the maintenance of a swimming pool is no small matter, which is why few private baths companies survived beyond 1914.

So to have survived into the 21st century, as Arlington and our two other featured Scottish clubs have managed – and to have done so whilst occupying historic buildings – represents even more of an achievement.

Of course members' fees have played a key role in financing this survival. But as Arlington's history illustrates, members' loyalty has proved just as pivotal.

For a sense of how that loyalty has evolved, Nanzie McLeod's collection of short stories, *Tales of Arlington* (*see Links*) contains a number of telling vignettes.

One of the club's 750 or so current members herself, McLeod describes a place of calm, of friendship and, above all, of orderliness. Outdoor shoes to be left in the boot room. Regulation 'pants' (or costumes) to be worn in the pool, blue for men, red for women. Misbehaving young members to be summarily suspended for two weeks by order of the bathsmaster. No raised voices in the Turkish room.

But if entry to this scrubbed but clubbable haven inevitably comes at a price, at Arlington this has at times gone way beyond the payment of annual fees.

Over the years members have often been called upon to dig deep, in particular during the 1960s and '70s when the installation of fire prevention measures compromised the original plenum ventilation system.

Indeed by 1987 Arlington had reached a crisis point.

The Glasgow Development Agency offered £184,000 for

repairs, but only if the members matched the grant pound for pound. This they agreed to do by setting up a debenture scheme.

But still this was insufficient, and after remedial work eventually started in 1993, a further crisis was only averted when Historic Scotland, who had listed the club in 1986, also pledged £130,000.

And still the building needed more, so in 1996 the club was grateful to receive another £561,000 from the Heritage Lottery Fund, awarded on condition that its facilities be open to the public (albeit partially, at set times), and that the constitution be amended so that if the club was ever wound up the proceeds would go to the National Trust of Scotland.

The problems seemed legion. Roofs needed repair. Plant needed replacement. Rampant rot needed treatment. And that was before health and safety measures had to be met and a new gym installed to try to boost membership.

By 2004 the most urgent work had been done, at a total cost of £1.2m, freeing the club to start clawing back the losses that had built up during months of closures.

There are sports clubs all over Britain, burdened, like Arlington, both by the stigma of elitism and the responsibility of maintaining an historic building.

That they survive is of course to the prime benefit of their members. But they indubitably enrich our wider heritage too.

▲ One example of how a club like Arlington has helped to protect a small part of our sporting heritage is its retention of the hanging **rings and trapezes** that were once common at British baths, public and private. They are reached via the steps seen here angled over the left side of the pool. What happens next is best explained by a clip available to view on *YouTube*, in which club members demonstrate how the rings and trapezes are used.

One feature of the pool, or 'pond' as known in Scotland, that has not survived, alas, is a decorative cast-iron ventilation unit from c.1900 that hung above the water until the recent refurbishment. This formed part of an unusual plenum heating and ventilation system that runs

throughout the building. Also gone is the former cast iron diving board, or 'dail' (the only surviving example of which is at the Western Baths Club, *see page 75*).

Arlington's magical **Turkish Room**, meanwhile (*above*) – with its domed roof and coloured glass lights evoking the sense of an Arabian night – has hardly altered at all since 1875, other than the removal of the original central fountain, and of course the admission of women to its hallowed sanctum.

Another reminder that this was once an exclusively man's world are the brass plates set into the terrazzo pool surrounds (*above*), reminding members to 'take off boots before crossing.'

Case Study

Western Baths Club, Hillhead, Glasgow

Opened April 24 1878
Address Cranworth St G12 8BZ
Architects Clarke & Bell
Cost c. £20,000
Pool 90' x 30'
Owner Western Baths Club
Listed Category B (1970)

There is an oft repeated tale that the Western Baths Club was formed by members of Glasgow's first indoor swimming facility, the Arlington Baths Club (*see page 70*), in protest at the club's refusal to admit women.

But as the Western's long serving secretary, William Mann, has pointed out in his history of the club – to which we are indebted (*see Links*) – Arlington did admit women. Instead, the Western's founders simply wanted a club of their own, within their own community.

Hillhead in the 1870s was still an independent burgh, a rapidly emerging suburb at the fashionable, western extremity of Glasgow. Many of the city's wealthiest families had moved there, drawn by the new university, the botanic gardens, West End (now Kelvingrove) Park, and a thriving network of cricket, bowls and golf clubs.

Arlington, although less than a mile away along the Great Western Road, towards the city centre, was just too far, and perhaps just not quite grand enough.

From *The Architect* magazine, reproduced somewhat belatedly in 1881, Clarke and Bell's plans for the Western Baths Clubs show a third of the ground floor dedicated to the Turkish bath. Under the billiard room lay a basement flat for the bathsmaster and his wife. The pool's marble surrounds and distinctive distance markers (*above left*) date from 1914.

But as the club's founding shareholders soon discovered, affluence and enthusiasm were no guarantees of success.

Following the launch of the Western Baths Company Limited in late 1875, with a capital of £10,000, the selected design, drawn up by prominent architects and Hillhead residents, William Clarke and George Bell, ended up costing nearer £20,000.

To add to the founders' jitters, five months after the club opened in 1878 one of Glasgow's leading banks crashed, causing financial meltdown. Only a loan of £6,000 from a wealthy merchant in 1880 staved off disaster, swiftly followed by a £4,000 debenture.

Four years later the club sank even deeper into the mire. Literally perhaps, for the area suffered, as did much of Hillhead, from subsidence, and it was said that the club's fractured pool all but drained away, as did the business.

Liquidators were appointed, and for the next two years the club stood boarded up, until new investors were persuaded to launch a rescue (despite the previous shareholders having lost their entire investment), and the club reopened in October 1886. But it had cost another £10,000 in repairs to achieve this.

Thereafter the club's fortunes improved, and by 1887 there were reported to be 657 members, including 86 women.

At last, the Western was able to settle into the routine of a typical Victorian club; musical evenings, billiards, games of Whist and lazy shampoos in the Turkish bath. Apparently on Sundays it was quite common for male members to stroll in from their homes in dressing gowns, having already changed for their morning dip.

In 1894 the club's more avid swimmers formed the Western Amateur Swimming Club.

Glasgow at that time could boast a particularly active swimming scene. Indeed by 1914 there would be 109 clubs in competition, spread across the city's now extensive network

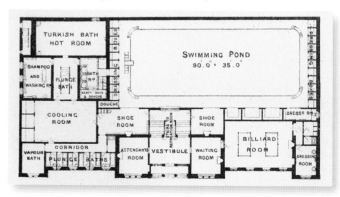

of public baths (the first one of which, at Greenhead, had opened in the same year as the Western).

The Western ASC nurtured a number of champions over the years. Norman Hamilton and his sister Margot won four medals at the 1934 Empire Games, while John Service swam at the 1948 Olympics. The club also produced eleven water polo internationals.

But as far as this book is concerned, the real star of the Western is its swimming pond.

That one of Britain's best preserved Victorian pools should be found in the private sector, and at a club which is considered a Glasgow institution – with all the innate conservatism that that implies – is hardly a surprise. This is, after all, a club where female

members had to fight hard and often to achieve parity with the men; where mixed bathing was allowed on a limited basis only in 1965; where there were quotas for Catholics and Jews, and a 'colour bar' until at least the 1960s, and where males of all persuasions were expected to wear the club's official red 'pants' or costumes when entering the pond. »

Variously described as Spanish Gothic, Venetian Gothic or Moorish in style, the Cranworth Street frontage of the Western Baths Club is little altered since 1878, other than the addition of a modern extension (to the left of this image). Inside, mosaic floors, red carpets, panelled rooms and a grand staircase create an air of refined opulence.

▶ Until Aberdeen's Esplanade baths opened in 1898, the pond at the **Western Baths Club** was, at 90' x 30', the largest indoor pool in Scotland. Even today it is one of the largest in the private sector.

But is not just size that makes the Western special. Members and visitors often remark at how hushed and calm is the atmosphere, almost as if it were a place of worship or for learning.

Successive bathsmasters – ever watchful and strict – have helped to ensure that that tradition continues. The pool hall's resemblance to a chapel might also be a factor.

Certainly it is a pleasure to swim in its tiled depths, surrounded by marble pool edgings and looking up at the filigree cast iron trusses of the roof, each with the letters W and B picked out in roundels.

As at Arlington, the club has retained rings and trapezes suspended over the water, once a familiar feature at public baths, but at the Western, alas, requiring support from an intrusive overhanging gallery.

It is also unfortunate that the ornate gallery and cubicles that once extended around both ends of the pond now only survive on one side (*as shown opposite*).

Yet there is a quiet simplicity about the pool too. If it is a chapel of swimming, it befits the Scottish ethos admirably.

>> Nevertheless, as at Arlington, there were also many occasions throughout the 20th century when members were called upon to save the club from ruin.

Hardest of all were the 1970s. As the building's fabric deteriorated – apparently cockroaches became regulars in the pool – subscriptions rose as losses mounted. Fuel levies were imposed, and twice there was talk of a merger with Arlington. By now the boiler was so erratic members used to call in advance before deciding whether to swim.

Then one Sunday in July 1977 the roof fell in. Quite literally. Over the deep end. No-one was in the pool, but it appeared to be the final straw. Over 40 per cent of members resigned.

And yet this low point also proved to be a turning point.

A more liberal approach at last – allowing mixed bathing at all hours, the opening of a bar, full rights for female members – brought in younger members.

The formation of a holding company, which leased the club back to its members, released £120,000 towards a modern boiler, a replacement filtration plant and a new laundry, gym and sauna.

In total, between 1977 and 1990 over £1 million was spent, so that by 2007 there were over 2,000 members and a waiting list. And as long as bathers behave with decorum, they can be any colour or persuasion they like, and wear any coloured costume they like also.

Even more shockingly, at certain times there are not only mixed saunas but sessions for naturists.

Naturists at the Western!

Could this be one further path towards redemption for the historic swimming pools of the nation?

Rings and trapezes, and original spittoons (*centre left*) are few and far between in pools today, as are corner steps such as these. But the pre–1914 cast iron diving stage (*above*) – once common at British baths – is believed to be the only one of its kind still in situ. Also possibly unique are the concave tiled walls (as seen under the spittoon), lining the tank.

Case Study

White Rock Baths, Hastings

Opened May 31 1878
Address White Rock, Hastings
Architects Jeffery & Skiller and
Cross & Wells
Cost c. £60,000 for complex
Pools 180' x 40' + 90' x 40'
Closed 1911
Re-opened June 27 1931
Architect S Little, Borough Engineer
Closed early 1970s (as pool)
Listed unlisted

Many a coastal town would build seawater baths, but none quite like that of the Hastings and St Leonards Baths and Aquarium Company.

Set up in 1875, its main backer was the Hastings MP, Thomas Brassey, son of a fabulously wealthy railway contractor, while one of its architects (and minority shareholders) was

Alfred Cross, whose son, also Alfred, and grandson Kenneth, went on to become leading baths designers of the early 20th century. (Coincidentally, the other Hastings firm hired as co-architects, Jeffery & Skiller, had until 1875 employed the man who became a rival Alfred Cross Junior, AH Tiltman.)

Assuming that the young Cross did become familiar with his

father's designs, he would surely have been intrigued.

The baths were built, literally, on the beach at White Rock, just east of Hastings' new pier, in such a way that its outer wall acted as a sea-wall, while its roof formed an extension to the promenade. In return for these benefits the council paid £1,500 towards the estimated costs of £27,000.

Completed in phases over a four year period, the building was essentially a 650' x 80' box, formed by cast iron columns and roof beams encased in concrete. The foundation block alone, laid in June 1876, weighed six tons.

Entry was down stairs leading from the promenade, and the only natural light came courtesy of lantern windows lining the roof.

First to open within this box in 1878 was the men's pool (*seen left in 1905*), followed in 1879 by a smaller ladies' pool. Slipper baths were added in 1880, joined two years later by Turkish baths and rooms for refreshment, billiards and reading. (The aquarium idea had long since been abandoned.)

It seemed a model development, and yet the company was badly undercapitalised and, as we learn from the Victorian Turkish baths website (*see Links*), in 1901 it offered to sell up to the Council for £40,000 (£20,000 less than the company claimed it had already spent). But no deal could be agreed, and in 1911 the enterprise collapsed. Or at least a section of the baths roof did, after a heavy storm.

One part of the building then served briefly as a cinema, but the site mostly lay empty until...

The year was 1926 when, onto the scene entered Sidney Little, new Borough Engineer, soon to be dubbed 'the concrete king'.

Roads, car parks, promenades, a lido; Little had big ideas for Hastings, and for White Rock Baths too. Some £100,000 was spent on shortening the main pool to 165', extending the balcony to make it easier to watch water polo matches, fitting a new suite of Turkish baths and one of the new miracle Zotofoam baths. 'Bathe in Foam and lose 1-3 pounds of superfluous fat within one hour!' claimed the adverts.

Resplendent in newly painted reinforced concrete, the baths reopened in 1931, with a second smaller pool following in 1938. One real touch of glamour, typical of Little, was the use of coloured glass mosaic on the pool floors.

But in common with the nearby Hastings lido (and, ironically, that of Kenneth Cross' in Morecambe, also built on sand), White Rock Baths fared badly after the post war holiday boom subsided, and in the early 1970s closed again.

Its third incarnation was as a skating rink, from 1980 to 1997, since when it has lain empty, prey to vandals and seepage, and deemed too costly to adapt by every one of the numerous developers shown round by its current owners, the Foreshore Trust.

One possible use might be as an underground car park, unless, that is, a rich, risk-averse and romantic reader has any other ideas...

Stairway to heaven – this was the entry to White Rock's Turkish baths (*top*), before Sid Little turned the building into a concrete cavern (*centre*). Note the water polo nets hanging over the pool. Few promenaders today realise what lies beneath their feet (*bottom*); only that, along with the pier, also closed, Hastings has untapped heritage crying out for investment.

Case Study

North Woodside, Glasgow

Opened August 13 1882
Re-opened May 2 1991
Address Braid Square, G4 9YQ
Architect John Carrick
Cost £18,757
Pools: men's 75' x 40', ladies 40' x 24'. Now single 25m.
Owner Glasgow City Council
Operator Glasgow Club for Cultural and Leisure Services of Glasgow
Listed Category B (1992)

Barely half a mile east of the Arlington Baths Club, and only a brief stroll from Glasgow city centre – yet set in a proverbial 'world apart', in the midst of a late 20th century, low rise council estate on the north side of the M8 motorway – the North Woodside Leisure Centre is an unexpected blend of old and new.

Scotland's oldest operational public baths, it was one of over fifty civic buildings designed by

John Carrick, Glasgow's first City Architect. In the 1860s Carrick had helped transform large swathes of Glasgow by clearing slums and widening streets under the City Improvement Scheme.

Following on from this, in 1875 the Corporation set up its new Baths and Wash Houses Committee, under whose auspices Carrick designed, in addition to North Woodside, the baths at Greenhead (opened 1878), Cranstonhill (1883), Townhead (1884) and the Gorbals (1885).

Of these, only North Woodside survives.

In order to reduce costs, Carrick's baths were relatively free from embellishment, and were all in the conservative Italian Renaissance style he clearly favoured. North Woodside's specifications also almost exactly mirrored those of Greenhead (which stood next to the famous Templeton's Carpet Factory, facing Glasgow Green).

In addition to pools for men and women (no first or second class distinctions here), there were 34 slipper baths (27 male,

seven female) and a wash house, or 'steamie' in local parlance, with 67 stalls.

Apparently one characteristic of early Glasgow baths was that, like much of the city, their water supply was drawn from Loch Katrine, and contained minute traces of clay. After a few days' use – this being in the days before filtration plants – sediment would therefore settle at the bottom of each pool, turning the tiles a murky brown. Committee minutes suggest, however, that this was considered much less of a threat to hygiene than the grime which bathers brought in on their boots.

Indeed what few photographs survive of North Woodside in the early 20th century show it to be an exceptionally utilitarian facility, with changing cubicles on two levels around the pool and virtually no adornments.

As at all public baths, Friday nights were the busiest, as queues of residents from the surrounding tenements waited for their weekly hot slipper bath. At Christmas and the New Year these queues would start as early as 6.00am.

Today North Woodside could hardly present a greater contrast.

A £1.6 million refurbishment completed in 1991 by Carrick's successor as City Architect, Christopher Purslow, has totally transformed the building.

Purists may quibble at the level of intervention; the blue UPVC window frames, the fountains and off-the-shelf statuettes (*see left*), the encasement of the cast-iron column bases in tiled surrounds, the reshaping of the pool ends and the generous use of coloured tiling and exposed brick.

But this is a reinterpretation of a Victorian baths, not an attempt at faithful preservation. There is a fitness suite in the former ladies' pool, a spa pool and a sauna in alcoves formed around the poolside. Changing rooms and lockers on the gallery level are light and airy. Indeed were it not for the handsome sandstone exterior and the open timber roof of the pool hall, this might easily be a private health spa on the outer ring road of a dormitory town.

Not to everyone's taste, perhaps, but hugely popular amongst those on its doorstep.

Thinking outside the box – North Woodside has been transformed from a dour public baths into an urban haven. But it will be interesting to see how well this marriage of Victorian functionalism and 1990s 'leisure' styling weathers the years, and the vagaries of fashion.

Case Study

Warrender Baths, Edinburgh

Opened December 17 1887
Address Thirlestane Road EH9 1AP
Architect Robert Paterson & Son
Cost £11,000
Pool 75' x 35'
Owner Edinburgh City Council
Operator Edinburgh Leisure
Listed Category B (1993)

On a quiet residential street in Marchmont, just south of Edinburgh's famous Meadows, stands the oldest of seven listed pools that are still operational in the city (more than any other local authority).

But although now owned by the Council, originally the pool was part of a private baths club, complete with gymnasium, slipper baths, Turkish bath and rooms for billiards and reading, not dissimilar in scale and spirit to Arlington Baths Club in Glasgow (*see page 70*) or Drumsheugh in Edinburgh (*page 90*).

As told in Jamie Gilmour's history (*see Links*), the Warrender club had been set up by exiles from Bellahouston in Glasgow and their Edinburgh chums, and opened by Sir George Warrender (the local MP from whom the plot of land had been bought).

Warrender swimmers soon made their mark, becoming the first winners of the Scottish Water Polo Championship in 1901.

But despite this being one of the smarter areas of town – Miss Jean Brodie territory indeed – the club as a whole struggled to survive, and in 1907 it was bought for just £3,000 by the Corporation. It re-opened two years later, in 1908, slightly remodelled so that the pool itself was no longer used as a plunge pool by users of the Turkish bath.

Thereafter the name Warrender Baths Club – note, not Swimming Club – became renowned in Scotland for producing a string of champions. Most notably among these was David Wilkie, gold medallist and world record holder in the 200m breastroke at the 1976 Montreal Olympics.

More recently another breaststroke champion, Kirsty

Balfour, European Gold medallist in 2006 and silver medallist at the 2007 World Championships, started her swimming career at Warrender as a child, apparently enthralled by the patterns formed by sunlight falling on the water.

Today the patterns are clearer than ever, following a 14 month, £1.6m refurbishment, funded jointly by Edinburgh City Council,

the National Lottery and Sport Scotland, and seemingly worth every penny. Since reopening in January 2006, user numbers have doubled from 89,140 in 2004-05 to 180,144 in 2006-07.

No need to explain why. Its revamp has been tastefully executed, retaining the best of the building's Victorian features; its mosaic floors in the impressive

foyer, its poolside cubicles and its inset curved steps, as seen above.

Of course the pool has also been rebranded, as the Warrender Swim Centre, but to local residents, regular school users and the many students in the area, it will always be plain Warrender Baths; an almost idyllic community centre that still has the intimate feel of the private club it once was.

Coaching from the sidelines – the famous Warrender Baths Club now hold most of their training and events at larger, competition sized pools in Edinburgh, such as at the nearby Royal Commonwealth Pool (*see page 250*). But Warrender is still their spiritual home, and the pool in which many a child, and future champion, has taken their first strokes.

Case Study

Westbury Baths, Wiltshire

Opened May 24 1888
Address Church Street BA13 3BY
Architect Mr Anderson
Cost £5,000
Pool 68' x 23'
Owner West Wilts District Council
Operator DC Leisure
Listed unlisted

Queen Victoria's Golden Jubilee in 1887 provided many a town with the incentive to build public baths. At Westbury, a small town on the western edge of Salisbury Plain, built around woollen mills, glove factories and an ironworks, the impetus came courtesy of a £5,000 gift from William Henry Laverton, owner of Angel Mill and maker of 'fancy woollen coatings and meltons'.

Westbury was then very much the Lavertons' domain. Indeed, the Laverton Institute (b. 1873) still houses the council offices.

As suggested by the address at the baths' opening in May 1888, signed by 300 loyal townspeople, Laverton was an archetypal Victorian capitalist-philanthropist.

'We believe that these baths will be conductive not only to the health and enjoyment of the people of Westbury but also to their moral elevation, and that as long as they exist their founder will receive the grateful remembrance of future generations.'

Laverton's wife, who had laid the foundation stone the previous year, then declared the baths open.

Quite how many swimmers were grateful, or felt morally improved when they realised that the pool water was piped in directly from Bitham Springs, and was not heated (at least not in the first few years), we cannot be sure.

But the boilers were soon in place and since then, these delightful baths have changed very little. Slate partitions forming changing cubicles along the north side (*the right hand side, as shown opposite*) have been removed, and the arched opening on the south (leading to the ladies' changing

Foundation stones often set the tone. This one, combined with the bath's spendid Church Street façade, seeks to ensure that no-one in Westbury will forget the Laverton family's munificence, or their loyalty to the monarch, whose portrait in bas relief sits above the date of her Jubilee, rather than the baths' opening date, which was a year later.

boxes) have been sealed off. The once exposed brickwork under the string course has been plastered and painted. The timber roof has also been painted white, to lighten the interior. But the roof's original decorative ironwork remains intact, still displaying the coats of arms of Westbury and, lest we forget, the Laverton family.

On Church Street the original male and female entrances have been boarded up and replaced by a wheelchair compliant entrance at the side of the building.

Most of these works date from a refurbishment programme carried out in the 1980s, shortly before the baths' centenary, and mean that the Westbury Pool, as it is now rebranded, can, through its sauna, fitness suite and hydrotherapy facilities – which replaced the original slipper bath areas – cater as much for people's health and enjoyment as their moral welfare.

Still, there remains one feature of the baths that no amount of modernisation has been able to eradicate.

Going by the name of George, he is Westbury Pool's resident ghost. One version of the tale has him as a tragic figure who jumped to his death from the balcony overlooking the deep end. Another reckons he was a boiler stoker, who can still be seen standing at the pool's edge in his overalls.

Case Study

Glossop, Derbyshire

Opened February 4 1889
Address Dinting Road SK13 7DS
Architect Mills & Murgatroyd
Cost £14–15,000
Pool size 82' x 32' (now 25m)
Owner High Peak Borough Council
Operator High Peak Leisure
Listed unlisted

The scene appears so idyllic. A graceful Italianate chimney rises, temple-like, above the sylvan heights and undulating lawns of a manicured Victorian landscape – Howard Park – where shrubberies and rockeries, serpentine paths and a cascading stream offer a lush contrast to the raw moorlands of the distant Peak.

But look closer, and the scene unfolds...

It is Saturday, July 30 1887, six weeks after Queen Victoria's Golden Jubilee celebrations in London. The streets of Glossop come alive with a procession of 26 carriages, led by a detachment of the 4th Cheshire Rifle Volunteers.

Among them is a young NCO, Robert Hamnett, who will later in life assume the mantle of Glossop's unofficial historian.

All the mill town's great and good are there, followed by the Sons of Temperance, the Ancient Order of Shepherds, plus sundry Oddfellows, Foresters and other Masonic societies, each with their sashes and banners. As Hamnett recalls, it was 'a brave show, never equalled before or since'.

The procession's destination is Barker's Clough, to the north of the town, where Lord Howard of Glossop has donated twelve acres for a public park, to be laid out by landscape architect Henry

Ernest Milner. But Howard Park is no ordinary park, for within its manicured borders a hospital and a public baths are to be built, to the designs of a Manchester firm, Mills and Murgatroyd.

Public baths so far out of town? Surely it should be down in the valley, where the millworkers live?

But there are over 40 mills there, and no room to move, let alone air to breathe, and although this has been much to the advantage of Lord Howard and his family, who effectively created this industrial new town, his offer of the park is too good to turn down. Whereas the Lord once tooketh, now he giveth. Besides, up on the hillside the air is clear. This is a haven. A Jubilee gift to the people.

So first stop for the procession is to lay the foundation stone for the hospital and to give thanks to its benefactor, Daniel Wood, joint owner with his brothers John and Samuel of the town's largest and most profitable cotton mills.

The Woods, together with Samuel's wife Anne (who hails from an even wealthier cotton dynasty), have pledged over £30,000 to this Jubilee project, having already given freely to other causes, including Holy Trinity Church, their first commission for Mills and Murgatroyd.

From the hospital site the party moves on to plant a sapling in honour of Lord Howard, who is, alas, absent, owing, writes Hamnett, to 'recent domestic affliction'. By the end of the year Lady Howard will be dead.

Absent also, through illness, is Samuel Wood. But his 15 year old son, also Samuel, home from Eton, is there to plant another sapling. Hamnett reports him as telling the crowd, 'They were both young, they were both Wood, and they both wished to grow.'

The Town Clerk then reads an address thanking the Woods, after which Anne is presented with a mallet, trowel and plummet to lay the foundation stone for the baths.

Cue the National Anthem, and the procession then makes its way back to town for Mr Herbert Rhodes and Captain Partington to be similarly honoured as they lay the third foundation stone of

the day. This is for Victoria Hall, in Talbot Street, which houses a library. Glossop's benefactors understand that bodies made healthy by the new park, baths and hospital, must also be possessed of healthy minds. Then it is off to the Town Hall banquet, where Hamnett counts 30 speeches.

Yet one year later, no fanfare at all accompanies the opening of Howard Park. Nor does any ceremony attend the opening of Wood's Hospital, in January 1889, or of the baths, a fortnight later.

In the centre of Howard Park lies the clue. Also unveiled in 1889 is a memorial to the brothers Daniel and Samuel Wood. Both

had died since the Jubilee. A shadow hangs over the park.

In 1896 the Wood family hands over the park and baths to the Council. Their work is done.

But in any case, by the time a chlorination plant is installed in 1928, the cotton industy has collapsed. Samuel Wood Jnr. has become Samuel Hill Wood MP and chairman of Arsenal FC.

Back in Glossop in 1961 a new balcony is constructed at the baths. In 1993 the building is sensitively modernised. The pool is shortened to 25m. The slipper baths are converted to changing rooms. A solarium is installed.

On the other side of the park,

which is now listed, the hospital still operates, and the library, also listed, is set for a £2m revamp.

This time the lottery will pay, rather than the aristocracy or the cottonocracy. Who stops to read a foundation stone these days?

Case Study

Dulwich, London

Opened June 25 1892
Address East Dulwich Road
SE22 9AN
Architect Spalding & Cross
Cost £25,895
Pool sizes 120' x 35' (now gym)
and 90' x 35'
Owner Southwark Borough Council
Operator Fusion Lifestyle
Listed Grade II (1993)

Since the closure of Forest Hill baths in 2006, the two oldest public baths still operational in London are at Dulwich and Camberwell, a mile or so apart from each other and both within the Borough of Southwark.

In fact Dulwich opened three months before Camberwell (*see page 91*). But they share the same architects and several characteristics (if not the same character), and were both built as a result of the Vestry of Camberwell adopting the Baths and Wash Houses Act in 1887. They were, in effect, part of a second wave of baths springing up in the new London suburbs. The railway had come to East Dulwich in 1868, and as the population rose steadily, so the Vestry had to catch up with its inner city counterparts.

As noted by the Dulwich Baths' historian Polly Bird (*see Links*), the newly appointed Camberwell Commissioners took their duties seriously, visiting twelve London vestries. One piece of advice that was to have a lasting effect came from Greenwich, who urged Camberwell to site their baths on main roads. This would boost income from bathing and from renting out the main pool as a public hall during the winter.

But sites on London's main roads were hard to find and costly to buy, which is why at Dulwich the Vestry was happy to settle on a well placed plot on East Dulwich Road, facing Goose Green, even though it was an awkward and irregular shape, barely 80' wide at the front and extending some 350' to the rear, where it was bound in by an end-of-terrace house and a mineral water works. To create a rear exit the Vestry therefore had to compulsorily purchase a 10' strip, leading onto a side road (Crystal Palace Road).

Given these constraints the Vestry played safe by appointing as their architect Henry Spalding, fresh from working on similarly narrow sites at Finchley Road, Hampstead, and Buckingham Palace Road, Westminster.

Spalding had just gone into partnership with an up and coming architect, Alfred Cross, who, as noted elsewhere, would soon emerge as a leading authority on baths. Spalding & Cross would work together on seven baths, of which Dulwich was the first.

Set back from the road, its public face is a Queen Anne style entrance block with the baths' name boldly inscribed below the eaves, and a clock tower topped by a cupola and weathervane. This is no shrinking violet.

Shell-moulded hoods mark the male and female entrances, both accessed via steps leading up from what was originally a garden. By raising the ground floor in this way Spalding & Cross were able to provide a full height basement to house the boilers and an establishment laundry. (As at Hampstead no wash house was deemed necessary.) A sensible idea in the 1890s, perhaps, but in the early 21st century, a real obstacle to providing disabled access.

Another clever idea was to position the water tanks in the attic, thereby concentrating all the services at the front of the site.

The upper floor, meanwhile, housed a spacious apartment for the superintendent, his wife (the matron) and their family.

Behind this entrance block, completely hidden from view other than from Crystal Palace Road, two pool sheds with lantern lights and timber hammerbeam roofs were ranged, end to end; first class at the front, second class at the rear, accessed via a long corridor. So tight was the site that at the far, south eastern corner of the second class bath the walkway around the pool narrows to only a few inches.

Unusually, this smaller pool was not heated until 1900.

The final third of the site is a jumble of extensions between the second class pool and Crystal Palace Road, formed after two houses were bought in 1910 to add extra slipper baths and wider exits, so that the capacity of the main pool, when used as a public hall, could be increased.

Indeed one theme throughout Dulwich's history is that its main pool and ancillary rooms have been consistently used as much for 'dry' sports (such as carpet bowls and boxing), concerts, dances and meetings, as they have for swimming or bathing.

This multi-functionality has been the key to its rebranding as the Dulwich Leisure Centre, and is now key also to its future.

In the early 1980s the main pool was boarded over once and for all, leaving only the smaller second class pool (which is of no great distinction), in operation. But it was not enough, and in 1990 the whole complex appeared to be doomed, only to be rescued after the newly formed Friends of Dulwich Baths persuaded Southwark to invest £250,000 on much needed repairs.

Since then the women's slipper bath area has been converted to a crêche, and the men's slipper bath area (in a corner of the entrance block) has been mothballed, but left intact for its historic value. Also lying empty is the first floor flat above the entrance.

Had nothing more been done, almost certainly the surviving pool would have closed too, putting

into doubt the whole complex's future. But Dulwich has too many friends to go down without a fight, and in 2007, after a long round of studies and consultation, Southwark announced a £5m renovation programme, due to start in late 2008.

Apart from a long overdue revamp of the old second class pool there will be new studios and treatment rooms, a café, and most radically of all, a new main entrance on Crystal Palace Road, to avoid having to compromise the integrity of the existing frontage by adding a wheelchair ramp.

What will happen to the old entrance block has yet to be determined. *Played in Britain* will thus return to Dulwich in our 2011 study, *Played in London*, to take a fresh view of this oddball survivor.

In the 1970s a suspended ceiling was fitted. In 1982 the pool was boarded over. But in 2002 Dulwich's new operators, Fusion, tore out the ceiling, restored the roof and fitted this modern gym. Note that piers support both roof and gallery, with space behind for cubicles. This was to allow for a wider pool and deeper gallery than otherwise possible on a narrow site.

Case Study

GWR Medical Fund Baths, Swindon

Opened June 11 1892
Address Milton Road SN1 5JA
Architect JJ Smith
Cost £10,000, plus £5,000 for slipper baths (1898) and £7,000 for Russian baths (1908)
Pool sizes 111' x 30' and 60' x 25'
Owner/operator Swindon Borough Council
Listed Grade II (2000)

As readers will have noticed, Victorian public baths share a number of similarities with railway stations. So it is ironic that the one set of baths built entirely by a railway company appears, from the outside at least, to resemble little more than a modest row of terraced houses.

The clue to Swindon's historic baths lies in the town's motto, *Salubritas et Industria* (Health and Industry). Swindon was, of course, established in the 1840s as the headquarters of Brunel's Great Western Railway, a company that over the years supported a number of welfare and educational institutions for its workforce. Chief amongst these was the GWR's Medical Fund, set up in 1847 by Daniel Gooch,

Superintendent of the Railway Works, and credited by many as not only the first industrial health care society in the world, but also as a source of inspiration to the founders of the National Heath Service in the 1940s, particularly Aneurin Bevan.

Every member of the workforce, over 14,000 at its peak, paid a few pence a week into the fund, not voluntarily but as a condition of their employment.

In return, all their health care needs, and much else besides, were provided for free.

The GWR built its first baths for the workforce in 1869. These were slipper baths, installed within the Mechanics Institute on Emlyn Square, opened in 1855. The building is still extant, although no trace of the baths survives.

These facilities were superceded by the building we see today.

Opened in 1892, this was a much larger establishment,

with two swimming pools and a wash house. But also within the building, uniquely, there was a medical dispensary and a range of private consulting rooms.

To this first phase were added slipper baths in 1898, and Turkish baths in 1908, so that the finished complex formed a complete block, 160' x 219', with entrances both on Faringdon Road, and (*shown left and below*) on Milton Road.

Perhaps because these were company buildings, little effort was made at embellishment.

Indeed as far as was possible, every element was either designed in the GWR's drawing office or supplied from the company stores. For example the stained glass, elements of which survive in the Turkish bath and in side rooms, was the work of one T Rice, an artist in the design office.

It has also been claimed that the wrought iron trusses in both swimming pools share the same

profile as standard railway lines. True or not, the truss designs are certainly unique.

Even the water was supplied by the GWR, piped in from its wells at Kemble in Gloucestershire.

Following the formation of the NHS and the nationalisation of the railways in the late 1940s, the Medical Fund was wound up and the baths handed over to the local authority. Since then there have been two refurbishment programmes, in 1963 and 1987, resulting in the loss of several internal features and the closing of the Faringdon Road entrance, but also in the restoration of the two pool halls and the Turkish baths.

Moreover, the founding spirit of the place lives on. Now rebranded by Swindon Borough Council as the Health Hydro, there is a modern gym and a natural health clinic, offering a range of complementary therapies.

The Hydro is also one of the few centres left in Britain where private baths and showers can still be had.

God's Wonderful Railway, they used to call the GWR. To which the healthy folk of Swindon might add, Amen to that.

Refurbished in 1987 the main pool has lost its poolside cubicles and stained glass, but otherwise retains its lofty, uncluttered lightness and its arched gallery overlooking the deep end. The adjacent learner pool (formerly the ladies') has similar clerestory windows with a central lantern light, one of nine roof structures of this type within the complex.

Case Study

Drumsheugh Baths Club, Edinburgh

Opened December 26 1882
Reopened February 6 1892
Address Belford Road EH4 3BL
Architect Sir John James Burnet
Cost £17,000
Pool size 70' x 35'
Owner Drumsheugh Baths Co Ltd
Listed Category B (1970)

Scotland's third surviving private baths club is a most unlikely proposition at first sight.

Entry is via a small lodge with a deep overhanging roof, perched on a steep ridge running down to the Waters of Leith and overlooking Dean Village.

Once inside the vestibule, white walls and Moorish arches lead down stairs that, via a lounge and gym, access a balcony overlooking the pool, well below street level.

Drumsheugh was the design of the eminent Sir John James Burnet (whose father was architect of the Arlington Baths Club). He chose the Moorish style, perhaps influenced by Turkish baths he had seen in Paris during his training.

Equally he might have visited the recently opened public baths at Whitfield Street in London.

To fund the baths shareholders had raised £12,000 in £5 shares, but in the end needed nearer £17,000. It cost a further £6,000 to reconstruct the baths after a disastrous fire in 1892. Ten years later the company then went into liquidation, only for the baths to be bought by its present owners, the Drumsheugh Baths Co Ltd.

Since then, as at Arlington, survival has required members to dig deep to match funding for upkeep. In the 1980s grants of £134,000 from Historic Scotland were needed for roof repairs. This was followed in 2005 by a further

£294,000 towards £1.15 million worth of refurbishment works.

But it has been artfully done, especially around the pool itself, which sits between cast iron columns, topped by red brick arches and a timber framed roof, top lit by two glass cupolas.

As at Arlington and Western, Drumsheugh retains its rings and trapezes. Its poolside cubicles have also remained in use, thanks to a rule requiring members to leave their shoes in the vestibule.

Eminently practical, as one would expect of Edinburgh's elite, but proof also that Victorian pools, if properly resourced and sensibly managed, can serve as the urban oases of the 21st century.

Camberwell, London

T ucked in at the end of a cul-de-sac of its own making, only yards from the busy Camberwell Church Street, the story of Camberwell Baths is closely intertwined with that of Dulwich (*see page 86*). It was opened in the same year (albeit three months later), built by the same vestry (Camberwell), designed by the same architects, is Grade II listed, and, above all, shoehorned into an elongated site, with two pool halls ranged end to end behind a stately entrance block (*above*).

This entrance would have been even grander had the Vestry not toned down the architects' original grandiose plans. But though plainer, the final, Flemish Renaissance style façade is far more appropriate, a lesson one of the architects, Alfred Cross, clearly took on board in his later work.

Inside the entrance an original pay box survives, and there is more recent decorative glazing (*below left*) above the main door.

Incidentally, Camberwell was one of the first baths to have electric lights, powered initially from the baths' own generator.

Like Dulwich, Camberwell currently has one of its two pools boarded over, although here it is the rear, second class pool (which, unusually, was the same size as the first class), now used as a sports hall. The first class pool remains in use (*right*), but boomed at 25m.

Again, in common with Dulwich, Spalding & Cross gained maximum width on the narrow site by supporting the shallow hammer beam timber roof on inset columns, which also support the upper gallery. There are now voids under this gallery, the changing cubicles having been moved to the former slipper bath areas.

But there are differences.

From its inception, the rear of Camberwell backed onto a road (Harvey Road), allowing for easy access to the wash house. There was also at the rear an apartment for an engineer, who served both here and Dulwich, and in 1895 was equipped with a private telephone line between his two posts.

But the major difference between Camberwell and Dulwich is that since 2007 the future of the former has hung in the balance.

Having estimated that a full refurbishment would cost at least £6m and require the building to close for two years, in 2007 Southwark pledged £200,000 'as a short term palliative', before entering talks with three bidders, each offering varying solutions for the future. Meanwhile a rapidly formed Friends group – whose website has more history (*see Links*) – launched a campaign aimed largely at ensuring that Southwark sticks to its preferred option of retaining at least one pool in whichever scheme is adopted.

Until those discussions can be resolved, Camberwell's future as a facility for swimming, if not as a building, remains uncertain.

Opened October 1 1892
Address Artichoke Place, SE5 8TS
Architect Spalding & Cross
Cost £28,575
Pools both 120' x 35'
Owner Southwark Borough Council
Operator Fusion Lifestyle
Listed Grade II (1993)

Case Study

Cambridge Street, Batley

Opened September 9 1893
Address Cambridge St, WF17 5JH
Architect Walter Hanstock
Cost £9,160
Pools 75' x 30' and 30' x 24' (now sports hall)
Owner Kirklees Council
Operator Kirklees Active Leisure
Listed Grade II (1993)

For over forty years the architect Walter Hanstock, first under the wing of Michael Sheard, then on his own account, and finally in partnership with his son Arthur Hanstock, had a hand in virtually every new major building in Batley.

Predominantly decked in the local sandstone that gives the townscape such a warm glow, these buildings, many of them listed, included the Town Hall, the hospital, the cemetery and several schools and churches, among them the Zion Methodist Chapel, known as the 'Shoddy Chapel', where local manufacturers were said to have done more business than praying. (Shoddy, on which the town's wealth was founded, was a form of recycled wool.)

But Hanstock also specialised in public baths. Batley was his first. Five more would follow for Leeds Corporation between 1895–99, and after his death in 1900, his son Arthur completed one more, in Selby in 1901. No other northern private practice was so active in the field (which from 1900 onwards would become increasingly dominated by City Architects; the likes of FEP Edwards in Bradford and Henry Price in Manchester).

None of these later baths survive – most were demolished in the 1960s and '70s – leaving Batley as the sole testament to Hanstock's versatility and bold approach to detail as a baths designer.

Dominating the building is the central three storey entrance block, which retains several original details, such as glazed screens, stained glass door panels, and in the former superintendent's flat, fireplaces and ceilings.

Flanking this block are single storey wings – each originally housing a range of slipper baths, Turkish baths, a Zotofoam bath and baths labelled pine and seaweed – while to the rear, either side of a spendid Italianate chimney, are two pool sheds. The smaller retains its original roof lights, but is now used as a sports hall, while the larger remains in use as a pool but is much altered.

In 1946 a new café was added to the viewing gallery, but then in 1981 a serious fire required the construction of a new roof and, for energy conservation, the fitting of a suspended ceiling (although the original viewing gallery survives out of view). Poolside cubicles were also removed and all surfaces upgraded, so that no trace of the pool's Victorian origins are visible.

A £300,000 revamp in 2004 took that process further, so that inside Hanstock's shell there now sits a modern leisure centre.

One story often repeated at Batley is that on the Technical and Arts College opposite the baths, also opened in 1893, there is a carved mermaid, which but for a builder's error should have been attached to the baths. There is no truth in this, but the two Victorian institutions facing each other make a handsome pair all the same. Clearly, there was brass to made from all that shoddy.

Case Study

Fore Street, Ipswich

As a once thriving inland port, Ipswich has, over the years, offered an unusually full range of aquatic experiences; swimming in the River Orwell at either the Stoke Bathing Place (1842–1953) or the West End Bathing Place (1893–1936); outdoor swimming at Pipers Vale (1937–79) and Broomhill Lido (1938–2002), and indoor swimming at Fore Street, at St Matthews (1922–84, *see page 170*), and Crown Street (opened 1984), where there is both a competition and a leisure pool.

Also in town is one of Britain's oldest operational private pools, at Ipswich School, opened in 1884.

But St Matthews is now a social club, Pipers Vale has been demolished, and Broomhill – its 50m pool lying empty – is subject to a long running campaign.

Thus Fore Street is the only historic public facility still in use.

Also referred to as St Clement's Baths, after the church to its rear (*see right*), Fore Street came about after three stalwarts of the Ipswich Swimming Club presented the Council with a 1,000 signature petition in 1888. They were the Rev Canon Bulstrode, Admiral Sir George Broke-Middleton (benefactor of Ipswich School's pool), and Felix Thornley Cobbold, of the Cobbold Brewery dynasty.

But only when Cobbold donated a site and a further £1,200 did the Council finally agree to pay the balance towards what was, even for its time, a modest baths.

Opened in 1894 with a grand gala (featuring a demonstration of

life saving skills by William Henry, co-founder of the Royal Life Saving Society), Fore Street had a single pool with a gallery, 12 slipper baths and a small laundry.

Cobbold, a fervent Liberal, had intended the baths to be classless.

'Clothes might be important in the outside world, but in the baths all were on an equal footing.'

Ipswich, he added, was not like 'some aristocratic towns' where baths were classed according to the water quality on certain days.

But that is exactly how Fore Street did operate. This being in the days before filtration, of the 28,265 who attended in the first year, 11,293 were men and boys on Saturdays, when entry was cheapest because the water was

at its dirtiest. But as DL Jones's history of swimming in Ipswich (*see Links*) points out, these figures also show how popular Fore Street was, at a time when the town's population was only 57,000.

Eventually a filtration system was installed, in 1933, and the pool lengthened to the standard 75' recommended by the ASA.

In the post war years the gallery and diving board were removed, and since the opening of Crown Street in 1984 Fore Street has played a subsidiary role as host to school groups, clubs and teaching – a role to which this compact, simple but charming pool, with its polished brass plate on the door, poolside cubicles and intimate atmosphere, is perfectly suited.

Opened March 1 1894
Address Fore Street, IP4 1JZ
Architect TW Cotman
Cost £4,300
Pool 72' x 22' (extended to 75')
Owner/operator Ipswich Borough Council
Listed unlisted

Case Study

Victoria Baths, Sneinton, Nottingham

Opened June 5 1896 (on site of 1850 original) with 1879 addition
Address Gedling Street/Bath Street, Sneinton, NG1 1DB
Architect 1879, MO Tarbotton; 1896, Arthur Brown, both Borough Engineers; extended 1928 and 1973
Cost in 1896, £18,000
Pools 110'x 35', 100' x 44' (now sports hall) and 70' x 30'
Owner/Operator Nottm City Council
Listed unlisted

In February 2008, Nottingham City Council's decision to close the Victoria Leisure Centre, on the eastern fringe of the city centre, sent protestors from the hastily formed campaign group (*see* Links) to the city's archives, in search of proof that, apart from the health and social issues raised by possible closure, the building itself and the site on which it sits are of historic importance also.

The trail goes back to the 1840s, when Nottingham was a densely populated and, according to the Borough Water Engineer, a more insanitary town than any other.

To alleviate these conditions the 1845 Nottingham Enclosure Act empowered the Council to put aside open land for people's 'health, comfort and convenience,' including a site of no more than five acres to be allocated 'for the purpose of forming... public Baths and Outbuildings and Gardens connected therewith, for the use of the inhabitants of the said town of Nottingham forever'.

Finally selected in June 1849, the site allocated was that on which the baths stand today, opposite Sneinton marketplace. There was, noted a Council report, 'probably no town where their value would be more felt than in Nottingham'.

The first baths, on what was now renamed Bath Street, was a modest affair, costing £2,713. Designed by Borough Surveyor Henry Moses Wood and opened on December 16 1850 (marginally before similar establishments in Birmingham and Liverpool), it

consisted of six slipper baths, two plunge baths, 52' x 12' for men and 27' x 12' for women, and a small wash house.

But by 1876 the facilities were showing their age, and so the new Borough Engineer, Marriott Ogle Tarbotton, was asked to draw up plans for a revamp.

As described opposite, this next programme of works, completed in 1879, included the covering of an existing outdoor swimming pool that lay between the baths and the rear of the adjacent Ragged School. Prior to 1876 the ownership of this outdoor pool, later to be called the Oval Pool, is not clear. Was it the school's or the baths' committee? As to its date of construction, that was most likely between 1858, when the school opened, and 1864, when the pool first appears on a map (*see* opposite).

By the 1890s the baths were once again showing their age, so Tarbotton's successor, Arthur Brown, prepared designs for an almost total reconstruction of the site, costing £18,000 and retaining only two existing elements, a suite of Turkish Baths, added in 1861, and the now covered Oval Pool.

Work began in 1894, as Brown was finishing off the layout of Victoria Park across the road, and on June 5 1896 the building reopened, also bearing the queen's name.

As can still be seen, the new Victoria Baths' most prominent feature was a clock tower forming part of a two storey entrance block. Behind this were two new pools; an Exhibition Pool and a smaller

Built in 1896 and modernised almost beyond recognition a century later, Nottingham's 33.3m Gala Pool is where Olympic gold medallist Rebecca Adlington did much of her training as a teenager.

ladies pool (parallel to each other and to Bath Street), plus the Oval Pool, now reserved for boys.

A small plunge bath reserved for Jewish women, known as a Mikveh, also formed part of the redevelopment, as did new suites of slipper baths.

Since 1896 there have been three major changes. In 1928 a new wash house was added on Bath Street, and from 1973–75, as part of a £336,000 modernisation, this same wash house and the ladies' slipper bath area was converted into a Turkish bath, sauna and solarium. At the same time the Oval Pool was infilled and converted into a sports hall (*right*).

Finally, during the 1990s, the main pool, renamed the Gala Pool, was shortened marginally to 33.3m, its gallery and cubicles removed and its roof reclad (*see left*). The former ladies' pool was similarly modernised, while a fitness suite and gym extension arose on the Gedling Street frontage, in a contrasting style.

The complex was also renamed, as the Victoria Leisure Centre.

Despite this extensive refit, in 2000 the Council decided to close the building, only to change their minds after a public outcry.

As noted earlier, they faced similar outrage in February 2008, before agreeing to keep the centre open at least until the end of the year, to allow time for further consultation. The main options at the time of going to press were either to build a new centre on the site, or start anew elsewhere.

Either way, even though an application to list the baths was turned down by English Heritage – too many alterations having taken place – it was agreed that the 1896 entrance block and clock tower would at least be retained.

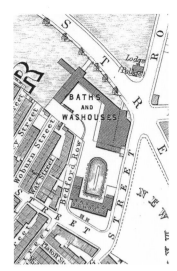

▲ The three lives of Nottingham's **Oval Pool** – first as an outdoor pool, as shown on Edward Salmon's map of 1864, lying between the 1858 Ragged School (still extant and now Grade II listed) and the 1850 baths; second as an indoor pool, covered in 1879, seen here (*top right*) c.1950, and finally, as a sports hall, converted in 1975 and photographed in 2008 (*right*).

These extracts from *The Builder* of May 17 1879 describe how the pool, which had 'been for many years an open bath', was covered by MO Tarbotton, engineer-in-chief to the corporation:

'The new building is 120' x 60' and is approached by a broad flight of stone steps from the present ticket-office at the Gedling-street entrance. The bath proper is 102' x 44', with semicircular ends...

'A continuous supply of warm water... is obtained from the condensing engine at Mr Windley's works in Roden-street, Mr Windley having placed this supply of water at the disposal of the corporation.

'The roof is... carried by seven wrought-iron ribs... semi-circular in shape... Each rib, for a height of 9' above floor-level, is of cast-iron; the remainder is wrought-iron with open lattice-work... giving the ribs a very light appearance. The weight of each rib is about 5½ tons.

'The building is ventilated by a louvre running the length of the roof... this louvre, nearly 20' wide, is entirely glazed, so that there is ample light as well as ventilation.

'Dressing-rooms, 38 in number, and a jumping-stage have been provided for the convenience of persons using the bath, and the woodwork of which these are made, as well as the underside of the woodwork of the roof, is stained and varnished.

'The bath is believed to be one of the largest in the kingdom, and the cost has been about £2,500.'

Case Study

Alloa, Clackmannanshire

Opened April 29 1898
Address Primrose Street, FK10 1JD
Architect Sir John James Burnet
Sons & John Archibald Campbell
Cost £40,000
Pool size 75' x 32' (now gym)
Owner Clackmannanshire Council
Museum and Heritage Service
Listed Category B (1972)

Glasgow architect John James Burnet was apparently a great stickler for detail, as we saw in his earlier designs for the private Drumsheugh Baths Club in Edinburgh (*see page 90*). But even that Moorish indulgence appears restrained compared with the public baths at Alloa, completed during Burnet's partnership with John Archibald Campbell.

Despite its size, Alloa in the late 19th century was, thanks to its position on the River Forth, a real hub of industry, particularly glass, brewing and wool spinning.

In September 1894, John Thomson Paton, philanthropist and owner of Kilncraigs Mill, which dominated the town, wrote to the Town Clerk saying that as there was now 'an abundant supply of water for Alloa' he wished to finance the construction of public baths and a gymnasium.

The sum he endowed for this was later given as £40,000. Paton also offered a further £3,000 to cover running costs.

Clearly the architects did not have to stint. Designed in an exuberant Scottish Renaissance style and faced in red ashlar with red granite details, the building was as well equipped as any of Scotland's private baths clubs, while both outside and inside it simply dripped with detailing and colour. It was also illuminated throughout with electric lights, fitted with Mavor & Coulson of Glasgow's all-important patented 'concentric water-tight system'.

Such was the interest that on opening day a public holiday was declared and the newspaper had to print 300 extra copies of its report to satisfy demand. In the first seven months nearly 30,000 admissions were recorded – this in a town of 13,000 inhabitants.

But who can blame them for being enchanted?

Entering from Primrose Street (*see left*) an unusually grand vestibule (*opposite*) gave access to a billiard room on one side and a cloakroom on the other. The hall then led into an atrium, brightly (or gaudily, according to taste) decked in maroon and ochre tiles and marble pilasters.

Carved in wood on the main staircase, fangs exposed, a dragon's head stared out – the first of many.

Inside the swimming pool, ten more beasties' heads extend from the roof beams, each one slightly different. Quite why they are there has never been explained. Perhaps they were Burnet's idea of Oriental exoticism. Certainly they are unique in a public baths setting.

As shown on page 50, the pool itself was equally arresting, with 35 poolside cubicles, rings and trapezes, hanging ferns, a gallery on three sides, and, overlooking the deep end, the balcony of a club room. This was designed so that performers in aquatic displays could step out dramatically, straight onto the diving board.

Behind the pool, with its own castellated entrance (*in the distance, left*), was a Turkish bath, while alongside the swimming pool were two first class and seven second class slipper baths (confusingly called plunge baths in the town's yearbook).

Finally there was a gymnasium, a slightly smaller version of the pool hall, measuring 76' x 28', with more, snarling dragon heads, an open timber roof and an 80 seat gallery at one end, under which were dressing rooms and showers.

By the 1960s Alloa's prosperity had all but ebbed away. Its harbour and station closed. Paton's, now part of Paton & Baldwin's, had shifted production elsewhere.

First to close at Primrose Street was the Turkish baths, damaged by fire in the mid 1960s. In 1986 the pool was closed, and in 1998 converted into a gym as part of a £130,000 refit. Meanwhile the building was renamed after Tommy Spiers, a stalwart of the Alloa gym and a Scottish boxing champion of the 1930s.

Since then the original gym has been used for storing artefacts from Paton's old works. The tower over the main entrance has also gone, as have the billiard tables.

Rather like the nearby Town Hall, also endowed by Paton, and the superb 1926 Paton & Baldwin's sports pavilion (to be featured in a forthcoming *Played in Britain* study, *Bowled Over*), here was a beautiful building desperately in need of a new role.

Fortunately, it appears to have found one. In 2008, at around the same time the town's railway station triumphantly re-opened, Malcolm Fraser Architects were tasked with drawing up plans for the pool to be converted into the town's public library, for the old gym to become a museum, and for other rooms to be used as a centre for Scottish traditional dance.

As we shall see in Chapter Nine, former baths elsewhere have been similarly adapted with great aplomb. Paton's wee gem deserves nothing less.

Wherever the eye turns there is something to enjoy at Alloa. The swimming pool (*top, and page 50*), currently a gym, is destined to become the town's library.

Case Study

Skibo Castle, Sutherland

Opened c.1900
Address Skibo Castle, near Dornoch, IV25 3RG
Architects Alexander Ross and Robert John Macbeth
Pool size 77' 6" x 26' 6"
Owner/operator The Carnegie Club at Skibo Castle
Listed Grade B (1984)

Andrew Carnegie is today best remembered for endowing over 2,500 public libraries around the world. He similarly financed public baths both in his home town of Dunfermline (*see page 132*), and in Braddock, Pennsylvania (home of one of his steelworks).

As detailed in Chapter Five, from 1913–18 his Carnegie UK Trust also funded the single most comprehensive study of British public baths ever undertaken.

But Carnegie built a pool of his own too, on the vast Skibo Castle estate that he had bought in 1898 as a Scottish retreat for himself, his young American wife and their one year old daughter.

As recalled in David Nasaw's biography (*see Links*), Carnegie

wrote to his Edinburgh friend and general factotum, Hew Morrison, thus: 'I wish very much to have a saltwater swimming bath (heated). Please ascertain who the man is in Scotland who has distinguished himself building these. I do not wish to get into connection with anyone who has not had great

experience... Should like some idea of cost, say 60' x 30'.'

Now John James Burnet, architect of the baths at Alloa and Drumsheugh, would have been the obvious choice. But perhaps because of Skibo's remoteness Morrison appointed an Inverness firm, Ross & Macbeth, who had designed baths for Inverness in 1889, but were hardly distinguished.

That said they did a fine job, designing a Scottish Baronial style detached block on the banks of the boating lake, with a pitched and fully glazed conservatory roof and a pool edged with white marble.

Changing rooms, bathrooms and showers were in a charming single storey sandstone entrance block with crowsteeped gables and a crenellated porch.

Before his final return to the USA in 1914, Carnegie played host at Skibo to Edward VII, William Gladstone, Edward Elgar, Rudyard Kipling and the Rockefellers.

Thereafter the pool fell into disrepair, before Peter de Savary bought the 7,000 acre estate in 1990, and spent £30m on its restoration, including £2m on the pool. Skibo then became noted for celebrity weddings, for example that of Madonna in 2000.

Today, only members of the exclusive Carnegie Club may cross the threshold of what Carnegie described as 'his heaven on earth'.

Yet it was here, ironically, that he also set about giving away as much of his wealth as possible to good causes. As he wrote, 'The man who dies rich, dies disgraced.'

Case Study

Portobello, Edinburgh

Hard though it is to imagine today, Portobello was once a seaside resort that also hummed with industry. Still, its leaders saw how the tide was turning and, in 1896, agreed that Portobello be absorbed by Edinburgh. One condition they set, however, was that £8,000 be spent on new baths.

In fact Edinburgh invested four times as much on a baths complex that was – after Infirmary Street (1887), Dalry (1895) and Glenogle (1900) – the fourth baths designed by the City Architect Robert Morham, although it is thought that his deputy, James Williamson, did most of the detailed work.

This included installing a pump to draw in seawater from a point 400 yards from the promenade and pass it through a mechanical filter.

Apart from its two pools, Portobello Baths was very much geared towards holidaymakers and leisure, with reading rooms, a smoking room, slipper baths, a gymnasium, Turkish baths and a tearoom offering sweeping views across the Firth of Forth.

Over the years the baths has proved to be a great survivor.

While Portobello's pier was lost in 1917 and a superb Art Deco lido – built just 800 yards along the shore in 1936 – was closed in 1979, the baths has undergone four major refurbishments.

In 1967 £48,000 was spent on a complete refit of the main pool. This was followed by £155,000 in 1984 and another £365,000 in 1986, when a fitness centre was built and the sea water pump

retired due to silting, and mains water connected instead.

Yet nine years later the baths closed again and this time the future looked bleak enough for a campaign group to form and put added pressure on the Council.

Finally, in 1998 – after a £4.5 million refit, part funded by the

Lottery and overseen by Percy Johnson Marshall architects – the baths reopened to great acclaim.

Indeed its rebirth, as the Portobello Swim Centre, was seen by those campaigning for other historic baths (such as at Warrender, *see page 80*) as a model scheme, and one that is now to repeated at Glenogle in late 2008.

By 2010 therefore, including the Drumsheugh Baths Club and the Leith Victoria Baths, built in 1898 and also revamped in the 1990s, Edinburgh will have six Victorian baths in operation, all Category B listed, and all highly prized.

Portobello may no longer be the seaside resort it once was. But as a heritage trail for swimmers, Edinburgh has no equal.

Opened 1901
Address Promenade, EH15 2BS
Architect Robert Morham
Cost £32,236
Pool sizes 75' x 35' (former Mens) and 50' x 24' (former Ladies)
Owner Edinburgh City Council
Operator Edinburgh Leisure
Listed Category B (1994)

Case Study

City Baths, Chester

Opened September 25 1901
Address Union Street, CH1 1QP
Architect John Douglas and Harold T Burgess
Cost £13,700
Pools 75' x 40' and 60' x 30'
Owner Chester City Council
Operator Cheshire Swimming Association
Listed Grade II (1972)

As other studies within the *Played in Britain* series have demonstrated, Britain's sporting landscape is awash with clubhouses and pavilions designed in the vernacular style known as half-timbered or 'Tudorbethan'.

Public baths of this ilk are, on the other hand, surprisingly rare.

But if one was to exist anywhere, Chester would surely be the place and, most likely, John Douglas would be the architect.

Douglas was a favourite of the the wealthiest man in Britain, the Marquess of Westminster, whose Grosvenor Estate encompassed (and still encompasses) vast swathes of Chester. Indeed the first of many 'black and white' designs that Douglas offered for his patron's approval was for the

lodge at Grosvenor Park, gifted by the Marquess in 1867. The lodge still stands, on the other side of the road from the City Baths, which Douglas completed 34 years later in a closely matching style.

It is a sham of course; mere decoration tacked on to a red brick structure, with stone dressings, leaded windows and Elizabethan chimney pots to complete the illusion. But as we can see from the baths, the park lodge across the road, and from dozens of other examples in Chester, Douglas pulled it off with genuine aplomb.

Initially he was not involved in the baths. Instead, the Council held a design competition, won by Harold T Burgess (who went on to design baths in Barnsley, Coventry and Wood Green, London).

That was in 1895. But by the time a site had been secured in 1898, Douglas had taken over.

Building took nearly two years, then just as the baths was about to open in August 1900, both its pools were found to be leaking.

Finally, a year later the opening took place, with races contested by corporation employees, members of the police, the fire brigade, and the Chester Amateur Swimming Club – a club formed in 1894 at Chester's floating bath (*see page 63*), which was scrapped soon after the City Baths opened.

The building is in two sections. On the corner of Union Street and Bath Street, the entrance block is pure Douglas. Inside the main door (the former men's entrance) sits an original Bailey's turnstile by the ticket office, in which the former electric console for the slipper baths (*page 121*) is also on display. Terrazzo flooring, carved timberwork and brass fittings all testify to the standards laid down by Douglas and the Duke (who had been the main contributor to the baths' funding).

Upstairs are the former living quarters of the superintendent and matron. Applicants for these posts in 1901 were told 'no children'. But that condition must have been dropped because the incumbent from 1904–13 and from 1920–32 was Albert Moody, whose three toddlers, Doris, Ada and Arthur, were known as 'the Chester Water Babies' for their aquatic displays, while their two year old brother Willy was said to be the youngest swimmer in England. Arthur eventually succeeded his father as superintendent from 1932–67.

By the end of Arthur's tenure, the City Baths appeared all but doomed. Half a mile to the north a new leisure centre was being planned on the site of the old Northgate station.

Shortly after it opened in 1977, the Council announced that the City Baths, despite being listed five years earlier, would close.

That it did not is in large part due to the legacy built up by the Moody family, and by successive generations of City Baths regulars.

Most of them, candidly, would have been only too happy to move to the Northgate Arena and Leisure Centre, until they saw during its construction in 1974 that the only facility for competitive swimming was going to be a four lane 25m pool with no space for spectators. (There was also a leisure pool, but that was hardly suitable either.)

Angered and bemused by this apparent design lapse, the city's two leading clubs, the Chester ASC and the Chester Dolphins formed the Chester Swimming Association, and spent the next three years fighting to keep the old baths open for club purposes.

Finally, on April 14 1977, a deal was agreed. The CSA would take over the management and routine maintenance of the baths, in return for which the Council would cover exterior repairs and any major structural faults.

Yet so successful was the CSA in building up business amongst clubs, schools and special interest groups (for example, sub aqua divers and triathletes), that the Council soon had to add to its contribution a subsidy for daytime staff too (the evenings being covered by volunteers).

Since 1977 the Association has spent £181,000 on major works, plus an average of £12,000 a year on routine upkeep. But with over 2,000 regular users per week, it has not once failed to make a small annual profit, and in 1997 was turned into a charitable trust.

Naturally the trust's president is the Duke of Westminster.

It has seldom been easy though. Most recently, in 2007 plans for a replacement to the Northgate Arena, since shelved, threatened the baths' future once again. And for both parties there will always be repair bills to meet.

But in 2008 a new 25 year lease was drawn up, thereby securing the CSA's position as a potential role model for campaigners at other historic baths to follow.

▲ A nice touch at the **City Baths** is that the gala pool, once reserved for second class swimmers and now used for training, has always been called **Atlantic** while, as indicated by the original signage (*left*), the smaller first class pool is named **Pacific**.

Neither pool has altered greatly since 1901, although compared with the entrance block the finishes are much more basic, suggesting that Douglas was not too concerned with the 'business end' of the operation.

Elsewhere in the building there is a members' social club in the former slipper bath area facing onto Union Street, and at the rear a gymnasium in the former laundry, financed by the CSA and opened by Sir Bobby Charlton in 1984.

Case Study

St Pancras Baths, Kentish Town, London

Opened October 9 1901
Address Prince of Wales Road, London NW5 3LE
Architect Thomas Aldwinckle
Cost £77,698 + £18,000 for site
Pools Originallly, Men's: 100' x 35' (1st), 100' x 35' (2nd); Ladies 75' x 25' (1st), 50' x 20' (2nd)
Owner Camden Borough Council
Operator GLL (after 2010)
Listed Grade II (1972)

Mention the name St Pancras and most architecture buffs think of William Barlow's Midland Railway terminus, now St Pancras International; a prime example of a Victorian structure brought back to life using a combination of 21st century building techniques and sensitive conservation measures.

But a mile and a half to the north of the station lies another

St Pancras building that, as this book went to press, was about to undergo a makeover of its own.

True, the £25.3 million pledged in 2007 by the London Borough of Camden for the refurbishment of St Pancras public baths – or the Kentish Town Sports Centre as known in recent years – might seem small beer compared with the £800 million invested in the

railway station. Yet it is the largest sum ever allocated to the revamp of an historic public baths and, as such, represents a significant watershed in the struggle to save Britain's dwindling number of heritage pools.

Here, not only was there a council prepared to listen to the views of swimmers desperate to keep this much loved facility in their midst, but a council that, under a previous administration, only a year earlier, had opened a £27 million leisure centre, barely a mile away, at Swiss Cottage.

Of course this being north west London, epicentre of the chattering classes and of many a vocal campaign group, the building of two new pools at Swiss Cottage and the restoration of three at Kentish Town has not been without its critics. Camden is as riven by extremes of opinion as it is by wealth and deprivation. But for those looking on from other London boroughs, or from towns and cities where pools, historic or otherwise, are being closed and not replaced, the situation in Camden appears enviable.

Camden, it should be noted, was formed in 1965 by the merger of three boroughs, Holborn, Hampstead and St Pancras, each of which had built public baths under the 1846 Act. So that although only a mile separates Kentish Town from Swiss Cottage, historically the former was part of St Pancras, and the latter part of Hampstead.

St Pancras had already built two baths, on King Street (now

Plender Street), Camden, in 1868, and, ten years later, on Whitfield Street (*page 55*). But this still left unprovided the working class and densely populated area to the north, around Kentish Town.

As in most parts of London, even in the 1890s finding a site was not easy, and in the end the vestry had to pay £18,000 for one, more than many local authorities would spend on construction costs alone.

But it was a prime site, if oddly shaped, in the midst of a residential area, close to a railway station and with all important street access on three sides.

Two Acts of Parliament coincided with the planning of the baths. Firstly, as detailed earlier, in 1896 an amendment to the 1846 Act allowed London baths to stage 'music or dancing' during the winter months. This greatly increased a baths' earning potential, but also meant that any pool hall used for such purposes had to meet London County Council regulations relating to ingress and egress at places of public assembly.

Secondly, the 1899 London Government Act resulted in the abolition of the old vestries in favour of new boroughs.

By pure chance, therefore, as St Pancras made the transition from a vestry to one of the 28 new Metropolitan boroughs, its plans for Kentish Town offered an ideal opportunity to demonstrate both its sense of social responsibility and civic purpose, and to build one of the first baths that would double as a purpose-built public hall.

As was common practice at the time, the Vestry held a design competition, with Alfred Hessell Tiltman, designer of three baths for neighbouring Islington, acting as the adjudicator. »

▲ Thought to be the work of sculptor WS Frith, the resplendent terracotta detailing at **Kentish Town**, supplied by Doulton & Co of Lambeth, is worth closer study. Watching over the men's first class entrance can be seen two mythical beasts known as 'grotesques', their function being to repel demons. (Notre Dame and many a New York skyscraper has them too.)

In the spandrels a pair of river gods (or at least Old Father Thames) offer a more benign welcome. Just visible in the top corner of the left spandrel is Tower Bridge, featured perhaps because it had been opened by the Prince of Wales in 1894.

The adjacent men's second class entrance has goddesses in its spandrels, named Aqua and Eura (goddess of the east wind perhaps).

The six blue doors on the corner (*see opposite*) served the men's first class pool when it was in use as a public hall. Above the three on Prince of Wales Road, at second floor level, are two more terracotta figures; of St Pancras, depicted wielding a feathered pen over a slain swordsman, and St George, who is of course in the process of spearing a dragon.

▲ Viewed from the south looking towards the Prince of Wales Road frontage, the daunting complexity of **St Pancras Baths** is evident.

Depending on how one differentiates between the different elements there are as many as 33 separate roof systems, many of whose gutters run off internally or into enclosed yards – a nightmare in terms of drainage and upkeep.

To keep all this in trim there were once 23 maintenance staff based here – enough to form their own social club. Three of them lived in flats within the complex.

The largest roof on the right, parallel with Willes Road, covers the former men's first class pool. At right angles to Grafton Road, on the left, can be seen the top-lit roof of the former ladies' first class

pool, converted in 1961 into changing rooms. Also dating from 1961 is the chimney, built when a neighbouring terraced house was demolished to make way for a new boiler house. Ironically, as part of the current renovations this will be demolished and new houses built in its place. The main entrance block will also be turned into flats to help finance the rest of the work.

» Of six entrants, the winner was Thomas Aldwinckle.

His credentials for the job were twofold. During the 1880s he had worked with Wilson & Son on two south London baths, at Ladywell (*see inside cover*) and Forest Hill. But just as importantly, Aldwinckle had also worked on numerous institutional buildings, such as hospitals, children's homes and workhouses.

Aldwinckle divided the site into two distinct parts.

In the southern section were two mens' pools, entered via a main entrance block on Prince of Wales Road (*see left*). On the first floor of this block were 29 first class slipper baths, with the superintendent's flat (with an attic floor) and committee rooms on the second floor.

The rear, or northern half of the complex, at right angles to the front, was itself in two sections.

At the far end stood the boiler room (with three massive, 30' long Galloway boilers), coal stores, a flat for the engineer and two bore holes to access an Artesian well. Also within this area was the mechanism for a Davidson's 'Sirocco' ventilation system, such as would become common in hospitals, colleries and other industrial buildings.

Truly, this was a Victorian structure, but with a foot lodged firmly inside the 20th century.

Wedged between the plant rooms and the mens' section was the ladies section, accessed via enrances on Grafton Street.

It says much about the area's demographic that when built St Pancras was one of only three baths in Britain to offer both first and second class pools for women. (The others were at nearby Hampstead and Hornsey Road.)

St Pancras also had a crèche, perhaps the first at any public baths.

As always both ladies' pools were smaller than the mens', and their section had only 10 first and 25 second class slipper baths.

Yet when all these facilities were combined, together with a wash-house containing 50 compartments and a drying room, St Pancras could claim to be one of Britain's best equipped baths.

Its total of 129 slipper baths was exceeded only by Hornsey Road, which had 139. And although two other four-pool complexes existed at Marylebone and Paddington (*page 54*), St Pancras offered more water area for swimming than any indoor baths in Britain.

St Pancras was also, at over £95,000 in total, the costliest building of its type yet built.

But clearly the investment was worthwhile. According to statistics compiled by the Carnegie UK Trust, for the year 1913–14 a total of 315,513 people used its facilities. Only Hackney Baths (built in 1897 and still partially in use for swimming) was busier.

During the winter the first class pool was also well used for concerts, dances, exhibitions, gymnastics and meetings. Among its visiting speakers were Lloyd George and Ramsay MacDonald.

But for all its community worth, St Pancras baths would prove immensely challenging to maintain and manage. Apart from the complexity of the fabric itself, the imperatives of class and gender segregation required staff to negotiate a warren of awkwardly routed corridors and stairways. Nor did it help that there was such a distance between the offices of the mens' and ladies' sections.

The Second World War placed a particular strain on the building.

Closed for the duration because it was so difficult to black it out entirely, its pools were used for water storage by the Auxiliary Fire Service. Inevitably maintenance faltered, and in 1949 both ladies' pools were infilled; the first class one being converted to a public hall and the second class to a café.

A survey carried out in 1954 revealed the full scale of the problem. Both mens' pools were found to be leaking while the boilers were outdated and the filtration system was beyond repair.

Had it not been for the fact that the borough's other baths at King Street and Whitfield Street had suffered bomb damage, that might have been the beginning of the end for St Pancras. But the building's shell remained »

◀ Because the **first class mens'** or **Willes Pool** at **St Pancras** had also to serve as a public hall it was, and still is quite different in character to its second class neighbour.

Apart from separate entrances and exits for the general public, its poolside cubicles, formed by lightweight enamel screens, were demountable (in order to create more floor space). It had a three sided spectator gallery, leaving a gap at the deep end for a stage. Behind this were two club rooms set aside for the use of 'artistes'.

Most interesting of all was the pool's unique hammerbeam roof shaped with a trefoil profile, which Aldwinckle hoped would absorb the echo usually suffered in pool halls.

By contrast the much cruder **second class pool** (*left*) had a plain steel-framed roof, with the first floor space above the poolside cubicles – these formed by fixed, slate partitions – being boxed in to house a range of 65 second class slipper baths along corridors on three sides of the hall.

These images were taken in early 1960, after the ironwork of the first class gallery had been covered by fascia boards, all poolside cubicles removed, and both tanks rebuilt in reinforced concrete. But these alterations were only a prelude, for when reopened later in 1960, as shown overleaf, the interiors had become all but unrecognisable.

▶ By today's standards the interior renovations carried out at **St Pancras Baths** in 1959–60 appear little short of municipal vandalism.

Only one area of Victorian tiling survived, and that was in a back stairs. Otherwise, every surface was retiled, repainted or boarded over, and almost every original roof detail concealed by suspended ceilings.

Most dramatic of all was the transformation of the second class mens' pool, now renamed the **Grafton Pool** (*bottom*).

However, before we judge too harshly, not only was this makeover mania absolutely within the spirit of the post-Festival of Britain age – most owners of Victorian houses were doing exactly the same at a domestic level – but also many of the alterations had quite valid operational reasons.

For example, now that there was no need for class or gender separation, and because poolside cubicles were now unacceptable on hygiene grounds, the former ladies first class pool was converted into changing rooms (*centre*). As there existed no direct route to this area from the former entrance on Prince of Wales Road, however, these were bricked up, alas crudely, and a new ultra-modern reception area created on Grafton Street (*top*).

At the same time the men's first class, now Willes Pool, was revamped, a learner pool created out of the former ladies' second class pool, a laundrette replaced the wash house, a new boiler house was built and 91 new slipper baths were installed (this still being an area with many bedsits and rooming houses).

Costing £180,000 in total, the renovations were unveiled in November 1960, with recent Rome Olympics gold medallist Anita Lonsbrough as guest of honour.

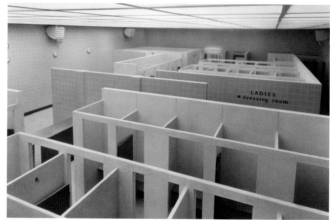

≫ structurally sound, and so in January 1959 the baths' first major refurbishment began.

Described left, this phase of works almost totally eradicated the building's Victorian interior.

For sure it gained the baths a new lease of life. But being neither fish nor fowl, neither pure Victorian or pure modern, it sat rather uneasily when compared with its newest neighbour in Hampstead – the £1 million Basil Spence designed Swiss Cottage sports centre, opened in 1964, a mile to the west (*see page 232*). Surely, once St Pancras, Hampstead and Holborn merged in 1965, it would only be a matter of time before the voters of Kentish Town would demand of their new masters at Camden something similar.

But they did not. The baths were listed in 1974, and over the next three decades, the fabric grew ever more dishevelled. In 1993 this decline was arrested when the slipper bath areas were replaced by health and fitness rooms and saunas, and the building was rebranded as the Kentish Town Sports Centre. Three years later a private leisure company, Holmes Place, took over its management.

But it was not enough, and the baths' shortcomings were further exposed in 2002.

The reason? That harbinger of the future just down the road, the Swiss Cottage Sport Centre, had been closed, after just 38 years' use.

During the four long years it took for its replacement to be completed, thousands of Swiss Cottage regulars decamped to Kentish Town, so that in 2004–05, for example, 260,000 users were recorded, even though the building was now clearly in a sorry state. On one occasion in 2004 a lump of concrete fell from the roof of the Willes Pool.

Understandably there were fears that once the new Swiss Cottage centre opened, the Council would close down Kentish Town, despite an election pledge in 2002 not to do so. But by 2005 that pledge appeared to crumbling. Holmes Place announced they were pulling out – they were later replaced by Greenwich Leisure Limited – and in March Camden closed the baths' laundry, deciding that it was more cost effective to buy a washing machine for each of the last 200 or so remaining regulars.

As the Council continued to consider its position, in December 2005 a newly formed action group handed into the Town Hall a 3,000 signature petition. Among regular swimmers adding their support were writer Hunter Davies, Culture Secretary Tessa Jowell, athlete Kelly Holmes, newsreader Jon Snow and the director of the Victorian Society, Ian Dungavell.

But the real turning point came in May 2006, when control of Camden changed from Labour to a Liberal Democrat–Conservative alliance, the former party having made its own pledge to fully refurbish the baths if elected.

To widespread delight, that pledge was confirmed in October 2006, not only for saving the two large pools but, as demanded by campaigners, the learner pool too.

A timely announcement it turned out to be, for the following February a pane of glass fell from the roof of the Grafton Pool, forcing the Council to close the building until the full programme of works could be completed.

Soon afterwards builders moved in to strip away all the suspended ceilings and at last, allow the building to breathe again.

For older regulars invited to tour the baths before the building work started in earnest in June 2008, it was an emotional sight, seeing the Victorian roofs exposed again after neary half a century.

The timber framed Willes pool roof in particular was greeted like an old friend, and was found to be in surprisingly good order.

Under plans drawn up by Limbrick Limited architects, this roof will be restored, as will the pool itself, but with the gallery remaining closed to the public.

The Grafton pool will be turned into a deck level pool, 25m in length and four lanes wide. Above the pool, a mezzanine floor will house a fitness centre.

The learner pool will also become deck level, 9m x 7m, with the original roof exposed to view.

Elsewhere there will be new changing rooms, a new studio and the Grafton Road reception will be extended with a full height roof.

To help offset the £25.3 million costs, 14 flats and 4 town houses will be built on parts of the site no longer needed, and in the former entrance block on Prince of Wales Road. It is also hoped to bring back into use the Artesian well.

All being well, the work will be completed in 2010 and revisited in our forthcoming *Played in Britain* study, *Played in London*.

Of course critics may argue that £25.3 million could have been spent on a brand new pool.

But Kentish Town is London's largest surviving baths complex of the pre-1914 era, and has outlived many of its modern counterparts for four very good reasons. It was well built, well placed, well used and very well loved.

Rather like that other building named after St Pancras, just down the road.

Stepping out in style – the gable end of the former ladies' first class pool on Grafton Street, and (*left*), in a hidden corner, the only area of original tiling to survive the 1960s.

The story goes that an American tourist once offered £10,000 to buy the ticket office at Bramley Baths, Leeds, which as it happens was only £600 short of the cost of the entire building when it opened in 1904. Fortunately the offer was declined and the baths went on to be restored in 1992. Alas, the original turnstiles in front of the ticket office have not survived.

Chapter Five

Edwardian 1901–1918

During the Edwardian era, it could be said, public baths well and truly came of age.

They were built in numbers and at a rate that outstripped all efforts during the previous century, and in certain quarters reached levels of opulence that, some would argue, is unlikely to be matched again.

As can be seen in this chapter at Bramley (Leeds), Beverley Road (Hull), the Carnegie Baths (Dunfermline), the Victoria Baths (Manchester) and Moseley Road (Birmingham) – all completed between 1904 and 1907 – this was a period of unprecedented exuberance and technological advancement, matched by ever greater levels of expenditure.

St Pancras Baths, opened 1901, had set a lofty benchmark, costing £18,000 for the site alone (more than many baths cost in their entirety), plus a formidable £78,000 for a four pool complex.

Now it was the turn of northern cities to demonstrate their own brand of municipal munificence.

Bradford, enriched by textiles and newly incorporated in 1897, led the way. With only two baths

to its name before 1900, it built no fewer than twelve public baths in an astonishing seven year burst from 1904–11. Nine of these had standardised pools measuring 60' x 20'. Three were operated in conjunction with the education committee. (To which we must add that between 1904–15 Bradford also completed an open air pool in Lister Park, and built or converted a further 15 buildings for use as baths and wash houses.)

Birmingham, which gained its charter in 1889, was similarly active. From four baths in 1900, it increased its stock by 1914 to eleven indoor baths with pools, three outdoor pools, and three 'cottage baths' (for washing only).

Birmingham's Baths Committee amassed this empire in part by stealth, the city having expanded its boundaries to take in three baths built by the neighbouring districts of Handsworth, King's Norton and Northfield.

Liverpool gained Woolton Baths by a similar expansion in 1913, to raise its total to 12 baths, of which four with pools were built in the five years from 1904 to 1909.

Other high spending baths committees were to be found in the town halls of Glasgow (18 establishments by 1915), Leeds (9), and Sheffield (7).

In terms of swimming facilities, however, Manchester became Britain's leading authority during this period. By building six new baths with pools between 1904 and 1913, it came to operate more indoor pools than any other authority – 32 pools divided between 14 establishments – not including one outdoor pool and two baths and wash houses.

Not all these buildings were paragons of modernity, however. By 1914 Mayfield and Leaf Street (*see page 42*) were both in excess of 50 years old, while Kent Street in Birmingham was over 60 years old. In Liverpool, Britain's first public baths, opened at the Pierhead in 1829 (*page 24*), was described as unfit by modern standards and was demolished in 1906.

For the Edwardians, therefore, historic baths were becoming almost as great an issue as they are today. As stated earlier, public baths had indeed come of age. »

Not only is terracotta highly decorative and hard wearing, but in the polluted air of an industrial city it was found to be easier to clean than conventional stonework. This terracotta tower is one of two intricately moulded ventilation outlets at the Moseley Road Baths, Balsall Heath, Birmingham, opened in 1907 and the oldest operational baths in Britain to be listed Grade II*.

▲ At the majority of public baths the convention was to limit external adornments to the front block, and erect basic pool halls, or sheds, at the rear, as at a railway station.

Not so at the Grade II* **Victoria Baths, Manchester**, opened in 1906, where no expense was spared in decking the entire exterior in a brash display of polychromatic bands of red brick and terracotta.

Yet this was also a supremely functional building. On the right, the entrance block housed offices, the superintendent's living quarters, a Turkish bath and first class men's slipper baths. In a row to the left are the three pools, each with slate roofs and skylights. Out of shot, further to the left, is the wash house.

Unrestricted urban sites such as this were rare, which made it easier for Manchester's in-house architects to incorporate the best ideas and latest technology. But what is perhaps just as significant is that they chose to cloak this in a style harking back to Jacobean and Baroque influences. As was typical of the Edwardian period, therefore, and as its very name suggested, here was a building with a foot in both the past and the present.

>> As for London, the Edwardian period was also one of continued development, but under a new form of local government.

Instead of 39 vestries of widely differing sizes, in 1899 London was reorganised into 28 metropolitan boroughs (plus the City of London), each of which appointed committees to take over from the Baths Commissioners.

Many areas were already well served the vestries having built, or rebuilt baths during the 1890s. But thirteen of the new boroughs chose to build afresh during their formative years, including Battersea, Camberwell, Chelsea, Fulham (see right), Hammersmith, Poplar, Shoreditch, Wandsworth and Woolwich. Indeed by 1915 – by which time London had a total of 51 baths – only one of the 28 boroughs, Finsbury, had yet to build at least one.

Camberwell's Old Kent Road Baths, opened in 1905 at a cost of £55,000, was possibly the most impressive of this new crop, but alas was bombed in 1940.

However one other Camberwell baths from the period does survive. That is the Grade II listed Wells Way Baths, opened in 1902 and now used as offices and by a boxing club. However, this was one of several from the period that, as a cost saving measure, had no pool (and is therefore not listed in the Directory). The Grade II listed Cheshire Street Baths in Bethnal Green (opened 1899), now flats and also home to a boxing club, falls into the same category.

Of course the building of public baths, with or without pools, spread far beyond the major conurbations, so that by 1912 Frank Sachs, author of *The Complete Swimmer*, was able to write that 'no self respecting city is satisfied >>

◀ Edwardian architects were happy to pick and mix their styles. At **Fulham Baths** (1902) on **North End Road, London,** the unusual narrowness of the site, shoehorned between a parish hall (on the left) and a bank, led E Deighton Pearson to apply a busy concoction of free classical detailing: square stone blocks intercut with half round pilasters; statues of Neptune and, presumably, Amphitrite, and above them, bulbous little Ionic columns set within a red brick and stone banded gable.

Free classical, free Renaissance, Edwardian baroque, they are all here in this chapter.

At **Green Lane, Small Heath, Birmingham** (centre), also opened 1902, J Henry Martin's red brick and terracotta treatment has been described as Gothic Jacobean, while at **Pitt Street, Portsmouth** (below), opened in 1910, GE Smith opted for a more pared down Art Nouveau façade.

But for all these examples' stylistic variety, this much they have in common. None still operates as baths. Fulham, or at least its front surviving section, is now dance studios. Small Heath is now a mosque and community centre (while the adjoining library, seen on the left, is vacant), and Pitt Street, having spent its final years as a gymnasium, was demolished in early 2008.

Patterned floor tiles, stained glass and an ornate set of Salford-made Ellison turnstiles welcome the public to Withington Baths – the only baths designed by the City of Manchester's architects department under Henry Price to remain in use. After opening in 1913 Withington was the first in the city to allow mixed bathing. Through these doors lay the future.

>> unless it contains a swimming bath, and few if any important towns in England are unprovided for in this respect'.

As to the overall number of baths built during the Edwardian period, sources vary. But we can be reasonably certain that in England, Scotland and Wales, not counting 'cottage baths' or stand alone wash houses, at least 160 public baths with pools were built between 1900 and 1915; that is, a rate of almost one per month, a rate that would not be surpassed until the 1970s.

This took the nation's stock of public baths with pools to approximately 378 by 1915, to which some 250 open air baths and bathing places must be added, plus at least 47 private establishments.

Nor do these figures include baths built in other sectors.

In 1875, at the suggestion of Joseph Chamberlain, Birmingham was possibly the first authority to introduce subsidised swimming sessions for schoolchildren, and offer free passes for those able to swim a length.

In the 1890s Bradford and Liverpool went further by building pools exclusively for children. By 1915 Liverpool had 17 school pools, Bradford had six. Also active in this area were Glasgow (8 pools) and Nottingham (4).

In the private school sector, where outdoor pools had long been in use – such as the famous 'Ducker' at Harrow, in use since 1810 and rebuilt in 1870, and at Malborough College since 1847 – indoor pools also started to become more commonplace.

In the 1880s Ipswich School, Cheltenham College, Uppingham, Charterhouse and Shrewsbury had all built indoor pools.

In the Edwardian period several more were completed; for example at Lancing College (1906), Kingswood School, Bath (1909), Cheadle Hulme (1911) and Bootham School, York (1913). All these still stand, and apart from Lancing remain in use for swimming (*see Directory*).

As detailed later in this chapter the Army and Navy also started to build baths at this time, as did the chocolate makers Cadbury, at Bournville and Rowntree, at York, for their workers.

But if indoor pools were now ubiquitous, and increasingly lavish in their design, were they actually any more advanced than their immediate predecessors?

For the answer to this we can consult two important publications from the period

The first, published in 1906, is *Public Baths and Wash-Houses – a treatise on their planning, design, arrangement and fitting* written by the architect Alfred Cross.

The second, published in 1918 but based on material collated before 1915, is the Carnegie United Kingdom Trust's *Report on Public Baths and Wash Houses in the United Kingdom*, by Agnes Campbell.

Both are seminal texts for understanding the operation of early 20th century baths.

Alfred WS Cross (1858–1932), whose father, it will be recalled, had a hand in designing the White Rock Baths in Hastings, was by 1904 one of Britain's most experienced baths architects, having formed a partnership with Henry Spalding, architect of Hampstead Baths, in 1889.

In London alone over the next decade Spalding & Cross worked *inter alia* on Dulwich, Camberwell Green, Marshall Street, Hoxton, Wandsworth and Walthamstow. >>

▲ 'My experience has convinced me that the best materials, *and the best materials only*, should be used throughout all departments,' advised EJ Wakeling, chairman of Shoreditch's Baths Committee in 1906. At the top of his list came glazed brickwork and tiling. Although adding to capital costs, he wrote, such materials would reduce maintenance costs considerably.

Here are some extant examples: at **Gibson Street, Newcastle**, 1907, now a sports hall (*above*), one of five painted tile panels in the entrance hall; on a staircase at **Hackney Baths, London**, 1897 (*top left*), now the Kings Hall Leisure Centre, and surrounding the cubicles at **Woodcock Street, Birmingham** (*left*), in the 1902 pool, now run by Aston University.

▶ Experiments with different roof structures continued throughout the Edwardian period as designers sought ways to maximise natural light yet avoid glare, and also to avoid the clutter of lattice girders and 'monotonous and ugly' lantern lights so excoriated by Alfred Cross (and by generations of maintenance crews ever since).

As shown here spanning the 1902 pool at **Woodock Street**, there emerged in Birmingham a distinctive roof form using bolted, elliptical iron girders, pierced with quatrefoil cut-outs.

Cross himself favoured a similar arched roof but with the steel framework concealed under panelled plaster, as at Haggerston in 1904 (*see page 126*). This reduced maintenance, created a cleaner, more reflective surface and also helped absorb noise.

In 1907 James Ernest Franck took the arched theme further by using, possibly for the first time at a British baths, reinforced concrete, as seen here at **Hammersmith Baths, Lime Grove**, in west London (*right*), opened in July 1907.

The pool tank was also formed in reinforced concrete which, given that it was still a relatively new material – having been showcased at the 1900 Paris exhibition – was a calculated risk. However Franck argued that it was more fire resistant than steel, and required less maintenance.

Not until the 1930s would it be used routinely at baths, but it did serve well at Lime Grove, albeit not as well as Birmingham's girder system, examples of which can be seen at Moseley Road and Tiverton Road, as well as Woodcock Street.

All that remains at Lime Grove, by contrast, is Franck's rather staid Edwardian Baroque entrance block, converted into flats in 1985.

Thereafter, on his own account Cross worked at Haggerston (1904), Finchley (1914) and, in the 1920s, on several other London baths with his son, Kenneth.

Cambridge educated and with an office in Mayfair, he was also elected vice president of the Royal Institute of British Architects.

Cross by name, in his 1906 treatise he frequently comes over as cross by nature.

'Conservatism is one of our national characteristics,' he griped, 'and that the guardians of our municipal enterprises are not, in all cases, the men best fitted for their responsibilities, is shown by their almost general inclination to employ their permanent officials to prepare the necessary drawings for public works...'

That is, instead of hiring an experienced architect, councils merely handed the work to their borough engineer or surveyor. (AH Tiltman had made the same point in his 1899 RIBA lecture.)

'The architectural value of the designs thus obtained may be gauged by an inspection of the markets, baths, fire stations, and other buildings which disfigure many of our cities and large towns.' This, he claimed, was because most of the designs were based upon buildings that the council official in question had inspected elsewhere, which had themselves been designed by someone with limited experience.

Yet somehow, Cross added ruefully, councils always seemed to take on trained architects when it came to the design of a town hall.

Clearly not a man afraid to insult potential clients, Cross also criticised design competitions. So many conditions were imposed, he wrote, that architects could hardly be blamed for poor standards.

Cost cutting was equally pernicious. 'The inquirer has only to visit an establishment of the average type, say twelve months after it has been opened to the public, to be in a position to judge of the truth of my remarks as to its non-durability.'

'Bath building continued on these lines cannot be expected to improve,' Cross warned.

Next he identified six major deficiencies in baths design.

The standard lantern light that capped most pool sheds he described as a 'wearisome iteration' of 'monotonous and ugly wood or iron excrescences, fatal alike, internally and externally, to the architectural dignity of the apartments in which they occur.'

Other deficiencies were overly narrow passages between slipper baths compartments; inadequate lighting in many second-class pools; insufficient headroom in the subways provided for the inspection of pipes; inadequate provision for bathers 'to properly cleanse their bodies with soap and water before entering the swimming ponds,' and finally the lack of space allocated to waiting rooms adjoining slipper baths.

Much of the rest of Cross's treatise is highly technical, but three further design issues are worth noting.

Firstly, wrote Cross, spectator galleries were rarely designed so that the occupants could gain an unobstructed or comfortable view of the entire pool (or 'pond' as he called it). In short, their sightlines were inadequate.

His solution, trialled at Hoxton Baths in Shoreditch, opened in 1899, was to create a gallery of amphitheatre seating along three sides of the pool, overhanging, rather than sitting above, the

changing cubicles. Its efficacy cannot be judged because Hoxton was damaged during the war and demolished in 1962. But at Cross's next design for Shoreditch, at Haggerston in 1904, he introduced another form of amphitheatre seating, at pool level (see page 128).

Changing cubicles were then erected behind the top row of seats, where, claimed Cross, they could be more easily observed by pool attendants. The arrangement also allowed 'juvenile frequenters' to change in the seated areas, leaving the cubicles free for adults.

For modern sensibilities such an arrangement seems untenable.

It also required bathers to walk up and down steps to get to their cubicles. Yet it remained in use at Haggerston until the 1960s, and although the cubicle arrangement Cross suggested was not copied elsewhere, pool level seating was adopted at several baths between the wars, once cubicles were moved away from the pool side (as explained in Chapter Six).

Another issue raised by Cross, concerned pool dimensions.

Before the 1890s no standards existed. Instead, designers simply fitted in whatever lengths and widths each site would allow.

But by the Edwardian era the majority of new first class and gala pools conformed either to a length of 75' (which was the ASA's preferred minimum for pools staging official events), or 100', with widths varying from 30-40'.

But there continued to be deviations, particularly when it came to lengths; for example, 81' at Small Heath, Birmingham in 1902, and 105' at Acton in 1904 and Hammersmith in 1907.

For race officials these variables must have been maddening, more so once British swimmers began »

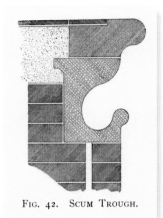

FIG. 42. SCUM TROUGH.

▲ For swimmers of a certain age, this poolside fitting will need no introduction. As illustrated in Alfred Cross' 1906 treatise on baths design, the glazed stoneware **scum trough** served as both a handrail and as a means of collecting 'floating impurities' on the surface.

For maximum efficiency, the scum trough at the deep end was positioned a few inches lower than at the sides and shallow end.

Note that the upper surfaces of the poolside gangway, or promenade, sloped down away from the water's edge. This was a further sanitary measure to ensure that any water contaminated by bathers' shoes, as they walked to and from their changing cubicles, did not enter the pool water.

▲ Before the Edwardian era, and at many pools until the early 1930s, the main method of providing fresh water was called the **'fill and empty'** system. This is how it worked.

Firstly, the pool tank itself was essentially like an extra large bath with a couple of plug holes.

On day one of the cycle the pool was emptied completely, the tank scrubbed down (as seen above at **Manor Place, Walworth**, in south London), and then refilled, often overnight, with fresh water.

Of course few bathers in those days showered or washed before swimming, and so as the days went by and the water became ever dirtier – however much chlorine or other agents had been added for sterilisation – the cost of admission was reduced accordingly.

Hence the last day of the cycle – 'dirty water day' – was also the cheapest, and the day on which the baths were usually at their busiest.

At second and third class pools the 'fill and empty' cycle would typically last a week, and end on Saturday nights, whereas in first class baths there would be two cycles per week. This, in addition to the fact that, on average, user numbers at first class pools were one eighth of those for lower class pools, meant that water quality in the former was appreciably superior.

Agnes Campbell identified four main sources of contamination in baths. Firstly, there was mud and dirt carried on bathers' shoes as they walked to their cubicles.

Secondly there were 'excretions due to objectionable habits' on the part of bathers. Thirdly, there were 'excretions from the skin' and long hairs. Fourthly, there was fluff and dye from bathing costumes.

Not only was the 'fill and empty' system potentially hazardous to health, it was inefficient in that heavy usage in the early part of

the cycle, particularly by children, could negate the benefits of a refill almost immediately.

It was also expensive, in terms of water charges, in labour charges (particularly where staff had to work overnight to make sure the pool was refilled by the morning), and in fuel costs (since each batch of water had to be heated from scratch). Lower charges on dirty water days also, patently, meant a drop in income.

A further flaw was that most pools emptied via outlets at the foot of the deep end, as above, whereas the worst pollutants gathered on the surface. Even where water was circulated therefore, much of the surface water lay undisturbed.

Filtration systems introduced in the early 1900s did go some way towards alleviating these problems.

But only in the 1920s were these systems perfected, thereby ending 'fill and empty' for good.

» entering overseas competitions, in which, outside the USA and Commonwealth, all distances were of course in metres.

Yet not even Cross dared to suggest that standards should be set, other than to state that in his view 100' x 40' would suffice in poor districts, and that 75' x 35' would suit everywhere else.

Ladies' pools, he added, without explanation, need not be larger than 60' x 30'.

Finally from Cross' book, we come to the issue of water management.

Cross described the main methods used to heat pool water as being either to inject steam directly into the water ('noisy and uncertain'), or to pre-heat the water and fill the pool as one would fill a bath (which required powerful and expensive boilers but was safer and more economical in the long run).

But there remained the more complex issue of how to circulate and filter the water so that it would be as clear as possible for as long as possible (assuming that some form of sterilising agent, such as chlorine, would also be in use).

Various filtration and circulation methods had been tried before the Edwardian period, for example at Lambeth in the 1850s. But it would seem that none had been effective, and so virtually all baths worked on the 'fill and empty' system (*see left*).

The first known reference to a system similar to the one that was introduced in the early 1900s, is in the form of a brief note attached to plans for the Infirmary Street Baths, Edinburgh, in 1891.

This states that 'foul water is drawn by pulsometer from ponds at 'A' to tanks at 'B' thereafter falls to filter at 'C', is purified and returns to ponds entering at 'D'.'

In essence, this appears to be the basis for the filtration system that starts to appear south of the border from 1904 onwards, developed by an engineering firm called Royle's, of Irlam, in Salford.

The first trials of this system, it is thought, took place at Newton Heath Baths (Manchester) and Bury Baths in either 1903 or 1904, after which it was also installed at the Girls' Bath at Bournville, Birmingham, in 1904 (see page 122), at both Hornsey Road and Caledonian Road baths in Islington, London, and in 1906 at the Victoria Baths, Manchester.

Cross wrote that the system 'consists primarily of a circulating pump, having its suction at the deep end of the bath, by means of which the water is delivered to a perforated distributing pipe or aerator, and thence through a series of perforated zinc trays to a galvanised iron tank.'

From this the water passed through a sand and gravel filter, and was then heated before being discharged into the shallow end.

In theory, Royle's system – which was developed further by two other companies, Messrs Bell's of Denton, Manchester, and The Turnover Company (thought to be from London) – allowed the same water to be circulated, filtered and cleansed over a period of 4-8 hours, without limit, thereby ending the need to 'fill and empty' and, in the process, improving water quality dramatically, and reducing running costs.

As such it constituted a major breakthrough in baths management. But was it effective?

For an answer we must turn to the Carnegie Report of 1918 mentioned earlier.

In this report, its author Agnes Campbell states that by »

TABLE II. A

Showing Public Baths and Wash-houses provision, etc., in towns with a population of over 200,000.   Year 1913-1914.

	POPU-LATION (1911 Census).	FACILITIES.			ATTEND-ANCE per 1000 of Population.	FINANCE.					
		Number of Establishments.	Number of Swimming Baths.†	Number of Private Baths.		Income.	Deficit.	Expenditure.	Income to Expenditure.	Capital Cost.	Rate Aid.
	000s.	1.	2.	3.	4.	5.	6.	7.	8.	9.	10.
England and Wales—						£	£	£		£	d.
[1] Birmingham,	840[3]	17	23 (3)	490	1600	11,235	25,812	37,047	30 %	260,979	1·7
[1][2] Liverpool, .	746	18	26 (4)	324	2114	12,513	17,138	29,651	42 %	236,652	·95
[1][2] Manchester,	714	18	33 (1)	742	2718	13,525	35,523	49,048	28 %	393,111	1·97
[1][4] Sheffield, .	455	8	11 (1)	201	1560	7,645	8,460	16,105	47 %	104,429	1·06
[1] Leeds, .	446	9	13	163	1008	5,308	7,960	13,268	40 %	111,967[5]	·96
[2] Bristol, .	357	10	12 (4)	203	1023	3,238	4,613	7,851	41 %	77,679	·66
West Ham, .	289	3	3	94	1147	3,287	3,150	6,436	51 %	*	·65
[1][7] Bradford, .	288	25	13	372	2335	7,710	14,353	22,063	35 %	116,744	2·75
Kingston-upon-Hull,	278	5[6]	9[6](2)	133	1344	3,799	4,800	8,599	44 %	53,000	*
[1][2] Newcastle-upon-Tyne,	267	6	8	119	1337	6,612	6,707	13,318	50 %	84,626	1·05
Nottingham,	260	3	5	54	1027	2,817	3,591	6,407	44 %	42,875	*
[1] Stoke-on-Trent, .	235	5	10	102	1036	2,542	5,028	7,570	34 %	47,175	1·56
[1] Salford, .	231	5	11	171	1890	2,802	6,013	8,814	32 %	78,700	1·4
Portsmouth,	231	2	2 (1)	40	*	*	*	*	*	10,727	*
Leicester,	227	7	10 (2)	132	1548	3,968	5,336	9,304	43 %	*	*
Scotland—											
[1][2] Glasgow, .	1011	21	18	475	1195	27,531	18,358	45,889	60 %	326,178	·74
[1][2] Edinburgh, .	320	9	7	150	1343	9,226	9,792	19,018	48 %	114,639	·81
Ireland—											
Belfast, .	387	5	8	144	872	3,250	3,782	7,032	46 %	57,773	·5
Dublin, .	305	1	2	40	383	1,378	1,220	2,598	53 %	12,489	·33

† Number of open-air baths given in brackets after the total number of swimming baths which includes them.
* Incomplete statistics.

[1] Turkish, Russian, or Vapour baths provided.   [2] Wash-houses provided.
[3] By Birmingham (Extension) Order, 1911.   [4] Baths closed during part of year for alterations.
[5] Excludes capital cost of Jewish bath.
[6] Includes open-air bath at King George V. playing-field, for which no figures are available.
[7] Figures for 1914-1915.

▲ Table IIA from the Carnegie United Kingdom Trust's *Report on the Public Baths and Wash-Houses in the United Kingdom*, an extraordinary piece of research compiled under extraordinary conditions.

Published in 1918, shortly before the Armistice, the study was based on the returns from 375 baths in England, Scotland and Wales (plus 8 in Ireland) for the period 1913–14. How useful it was by 1918, at a time when few local authorities had the resources to act upon its findings is arguable. Nor did anyone need reminding of one of its main conclusions, that 'It is evident that baths establishments are run at a loss.' But historians at least can be thankful of its existence. It is a *tour de force*.

▶ 'After enjoying sea dips with his family during the holidays, the Londoner can continue his water pleasures at will,' reported *The Graphic* in December 1911, by which it meant that 'mixed bathing' was now being permitted at **St Pancras Baths** in Kentish Town (albeit only on Wednesday afternoons, hardly ideal for working men or women).

Entry was by ticket, available via the council, or through membership of a recognised swimming club.

Despite widespread disapproval in some quarters, mixed bathing had already caught on at the seaside – Bexhill in 1901 being the first resort to allow it officially on its beaches – leading to mixed club sessions at Manor Place Baths in Walworth, London, in 1904. But when 423 people signed a petition asking for Liverpool's Baths Committee to do the same in 1906 they were turned down.

Kensington then experimented with supervised sessions at its Silchester Road Baths in 1910, followed by Kentish Town in 1911, by Withington Baths, Manchester in 1913 (after a petition), and finally by Liverpool a year later.

At Withington, the rules, drawn up by General Superintendent John Derbyshire, were explicit.

Males had to be accompanied by one or more females. (In Kentish Town 'a lady relative or family friend' was stipulated.)

Under 16s, male or female, had to be accompanied by a parent or guardian, but females over 16 could attend unaccompanied.

Changing cubicles were strictly segregated on opposite sides of the pool, while curtains placed in front of the cubicles (as illustrated at St Pancras) had to remain drawn and cubicle doors kept shut while bathers changed.

THE POPULARITY OF MIXED BATHING IN LONDON

All bathers had to enter and leave the water on their respective sides of the bath and, after leaving the water, proceed directly to their cubicles. Once dressed they had to leave the cubicle door open and 'leave the building without delay'.

As to swimwear, all males had to wear regulation ASA costumes, either dark blue or black, with 'bathing drawers underneath'. Females had to wear either the recognised ASA costume or another 'of approved pattern'. No light coloured costumes were permitted.

Any person breaching these rules or 'endangering the good conduct of the bath' was liable to be excluded by the Superintendent.

Writing the Carnegie UK Trust Report of 1918, Agnes Campbell remained cautious however, advising that 'Ancient and medieval experience points to the necessity for strict supervision where (mixed bathing) is practised.'

She was not alone, and the idea spread only slowly in the 1920s, and became the norm only after the Second World War. Indeed in some areas, such as Worthing, single sex sessions continued well into the 1960s.

More recently they have been revived in areas where Muslim men and women – but many non-Muslims also – have specifically requested segregated sessions.

≫ using circulating and filtering systems, 'water may be kept in a bath for months or even years without apparent deterioration'.

Campbell goes on to say that although the plant could cost between £800–£1,300 to install, the savings on water charges, heating and labour costs could balance that out in the long run.

She also adds a table – one of 54 in this most exhaustive of reports – outlining the responses from over 50 local authorities where such systems had been installed by 1914. For example Eccles reported of their Bell's system, 'Exceedingly good. The water kept very clear with the use of little sulphate of alumina and lime. In summer the filters are cleaned out daily and in winter three times a week. The water in the swimming pond is changed annually.'

Of their Royle's system, the Middlesbrough Committee noted, 'The water is pumped out at the rate of 12,000 gals per hour and the whole of the 60,000 gals swimming bath water thus treated every five hours. Previous to inauguration of the system bath filled twice a week. Water was peaty, now pellucid. Economy in water and heating.'

Given that in some locations these systems had been in place for several years before Campbell's report, it would seem that the days of 'fill and empty' were now over.

And yet by the 1920s we learn from the Victoria Baths in Manchester that admission prices were still being dropped on the 'dirty water days' of Wednesdays and Saturdays. Similarly at Bradford's Central Baths, where filter systems had been installed before 1914, adverts by the Paterson Engineering Company in the early 1930s suggest that only by then had the problem of 'dirty water' been finally eradicated.

There might be a number of explanations for this. Perhaps the early systems gradually deteriorated, possibly owing to inadequate design or insufficient maintenance. Or perhaps, no matter how clear the water was, accumulated grime from bathers still required the regular scrubbing down of tank floor and sides.

Pending further research this issue, like the water itself, must remain somewhat unclear.

In contrast, the issue of water sterilisation is fully documented.

Again, this was an issue first tackled scientifically during the Edwardian period. Apparently the person to blame, or rather thank, for the initial use of chlorine as a sterilising agent in swimming baths – the cause of so much discomfort to swimmers over the generations – was Dr FW Alexander, Chief Medical Officer for the London Borough of Poplar.

Following an outbreak of conjunctivitis amongst swimmers, he started experimenting with various dosages of chlorinated solutions in 1908, until he arrived at a dosage which killed off any bacterial content yet could still be tolerated by swimmers.

Evidence from as recently as the 1980s suggests that baths managers did not always get this right. Stinging eyes and sickness were often reported.

But the alternative was worse. According to Agnes Campbell non-sterilised water had, in extreme cases, caused eye and ear infections, intestinal disorders, and in one case, a dose of gonorrhea. Infection from rented towels was another cause for concern.

Not that any of this seemed to deter Britain's swimmers. »

▲ Wearing costumes oddly similar to the full-body, hi-tech racing suits of today, three of Britain's greatest swimmers, **Rob Derbyshire, Henry Taylor** and **Jack Jarvis** pose at the **Olympic Games pool, White City,** in 1908, where Britain topped the aquatic medals table, a feat that has not been repeated since.

Paradoxically, at a time when Britain also led the world in baths construction, the 1908 Olympic pool was a temporary, open air tank, dug in front of the stadium's main grandstand. At 100m x 15m it was also Britain's first metric pool, and the first man-made pool used at an Olympiad. Previous aquatic events had been staged in the sea (Athens 1896), a river (Paris 1900) and a lake (St Louis 1904). As such, unheated water in 1908 was not an issue, although owing to the cold, one Hungarian almost lost consciousness in his relay event.

John 'Rob' Derbyshire (*left*) was the son of John Derbyshire, superintendent of Osborne Street Baths, Manchester, where, as 'the little Robin' he first performed in one of his father's displays as a three year old. He competed at four Olympic Games, and was a key member of the water polo team, trained by Derbyshire Senior, that won a gold in 1900. (Indeed Great Britain would not lose a water polo match at the Olympics until 1924.)

After retiring he followed in his father's footsteps and became superintendent at Lime Grove Baths, Hammersmith, from where he coached many an Olympian up to and including the 1928 Games.

Henry Taylor, with four Olympic golds and three world records, was an orphaned mill worker from Oldham who learnt to swim in local canals and at Chadderton Baths on 'dirty water days'. His skills also

helped save lives during the Battle of Jutland in 1916. After his ship was sunk, Taylor kept swimming and encouraging survivors for two hours before help arrived.

In later life he struggled, however, sold all his medals, and died impoverished in 1951. He is remembered by a plaque at Chadderton Baths, unveiled in 2002, and by a display inside the adjacent sports hall.

Arthur 'Jack' Jarvis, who had won two golds at Paris in 1900, also learnt to swim in canals, a background which made him dedicate much of his life to the cause of life saving.

Described as a man of 'magnetic personality with irrepressible bonhomie', together with his sister and his four daughters he was at the centre of a Leicester coterie of swimmers and coaches that trained many a champion in later years.

During the Edwardian period swimming's popularity rose to unprecedented levels. In London alone, the number of admissions to pools rose from 3.27 million in 1905 to 4.45 million by 1914.

Millions more schoolchildren swam for free, while the number of swimming clubs registered with the ASA reached a peak of 1,468 in 1914. Manchester had 134 clubs for men and 30 for ladies, Liverpool had 75 and 63 respectively, while Islington's three public baths were home to nearly 100 clubs, each allocated specific times over evenings and weekends.

No doubt the 1908 Olympics fed this interest. Indeed swimming's governing body, the Federation Internationale de Natation Amateur (FINA), was formed after the games at a London hotel, with an Englishman, George Hearn, as its first general secretary. Several FINA rules were copied directly from those of the ASA.

Ladies swimming also advanced considerably during these years.

In 1902 the ASA finally buckled to pressure by staging the first Ladies Championships. After further pressure from female swimmers the ASA even allowed men to attend. (However, competitors were ordered to keep on their robes until immediately before each race, and put them on again as soon as they finished.)

A further breakthrough came in 1912 when, despite de Coubertin's reservations, ladies were allowed to compete at the Stockholm Olympics. Britain's ladies' first gold came in the 4 x 100m relay, while Belle White took a bronze in the diving.

How appropriate, therefore, that our first case study from the years 1901–18 should be a baths built exclusively for women.

▲ In 1906 the Admiralty decreed that all recruits should be given instruction in swimming and life saving for half an hour a day, an edict which led to the construction of at least seven pools at naval establishments around the country.

This is the **Royal Naval School of Physical Training Baths** on **Pitt Street, Portsmouth** (*see also page 111*), opened in 1910 and later known as HMS Temeraire.

On the left a cadet learns to swim in a harness, suspended on a rope, while at the far end five recruits practice in harnesses attached to a pole spanning the width of the pool. On the right are trapezes, accessed from a platform also suspended over the water.

Other naval baths were built at Eastney Barracks in 1904 (also in Portsmouth and now a public pool run by the council); at Dartmouth in 1905; at Shotley Barracks, Suffolk in 1908, at Devonport in 1910 (still operating under the name HMS Drake), and at Chatham in Kent (1911).

The army also built pools. Its first was at Aldershot in 1900, built from the proceeds of the Royal Military Tournament. Although closed in 1984 the building still stands and is Grade II listed.

Other army-related baths were at the Duke of York's Royal Military School, Dover, opened 1909, at Chelmsford in 1914, and the former Light Infantry baths at Gosport, opened 1922, now part of St Vincent College.

Training aids such as those seen above were also once common at public baths, but only two trapezes are known to have survived, at the Arlington and Western Baths Clubs in Glasgow (*pages 71 and 74*).

Also once common at public baths – installed for fun rather than for instruction – were **Newman's water chutes**, as seen right at **Knightstone Baths, Weston-super-Mare**, in c.1913. Devised by a Mr Newman, superintendent at Westminster Baths, the earliest versions were bolted to the balcony, whereas Knightstone had

a manufactured chute (possibly supplied by Thomas Bradford & Co.) with its own frame and steps.

In this photo the water hose at the top appears to have been turned off to allow two members of the Weston swimming club to pose without sliding down. Note that one of the girls appears without her swimming cap, the wearing of which was otherwise obligatory.

In all cases of FAINTNESS, DROWSINESS, or SICKNESS of any kind, **RING BELL**, and IMMEDIATELY **STEP OUT OF BATH**.

NOTICE.

Bathers occupying a Bath Room more than thirty minutes are liable to a second charge for admission.

▲ Surviving suites of Edwardian slipper baths are now rare, most having been converted into other uses, or modernised (as at Dulwich and Govanhill) before being mothballed in the late 20th century. But some elements have survived, such as this electric bell system (now disused) at the **City Baths, Chester**, which allowed bathers to request assistance or more hot water.

Best preserved of all are the slipper baths at **Moseley Road, Balsall Heath, Birmingham** (*above left*). The second class baths there were last used as recently as 2004. The rope (*left*) was for hauling oneself out of the bath. The chain pull was to request more hot water.

Agnes Campbell noted in 1917 that even in houses fitted with baths, the occupants found them expensive to run and lacking in privacy, and often used them to store coal or clothes instead.

Case Study

Cadbury's Girls' Bath, Bournville, Birmingham

Opened 1904
Address Bournville Lane B30 2LU
Architect GH Lewin
Cost not known
Pool 80' x 46'
Owner Cadbury Trebor Bassett
Closed 1982
Listed Grade II (1980)

When the Quaker chocolate manufacturers Richard and George Cadbury first set up their 'Factory in a Garden' in 1878, on farmland straddling Birmingham's Bourn Brook – hence the name Bournville – the moral, social and recreational needs of their workers were of paramount concern.

So much so that by 1905, the year Cadbury's trademark Dairy Milk brand was launched, nearly a third of the company's outgoings was spent on activities other than production. Bournville could boast, as a result, one of the finest cricket grounds in the Midlands, a superb pavilion and gymnasium (built in 1902),

bowling greens, tennis courts, an open air swimming pool for men (opened in 1898), and this quite magnificent indoor baths, designed by the works architect GH Lewin and company engineer Louis Barrow.

Nikolaus Pevsner described it as the 'most impressive extravaganza of the whole Bournville estate'.

But its qualities were more than skin deep.

Firstly, this was a very rare beast – a high specification indoor pool built expressly for women (even if the company did rather patronisingly call it the Girls' Bath). Apart from school or college pools, only two other female-only baths establishments

are known to have been built before 1914; at King's Meadow, Reading (1902) and Blakey Moor, Blackburn (1912).

The Girls' Bath at Bournville was also technically advanced, featuring as, mentioned earlier, one of the first Royle's filtration systems, which Barrow had seen in action at public baths in Bury and Manchester. Apart from the system's other advantages, filters were deemed advisable because the Girls' Bath was sourced directly from the Bourn, whose waters had a yellowish tint.

Not only did Cadbury girls have the cleanest water possible, they also had the warmest. Most public pools at that time were heated to no more than 68-70° F. At Cadbury the temperature was set to 74° in summer and 76° in winter.

A further advance was the supply of 22 'spray baths', or showers, plus a poolside design that ensured that no swimmer could enter the water without first showering and passing through a foot bath. This was 25 years before such provision became obligatory at public baths.

There were even hair dryers.

Not that this was any place for idlers. Every employee under 18, male or female, had to undergo two half-hour periods of exercise per week, and everyone was expected to learn to swim, in the company's time. Also within company time each girl was invited to take one slipper bath per week.

At a time when female workers outnumbered males by three to

one, and there was also strict segregation of the sexes in the workplace – there were even separate dining rooms – these privileges had the men, shivering in their outdoor pool, casting envious eyes towards the new aquatic temple in their midst.

Within a year they were able to extract a concession. Male staff were to be allowed their own sessions in the Girls' Bath, but only before 8.00am on weekdays and from 4.00–9.00pm on Fridays.

This Cadbury assortment of paternalism and progressivism soon caused ripples. For example the firm's long lasting association with the pioneering Anstey College of Physical Education, founded for women in 1897, in Halesowen, led to many a Cadbury girl teaching other women to swim at local public baths in the region.

Nor did the firm's investment in swimming stop with the Girls' Bath. In 1911, a few hundred yards down Bournville Lane, Stirchley Public Baths and Library opened on land donated by the firm. And in 1936 the men's pool was converted into a small indoor pool.

Finally, in 1937 the Bournville Village Trust opened a modernist lido at Rowheath, a nearby 75 acre site gifted by the Cadburys as a park and sports ground. (For more information on all these facilities, see *Played in Birmingham*.)

Today, alas, only the 1936 indoor pool remains operational, run by Birmingham City Council as a teaching pool. Otherwise, the Bournville Lido closed in 1987, as did Stirchley Baths in 1988.

As for the Girls' Bath, this closed too, in 1982, and although its exterior has since been lovingly restored, in 2005, the interior, as shown above, remains in limbo.

George Cadbury, as his biographer wrote, was never purely an altruist. He 'loved games for themselves, but he loved them still more as a physical training necessary to keep one fit for the real business of life'.

Today it would seem, with both the Girls' Bath and Stirchley Baths lying empty within a few hundred yards of each other, the business of life has rather more pressing matters to deal with than swimming.

Arts and Crafts styling informs many of Bournville's buildings. This panel on the Girls' Bath, in the shadow of the square clock tower, was carved by Benjamin Creswick, a leading member of the Century Guild and of the Birmingham School of Art.

Case Study

Acton, London

Opened June 11 1904
Address Salisbury Street W3 8NW
Architect DJ Ebbetts, Borough Surveyor
Cost £15,398
Pools 105' x 30' and 75' x 30'
Owner Ealing Borough Council
Operator Greenwich Leisure Ltd
Listed Chimney only, Grade II (2003)

Acton Baths merits attention not because it is of architectural merit – although uniquely its freestanding chimney is listed – but because it forms one element within a block consisting of Acton Town Hall and various extensions, erected between 1909–39.

Facing onto Acton High Street, with the baths at the rear, this assortment of municipal buildings occupies a prime location whose value the Borough of Ealing (into which Acton was absorbed in 1965) would ideally and understandably like to realise.

But of course it is no simple matter. Twice the baths have been close to closure, first in 1968, and again in the late 1980s when, after years of under investment, its future was made into an election issue by the Friends of Acton Baths. That pressure, and a change of administration, culminated in a refurbishment costing £2.5m.

But even as the baths reopened in 1990 there was a caveat. Here, it was warned, was a building that had been erected cheaply even by the standards of 1904, and suffered serious shortcomings, not least to its drainage.

Had a full refurbishment been carried out the bill would have been nearer £10m. As it was, the repairs were a quick fix only, and would last no more than 20 years.

As these years passed by, various schemes were proposed for the entire block, including the construction of a new pool within, and subsidised by, a sizeable retail and residential development.

But in 2003 the listing of the Town Hall (and the baths' chimney) rather stymied those plans, forcing a rethink that remained unresolved as this book went to press.

In the interim, £600,000 more had to be spent, on top of an annual subsidy of £250,000.

And so time compresses. Ealing needs to yield the maximum return from the site in order to finance a new pool elsewhere in Acton, and to do so before the baths' operator's contract ends in 2012, in order to avoid spending yet more on another patching up operation.

In short we must enjoy Acton's ivy clad walls while we can and trust that from this intricate web of planning, the surviving chimney will at least find some consolation as the oldest kid on the block.

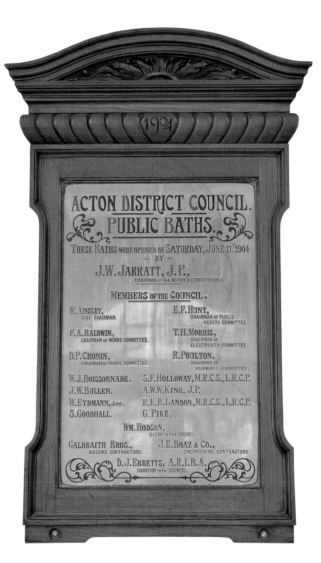

For all the ongoing problems with its fabric, Acton Baths retains several of its admirable Edwardian features, including this splendid brass plate in the main reception, commemorating the opening in 1904, the poolside balcony in the former First Class pool, and the free-standing chimney in the back yard, seen here with steel ties protecting its terracotta cladding.

Case Study

Haggerston, Hackney, London

Opened June 25 1904
Address Whiston Road, E2 8BN
Architect AWS Cross
Cost £60,000
Pool 100' x 35'
Owner Hackney Borough Council
Listed Grade II (1988)
Closed February 2000

Writing in his seminal treatise of 1906 – noted earlier in this chapter – Alfred Cross bitterly criticised those town hall officials who preferred to entrust baths design to borough engineers or surveyors, rather than to architects.

Haggerston Baths, in the east London district of Shoreditch, was his riposte to that conservatism, and a triumphant one at that.

It may not be large, having only one pool. It may not be highly decorative. But Haggerston is a building of undeniable, yet subtle quality, built to high specifications at a time when Cross, after 15 years in the baths business, was starting to challenge many of the norms of the late Victorian period.

In fact Haggerston was the second baths Cross worked on in Shoreditch, the first being at Pitfield Street, Hoxton, completed in May 1899, just as his ten year partnership with Henry Spalding was coming to an end.

Grouped with a fine Passmore Edwards library by Henry T Hare, Pitfield Street had two pools, 76 slipper baths and a 50 stall wash house. In a densely populated and poor parish where fewer than one in 20 homes had a bath, it became one of Britain's five best attended establishments, used by over 280,000 bathers annually, plus almost 50,000 for the wash house.

Although its exterior was styled in the familiar Free Renaissance garb of the period, Pitfield Street was a highly innovative building.

It was, for example, the first baths to be powered by electricity generated by a 'dust destructor', or refuse incinerator, built next door. It was also the first baths to stage cinematographic performances.

Moreover, instead of the usual narrow spectator gallery placed on top of poolside cubicles, Pitfield Street had overhanging galleries of three rows on the sides and eight rows at one end.

Another step forward was the use of steel arches to form the roof. But rather than leaving them exposed, as at Birmingham's Woodock Street, for example, at Pitfield Street the trusses were boxed in, with plastered, curved ceiling panels in between.

A simple decorative device, for sure, but one that added lightness, reduced echo, and represented a clear departure from the usual utilitarian brick and iron shed.

Now had Pitfield Street survived, it might well have ranked as highly as St Pancras Baths. But although the library survives (now housing a theatre), as does the neighbouring power station (now a circus training centre), the baths were damaged beyond repair during the Second World War.

This therefore leaves Haggerston as the only surviving baths of Cross' mid career; that is, after Dulwich and Camberwell (both completed in partnership with Spalding), and before 1922, when his son Kenneth joined him in practice.

But Alfred Cross was not the only guiding hand at Haggerston.

In most cases the names of Baths and Wash Houses Committee members are of only passing interest to historians. But at Shoreditch the name of the committee vice chairman EJ Wakeling stands out.

Wakeling was unusual in that, as a keen swimmer and secretary of a swimming club, he had entered local politics in 1887 with the specific intention of getting baths built on his home patch.

That it took so long to get Pitfield Street built 'after repeated disappointments' and 'much opposition' clearly frustrated Wakeling, as did the design competition process. Pitfield Street ended up late and over budget as a result.

Chastened by this experience, Shoreditch's committee thus hired Cross directly for Haggerston, with no competition, and were clearly led by their architect when it came to the brief.

For example, the Committee had hoped to fuel the entire baths operation, as at Hoxton, from a nearby power station (built along the road between Whiston Street and the Regent Canal). But Cross persuaded them that three standard, coal-fired Lancashire boilers and a 90' chimney stack would be more economical.

Cross also insisted that glazed bricks and tiling should be used throughout the interior (to reduce maintenance costs), although for the exterior he had to settle on Portland stone rather than granite.

Nevertheless, the final bill of almost exactly £60,000 was £5,000 over budget, seemingly costly for a single pool establishment. But then Haggerston did also have 91 first and second class slipper baths and a 60 stall wash house.

Hoxton, by comparison, had cost £75,765 for fewer baths and a smaller wash house. But it did have two pools, whereas at Haggerston the provision of a single pool meant that, as always, women had to put up with only limited access, on one day a week.

But for the people of Haggerston, Wakeling is best remembered for his contribution to the baths' opening ceremony.

According to the *Hackney and Kingsland Gazette*, after the opening speeches Wakeling apparently surprised everyone by diving in and swimming a complete length of the pool, 100', underwater. (Not bad for a man aged at least 40.)

Haggerston Baths would go on to enjoy a robust life too. Charmed even, as it somehow managed to escape serious damage during the Second World War, despite the rest of the surrounding houses being virtually flattened. The pool also became popular as a boxing venue.

But inevitably, changing social factors brought about the need for alterations. As detailed overleaf, these were carried out between 1960–64 and 1985–88, after which the baths reopened in fine fettle, having been newly listed Grade II.

Come the late 1990s, however, and regulars at Haggerston began to feel nervous. The baths' fabric was clearly deteriorating through lack of maintenance, and in 1999 a users group formed to convey its concerns to Hackney Council.

(Hackney, incidentally, had been created in 1965 by the merger of three boroughs, Stoke Newington, Hackney and Shoreditch.)

The axe finally fell one Friday night in February 2000, when children turning up to their weekly

session found a notice stating that for health and safety reasons the pool was now closed.

As pool campaigners swiftly marshalled support, it emerged that the Council had chosen this route rather than spend an estimated £300,000 on repairs.

Yet everyone in Hackney knew full well why such tight budgetary controls had suddenly become so important. Two miles to the north, the borough's newest leisure project – hailed by the Millennium Commission as one of twelve schemes to showcase modern British architecture – was running massively over budget and three years behind schedule.

Haggerston Baths, it was clear, had been just one sacrifice among many made in a desperate attempt to keep the flagship afloat.

Even more frustration was to follow when the admittedly »

▲ To appreciate just how much its red brick and Portland stone façade once dominated the streetscape, it should be noted that Haggerston Baths was, until the Second World War, tightly wedged between humble terraced houses on both **Whiston Road** and, to the rear, on **Laburnum Street** (*below*).

In fact both neighbouring terraces on Laburnum Street were flattened during the Blitz, making the baths' survival all the more remarkable.

Nowadays its flanks are exposed and the building is dwarfed by tower blocks. Even so, its once gilded **weathervane** (*opposite*), by the Salford firm of George Wragge Ltd (who also worked at the Victoria Baths in Manchester) remains a prominent feature on the skyline.

▶ From his 1906 treatise, Cross' plans for **Haggerston** show the poolside amphitheatre seating which, he argued, provided better sightlines than first floor galleries.

Cross had already tried gallery level amphitheatre seating at Hoxton, which as a result became a popular venue for London galas. But as can be seen in the section below, at Haggerston the seats started at pool level, with teak changing cubicles placed at the rear of the three tiers of seats.

But for all Cross' claims that this arrangement made it easier for attendants to keep an eye on the boxes, and that the seats in front could be used by children wanting to change when there were no boxes free, the system did not catch on. Amphitheatre seating only started to make sense in the 1930s, once cubicles were moved away from the pool hall.

The current layout at Haggerston dates from the 1960s. In 1961 a new laundry was built in the north west corner of the site (previously occupied by houses bombed in the war). In 1964 the old laundry was converted into changing rooms, the amphitheatre seating was removed and replaced (ironically) by a gallery, and the men's and women's entrances on Whiston Road replaced by a single entrance at the west end of the former men's first class slipper baths.

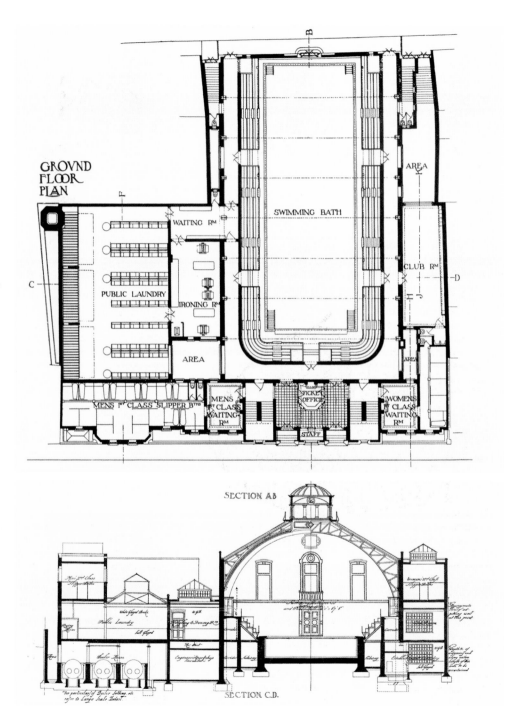

» ultra-modern but, by now infamous Clissold Leisure Centre did finally open in early 2002. So plagued was it by technical and structural faults that it had to close in late 2003 for an overhaul which took another four years to complete and saw the total bill spiral from an original estimate of £7m in 1996 to £45m in late 2007. (Not even Wembley Stadium or the Millennium Dome had risen in cost by sixfold.)

Although over £10m of this outlay was covered by the Lottery, and an undisclosed portion of the remainder was later clawed back by out-of-court settlements, the damage to Hackney's coffers, and to its reputation, was immense.

Nor did it help that the borough's other historic baths, the former Hackney Public Baths (now the King's Hall Leisure Centre), dating from 1897 on Lower Clapton Road, was also absorbing costs, despite the fact that only one of its three original pools remained operational. It too was then listed Grade II in 2003.

At Haggerston meanwhile, as a stoic, candlelit vigil outside the bath marked its forlorn centenary in June 2004, the likely repair bill steadily escalated to over £5m.

Initially the campaigners hoped the building might be handed over to a specially formed trust.

Then for a while hope resided in a scheme to build a City Academy next door, with the baths forming part of its sports facilities.

But this plan collapsed in early 2005, after which a structural survey funded by English Heritage found that although the building remained basically sound, there were nevertheless severe problems with its floors, ceilings and the drainage system, and that asbestos was also present.

For its part Hackney conducted a feasibility study. This concluded that its preferred option – which includes the retention of the pool and the conversion of other parts of the building to a medical centre and various community facilities – would cost around £21m.

As this book went to press, discussions on how to implement this option continued, while the campaigners continued to meet, to stage their now famous annual street parties, and to put their faith in the hope that, in an area with such acute and diverse needs, the social and health benefits of having a pool of genuine national significance in their midst could surely not be denied.

After all, looking east, they could spy on the £303m Aquatic Centre being built for the 2012 Olympics, three miles away, while looking north, the Clissold Centre was now busy and popular.

But actually a much brighter ray of hope lay even closer to hand, barely half a mile to the north east.

In October 2006 London Fields Lido, built in 1932, re-opened to great acclaim after a £2.5m refit.

And how long had campaigners waited for that glorious moment?

Eighteen years.

In the meantime, we can only hope that someone senior at Hackney Council is practising their underwater swimming, ready for the big day at Haggerston.

▲ Seen here in 1992, Haggerston's pool hall remains an outstanding example of early 20th century baths design. To judge how advanced it was, flick through the images on the previous 30 or so pages, paying close attention to the internal roof structures and finishes.

To understand how it influenced baths that came later, do the same over the pages that follow.

By the simple expedient of boxing in the steel arches, panelling the ceiling in plaster and recessing the skylights, Cross created a quite different ambience – brighter, with less echo, and with a softer, more discreet natural light.

Another innovation was the use of non-slip rubber flooring.

Case Study

Bramley, Leeds

Opened October 17 1904
Address Broad Lane LS13 3DF
Architect J Lane Fox
Cost £10,600
Pool 75' x 30'
Owner Leeds City Council
Operator Bodyline/Leeds City Council
Listed Grade II (1996)
Reopened April 30 1992

Once a village in its own right, but now a suburb on the north west edges of Leeds, Bramley's streetscape has altered so radically since the 1960s that the survival of its Edwardian baths seems almost miraculous. Truly, the image above, apart from the smoking chimney and the lack of traffic, might easily have been taken in the last few years, rather than in c.1904.

Here is a superbly preserved, but also archetypal single pool, district baths of the early 20th century. It is, moreover, the sole survivor of seven such baths constructed in Leeds between 1895 and 1904.

Like Bradford, Leeds adopted the policy of having one large central baths, in its case Cookridge Street (*see page 44*), with smaller

district baths distributed around the suburbs.

Batley architect Walter Hanstock (*page 92*) designed five of these, at Union Street and Kirkstall Road (1895), Joseph Street and Holbeck Lane (1898), and Meanwood Street (1899). Each followed a similar plan, with a pair of pools of almost identical sizes, typically 75' x 30' and 62' x 24'.

Hanstock died in 1900, so for the next two baths, at York Road and Bramley, the corporation held a competition, inviting only Leeds architects to apply.

HA Chapman was selected for York Road which, combined with a library, was opened by the Leeds Mayoress on October 11 1904.

J Lane Fox won the commission for Bramley, which the Mayoress' husband opened a week later.

While Lane Fox took no risks, the result was a well proportioned, single storey range of buildings with a two storey entrance block, dressed in the distinctive gritstone of West Yorkshire.

In addition to a single pool (once again 75' x 30'), there were 20 slipper baths (16 for men, four for women) and a suite of Russian baths, for men only. All departments were finished in glazed bricks with skylights.

But what stands out today – shines out even – is the extensive use of stained glass, in the pool hall, in the corridors, and in the baths' quite magnificent entrance hall (*shown on page 108*).

That all this survives is largely thanks to local councillors.

In November 1988 Bramley Baths closed. Most people expected it to share the fate of Leeds' other historic baths, all of which were demolished, other than York Road (where the baths closed in 1968 but the entrance block and former library, listed Grade II, survive in a parlous state).

But at Bramley councillors and local residents did not give up.

A grant of £1.5m was attained from the Sports Council, and after nearly four years of closure, in April 1992 the baths re-opened, looking almost as good as new.

Under an extensive renovation programme carried out with great sensitivity by Cementation Construction and surveyors Derrick Wade Waters, the pool's tank was repaired, the men's slipper bath area converted into a dance studio (now a gym), the laundry became a fitness studio and the Russian baths were revamped.

Other changes have seen the manager's living room turned into a refreshment area, his kitchen turned into a locker room, his garden into a car park, and a room off the gallery into a beauty salon.

Some 146,000 people a year now pass through the entrance hall, and who can blame them for coming back again and again.

And just to top it all, since its re-opening there has been none of the usual 'leisure centre' rebranding.

This being Yorkshire, where a spade is a spade, Bramley Baths is still Bramley Baths, and there's nowt wrong with that.

▲ Authentic Edwardian, but with a modern twist – **Bramley Baths** retains its original ironwork, stone pool surrounds and, at each end of the pool, its delightful arched stained glass windows (by an unknown artist).

But as a result of its 1990s refit, the tank's tiling is new, as are the poolside cubicles and the light fittings, carefully chosen to echo the originals. Also sensitively styled are the ventilation units lining the back of the gallery, and the jacuzzi, inserted into the area formerly designed to store the wooden floor used during the winter months.

No less admirable is the restored entrance block (*left*). On the Dutch gable are two sculpted owls, the symbol of Leeds.

Case Study

Carnegie Centre, Dunfermline

Opened March 31 1905
Address Pilmuir Street KY12 0QE
Architect Hippolyte Jean Blanc
Cost £46,748
Pools 75' x 30' (original), plus
25m x 12.5m and 12.5m x 12.5m
toddlers' pool added in 1984
Owner Fife Council
Operator Fife Sports & Leisure Trust
Listed Category B (1979)

Having sneaked a look at the sumptuous indoor pool that the steel baron and philanthropist Andrew Carnegie built at Skibo Castle (*see page 98*), we now turn to the public baths that he gifted to his home town of Dunfermline; a building that, at the time of writing, is about to undergo a £19m refurbishment, due for completion in late 2010.

Known as the Carnegie Leisure Centre – since a major expansion in the 1980s – the building is actually the second of two Dunfermline baths to have been endowed by Carnegie.

The original one, on Schoolend Street, close to the current site, was built in 1877, by which time Carnegie, then aged 42, was based in New York (and had just opened the world's largest steel mill, in Pittsburgh). Indeed the baths, designed by local architect Andrew Scobie and costing £5,209, constituted Carnegie's first formal act of philanthropy.

He even sailed over for the opening, in July 1877, declaring that he wished the baths and its adjoining gymnasium to be of benefit to the working classes, and also to be evidence of the 'deep and abiding interest he had always had, and ever would have in the prosperity of his native town'.

Almost immediately a Carnegie Swimming Club formed, making full use of the 68' x 30' pool and, in 1884, becoming a founding member of the Scottish Amateur Swimming Association (in which it remains actively involved today).

Carnegie himself enjoyed swimming, and in retirement was said to have swum every day. As a good Scotsman he also grew to love golf. But his main passion was reading, and so it was that in August 1883, thanks to a further donation of £5,000, the first of what would become a network of over 2,500 Carnegie libraries around the world also opened in Dunfermline, only a short distance from the baths, on Abbot Street.

As the years went by it became apparent that the original baths, which had only seven slipper baths and no wash house, was too small. Hearing of this, in 1899 Carnegie offered the Council £20,000 for the erection of a larger establishment, 'as a Christmas gift' from a 'loyal son'.

For a man now donating money freely and in vast amounts, such a sum was relatively trifling compared, for example, to the £1m he had just given to his Carnegie Institute in Pittsburgh. But even this level of generosity would pale into insignificance once Carnegie sold out his steel interests in 1901 and, as arguably one of the two or three richest men in the world, became a full time philanthropist. His aim, he said, was to give away his entire fortune before he died.

It was in this spirit that, two years after purchasing Skibo, in 1903 he also bought the 76 acre Pittencrieff estate on the edge of Dunfermline town centre, and through the newly formed Carnegie Dunfermline Trust transformed it into a public park.

The same Trust was also tasked with running the new baths.

Its architect, awarded the commission after a design competition had been abandoned, was Hippolyte Jean Blanc, born of French parentage in Edinburgh, and very much an establishment figure in Scottish architecture.

Blanc was a keen antiquarian and had designed numerous churches, but never a baths, and it soon became apparent that £20,000 would not be sufficient to deliver his elaborate proposals. Needless to add, Carnegie covered the shortfall, having visited first in July 1902 for the laying of the foundation stone, and again to inspect progress in May 1904.

The following October, after Carnegie, who was now nearing 70, and his American wife Louise (22 years his junior) had returned to New York, the first part of the building, the gymnasium, was formally opened by Carnegie's Dunfermline solicitor, John Ross.

Five months later the baths section of the building was opened by Provost Macbeth, amid scenes described by the *Dunfermline Press* as 'probably the most magnificent of its kind ever seen in Dunfermline'.

To commemorate the event silver medals were issued bearing the inscription, 'Let there be Light – The Carnegie Dunfermline Trust Swimming Baths'. Shown opposite is one of them, held by the National Museums of Scotland.

As to the baths itself, the building seemed little short of the gold standard; opulent »

◀ July 16 1902, and Andrew Carnegie's wife Louise prepares to unveil the **foundation stone** for the new Carnegie Baths. The stone, which was laid on the left hand wall inside the main entrance porch, is seen here draped in a white cloth, in front of where Louise sits, dressed in black. Her husband, white beard trimmed as always, stands proudly to one side, in front of an opening that would become the window to the left of the main entrance.

Just behind him, wearing a top hat and chain of office, stands Andrew Scobie, architect of the original Carnegie Baths who, by that time, had become Provost.

Once completed, as shown below in 1906, the new baths presented a handsome 260' long frontage on **Pilmuir Street**.

Since then the railings have gone and the leaded windows replaced. Behind the building a large new sports centre has emerged. But the front block has barely altered at all.

Built in grey sandstone quarried from nearby Swallowdrum, its entrance is flanked by octagonal towers, each bearing a bronze panel by sculptor Richard Goulden. The one on the left reads *In Infantia Purdor* (purity in childhood). The one on the right reads *In Viro Virtus* (moral strength in manhood).

At the far end can be seen the pyramidal roof of the Turkish baths.

Carnegie Baths, Dunfermline.

▶ Following the pattern of private baths clubs in Scotland, such as Arlington and Western, but also that of the public baths at Alloa, the **Carnegie Baths** in **Dunfermline** was the Edwardian equivalent of a modern sports centre. That is, it combined wet and dry facilities with areas for health treatments, refreshments, games and socialising.

On the wet side there were 20 slipper baths and three spray baths (or showers), but no wash house.

The pool, or pond (seen here in a series of postcards thought to date from 1906), measured 75' x 35' and was surrounded by 50 demountable cubicles and a three-sided gallery. Even in black and white the quality and exuberance of the tilework and ironwork can be sensed. Note also the choice of 'artistic electric lamps'.

For reasons unknown the chute by the diving stage was described as 'Canadian'. But the hanging ferns and rings gave the pool hall a decidely Scottish appearance.

Less ornate but larger in area was the wood-panelled gymnasium.

Measuring 103' x 45', this too had a three sided gallery, able to hold 1,000 spectators.

Under plans for the centre's refurbishment in 2009–10, the gymnasium will be converted into a changing village, with a mezzanine floor added to accommodate an aerobics studio.

Swimming Pond, Carnegie Baths, Dunfermline. 4002 5.

The Gymnasium, Carnegie Baths, Dunfermline.

»» enough to be considered first class throughout, and in several respects as well equipped as many a private baths club.

All the same it did only have one pool, which is why the Trust decided not only to keep the old baths open, but also to make use of it free of charge.

Thus they could be seen to be fulfilling their philanthropic duty, while at the same time ensuring a certain level of exclusivity was maintained at the new baths. (A similar two tier system operated in York and in Liverpool, where there were three free baths for juveniles.)

Certainly there was more than enough demand for the two establishments to co-exist.

For the year 1913–14, for example, 34,696 bathers took advantage of the Free Baths, while 90,859 paid to use the new baths.

There being no other indoor baths in the whole of Fife, and a population in Dunfermline of only 28,000, this made Carnegie's baths amongst the busiest per capita in Britain, and, moreover, with a higher ratio of female users to males than anywhere in Scotland.

How do we know this? Because of statistical research carried out by yet another Carnegie endowment, the Carnegie UK Trust, whose report by Agnes Campbell we referred to earlier.

One of the report's aims was to decide whether the Trust should subsidise the construction of more public baths in Britain.

Compared with all the many libraries Carnegie funded, he had, to date, gifted only three baths on this side of the Atlantic; the two in Dunfermline and one in Forfar, which he opened personally in October 1910. (Designed also by Hippolyte Jean Blanc, Forfar baths is still open today.)

But world events rather overshadowed the report's aims, and by the time it was published in 1918 the Trust had other priorities.

Added to this, Carnegie died the following year. He had, by then, managed to dispose of some 90 per cent of his fortune.

But there would be no more baths to show for it.

Back in Dunfermline the Free Baths remained open until 1926. Thereafter it was used as an art gallery, then, under the name of Pilmuir Hall, as a theatre and dance hall. Finally, in 1957 the Ministry of Pensions rented it, before its demolition in 1971.

The 'new baths', meanwhile, were no longer so new, and in 1946 the Carnegie Dunfermline Trust paid £10,000 for repairs and then handed over full control of the building to the town council.

Since then it has undergone three phases of major works.

The first was an emergency procedure, after the pool started leaking and had to be closed in November 1975. It reopened the following May, a new, smaller tank having been installed inside the original. At the same time the poolside cubicles were removed and the roof and ironwork restored. Also in the 1970s the Turkish baths and gymnasium were renovated, albeit with no great sensitivity.

Phase Two saw the building's footprint virtually double, with the addition of a completely new block on the north, or Campbell Street side, housing a 25m pool, with a toddlers' pool alongside.

Costing £1.2m, both pools were opened in April 1984. The original pool, meanwhile, was renamed as the Training Pool.

Phase Three saw the addition of yet another new block at the rear of the site, on Inglis Street. Named

Interior of Turkish Baths, Dunfermline.

Billiard Room, Carnegie Baths, Dunfermline.

the Asda Arena and completed in May 1991, this consisted of a large sports hall and squash courts.

But if in terms of its facilities the Carnegie Leisure Centre now had plenty to offer, as evinced by its 450,000 annual users, architecturally the result was a hotch-potch of styles, elevations and roof levels, with a complex and wasteful web of circulation routes that occupied almost a third of the centre's total area.

More worryingly, several of the renovations from the 1970s proved short-lived. For example, by 2007 the tank installed in the original pool started to leak, which in »»

Dunfermline's Turkish baths were possibly the finest at any public baths in Britain, and certainly the finest to have survived. The equally splendid billiard room is now a dance studio.

▶ Let there be light – this grand **hallway** and stairwell provided a theatrical entrance to both the pool and gymnasium, and, via stairs, to their first floor galleries.

In contrast, in the south west corner of the building the **Turkish baths** (*below*) formed a self-contained, Moorish-style cocoon, a world apart from life out on Pilmuir Street, only a few feet away.

As always the suite contained a sudatorium, tepidarium and cooling room, together with a plunge pool, shampooing room and a steam bath. But in terms of its decor, even compared with the opulent standards of the day, the lavish use of glazed tiles and polychrome faience, particularly on the Moorish arches, was quite outstanding.

Unfortunately the equally gorgeous mosaic floors were concreted over during the 1970s.

As part of the refurbishment planned for 2009–10, the fabric of the Turkish baths will be restored, but no longer as a wet area. Instead, it will be used for various therapies and treatments, while in the centre of the complex (where formerly there were changing rooms), a modern spa, with sauna, steam room and plunge pool, will be created. Regrettable though the loss of the Turkish baths is, the new spa area will at least be more accessible to those using the two main swimming pools.

≫ turn caused the original tank to leak also. Meanwhile, most of the building services, old and recent, were starting to fail, a new filtration plant was required, and the Turkish baths had reached the end of their useful life.

Inevitably the question arose of whether it would be wiser to start afresh on a larger site elsewhere.

That, however, it was estimated by Fife Council, would have cost £30m. It would also have left the Council with an unused listed building on its hands, whilst also detracting from its efforts to rejuvenate the town centre.

As is increasingly the case, issues relating to sustainability also favoured renovation.

After all, Dunfermline's centre is well served by public transport, and while checks confirmed that much needed to be done to improve the Carnegie Centre's energy efficiency, there appeared to be little wrong with its actual structures. Not only that but thermographic images showed that the Edwardian sections were the most efficient.

Thus the decision to renovate was confirmed in mid 2008.

Inevitably there have been criticisms. As at Kentish Town (*see page 102*) the Carnegie Centre will need to be closed for at least 18 months, leaving many sports clubs and regular users without an easily accessible alternative.

But the ends will surely justify the means. For make no mistake, even disregarding the sporting and community benefits of the centre's late 20th century additions, the surviving Edwardian elements rank amongst the finest to be found at any historic baths in Britain.

Carnegie's baths – one good act among many – now richly deserves another.

▲ Having been renovated once before in the 1970s, the original pool at the Carnegie Leisure Centre, now called the **Training Pool**, is to be revamped again in 2009–10, under plans drawn up by Fife Council's Property Services division.

The plans include the removal of various fittings and glass divisions added during the 1970s – which may perhaps lead to some of the original tiling being uncovered – and the introduction of openings at pool level to create better links, physically and visually, with the two other pools and the new spa planned in the former changing area.

At the same time the 1970s tank will be removed and the pool lengthened from the original 75' to 25m, and widened beyond its original width of 30' to allow for six lanes to be fitted between the cast iron columns. A moveable floor might also be added.

Most intriguing of all, the tank is to be replaced by a stainless steel liner, such as is now common in private and school pools, but is so far rare in the public sector.

That old Scottish man of steel, Andrew Carnegie, would no doubt have heartily approved.

Case Study

Beverley Road, Kingston-upon-Hull

Opened May 29 1905
Address Beverley Road, HU5 1AN
Architect AE White (City Engineer)
Cost £27,000
Pool 100' x 35' (former Men's).
Former ladies, 65' x 30' and boys,
60' x 40', both closed
Owner Hull City Council
Operator Hull Leisure
Listed Grade II (1990)

Beverley Road baths, according to a booklet published to mark its opening in 1905, represented 'the crowning achievement of the Corporation,' one that 'would be difficult to surpass either from an architectural or utilitarian point of view'.

And so it proved, at least as far as the city's Baths and Wash Houses Commitee was concerned.

In Hull, as in so many other provincial cities, the great pools of splendour built during the Edwardian era represent a high point in the history of public baths provision. We have already highlighted the 1898 entrance hall at East Hull (*see page 4*). Beverley Road was even more lavish, and a century later ranks amongst the finest survivors of the period.

The port city of Hull may also take credit for being Britain's first local authority, after Liverpool (perhaps not coincidentally its west coast rival), to provide public baths with swimming facilities.

Opened shortly before the passing of the 1846 Act, Hull's first venture was at the Stoneferry Waterworks. This attracted 22,000 bathers in its first year but was too far from those densely populated areas around the docks where the need was greatest. In 1847 therefore the newly appointed Baths and Wash Houses Committee started looking for a more central site.

Trippett Street baths was the result. Based on plans drawn up by the engineer Price Prichard Baly – his first and apparently only baths commission outside London – and finished in 'Tudor-style' by local architect David Thorp, the £12,000 baths opened on April 22 1850; that is, before any other provincial baths built under the terms of the 1846 Act.

But as researcher Peter Ablitt has pointed out (*see Links*), despite its location, and the provision of 73 slipper baths and pools measuring 75' x 21' and 36' x 23', (each supplied with warm water from the engine of a nearby oil mill), Trippett Street struggled.

In its first year, income from the expensively fitted wash house, which had 56 stalls, amounted only to £62 17s 1d. And even when the Hull Kingston Swimming Club formed in 1886 it appeared to prefer using the often dangerous timber ponds down by the docks.

Because there appeared to be more demand in west Hull, the next baths to open was in Madeley Street, in 1885. This was followed by East Hull in 1898.

Trippett Street, meanwhile, was converted in 1904 into an exchange for the famed Hull Telephone Department, the only telephone company in Britain that would remain in municipal ownership.

Beverley Road, the successor to Trippett Street, should have opened much earlier than 1905, but it took the Baths Committee, under its chair Councillor John Shaw (*see right*), three years just to

buy the site, which although only 4,500 square yards in area, was split between 17 different owners.

As at East Hull, the design work was carried out by AE White, the City Engineer, but this time with a brief to provide three pools, compared with two at East Hull.

Rather than being categorised according to class, the largest, gala pool, was reserved, unsurprisingly, for men, and the two smaller pools for ladies and boys. Ladies entered via a separate door on Epworth Street, while the boys' pool was described at the time, somewhat bluntly, as being 'finished off in a way to adapt itself to the habits of those that use it'.

There was also a gymnasium (opened in 1906), and 48 slipper baths, but no wash house. (Indeed after the loss-making venture at Trippett Street none of the later Hull baths would have one.)

In later years Russian vapour baths were also added.

One aspect of life at Beverley Road that seems to have elicited most memories from older users was the baths' popularity as a dance hall during the winter.

According to oral histories recorded by the City Council's *Hull in Print* project, the baths formed part of what was called the 'taffeta trail', a string of dance halls up and down Beverley Road.

Whereas most public baths had one pool boarded over for the winter, Beverley Road had two. Apparently during the 1940s and '50s there would be modern dance music on offer in the large pool hall, while in the ladies' pool the accent was on Old Time dancing.

But undoubtedly the most illustrious musical night of the baths' history occurred on October 12 1933, when, as described in the *Hull Daily Mail*, 'trumpet wizard'

Louis Armstrong and his Harlem Band entertained over 300 'lovers of "hot" rhythm' on the occasion of Hull's annual Civic Week. (Satchmo had apparently been playing at Hull's Tivoli Theatre during the previous week.)

Beverley Road was said to have been similarly hopping during the Second World War, when Hull's braver souls would dance their way through air raids with fatalistic abandon as the docks were pounded by German bombers.

Saturday night dances continued at the baths right up until 1969, by which time the numbers were insufficient to justify the £3,000 costs of converting the pool.

But the dance nights are not forgotten. In the entrance hall a plaque commemorates bandleader Tommy Fisher, who played at the baths many times and died in 1986.

That same year also sounded the death knell of Hull's oldest baths on Madeley Street, demolished to make way for a new overpass.

There would also be partial demolition at Beverley Road.

While extensive, and ultimately award winning renovations took place at East Hull during 1986, both the smaller pools at Beverley Road were closed in 1985.

The ladies' pool was demolished to make way for a car park. The boys' pool was infilled and became the plant room for a new heating and filtration system for the main pool, which itself was modernised as part of a £1.8m refurbishment.

Thus within a few years the city of Hull lost four of its seven Victorian and Edwardian pools.

On the other hand, both East Hull and Beverley Road, which was listed in 1990, were now in a much improved state, and one which, happy to report, has continued until today.

Rarely are the chairmen of baths committees commemorated in quite the fashion accorded to John Shaw (1832–1923), whose portrait, crafted in brass by Leeds sculptor Edward Caldwell Spruce, is set in a tiled niche in Beverley Road's entrance hall. Chairman of the Baths and Wash Houses Committee and a councillor for 29 years, Shaw had started out at the age of 18 as Trippett Street baths' first engineer. He later ran a shop on Dagger Lane in the city centre.

Everywhere one looks at Beverley Road there are details to savour – art nouveau doorways, the barrel-vaulted entrance hall (albeit lacking its original ticket office), a piece of stained glass or a splash of mosaic. The Hull crest, with its three crowns, appears in several places; including over the door to the vapour suite (*above*) and on the floor by the main entrance (*right*).

▲ After the barely restrained flamboyance of Beverley Road's Edwardian Baroque exterior and its sumptuous main entrance hall, the **main pool hall** itself has a more typical, functional simplicity.

Following its renovation in the 1980s, the pool is divided into two sections, of 25m in length, with a small teaching pool beyond. The poolside cubicles have also

been modernised, with, as can be seen in the centre, locker areas for added flexibility. The poolside tiling and gallery floor is also modern.

Otherwise the polychromatic brickwork, gallery seating and balcony railings have all been faithfully restored, as has the original mechanism used for lowering the electric lights over the pool.

Elsewhere, other sections have been converted into a fitness suite, solarium, TV room and conference room. But the vapour suite is the original, and there is also a surviving section of the slipper baths area, although without the baths.

As to those plastic dolphins suspended from the pool roof, there are no doubt various schools of thought...

Case Study

Victoria Baths, Manchester

Opened September 7 1906
Address Hathersage Rd, M13 0FE
Architects T de Courcy Meade, Arthur Davies and Henry Price
Cost £59,939
Pools Men's 1st class 75' x 40', 2nd class 75 x 35', Ladies' 75' x 30'
Owner Manchester City Council
Operator Victoria Baths Trust
Listed Grade II* (1983)
Closed 1993

Behold the Taj Mahal of British swimming!

One of only five public baths in England to be listed Grade II*, the Victoria Baths was described by the *Manchester Guardian* at the time of its opening as 'probably the most splendid bathing institution in the country'.

The Lord Mayor aptly called it 'a water palace'.

Over a century later, and despite its closure as a bathing facility in 1993, those words still ring true.

It is no hyperbole to state that the Victoria Baths is the most lavishly constructed and most richly detailed pre-1914 baths that still stands in Britain, outstanding even by the extraordinarily high standards set elsewhere during the Edwardian era.

Thanks to its exposure on national television as the runaway winner of the BBC's *Restoration* series in September 2003, the Victoria Baths is also possibly the best known historic baths in Britain – a winner partly because, as many of those 282,000 viewers who voted for it later said, whether Mancunians or not, it reminded them of the much loved baths they had lost from their own communities. Baths that were built by the people, for the people.

But if all that were not enough, the Victoria Baths is of even greater significance when placed within the wider context of Manchester's standing as one of the great world cities of the early 20th century.

Already established in the early 19th century as the first great city of the industrial revolution, enriched initially by cotton and, in the 1890s, by the Manchester Ship Canal – itself a scheme of exceptional engineering and commercial audacity – Manchester entered the new century with a bravura that quickly manifested itself in sport and recreation.

As previously recounted in *Played in Manchester (see Links)*, in 1902 Manchester businessmen combined to build Britain's first purpose-built racecourse of the century at Castle Irwell. In 1910, a local brewing magnate bankrolled the construction of Old Trafford, Britain's first genuinely modern football stadium, home of Manchester United.

That same year the Manchester Ice Palace opened. Second only to Berlin's *Eispalast*, it was the largest and most advanced ice skating rink in Europe.

Add in theatres, cinemas, dance halls, billiard halls and sports grounds, and a picture emerges of a city that worked hard, played hard and was not afraid to splash out on its pleasure palaces.

And splash out is exactly what the Corporation did do, on Victoria Baths.

Fifty years earlier, Manchester had shown reluctance to adopt the 1846 Act, leaving it to the Manchester and Salford Baths and Laundries Company to build the city's first establishments.

Only in 1877 did the Corporation take over the company's assets (which by then included Mayfield and Leaf Street Baths), and begin its own building programme, so that by 1894 it had nine baths under its wing. (Of these, three, at Gorton, Newton Heath and Openshaw, had been built by district councils absorbed by the city in 1890.)

One characteristic of the city's swimming network was its lively inter-club rivalry, manifested in a regular programme of galas and water polo matches, particularly at New Islington Baths (where, as noted earlier, the world's first swimming record was recorded in 1889), and Osborne Street, whose water polo team represented Great Britain at the 1900 Olympics in Paris, and won the gold medal.

One of that famous team was John 'Rob' Derbyshire (*see page 119*), whose father, also John, was Superintendent at Osborne Street and later General Superintendent for all Manchester Baths. As told by Prue Williams in her history of Victoria Baths (*see Links*), Derbyshire used to do the rounds of his baths each Friday in his Corporation pony and trap, to pay wages and to check up on staff.

Derbyshire was one of several advisers called upon during the planning for the Victoria Baths, which seemed only fair as the building was not only going to serve as his new headquarters, but also his family home.

Planning started in 1895. In the minutes of the Baths and Wash Houses Committee there is no indication that the proposed building was to be particularly grand. The brief was simply for three pools, as at Leaf Street, New Islington and Osborne Street, with slipper baths, a public »

▲ Photographed before flats were built on the adjoining car parks in 2008, the linear efficiency of the **Victoria Baths** layout is evident.

Given a site that many baths architects of the period would have envied, particularly those in London, its designers opted for a conventional front block with three separate entrances, for first and second class males and for females, behind which were ranged the three respective pools. The Men's first class or Gala Pool, the widest of the three, is at the top.

Also in the front block were Turkish baths and 16 men's first class slipper baths. On the upper two floors was a committee room and a four bedroom apartment for the superintendent and his family.

Along the galleries of both the second class men's pool (*in the centre*) and the ladies' pool were more slipper baths, 23 for each.

At the rear of the pools (*on the right, above*) stood the filter room and boiler house, both topped by water storage tanks, and a laundry.

In the early 20th century the area around the baths, known as Chorlton-upon-Medlock, was quite different from today, with a more settled population and predominantly terraced housing.

Hathersage Road, meanwhile, on which the baths is built, was known until c.1960 as High Street.

Much of the area westwards, beyond Oxford Road, was poor and densely populated. But to the immediate south lay Victoria Park, a once gated, exclusive estate. Charles Hallé, Ford Madox Brown and Elizabeth Gaskell had all lived in the neighbourhood. The actual site of the baths had been a lawn tennis club.

The arrival of Owen's College (later Manchester University) in the 1870s, and the Royal Infirmary, opened at the same time as the baths, drew a new breed of professionals to the vicinity.

By the mid 20th century these middle classes had largely moved on, but the baths still attracted a wide spectrum of users, many of whom worked on or around Oxford Road. For them, the Victoria Baths was the nearest to a city centre baths that Manchester could offer.

Supplied by the Welsh firm of JC Edwards of Ruabon, the terracotta detailing at the Victoria Baths is rich with detail. The face of the sea creature appears several times, while above the windows of the Turkish baths section (at the west end of the front block) a mermaid and her mate appear to be enjoying some net gains.

>> hall, but no wash house or establishment laundry.

In the end it took three years to settle on a site – the grounds of the Victoria Park Lawn Tennis Club – and a further year before a deal could be struck for £750, in December 1899.

Visiting the location today it seems an odd choice for such a landmark building; a backwater almost. But at the time it lay on a tram route, on what was then known as High Street (even though that stretch of it remained predominantly residential).

Most important of all, from both a political and demographic point of view, the site straddled the borders of three wards, Longsight, St Luke's and Rusholme.

Once the site was purchased there followed three further years of planning whilst members of the Committee, and John Derbyshire, visited baths in Nottingham, Leicester and London.

One consequence was a decision to follow Leicester's example by sourcing water for the new baths from a bore hole. Drilling added £4,788 to the bill, but in the long run saved on water charges. It also avoided the criticism levelled at other Manchester baths that the water drawn from the mains supply was often yellowish.

As will be seen from the plaque (right), the architect's name usually ascribed to the Victoria Baths is that of Henry Price, who had been appointed to the new post of City Architect in January 1902.

But research carried out by the Architectural History Practice has confirmed that most of the basic design work was drawn up before 1902 by the City Surveyor, Thomas de Courcy Meade, and one of his assistants, Arthur Davies.

Price would nevertheless play a crucial role in honing the details and steering the project to completion.

Davies' plans of July 1901 were originally costed at just under £40,000 (having originally stood at £57,000, until it was agreed to omit plans for the public hall).

A year later work commenced, and in 1903 the foundation stone was laid, unusually, inside the largest of the three pools.

But as work progressed, by May 1905 costs had risen by £20,000; that is, 50 per cent over budget.

Much of this apppears to be down to Price's insistence on using – as recommended by the likes of AH Tiltman and Alfred Cross – superior materials, in order to reduce long term maintenance costs. For example, glazed bricks were used instead of pitch pine for certain partitions, porcelain slipper baths instead of zinc, terrazzo floors instead of spar, and wired glass in the skylights instead of ordinary glass. Watertight piping to convey the electrical services also added to costs, as did a late decision to add a laundry, and the choice of mahogany for all rails and balustrading.

Even so, the additional and extensive use of faience, decorated tiles, terracotta, mosaics and stained glass had nothing to do with durability. They were ostentation, pure and simple. Art for art's sake. Municipal bling.

Hardly surprising then that eyebrows were raised at the final bill of just over £59,000, even if, compared with its contemporaries in London, for example Haggerston – which cost a similar amount for one pool – the Victoria Baths was not exactly reckless.

The baths also served as a wonderful showcase for the

various Lancashire firms and artists whose products and designs were on display.

In that sense, as the images on these pages demonstrate, the Victoria Baths today is not simply a former public utility or swimming venue. It is a repository of British industry and of decorative arts.

Among the suppliers are several that crop up repeatedly in the field of public baths provision. Messrs Galloway, for example, supplied 'Lancashire' brand boilers to dozens of baths. They were based off Hyde Road, next to the then ground of Manchester City, half a mile east of the Victoria Baths.

The turnstiles came from WT Ellison's of Irlams o' th' Height, Salford, whose recently patented 'Rush Preventatives' were to be

found at virtually every major football, rugby and cricket ground.

But perhaps the most significant supplier, also from Irlam, was Royle's, suppliers of the Victoria Baths' water filtration plant, and soon to become a leader in the field. Described earlier (*see page* 117), the Royle's system gained the favour of the Baths Committee after they had seen it in operation, most likely at Bury, where it had been in use since at least 1904. It is thought that Manchester also trialled it around 1904 at its baths on Oldham Road, Newton Heath.

In theory the system – whereby water was pumped from the deep end, aerated via a large spray, filtered, reheated and then returned to one of the pools – should have put an end to the »

Crafted by George Wragge of Salford, this copper plaque, marking the opening day, is typical of the detail found throughout the Victoria Baths. Note that 19 councillors sat on the Baths Committee, far more than in most cities. On the other hand, Manchester did have 155 councillors overall, and the Education Commitee was even larger.

'fill and empty' system. Yet there is plenty of evidence to suggest that 'fill and empty' remained in operation at the Victoria Baths and elsewhere well into the late 1920s, when Royle's, Bell's and other companies finally perfected the filtration process. But in 1906 the prototype was clearly considered state-of-the-art, along with the boilers, electric bells and all the other modern devices of which the Corporation were clearly so proud on the baths' opening day in 1906.

In fact the Victoria Baths was not the only Manchester baths to open on September 7.

In the morning, a mile to the west, the Mayor also officiated at the opening of Moss Side Baths, on the corner of Broadfield Road and Bowes Street (close to Maine Road, where Manchester City were destined to move in 1923).

This smaller establishment, with one pool and 32 slipper baths, cost only £12,832 but was in truth more the product of Moss Side Urban District Council. (On its foundation stone, laid in 1904, the building was credited to District Surveyor, Henry Longley.) But that same year Moss Side lost its independence to its larger neighbour, and so once again Henry Price was tasked with finishing another man's work.

(In 1904 the districts of Withington, Chorlton-cum-Hardy, Didsbury and Burnage also became part of Manchester.)

After the Victoria Baths, Price went on to oversee four more baths before 1914. These were at Barmouth Street, in the east Manchester district of Bradford, in 1909, Harpurhey in 1910, and Withington, in 1913.

Of these, Harpurhey (closed in 2002 but Grade II listed), was the closest in scale to the Victoria Baths, having three pools, 66 slipper baths and a wash house, yet cost £20,000 less.

Withington, with two pools, 28 baths and no wash house, was even cheaper at £17,426 (and is in fact the only one of Manchester's pre-1914 baths still in use).

So was the Victoria Baths worth the expenditure?

Certainly it was popular. Agnes Campbell's figures for 1913-14 show it to have been the second busiest in the city after Leaf Street (in the more densely populated and poorer Hulme area), attracting 199,770 users (compared with 240,166 at Leaf Street). Outside London, only one other baths in Britain had comparable figures, that of Glossop Road in Sheffield.

Within the Victoria Baths' total, the Turkish baths recorded figures of 4,643 (including 1,237 women), which although less again than Leaf Street, and indeed several other provincial Turkish baths, was still highly respectable.

But what really stands out from Campbell's figures is the number of female swimmers.

Manchester, together with certain vestries in London, had started providing separate pools for women in the 1880s. But as we have noted before, these pools

This sumptuous hallway leading to the Gala Pool, is lined by tiling supplied by Pilkington's of Clifton, near Manchester. Designed by Frederick C Howells, similar examples can be seen at Lister Drive Baths in Liverpool, opened in 1904 (*see Chapter Nine*). The stained glass window (crafted by Christine Bedwell) and mosaic detail are also in the hallway.

were all much smaller than their male counterparts.

The ladies' pool at Victoria Baths, by contrast, was the same 75' length as both mens' pools and only five feet narrower than the mens' second class. This near parity was exceptionally rare, and was rewarded by the attendance of 40,435 female swimmers in 1913–14, far higher than any other baths in the provinces. Barmouth Street and Harpurhey, which also had good sized ladies' pools, also recorded high levels of usage, thereby confirming what many had refused to believe until then, that women wished to swim no less than men, but simply needed decent facilities.

In time of course the rationale for separate pools decreased. Mixed bathing on one day a week was introduced at Victoria Baths in 1922 (after the earlier trials at Withington), rising to two days a week by the 1930s. By then there was also less distinction to be made between the men's first class and second class pools, because improvements to the filtration system ensured that water quality was the same in all three pools.

But even after mixed bathing became the norm after the Second World War, the Victoria Baths' capacity to allocate one pool for girls and another for boys (the second class pool) made it ideal for school swimming sessions.

As a competition venue, the Victoria Baths also earned its keep, becoming the city's premier gala venue. One particular highlight in the Gala Pool was an appearance in 1912 by the Hawaiian Duke Kahanamoku, 'the human fish', who gave one of the first demonstrations in Britain of the then little known stroke called front crawl.

This and many other stories of life at Victoria Baths over the years may be found in Prue Williams' book. They cover the baths' usage as a dance hall, when the likes of Frankie Vaughan and Dicky Valentine would guest for the Phil Moss Orchestra (whose party piece was to dim all the lights so that the bands' fluorescent suits would glow in the dark).

There are tales of Sunny Lowry, who swam the Channel in 1933 (and later became an ardent supporter of the baths campaign), and John Besford, a member of the South Manchester Swimming Club, who famously won the European 100m backstroke title in Magdeburg in 1934, and with it a huge trophy which Adolf Hitler had commissioned, thinking that a German was bound to win it.

Remembered too is the go-ahead baths superintendent Frank Botham, who in the 1950s introduced carpet bowls during the winter, and in 1952 ordered England's first Aeratone Bath, an early form of jacuzzi, invented in Scotland. It became a favourite treatment for injured Manchester United and City players, just as the Turkish baths became a regular haunt for Manchester businessmen.

As the city's premier baths, by the mid 1930s the Victoria Baths also found itself to be the hub of Britain's largest municipal baths empire. The construction of four more baths during the inter war years meant that, including two outdoor pools, Manchester's Baths Committee, with its board room at Victoria Baths, held sway over 22 establishments, with 35 pools and 885 slipper baths between them. (Birmingham had more sites but fewer pools or baths.)

But it did not last. German bombs put paid to the city's two oldest baths, Mayfield and Leaf Street. »

There are more lavish Turkish baths, at Dunfermline and Harrogate for example. Yet there is a classic simplicity to those at the Victoria Baths, located in the centre of the front block. This is the view from the Calidarium, looking through to the Tepidarium, with the Russian bath and shampooing room beyond. As well as aiming to re-open at least one of the swimming pools, the Victoria Baths Trust is committed to reopening the Turkish baths as soon as funds will allow.

Gloriously restored in 2008, the Victoria Baths' extensive array of art nouveau stained glass flits between various themes. In the Cooling Room of the Turkish baths suite, the main window depicts a so-called Angel of Purity (*below*), while dotted around elsewhere are six panels showing sportsmen in action (*opposite*), but oddly enough no swimmers. The footballer is said to have been modelled on Reg Pointer, son of William Pointer, whose local firm almost certainly designed the windows. Reg died in action in the First World War.

》 The economic downturn of the 1970s and '80s would see eight more baths close between 1970–90.

At Victoria Baths, meanwhile, the laundry closed during the 1980s, the men's second class pool was converted into a sports hall and its slipper baths removed. The baths was also listed, in 1983.

By then, only two of the city's other pre-1914 baths remained operational, Harpurhey (listed in 1994) and Withington.

But Victoria Baths was the next to fall. Faced with repairs of at least £500,000, the Council preferred to close it, finally locking its doors on March 13 1993.

No matter that 16,000 people signed a petition in protest, the city's priorities now lay elsewhere; first with a bid for the Olympics, which failed in September 1993, then with a successful bid for the

2002 Commonwealth Games, which resulted in the opening of the £32m Manchester Aquatics Centre on nearby Oxford Road in September 2000. With its two 50m pools and a perfect location between the university and the city centre, the Aquatics Centre's credentials seemed to have eliminated any hope of a rescue plan for Victoria Baths.

Back on Hathersage Road, however, a quiet storm was brewing. Such was the affection for this water palace that within five months of its closure a Victoria Baths Trust had been set up. Its aim? To secure the fabric of the building so that, in the long term it might ultimately be brought back into use, partially or wholly.

Around the same time the Friends of Victoria Baths was established to support the Trust.

Briefly, this is what has occurred since. In 1998 the Trust, consisting entirely of volunteers, formed a partnership with the City Council, the local healthcare NHS Trust and a voluntary sector company, to bid for two tranches of Lottery funding, in order to turn the baths into a healthy living centre.

Both bids were rejected for failing to show how long term viability could be achieved.

But the Trust did achieve one breakthrough. In March 2001 they signed an agreement with the Council for the Trust to actually manage the empty building.

Regular clearing-up operations, partly funded by the Council, could then start in earnest.

But volunteers can only do so much. Faced with serious water penetration and dry rot, an appeal for emergency funding resulted in grants of £161,000 from English Heritage and £96,000 from the A6 Corridor Partnership, to allow at least some remedial work to start in 2002.

But this was only a holding operation, reckoned to secure the building for three to five years.

In 2003, ten years after the baths had closed, the Friends group stepped up its efforts by organising monthly Open Days, which proved extremely popular.

And then, in September 2003, to the delight and amazement of all the Trustees and Friends, the Victoria Baths hit the headlines by winning, by a clear margin, the BBC's first series of *Restoration* (in which the public were invited to vote for one of 30 buildings at risk). The prize? Lottery funding worth £3 million, plus nearly £500,000 raised by the *Restoration* fund from the phone-in votes.

But of course television is not like real life, and the victory was

by no means a panacea. Superb publicity, no question – a month after the programme Prince Charles popped by, as did the *Antiques Roadshow* in 2004. But in truth all the Trust and its partners had won was the *right* to bid for that Lottery money. It still had to submit a convincing project plan.

Moreover, £3.5m was not enough to realise the first of the Trust's stated aims of re-opening the Turkish baths and one pool. To do both, it was now reckoned, would cost in the region of £20m.

Nevertheless, as the restoration plans took shape, the building took on a whole new lease of life.

It became an educational resource for local schools.

In addition to tours and open days it become an arts venue (*see for example page 1*). A whole series of artists, photographers, musicians, dancers and performance artists filled the pool halls with their work, often with magical results.

The baths also became a popular location for television and film productions, such as *Life on Mars*, having already featured in a 1984 video called *Now Voyager* (in which Mancunian Barry Gibb of the Bee Gees tries out the Aeratone), and in the TV series *Cracker* and *Prime Suspect*.

On the baths' centenary a dance band recreated the atmosphere of Phil Moss and his band's 'Dancing in the Dark' nights from the 1950s.

Overall, an average of 10,000 visitors per year have passed through the doors since 2003.

But welcome though all this attention has been, it is only a means to an end, and so efforts continued behind the scenes to ensure that, finally, in March 2007, nearly two years later than planned, work was at last able to start on Phase One of restoration.

Lloyd Evans Prichard were the architects, joined by Buro Four as project managers, Firmingers (as quantity surveyors), Wright Muttershaw (structural engineers) and William Anelay (contractors), with a number of other expert craftsmen and women on hand.

Unveiled in September 2008, some of the results of this work can be seen on these pages; the restored stained glass, for example, the restored brickwork, roofs, terracotta, clocktower and skylights of the front block. Mosaic floors have been repaired, roof timbers replaced, and the clock now works again.

Combined, this cost £3.8m, split between £3m from the Heritage Lottery Fund, £450,000 from English Heritage, £150,000 from the BBC's *Restoration* kitty, £88,000 from Manchester City Council (still the building's owners), £62,750 from the Landfill Tax Credit scheme, £14,200 from charitable trusts, and £14,650 from the Victoria Baths Trust itself (primarily used for the stained glass windows).

The results are stunning, and should be inspected in person, by all readers, as soon as they have finished *Great Lengths*, and certainly by everyone who voted for the baths in 2003. After 15 years of being boarded up and weed infested, the Hathersage Road frontage has come alive, just as it must have appeared in 1906.

But, and of course there had to be a but, Phase One of the restoration still did not include the re-opening of the Turkish baths, as the Trust had hoped back in 2003. Instead, the work was confined largely to the fabric and basic services, and, what's more, to the fabric and basic services of the front block alone. »

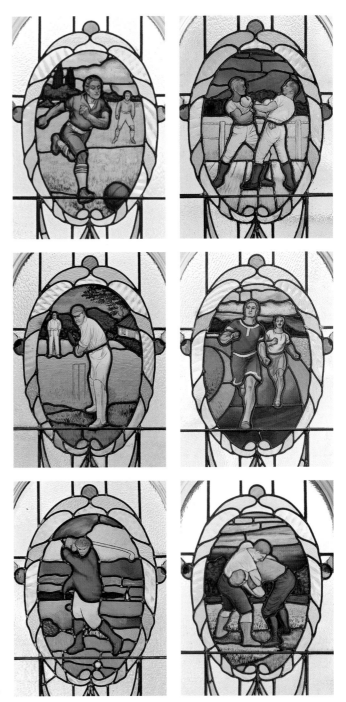

The Men's First Class, or Gala Pool – with the city's crest on the far wall, and its 45 surviving cubicles. On the right is the entrance to the gallery, where spectators would pay an extra few pence to watch galas, or one of the regular Friday night water polo matches.

›› In short, that still left the major task of restoring the three pool sheds, before the Turkish baths, let alone the Gala Pool, can be recommissioned .

It was with that in mind that in early 2007 the various partners involved with the baths appointed what is called a 'preferred developer', a company called Artisan Ship Canal Developments, whose constituent elements include property developers and Manchester City Council.

The developer's brief is to find ways to redevelop part of the site – notably the rear, where the old boiler house and laundry are situated – in order to raise enabling funds to complete Phase Two. Converting two of the pool sheds to other uses must also be considered as part of that process.

But a crash in the property market rather put all that on hold, so that yet again, by late 2008, the baths faced an uncertain future.

In 1906, £59,000 was deemed a hefty sum to pay for a public baths. Today, that figure is the equivalent of between £30-40m.

And now the Trust need to find in the region of £16m.

It may seem a vast amount. Yet in a city where sums of that scale are spent frequently on footballers, and in a part of the city where health care and education are the largest employers, surely it can be found.

The Victoria Baths, lest we forget, was a product of Mancunian drive and determination. It embodies so many of the qualities, beliefs and talents that made British urban life the benchmark for other nations to follow at the dawn of the 20th century.

It is a building of national, and even international importance.

To stop now in its restoration is quite simply unthinkable.

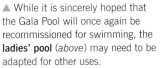

▲ While it is sincerely hoped that the Gala Pool will once again be recommissioned for swimming, the **ladies' pool** (*above*) may need to be adapted for other uses.

Needs must of course but this is much to be regretted, for the pool retains several original, and now quite rare features, such as the steps leading down into the deep end (which at most other historic baths have long since been replaced by less intrusive ladders), and, surprisingly, spittoons along the side of the pool. Clearly not all Edwardian ladies were so ladylike.

In common with the Gala Poool the ladies' also retains many of its cubicles, each with cast iron frames, wooden doors and curtains.

Note also that the gallery was designed not for spectators but for 23 slipper baths, since removed.

The slipper baths on the gallery of the **mens' second class pool** (*above right*) were also removed in the 1980s to provide extra space for sporting activities.

At the same time the pool was boarded over – using the same structure that had for many years been used as the winter dance floor in the Gala Pool – so that the area could be used as a sports hall.

This area now serves as a useful space for meetings, exhibitions and displays. Alison Kershaw's iconic *Well Loved* rope light sign (*see also inside cover flap*) now hangs on the far end balcony.

Case Study

Chelsea Manor Street, Kensington and Chelsea

Opened April 4 1907
Address Chelsea Manor Street,
SW3 5PL
Architect Wills & Anderson
Cost £33,000
Pools Men's 100' x 30' (now 25m
plus learner pool), Ladies' 95' x 28'
(now sports hall)
Owner Royal Borough of
Kensington and Chelsea
Operator Cannons Leisure
Management
Listed Grade II (1984)

Mention the name Chelsea and a host of associations come to mind; the football club and the arts club, the flower show and the Pensioners, Sloane Rangers, chic bars and fashionable boutiques.

But step back a few yards from King's Road, and there, in what looks more like municipal offices, stands the Chelsea Sports Centre, formerly the public baths of the Borough of Chelsea.

What we see now is actually the second baths to have been built on the site. The first, opened in 1877 and designed by E Perrett, engineer also of the floating baths at Charing Cross (*see page 62*), was

built by the Chelsea Swimming Baths Company. Not having any slipper baths, clearly it was not aimed at poorer residents in the area. (There was both a workhouse and a Peabody Estate close by.)

But nor did the rich support it in sufficient numbers and, in 1889, the baths went out of business.

In response, the following year the Chelsea Vestry finally adopted the 1846 Act and tried to buy the baths. This proved harder than anticipated, however, and in 1896, under pressure from ratepayers in the more deprived northern part of the Vestry, it instead commenced building baths in Kensal Town,

on Wedlake Street (backing onto the Grand Union canal). Costing £27,000, its architects were Harnor & Pinches, who had earlier designed baths in Bow, and would go on to design the Central Baths in Hackney in 1897.

Meanwhile the Vestry did eventually manage to purchase the Manor Street site, and after a design competition (assessed, incidentally, by the eminent architect Norman Shaw), Harnor & Pinches were commissioned again.

But before work could start, local government reorganisation resulted in the Vestry becoming the Borough of Chelsea, and having deemed Harnor & Pinches' plans to be too expensive, the new administration decided to hold a fresh competition.

This time the winner was the partnership of Herbert Winkler Wills and John Anderson.

Now had their winning scheme been implemented, there can be little doubt that the new Chelsea Public Baths would have become one of the finest establishments of the period. There were to have been three pools, a basement Turkish bath, 142 slipper baths, a laundry and superintendent's flat. But above all was the grandeur of its English Renaissance elevations, centred upon a dignified entrance on King's Road, complete with a double height inner courtyard.

The architects had been directed towards this style and the use of red brick and Portland stone dressings in order to marry it with the adjoining Old Vestry Hall (completed by John Brydon in 1886 and now listed Grade II*). The same style was also to be adopted for the Town Hall, destined to be built alongside the new baths.

But once again the plans were called back – too expensive still at £60,000 – and when the final drawings were agreed in 1904 it was clear what had occurred. The Borough had decided to give the Town Hall pride of place on King's Road, and relegate the entrance to the baths to Chelsea Manor Street.

The plans were also scaled back to two pools, 90 slipper baths and no Turkish baths, and turned by 90 degrees (*see right*). To save further costs a bore hole, 470' deep, was drilled, and an underground concrete storage tank built under the Chelsea Manor Street frontage.

Completed for half the budget of the earlier proposal, the baths opened in 1907, just as work started on the Town Hall next door. (Designed by Leonard Stokes and now listed Grade II, this still stands, although used for other purposes since Chelsea and Kensington merged in 1965.)

Since then there have been few major changes. In 1978 the ladies' pool was converted into a sports hall, and the main pool boomed to 25m, with a small learner pool at the end. The poolside cubicles were removed and one of the slipper bath areas converted into a gym. Elsewhere in the building, a solarium, café, crèche and therapy suite have been installed.

Compared with many of its contemporaries, Chelsea's baths appears quietly dignified, even restrained, which is hardly what one would expect of King's Road.

But for those of today's Chelsea set who cannot afford the area's private health clubs, its merits go well beyond fashion.

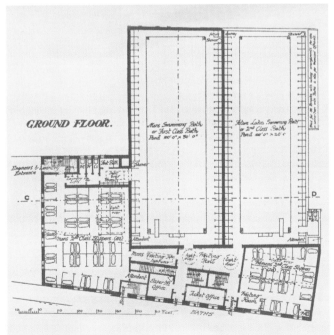

In 2008 the pool at Chelsea (in the centre of the plans on the left) was relined as part of a £700,000 refurbishment, which also gave new life to the polished, pew-like benches in the gallery. Other original features include the balcony, open iron framed roof, iron columns and a fireplace and safe in the ticket office. Next door to the baths is the Old Vestry Hall, whose cupola can be seen on the left of the exterior view opposite.

Case Study

Moseley Road, Balsall Heath, Birmingham

Opened October 30 1907
Address Moseley Road, B12 9BX
Architect William Hale & Son
Cost £32,924
Pool sizes first class 81' x 32'
(closed), second class 71' x 33'
Owner/operator B'ham City Council
Listed Grade II (1982) II★ (2004)

Of Britain's surviving public baths built before 1914, the Victoria Baths in Manchester is, as previously noted, the most lavishly constructed and most richly detailed.

But some experts would argue that Moseley Road Baths, which opened thirteen months later and cost barely half as much to build, is at least Victoria Baths' equal in architectural importance, if not in scale or detail, and is even superior in terms of how much of its original form, layout and fabric remains intact. Not least, uniquely, it possesses not one but three slipper bath departments (*see page 121*), one of which was in use as recently as October 2004.

Moseley Road has further significance in that it is one of a pair of buildings on the site; the baths, as opened in 1907, and the adjoining public library, completed eleven years earlier.

Despite this gap, and the fact that different architects were involved, the pair share not only a party wall, but also a single listing.

The combining of public baths and libraries on one site dates back to ancient Greece. In Britain, one of the first joint schemes after the 1846 Act was just north of Birmingham, at Wednesbury in 1878, while two miles from Moseley Road is one of the finest examples, on Green Lane, Small Heath (opened in 1902). Other joint schemes of this era were at Dewsbury, Duke Street (Sheffield), York Road (Leeds) and East Hull.

But in all these cases either the baths, or the library, or both, have ceased to function. Indeed, apart from Moseley Road, the only other functioning example from pre-1914 is at Upperthorpe, Sheffield, now a Healthy Living Centre.

For its rarity value as a working baths and library combination, therefore, and because of the baths' architectural integrity, in August 2004 Moseley Road's combined listing was upgraded from Grade II to II★.

Only four other public baths are similarly ranked. One is the 1964 National Recreation Centre at Crystal Palace (*see Chapter Seven*). The others, all featured earlier, are at Collier Street (Salford), Ashton-under-Lyne and the Victoria Baths.

Moseley Road is therefore the only Grade II★ baths that predates 1914 and remains in use.

Now of course this should be cause for celebration, as should the fact that Birmingham also boasts two other Edwardian pools where one can still swim: Woodcock Street (built in 1902 by the Council but now part of Aston University), and Tiverton Road, Selly Oak (built by King's Norton and Northfield District Council in 1906 but taken over by Birmingham in 1911).

No other British city has three Edwardian pools still in use.

Like the curate's egg, however, Moseley Road is only to be enjoyed in parts. In fact, only one part; that of the former second class pool.

Apart from the lobby and certain staff and plant areas, every other section – the main pool, the three slipper bath areas, the laundry, club room and flat – are, as of 2008, out of use, suffering from faults that range from minor, to worrying, to sufficiently serious for the baths to have been placed on the *Heritage at Risk* Register in 2005. (That means that although occupied, it is still vulnerable through neglect and decay, rather than from demolition.)

Moseley Road baths is also the only building to have featured on the Victorian Society's *Top Ten List of Endangered Buildings* twice in succession, in 2007 and 2008.

Assuredly, this was not what the people of Balsall Heath signed up to when the baths were first proposed in May 1890. »

▲ Lacking a local stone of its own, Birmingham embraced terracotta with such enthusiasm that it has often been described as a symbol of the city's 'Civic Gospel'.

Here at the **Moseley Road Baths and Free Library** its impact can be readily appreciated. Buff terracotta (supplied by Jabez Thompson & Co. of Northwich), added colour, especially next to red bricks, was easily cleaned in polluted air, and lent itself perfectly to the prevailing trend for Jacobean and Flemish Renaissance detailing.

On the right is the 1896 library, by Cossins & Peacock, with its clock tower counter-balancing the entire composition. In the foreground is the baths, with its two octagonal ventilation towers serving the three slipper bath sections, each with their own entrance and large windows facing the street. Both pools are behind this block.

And just in case any Balsall Heath residents should forget who provided this magnificence in their midst, above the door to the women's baths (*opposite*) was displayed the city's crest.

This was sculpted by Benjamin Creswick of the Birmingham School of Art, a man whose own life had itself been an expression of 'Art and Industry'. Creswick had been a knife grinder in Sheffield when his creative skills were spotted by no less a figure than John Ruskin. He was also, as may be discerned from the two figures on the crest, a member of the Century Guild, one of the foremost societies of the Arts and Crafts movement.

Moseley Road's chimney stack, partially restored in 2005, rises up from between the two swimming pools and is 110 feet tall with a cast iron ornamental cap. The brickwork was described as a mixture of 'dull red sand bricks' and 'picked Oldbury bricks'.

» At that time Balsall Heath still came under the jurisdiction of King's Norton, but had its own Local Board of Health, set up in 1862. The area also once had its own subscription baths, opened in 1846, with private baths priced at one shilling, and access to a 100' x 40' open air pool, costing 6d, or 10s 6d for a season. This first Balsall Heath Baths also offered 'stabling and other conveniences for the accommodation of gentlemen attending in carriages or on horseback'.

After the death of the owner in 1873 the baths was offered for sale to the Local Board. But the Board felt that Kent Street Baths in central Birmingham was near enough, and the baths never re-opened. (Its location, off George Street, just west of Moseley Road, is however marked by Bath Walk.)

As Balsall Heath meanwhile developed into a moderately well-to-do district, in May 1890 the Local Board – which only three years earlier had voiced strong opposition to any overtures from its larger neighbour – received a letter from Birmingham's Town Clerk offering to build both baths and a free library, if Balsall Heath threw in its lot with the city.

Birmingham also made offers of libraries to two other districts it coveted, Saltley and Harborne.

Clearly the offer struck a chord in Balsall Heath, because in November 1890 'a meeting of ratepayers and owners of property' assented to the proposal.

All three areas subsequently joined Birmingham in October 1891. Accordingly, Saltley library was upgraded in 1893. Harborne gained its library in 1892. But in Balsall Heath progress was slower.

The site on which the library and baths were to be built could hardly have been better. Bought for just under £4,000, it was on a busy high street, served by trams, and there was a road at the rear to allow for coal deliveries.

Of its total of 3,247 square yards, one fifth was allocated to the library, which was duly completed in April 1896, at a cost of £5,243.

Yet it would be eleven years before the baths followed suit.

The reason for this delay, quite literally, was boring.

Being naturally blessed with an intricate web of streams and rivers, water is never far beneath the surface in Birmingham, which is why all four of the city's baths, at Kent Street (1851), Woodcock Street (1860), Northwood Street (1862) and Monument Road (1883), were fed by boreholes.

But for some reason, at Balsall Heath tenders for drilling were not prepared until late 1897, and it would be another five years before the contractors, Messrs Timmins & Son of Runcorn, were finally able to report success.

Why so long? Apparently two or three times boring tools became detached underground, setting back the search for water by months at a time. Then, at about 500 feet down, the drillers met a bed of rock, which distorted the steel tube liner of the hole and jammed the whole operation.

But Timmins persevered, and by mid 1903 eventually, at a depth of 725 feet – deeper than any other well used by a baths in Birmingham– struck a source that yielded 8,250 gallons per hour.

While all this had been going on below ground, on the surface Moseley Road was becoming a hub of communal activity.

A short walk to the north of the drilling site a Friends Institute, designed by John Bowen and also

decked liberally in terracotta, opened in 1898. Opposite the library, the handsome Moseley School of Art, by WH Bidlake, followed in 1899. Elsewhere in the city, meanwhile, by the end of 1902 the Baths & Parks Committee had overseen the successful reconstruction of Woodock Street (*pages 113-14*), and, in conjunction with the Free Libraries Committee, the opening of the new baths and library in Small Heath (*page 111*).

Yet still the ratepayers of Balsall Heath waited for their promised baths until, finally, in March 1904, a year after having been assured of the water supply, the Council invited architects to submit plans.

From a shortlist of twelve, the winning plans were from William Hale & Son of Colmore Row, Birmingham. For Hale senior, who was President of the Birmingham Architectural Association, this was his second major commission in the area, having designed the Balsall Heath & Moseley Institute – another great centre of improvement – a short distance along Moseley Road, in 1876.

But it was the firm's first baths, so no doubt the Hales were glad to work alongside the Birmingham Baths' experienced Superintendent Engineer, Job Cox, who oversaw the engineering works.

The brief was as follows: on the ground floor two pools, first and second class; 16 first and 16 second class slipper baths for men; six first and eight second class baths for women, and on the first floor, a committee room, establishment laundry and flat.

Instead of allocating this flat to the baths manager and his family, as was the norm elsewhere, at Moseley Road the accommodation was allocated to the baths' money-taker, who had only to descend »

▲ Originally, the hatch seen here, in what is now the baths' sole entrance, was where an attendant dispensed towels and costumes to users of the **first class pool** or the **mens' first class slipper baths**, which were accessed through the door on the right (*and also illustrated on page 121*). Tickets for both were meanwhile issued from a central ticket office, which had similar bowed fronts with windows serving each of the three departments. In the late 1950s, this central office was partitioned to form a waiting room (*to the left of the camera*). The attendant's office then became the main ticket office.

The former curved front of the original ticket office in this area can still be made out, however, in the patterning of the terrazzo floor.

Note that to the left of the ticket window there is an archive photograph of the slipper baths. Further images are displayed in the waiting room, along with other examples of memorabilia, potted plants and community notices.

This is a lived-in building whose history and pedigree, despite all its current drawbacks, are much treasured by its staff and regulars.

▲ Closed since August 2003, the former **men's first class pool** at **Moseley Road Baths** is surely the most dramatic Edwardian pool hall in Britain. Certainly its 'balconettes' overlooking the deep end (*see also opposite*) – reminiscent of French baths of the early 20th century – are unique in this country, while below them at pool level, similar round-headed, tiled cubicles are found only at Woodcock Street (*see page 113*). Also of note are the iron roof trusses, which although again similar to those at Woodcock Street (and Nechells and Green Lane), are of a particularly large span and with more elaborate perforations.

Overall the roof is thus a rare deviation from the standard form of the day (as seen at, for example, the Victoria Baths in Manchester).

Yet the pool hall is in a parlous state. As can be seen, the spectator gallery has had to be propped and the end gable windows boarded over, while, unseen, the roof is leaking in sections and, worst of all, the bases of the cast iron trusses are rusting within their tiled brick surrounds. And of course the longer remedial works are delayed, the greater the risk to the fabric.

>> a flight of stairs from the flat to go directly down into the ticket office. How confined his or her daily routine must have seemed.

On an invitation to the baths' opening on October 30 1907, now held by the Birmingham archives, someone scribbled, 'Lord Mayor absent through illness, ceremony performed by Deputy, Ald. Reynolds… weather inclement.'

But the baths' prospects were excellent. Within six years Moseley Road's annual usership topped 144,000 (including over 20,000 female swimmers), second only to Kent Street and Monument Road, both of which were in more populous districts.

Thanks to the completion of additional baths at Nechells in 1910, plus the annexation of four others in 1911 when the city once again expanded its boundaries – to take in Victoria Road, Aston (1892), Tiverton Road, Selly Oak (1906), Grove Lane, Handsworth (1907) and Bournville Lane, Stirchley (1911) – by the First World War the city's Baths Department was Britain's third largest, after Manchester and Liverpool.

It included eleven indoor baths, three outdoor pools and four cottage baths, making a total of 23 pools, 490 slipper baths and three Turkish baths. Combined, these facilities drew 1.3m users in 1913–14, and played host to 41 swimming clubs.

Birmingham was also at the forefront of adapting its baths for winter usage. In 1905 a Social Institutes Committee – set up to offer 'recreation of the broadest and most comprehensive character, on neutral ground, for both sexes, unassociated with any sect or political party' – started staging events at Northwood Street, spreading to five other

baths by 1911. At Moseley Road activities included bagatelle, cards, chess, draughts and whist drives.

So successful was this initiative that delegations from other cities came to study the scheme, which, claimed the police, did much to improve public order.

The Social Institute Committee was eventually wound up in 1945. But under the city's new Baths Superintendent, Jack Moth (appointed from Woolwich), dances and indoor bowls continued at Moseley Road well into the 1950s. (Indeed so many winter dances were there at Birmingham baths – Wednesday night being the Moseley Road slot – that there was even a Baths Ballroom Trophy.)

Under Moth, annual usage of the city's baths exceeded three million in 1951 (six times the total when Moseley Road opened). >>

Moseley Road's unique balconettes were linked by stairs to a club room for members, and lined with ivory white glazed bricks with dark green banding supplied by the Stourbridge Glazed Brick Company. Elsewhere, the lobby and circulation areas are finished in cream coloured glazed bricks, with faience and vitreous tile work supplied by Doulton. Cracks in the balcony floor can just be seen.

Refurbished in 2005 and now the only department in use, the former second class pool at Moseley Road lacks the decoration of its larger neighbour and, before 1963, lacked cubicles altogether. Instead, bathers changed on one of 98 oak seats along the sides, behind a communal curtain if they wished, and with only a shelf for their clothes. Also, until the 1930s all the windows were leaded and had stained glass, to provide 'a pleasant and cheerful aspect to the interior'.

›› Particularly popular still were the slipper baths at Moseley Road.

According to a 1946 survey, only 35 per cent of households in Balsall Heath had a bath, compared with a national average of around 50 per cent. (In the semi-detached, inter war estates of nearby Hall Green the figure was 99 per cent.)

Even as recently as May 1973, a total of 1,091 people took slipper baths in one week at Moseley Road.

Yet ten years later this figure had dropped to 280 per week.

No doubt this was mainly owing to better housing. But in other respects these were tough years for Balsall Heath, as unemployment and crime blighted the area.

The baths suffered too, its state of repair made worse by local government cutbacks and by the refocusing of resources on the new generation of leisure centres.

In fact in the circumstances it could be said that Moseley Road was lucky to survive at all. Grove Lane closed in 1975, as did both Green Lane and Kent Street in 1977. In the late 1980s the axe then fell on Bournville Lane and Saltley and on two inter war baths, at King's Heath and Kingstanding. Monument Road closed in 1994, followed by Nechells in 1995.

Birmingham was hardly unique in closing older baths. But the effect was to place Moseley Road's

deteriorating condition into even sharper relief.

So when Moseley Road also closed in October 2004 – for emergency repairs, it was stated – most users feared that it would never reopen.

Yet it did, after a public outcry and pressure from various bodies led to the Council spending £1.25m on short term remedial works. These included repairs to the chimney, to the filter systems, to terracotta window details and to the second class pool.

But when the building re-opened in October 2005, relief in the community was tempered by disappointment. Only the smaller of the two pools remained in use.

The first class pool had been sealed off, as had the last remaining section of slipper baths (the former men's second class area), even though this had been in use, albeit fitfully, until 2004.

Given that the nearest public pools were some distance away, the effect was marked. Particularly hard hit were local faith groups whose access to single-sex swimming sessions became increasingly restricted, while staff at the baths were forced to turn away individual swimmers because the single pool was pre-booked by schools or clubs.

Even so, the single pool was used by some 30-35,000 people in 2007.

There is not space to explain fully what has occurred since, or why, it would seem, the building's fabric has been allowed to deteriorate further since 2005.

Like so many historic baths, Moseley Road has become trapped in the midst of a seemingly intractable political and funding battle, one that has divided not only members of the Council's

SHALLOW WATER

ruling Conservative-Liberal Democrat coalition, but local community groups too.

In November 2006 the setting up of the Friends of Moseley Road Baths added another voice to the debate, along with those of the Victorian Society and English Heritage, all anxious for at least some resolution so that crucial remedial works could begin.

The issue has been further complicated by a city-wide debate on swimming facilities generally.

Nechells, closed in 1995, re-opened in 2006 as an Enterprise and Community Centre (*see Chapter Nine*), but without swimming facilities. Both Tiverton Road and Harborne Baths (b.1923) remain in need of attention, while in 2006 the Wyndley Leisure Centre (1971) closed in order for asbestos to be removed, followed in 2008 by Sparkhill (1931), for repairs to its roof. (Both, however, are expected to re-open in 2009.)

At the same time, the Council repeatedly delayed a decision on whether to proceed with building the city's first 50m pool, whose location would clearly have an impact on existing pools.

Back at Moseley Road meanwhile, a series of consultants' reports resulted in the drawing up of three main options in 2008.

In brief, the first, costed at £2–6m, was to mothball the building, erect a temporary cover to prevent further water penetration, and then either set about more detailed studies as to what the next stage might be, or carry out all urgent works to at least secure the fabric, but with no long term goal set.

A second option was to restore the building in full, including bringing both pools back to use.

This, it was estimated, would cost between £20–22m.

Finally, a third option proposed to restore the gala pool, but convert the smaller one to community space, at costs ranging from £22.7m – £23.3m.

In defence of the second option, the Friends group (whose website carries an excellent virtual tour of the building – *see Links*) argued that Balsall Heath needs two pools.

In support of the third option, some local residents and Council representatives contended that the area equally needs community space, and that the single pool option would result in lower maintenance costs.

In terms of conservation, clearly Moseley Road is rich in assets. Its slipper baths, attendants' offices, its ticket office, drying racks, water tank and first class pool are all rare surviving features of a way of life that was once common to millions of British people.

Moseley Road itself, it must also be said, is richly endowed in historic buildings. In a one mile stretch either side of the baths, from Highgate Park and the Friends' Institute in the north, to a former Tram Depot in the south, there are 15 Georgian, Victorian and Edwardian buildings of note, ten of which, dating 1810–1906, are listed by English Heritage.

Of course Balsall Heath must look to the future. But with such historic treasures in its midst, here surely is an opportunity for regeneration based on existing assets, with the baths and library forming the central focus.

When the people of Balsall Heath threw in their lot with Birmingham they waited 16 years before their baths were ready. A century later they find themselves waiting again.

Only this time, the whole nation is watching.

Moseley Road's drying racks in the former establishment laundry are unique survivors. The ticket office for the women's slipper bath area is also rare. No one questions the need to bring the building back to life. But if by doing so features such as these are lost, then they are lost forever, not only to Balsall Heath or Birmingham, but to Britain as a whole.

Case Study

Royal Automobile Club, London

Hidden away from the gaze of Joe Public, there are over 1,600 private indoor swimming pools in Britain today, in hotels, health clubs, corporate headquarters and government buildings.

Some of the grandest that London has known – such as at the Bath Club, Dover Street (b.1894), the Ladies' Carlton Club, Grosvenor Place (b.1931 and designed by Clough Williams-Ellis), and at the offices of Bourne & Hollingsworth, Gower Street (also 1930s) – are no more.

The 1884 pool at the London Polytechnic on Regent Street is now a University of Westminster bar called the Deep End, while the pool at the YWCA (by Sir Edwin Lutyens in 1932) on Great Russell Street, is part of a Jury's Hotel.

Among those operating today are pools in the Shell Centre (on the South Bank), Senate House (Malet Street), Tower 42 (formerly the NatWest Tower) and, hardly surprisingly, Buckingham Palace.

But not one of these (with great respect Ma'am), is as fine as the pool of the Royal Automobile Club on Pall Mall.

Opened March 23 1911
Address 89 Pall Mall, SW1Y 5HS
Architect Charles Mewès and Arthur Joseph Davis, with Edward Keynes Purchase
Cost £250,000 (complete building)
Pool 86' x 30'
Owner Royal Automobile Club
Listed Grade II* (1970)

Founded in 1897, and granted its royal status by Edward VII, himself a keen motorist, the club's aims were 'the protection, encouragement and development of automobilism'.

But in the spirit of the Edwardian age, the enjoyment of pleasure was also high on their agenda, and as, for the elite of the day, high style meant French style, the club turned for their new headquarters to the fashionable Anglo-French partnership of Charles Mewès (1858–1914) and Arthur Joseph Davis (1878–1951).

Both hailing from Jewish families, Mewès, later described in the RIBA Journal as 'the best type of the intellectual Frenchman', and Davis, a refined *bon viveur* who lived in Mayfair, trained at the Ecole des Beaux-Arts in Paris (as did Sir John Burnet, architect of the Drumsheugh Baths Club in Edinburgh, *see page 90*). Mewès had been the architect of the Ritz Hotel in Paris, opened 1896 (also with a wonderfully indulgent swimming pool), while as a partnership the pair went on to design the London Ritz (without a pool), ten years later.

As at the Ritz, behind its Beaux Arts finery and classical pomp – much of it modelled on an 18th century Parisian palace in which the Automobile Club de France was based at the time – the RAC Club was actually a thoroughly modern building.

Built on a concrete base with a steel frame, it featured central heating, air conditioning, lifts, a telephone switchboard and its own private post office (still in use, and the only one of its kind other than at Buckingham Palace).

There were also Turkish baths, a gymnasium and a billiard room, to which squash courts have since been added.

As to the pool's luxurious decor – much of which was apparently completed by French workers

'invariably smoking' and wearing smocks and sabots – it has been variously described as Roman, Pompeiian and Egyptian.

Yet it might easily, for 1911, be considered also daringly modern.

Whichever, so greatly was it admired that Mewès and Davis were immediately asked to repeat the theme for the *Imperator*, the world's first ocean-going liner

to have an indoor pool, launched by the Hamburg-Amerika line in 1913, then again for one of its sister ships, the *Vaterland* in 1914.

That same year, shortly before the First World War broke out, Davis also designed a pool for Cunard's *RMS Aquitania*.

None survives, of course, which makes the RAC pool, seen here after its recent refurbishment, all

the more precious, and enticing.

Apparently Winston Churchill and George Bernard Shaw were once regulars. And if you know the right people you too can enjoy the experience, as a guest, or, should the fees be no obstacle, as a member.

But be warned. The rules state quite categorically, no cravats to be worn.

'Like stepping into a painting by Sir Lawrence Alma Tadema,' was the description of one RAC Club member. The *Architectural Review* thought that the pool, with its mosaic columns, marble walls and shimmering green water, glimpsed as one stepped down into the club's lower vestibule, was 'the most impressive *coup d'oeil* in the whole building'.

Case Study

Govanhill, Glasgow

Opened 1917
Address Calder Street, G42 7RA
Architect AB Macdonald
Cost £13,000 approx.
Pools 75' x 35', 50' x 25', 25' x 12'
Owner Glasgow City Council
Listed Grade B (1992)
Closed 2001

Among Britain's dwindling number of Edwardian public baths, Govanhill does not immediately stand out for its architectural qualities.

Though handsome enough on its Calder Street frontage (*above*), and with a first class pool still admirably intact (*opposite*), it is hardly an arresting building in the same way that the Victoria Baths or Moseley Road Baths catch the eye.

And yet in the wider story of how historic baths have been saved from demolition, Govanhill is of immense national significance.

During the spring and summer of 2001, Govanhill was the scene of an epic 140 day occupation by campaigners.

They were protesting against Glasgow City Council's decision to close the baths rather than invest £750,000 for immediate repairs, let alone an estimated £3 million for a more thorough overhaul.

That this occupation endured for so long, and was followed by an eight month picket outside the building, marks out the South Side Against Closure group (SSAC) as amongst the doughtiest of baths campaigners on record; second only to those who occupied Fulham Baths for over a year in 1979–80 (*see Chapter Eight*).

But whereas the Fulham campaign ultimately resulted in only parts of the building being saved, and not for swimming,

the campaign for Govanhill has scarcely abated in its intensity since 2001, and in late 2008 appeared to be on the brink of a major breakthrough.

As a result, there is now a good chance that Govanhill will reopen for swimming, and much else besides, under the auspices of a specially formed Govanhill Baths Community Trust (GBCT).

But before summarising the Trust's intentions, some background is necessary.

Govanhill's first baths, built in 1877 on Butterbiggins Road, was privately run. Meanwhile, between 1878 and 1902 Glasgow Corporation erected ten public baths with pools, followed between 1904 and 1916 by a further 12 baths and wash houses.

Planning for a public facility in Govanhill started in 1912 under the auspices of the City Surveyor, Alexander Beith Macdonald. An elaborate foundation stone (between the entrance doors for men and women) was then laid on July 2 1914 by the Lord Provost, Sir Daniel Macaulay Stevenson. Behind this, intriguingly, was placed a casket containing 'documents' of an unspecified nature.

Within weeks of the ceremony the First World War erupted. A year later Macdonald died. And so, when the baths did finally open in 1917 (the exact date is unknown), there were no celebrations, and for the next 83 years Govanhill Baths served its purpose without troubling either the history books or the headline writers. ›

▲ Despite eight years of disuse, the **main pool** at **Govanhill**, seen here in 2008, remains in good order. Apart from the addition of modern ventilation units and lighting, it is also little altered. Note for example the recessed steps at the deep end and the high backed seats at the rear of the gallery (which created a barrier for an extra row of standing spectators to lean against).

Also of interest, under their layers of peeling red paint, are the reinforced concrete roof trusses.

Although this material became commonplace at swimming baths between the wars, few examples from before 1918 are extant.

The same roof form can also be seen in Govanhill's second pool (which has no gallery), while the much smaller third pool has a flat roof with skylights. All three pools retain their original spittoons.

In 2006 a Buro Happold survey of the baths found that although the spectator gallery requires some £250,000 worth of strengthening work, the rest of the building was essentially sound.

As illustrated opposite, the baths' **Calder Street** frontage is of an Edwardian Baroque style, faced in the red sandstone ashlar that is common in Glasgow.

Within this entrance block there were originally 40 slipper baths for men, 10 for women and Turkish baths. Reduced and refitted in the 1970s, these departments all remained in use until 2001.

The peak of the main pool roof can just be seen behind the parapet of the entrance block.

》 As with most baths of this period, the building was divided into three departments.

On a rectangular site there were slipper baths and Turkish baths in the front block, behind which were three pools – one full size, one medium and one small (effectively for men, women and children) – with a 68 stall wash house, or 'steamie' at the rear, accessed directly from Kingarth Street.

Although not large by London or Manchester standards, and certainly not costly to build, this combination of facilities made Govanhill the largest single baths complex in Glasgow.

In 1971 the wash house was converted into a laundrette, and later still into a gym. Otherwise, the only other major alterations have consisted of new fixtures and fittings in the slipper baths and Turkish baths areas, the modernisation of the heating and filtration systems, and the replacement of the brick chimney with a modern steel version.

Thus while the likes of Maryhill Baths (1898) and Whitevale (1902) closed during the 1970s and '80s, Govanhill remained operational, and when listed Grade B in 1992 was in fact the city's second oldest functional baths, after North Woodside (see page 78).

Govanhill even managed to outlive all four of the baths built between the wars, at Whiteinch and Pollokshaws in 1923, at Govan (1925) and at Shettleston (1929).

But not for long.

Rumours that the Council was considering closing Govanhill started to circulate in mid 2000 amongst parents of children who belonged to the resident Kingston Swimming Club, which had formed in 1892 and numbered around 240 members.

Confirmation of the closure plan was eventually announced by the Council in January 2001. A 12,000 signature petition had no effect, and so on March 21, eight days before the official closing date, a group of activists went for a swim… and did not go home.

Over the next 140 days, a core group of up to 200 individuals took turns to maintain the occupation. But if their actions failed to reverse the Council's stance, they did help to create an extraordinary rebirth of community spirit.

Govanhill, it should be noted, falls within the constituency of Shettleston, which according to various indicators has been assessed as not only one of the poorest constituencies in Britain, but also one of the unhealthiest.

Nerves were already frayed in the area owing to the recent closure of a social work office and a school. Threats to the local library were also ongoing. If the baths also closed, it was felt, this would be the last straw.

The area's Muslim community was further worried because whilst single sex swimming sessions were perfectly feasible at Govanhill, the nearest alternative pools, at Bellahouston and the Gorbals, featured large expanses of glazing and were therefore not deemed suitable for women.

Both during and after the occupation Calder Street and the Peace Park adjoining the baths staged a regular series of street parties and demonstrations. A fund raising shop set up across the road by the Friends of Govanhill Baths became the nerve centre of the campaign.

But there was a sorrier side to all this activity.

Of thirteen individuals charged with various offences by the

police following the ending of the occupation in a dawn raid, only one campaigner was actually fined. But the fallout left many in the area distrustful of the police.

Similarly fractured was the relationship between the community and local politicians, in a constituency that had already recorded the lowest turnout in Scotland at the last general election.

Had there been full and frank consultation throughout the process this breakdown of trust might just have been averted. But equally, had the campaign leaders not been so determined, and seemingly so indefatigable, Govanhill Baths would not now have any future as a facility for swimming.

Year after year their efforts – commissioning reports, drawing up business plans and galvanising support – ground down the Council's resistance, until in August 2006 it finally agreed to grant the Trust a 99 year lease.

In early 2008 another hurdle was crossed when representatives of the Council formally met with Trustees to establish a project team aimed at the re-opening and refurbishment of the baths.

That in the meantime the City Council had announced a £6m refurbishment of Maryhill Baths, on the other side of the city, while still refusing to invest more in Govanhill, was frustrating. But then, to be even sitting around a table with Council representatives was deemed by the campaigners to represent progress.

As of late 2008, the plans for Govanhill Baths, drawn up by Nord Architects, envisaged a blend of newbuild and existing elements, to create what they described as a Wellbeing and Sporting Complex.

This would include restoring the two main pools for swimming, while converting the third into a hydrotherapy pool.

Other areas of the building would be converted into a gym, a café with roof garden, a crèche and an asthma clinic, with the rear section cleared to make way for a social housing development.

The front block would be linked more directly to the adjoining open space, while newly created circulation areas and a new side entrance would open up the building's interior to make it lighter and more welcoming.

Estimates for these plans ranged between £7.5m to £9m, but the Trust was at pains to emphasise that the opening of the pools was its first priority.

Earlier we noted how the Chester Swimming Association has taken over the running of the City Baths.

The GBCT may have to go one further by not only running Govanhill Baths but owning it too.

This was hardly what the campaigners set out to do when they first challenged the Council, nor even when they secured the promise of a 99 year lease.

But in 2008 the Trust was told that in order to be eligible for vital funding from the Lottery, it, and not the Council, had to own the building.

Yet, not unreasonably, the Council would not hand over the building until it was sure that the Trust had gained all the necessary funding.

In October 2008 the baths were opened to the public for the first time in over seven years, for the first of what was hoped might be a regular series of Open Days.

In the end, nearly a thousand people attended: some who had swum there as children and wanted to show their own children and grandchildren; some who had never been but wished to show support; some who not been inside the building since the occupation – and whose lives had been transformed by the experience – and many local swimmers for whom the nearest alternative pools are inaccessible, and who have therefore given up altogether.

Govanhill Baths, they agreed, had long been at the heart of the community, but in many ways the battle for its future had brought the community closer together than ever before.

As the American bluesman WC Handy once sang, 'You don't miss your water till your well runs dry.'

The Trust aims to have at least some of that water back in the building by March 21 2011, the tenth anniversary of the start of the occupation.

Occupational therapy – Govanhill's ladies' pool and the former slipper baths corridor await their makeovers.

One of the most bitterly contested baths closures of recent years was that of Bristol North, Bishopston, in October 2005. Protestors briefly occupied the building before being evicted. Another campaigner stood as an independent in that year's general election. But his efforts, together with a petition signed by 6,400 local residents, failed to sway the council, and the Grade II listed building is now destined to be converted into other uses. Designed by the City Engineer Lessel McKenzie, Bristol North Baths was actually half completed before the First World War, before being opened for swimming in August 1922. In total six baths were built in Bristol between the wars, of which by late 2008 only two survive (*see page 178*).

Chapter Six
Inter War 1918–1945

As Britain emerged from four years of conflict in November 1918, the prospect of a renewed surge in public baths provision looked highly unlikely.

The Carnegie UK Trust's Report, published in 1918, arrived too late and at the wrong time to have a meaningful impact, while its author, Agnes Campbell, went off to become a head mistress in Jamaica, leaving behind a Britain not so much 'fit for heroes' as promised by Prime Minister David Lloyd George, as one plagued by shortages and social unrest.

To compound the nation's sorrow, after the loss of nearly 660,000 British combatants – including Olympic water polo gold medallist Isaac Bentham and breaststroke record holder Percy Courtman – 230,000 more Britons fell victim to the flu pandemic of 1918–19. Amid widespread health fears, swimming in a public pool cannot have held much appeal.

Reflecting these grievous losses, the Amateur Swimming Association's handbook for 1914 had listed 1,468 swimming clubs. By 1920 this had dropped to 875.

Yet such was swimming's enduring popularity that it took only nine years for club numbers to return to their 1914 level, while user numbers at public baths as a whole – for swimming, slipper baths and wash houses – also rose steadily. Just two examples: between 1914 and 1932 the annual total of users at Liverpool's public baths rose from 1.32 million to 2.23 million, and in Birmingham from 882,000 to 1.69 million.

An increase in population during that period – despite the carnage of the First World War – can account for only a small percentage of that rise.

Instead, other factors were at play, as indeed were the British people, or at least those fortunate enough to be in full time employment.

For them, famously, the 1920s was the decade of the *palais de danse*, of booming attendances at cinemas and football grounds. The Empire Exhibition at Wembley in 1924–25 attracted an extraordinary 27.1 million visitors.

As the 1920s wore on, a whole range of sporting novelties captured the public's imagination: greyhound and speedway racing, darts, snooker, ice skating and ice hockey. Cycling, rambling and camping took off too, as did, from 1930 onwards, youth hostelling.

Britain's seaside resorts, meanwhile, thronged with pleasure seekers.

Partly this reflected the extension of workers' rights to paid holidays, increasing from 1.5 million eligible in 1925 to at least 9 million by the mid 1930s.

No doubt the fashion for sport, exercise and outdoor life in general was also borne out of a longing for fun and freedom after the privations of the war and its troubled aftermath.

But whatever people's motivation, it was a trend that government was keen to foster.

During the war, the armed services had been shocked by the poor health and lack of fitness of home grown recruits, particularly compared with troops arriving from Australia, New Zealand and other colonies.

Now, following the creation of the new Ministry of Health »

Launched by Capt Bert Cummins from his home in Croydon in 1922, *Swimming Times* evolved into an international treasure trove of news, results, titbits and adverts. Its tone between the wars was often jaunty. Club events went 'swimmingly'. New divers 'took the plunge', or in winter were 'wrapped by enthusiasm, a very fine blanket'. In 1971 *Swimming Times* became the offical organ of the ASA.

Opened in 1922, St Matthew's Street Baths in Ipswich illustrates the transitional stage between designs of the pre-1914 period and those of the 1930s. Note the arched and plastered ceiling with recessed lantern lights, and the proscenium arch framing the diving stage – both features characteristic of the inter-war years – while following the pre-war trend the upper gallery sits above old-style poolside cubicles (screened off here in readiness for a gala). The ceiling and neo-classical columns are the only recognisable features that survive since the building was converted into a social club in 2006.

» in 1919, it was time to build a healthier Britain; fitter, leaner, and more efficient in the workplace. A workplace, incidentally, where as a result of the wartime economy there were now greater numbers of women, some of whom, aged over 30, had, in December 1918, voted in an election for the first time. There was also, consequently, a growing number of women now serving on local councils, where they were able to lobby for equal rights at swimming baths.

School swimming came to the fore too. As noted earlier, Birmingham was possibly the first authority to offer subsidised swimming sessions for schoolchildren in 1875, followed by several other provincial cities.

In 1890 London school boards extended this provision by allowing schools to offer swimming lessons within school hours. Now, following the 1918 Education Act, this right was granted to all school boards (although swimming did not become an official part of the curriculum until the 1944 Education Act).

A visit to the baths thus became an increasing part of the nation's collective experience, loved and loathed in equal measure. Moreover if they lived in Bradford, Liverpool or Glasgow, children were just as likely to learn to swim in specially built school pools. At its peak between the wars, Liverpool's Education Committee operated 32 such pools on its premises.

As to the construction of new public baths, at a time of acute economic hardship – punctuated by the General Strike of 1926 and the economic crash of 1929 – indoor pools were an expensive luxury for local authorities.

Consequently, there appeared on the scene a new generation of baths, different from those we have been featuring so far in one key respect. They were open air.

Many of these outdoor pools, it is true, were built not only to cater for swimming but to respond to the new cult of sun worship. Exposure to sunlight, it had been discovered, helped combat rickets and tuberculosis. Suntans, meanwhile, once derided in fashionable circles, became a badge of health and glamour.

Equally important was that pool construction created work. By 1922, it was estimated, one million ex-servicemen were still jobless. To help counter this, the Ministry of Labour (itself formed in 1917) offered grants to local authorities prepared to engage unskilled men in building works. Open air pools suited this policy perfectly, being cheaper and simpler to build than indoor baths, and cheaper to run.

Among the first authorities to adopt this scheme were Cardiff Corporation, which built two open air pools in 1922 at Splott Park and Llandaff Fields, and London County Council, which built three, at Highbury Fields, Peckham Rye and Southwark Park, all opened in 1923. Also in 1923, six weeks after the opening of Wembley Stadium, Britain's largest outdoor pool, 376' x 172', opened in Blackpool.

This trend towards outdoor provision was to gather further momentum during the 1930s.

Some outdoor facilities, it has to be said, were comparatively basic

bathing places created alongside lakes or rivers, or as seaside tidal pools. But the majority were fully enclosed, and from 1931 became known more commonly as 'lidos'. That is, they were urban beaches, with pools, cafés and sun terraces.

A more detailed appraisal of Britain's lidos and open air pools can be found in the companion study to this book, *Liquid Assets* (see Links). But in this context, a number of issues are noteworthy.

Firstly, for the only time in the history of public baths provision, the construction of open air pools outstripped that of indoor pools.

An estimated 300 outdoor facilities were built in Britain between 1918–40. This compares with some 135 indoor public baths during the same period. (Note, however, that owing to the economic climate only 41 of these were built during the 1920s.)

Secondly, unlike their indoor counterparts, shaped as they were by Victorian conventions, outdoor pools were designed without class distinctions. As Sir Josiah Stamp said at the opening of Morecambe's lido in 1936, 'When we get down to swimming, we get down to democracy.'

Thirdly, a key attraction of open air pools was that they were more geared towards mixed bathing.

As noted in the last chapter, mixed sessions had been trialled at selected indoor baths in London and Manchester before 1914. After the war this trend spread slowly. At St Matthew's Street, Ipswich, for example (see opposite), mixed sessions were restricted to 7.00-9.00am on weekdays and 7.00-10.00am on Sundays.

Scotland's first trials followed in 1927, while by the early 1930s sessions had been extended to 13 of Manchester's 19 baths.

Even so, the numbers of people taking advantage of the sessions remained small. During 1936–37, of the total 1.68 million admissions in Manchester, only 77,344 attended mixed sessions.

The trend nevertheless had an impact on the design of new baths. No longer requiring separate entrances or complex circulation routes to keep the classes and sexes apart at all times, modern baths could be cheaper to build and more efficient to operate.

One of the last multi-pool baths to have distinct pools for first and second class men, and for ladies, was Greenwich, opened in 1928.

Thereafter we begin to see pools given different names. In 1931, at Sparkhill in Birmingham (see right) comes the first known reference to a 'learner pool'. At West Ham in 1934 the three pools were labelled 'major', 'minor' and 'schools'. (This last pool featured the novel concept of twin shallow ends, to enable more children to be taught at the same time.)

But there was another reason why it was no longer appropriate to ascribe class distinctions to different pools. In the preceding chapter we learnt how filtration systems before 1914 had failed to bring an end to the 'fill and empty' system. That all changed in the mid to late 1920s.

It is impossible to credit one engineering company or one local authority with the breakthrough.

But we do know that the Porchester Baths in London (see page 186), opened in 1925, had as its motto, 'every day is clean water day', and that the London Borough of Islington felt sufficiently proud of its new water filtration and purification plant at Hornsey Road to stage a formal opening ceremony on October 29 1927.

It is also known that the nearby Highbury Fields outdoor pool was similarly equipped by the LCC.

Clearly these improved systems worked better than any of their predecessors, because in August 1929 the Ministry of Health issued a circular, *The Purification of the Water of Swimming Baths* (see Links).

Although an advisory rather than a statutory document, it made clear that any local authority wishing to raise loans for indoor or outdoor baths would have to build into their plans 'an adequate filtration plant' operated by 'qualified supervisors' who would be expected to keep 'concise records' on a regular basis.

The circular also made practical suggestions, all of which would become standard in new baths.

Most important of all in design terms was that cubicles were to be located away from the poolside, »

Sparkhill Baths, Birmingham, opened in July 1931, featured the earliest known 'learner pool', positioned so that children of all ages could swim under the same roof. In the single sex pool beyond, doorways led to separate changing areas. Birmingham's Baths Committee, it was said, had learnt much from their trip to Continental baths, especially in Germany. The crystal clear water was, however, an advance 'Made in Britain'.

WINDSOR CENTRAL BATHS, BRADFORD.

BEFORE Installation of Paterson Filters.

AFTER Installation of Paterson Filters.

▲ Engineering companies such as Royles of Irlam, Bell Brothers of Denton, Berry & Sons of London and Paterson's of London all placed regular advertisements in *Swimming Times* and *Baths and Baths Engineering* during the late 1920s and 1930s.

The efficacy of each system was measured in terms of its 'turnover period', that is, the time it took for the whole body of water to pass through the filters. For busy indoor baths (used by perhaps 1,300 – 2,000 bathers per day), a turnover period of not more than four hours was recommended, or 3.5 hours if there was to be an evening gala. Six hours was probably sufficient in less busy locations, but not in hot weather, when a sudden inrush of hot, perspiring bathers could add extra pressure on the filters.

Water was drawn from the deep end by pumps, through a strainer, and into the sand-filled filter tanks. After passing through the sand, the water would then be warmed, aerated and chlorinated and returned back to the pool via inlets in the shallow end.

Baths operators thus saved money on water charges, on re-heating, and on paying overtime to staff who would otherwise have to work at night, maybe twice a week, to fill and empty each pool and scrub it down in between.

They could also expect more paying customers, drawn to the better quality of water on offer.

Paterson's 'before and after' photos above provide evidence enough of the difference filters could make. But consider also this story from London in August 1927.

An eleven year old had drowned in the open air pool at Willesden. So cloudy was the unfiltered water – 'It was absolutely black,' said the boy's father – that the attendant dived in but could see nothing, and it took a policeman a further 20 minutes before he found the body, in six feet of water at the deep end.

An extreme case, perhaps. But a powerful endorsement for filtration.

» while showers and footbaths, each provided with soap, were to be placed at poolside entrance points.

The circular further noted that in busy periods and during heatwaves the staff at some baths were merely drying costumes and towels before hiring them out again, rather than washing and sterilising them after each use. This, it emphasised, was 'a disgusting practice likely to transmit infection'.

Stricter regulations and the capability to provide clean water seven days a week, clearly represented a leap forward. But it also meant that there was no longer any meaningful distinction between the first class and second class bathing experience (other than perhaps the quality of the cubicles and the size of the tanks).

The advances in water treatment also had ramifications for the management of baths.

One of the first measures taken by the Ministry of Health, in 1921, had been to set up a National Association of Baths Superintendents. Now, to add to the duties of superintendents came a legal responsibility for water quality and general hygiene.

In other words, a job that had once been mainly managerial now became also highly technical.

This was a trend endorsed by a leading spokesman for the baths movement, architect Kenneth Cross, son of Alfred (see page 112).

Kenneth Cross (1890–1968) had joined his father's architectural practice in 1922, and in 1927 delivered a lecture, *Public Baths and Their Future Development*, to the Royal Society for the Promotion of Health (see Links).

Parts of it clearly rehashed his father's views. But there were some interesting new details too.

For example we learn from Cross that the desired water temperature of pools at that time was 72-75° F (or 22-24° C).

By comparison, in his 1906 book his father had alluded to a norm of about 70°(21° C), which suggests that by the 1920s, thanks to improved boiler systems and better insulation, water temperatures had risen by 2-3° C.

But when we compare those 1927 figures with today's norms of 28-30° C, we see that not only are modern swimmers more cosseted, but that our pre 1939 pools are operating at temperatures some 4-7° C higher than those for which they were designed.

Cross's 1927 lecture also noted how, prior to 1914, the brickwork forming the typical pool tank had needed to be around 2' 3" thick. Now, reinforced concrete had reduced this to a mere 4-5".

As to the future, Cross envisaged baths forming part of modern civic centres.

'The town hall, the public library, the baths, municipal gymnasium, club rooms, restaurant, dance hall, theatre, art gallery and cinematograph might well form such a group of co-ordinated and well-designed buildings in which the jaded ratepayer might find consolation and relief according to his taste.'

He could well have been describing the Billingham Forum, opened in 1967.

Cross had a further chance to comment on developments in his next publication, commissioned by the ASA and titled *Modern Public Baths and Wash Houses*.

The book – to which we shall return – was well timed, for around 1930 the pace of change and of baths construction quickened considerably. It will »

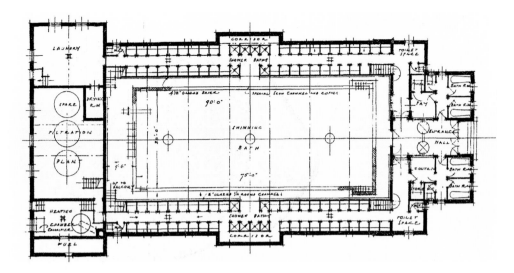

▲ **Ashington Baths, Institute Road, Northumberland,** opened 1931, was a typical low cost layout of the period, notably with pool access via showers, as per the Ministry of Health's 1929 guidelines.

Designed by Marshall & Tweedy of Newcastle and costing just £12,000, Ashington was one of around 20 indoor pools funded by the **Miners Welfare Fund**.

Overall, between 1920–39 the MWF invested some £30m in mining districts, mostly on pithead baths (as legislated for by the 1911 Coal Mines Act), but also on health centres, canteens, sports grounds, community halls, libraries and even bus shelters.

Initially its funds derived from a 1d levy paid by colliery owners on every ton of coal produced, rising to 2d in 1926, but dropping to a halfpenny per ton in the 1930s. To be eligible for funds each project had to be set up as a charitable trust, and with an agreement that the miners contribute, typically 3–4d a week towards the costs.

As of 2008, only five MWF funded swimming pools remain in use, all run by local authorities; at Ashington, Creswell (*below*) and Sutton-in-Ashfield (both 1924), Scisset, near Huddersfield (1928) and Sherwood, Mansfield (1934).

A sixth MWF pool survives at Buckley, Flintshire (1928), where it is hoped that the building, which closed in 2005, might be adapted for community use. (There is also a former MWF outdoor pool in the Castle Grounds, Tamworth, now used as a play centre.)

That it took until the 1920s for Britain's coal mine owners to match their European counterparts by providing pithead baths, and even then only aided by contributions from the miners themselves, is

in itself an indictment of their attitude, especially given the lack of bathrooms in miners' homes. Yet here were miners also contributing towards swimming pools.

At Sherwood in 1934, for example, in addition to the pool, pithead baths were built for 2,000 men, together with a canteen, a bicycle shed and an 'electrical apparatus for boot cleaning and greasing'. Of the total costs the Sherwood Colliery Company paid £20,200, and also agreed to supply water and energy free of charge. But the MWF still had to contribute £12,250.

In 2009 Sherwood Pool will undergo a £4.5 million revamp funded by Mansfield District Council. But without the miners' pennies there might have been no pool at all. For this reason, of all the nation's historic pools, those funded by the MWF represent a unique category.

Sherwood has one other claim. It was once the home pool of Rebecca Adlington, star of the 2008 Olympics, whose thoughts can be read on page 7.

▲ In an attempt to add a dash of modernity, around 20 London baths were lit up by neon signs during the 1930s. This is the last known survivor, at **Hornsey Road, Islington**, which in 2008 was being restored as part of the building's redevelopment into flats.

Meanwhile two rather brutalist baths – at **Poplar, Tower Hamlets**, opened 1934 (*top right*), and at **Kent Street, Birmingham**, 1933 (*right*) – have not operated as pools since 1988 and 1977 respectively.

Urmston Baths, opened 1933 (featured in *Played in Manchester, see Links*), with its unique central glazed dome over a round pool with rectangular wings (*bottom right*), was demolished in 1987.

» be recalled that only 41 public baths were built in the 1920s. Over the following decade that number would increase to at least 94.

In the midst of that flurry, in 1934 the baths industry – for it had become exactly that – even gained its own monthly journal, *Baths and Baths Engineering*, packed with advertisements, reviews of new products and articles on the latest baths designs.

There was much to report.

Between 1934 and 1937 just over £2.5 million worth of loans were sanctioned for baths construction by the Ministry of Health, an unprecedented level of spending. Baths costing in excess of £100,000 were now common.

Moreover, as the case studies that follow will demonstrate, the 1930s could well be considered the most exciting era ever in swimming pool design. As Harold Fern, President of the ASA wrote in *Swimming Times* in February 1935, 'Some of these new baths are of a character which even the most optimistic of us never thought was possible a few years ago, and, indeed, it can with truth be said that they are unsurpassed in any other part of the world.'

The 1930s was the decade that reinforced concrete construction and Art Deco – a style that lent itself so well to recreational architecture – brought added glamour, lightness and grace to the swimming arena.

It was a time when underwater lighting (at Doncaster in 1932) and wave machines (at Wembley in 1934) were introduced. At Airdrie in 1936 porthole windows were installed so that spectators could view people swimming from a basement level (an idea borrowed from the Netherlands). Loughborough College did the same at its new pool in 1939 as an aid to swimming instructors.

In May 1933 Watford Central Baths became the first baths to be powered solely by electricity, and therefore require no chimney. Elsewhere, pre-war high pressure steam boilers were replaced by more efficient low pressure boilers powered by coke, gas or oil.

Also much reported on during the 1930s were two pieces of legislation affecting public baths.

Part Eight of the 1936 Public Health Act was in effect a complete redraft of the original 1846 Act and all its subsequent amendments. From an accumulated total of 68 sections, the new Act reduced these to 14, and in doing so cleared up many of the anomalies arising from changes to local government.

Regarding baths management, the main changes were as follows.

Charges for swimming, slipper baths and wash houses were now to be at the discretion of the local authority, rather than being set by government as a scale of minimum charges. (Despite this, charges stayed remarkably low, even when compared with pre-war levels.)

Local authorities were now empowered to draw up byelaws for the regulation of their baths, particularly in relation to water quality and the conduct of bathers.

They were also, significantly, given the power to regulate private swimming baths for which entrance charges were made. (This was to target the growing number of roadhouses that offered open air pools of often dubious quality.)

One aspect of the new Act did not please the swimming lobby, however. The ASA had lobbied Parliament to withdraw the clause permitting local authorities to board over pools between October and April.

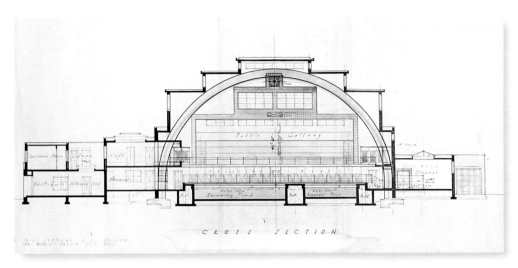

CROSS SECTION

They failed, even though baths in Scotland – most of which stayed open during the winter – had proved that there was demand.

But at least the Ministry of Health appeared to have noted the ASA's concerns, for also in 1936 it issued its own memorandum urging that baths should at least be kept open as long as possible, in order to improve 'the physique of the youth of the country'.

This renewed emphasis on fitness, clearly influenced by reports of German militarisation, resulted in the 1937 Physical Training and Recreation Act, whereby local authorities could apply for grants to create playing fields, gymnasiums, swimming baths, bathing places and holiday camps.

A *Times* editorial, entitled The Cult of Fitness, on April 8 1937, argued that the 'Fitter Britain' campaign was not an attempt to emulate 'the militarism of totalitarian states' but to ensure that 'a democrat should not be distinguished by his debility.'

Yet in truth, when it came to strategically planned sports

provision, Britain had fallen behind its European neighbours, Fascist and democratic alike.

In the case of swimming, for sure before 1914 it could be said that Britain's public baths led the world. But clearly several of the innovations introduced to Britain during the inter war period were pioneered on the Continent, where Germany, Austria and Hungary were particularly active in baths construction during the 1920s.

So too was France.

According to one source, in 1922 there were only 20 public baths in the whole of France, of which seven were in Paris. This compared with some 700 in Britain, indoor and outdoor, and an estimated 1,360 in Germany. But the French soon made up for it, in style if not in numbers.

At Tourelles on the outskirts of Paris, for the 1924 Olympics they built the world's first aquatic stadium. Measuring 50m in length, with heated water, lane markers and four concrete stands seating 10,000 spectators, Tourelles – albeit an outdoor facility – set the standard for all long course »

▲ Liverpool City Surveyor Albert Jenkins borrowed an idea from Germany for identical baths he designed for the new suburbs of **Norris Green** and **Dovecot,** both opened in 1936 and named after Baths Committee members William Roberts and Harold Davies respectively. (The latter is illustrated on this book's cover).

Within a single hall measuring 131' x 90', there was a main pool (100' x 35'), children's pool (45' x 20') and, for first time in Britain, a separate diving pool (42' x 20', with a depth of 10' 6").

As at Poplar (*opposite*) and several baths of the 1930s, the pool hall was lit by stepped, clerestory windows.

The three pool format was not a success however. Both Liverpool baths were plagued by high energy and maintenance costs. Safety concerns led to the diving pools being converted into teaching pools, and in the 1980s acoustic dampers had to be installed to counter the echo chamber effect.

Dovecot closed in March 1988, followed by Norris Green in 1995, and both were later demolished.

▲ 'Fresh air, sunlight, exercise and companionship are essential to the fullness of life,' wrote Kenneth Cross, architect of the **Pier Approach Baths, Bournemouth,** opened in 1937, closed in 1984, and replaced, ironically, by an IMAX cinema that itself closed after only three years and was voted Britain's ugliest building by Channel Four's *Demolition* programme in 2005.

Cross also argued that pools should not be designed to cater for music. Proscenium arches, such as at **Kent Street, Birmingham** (*above right*), opened in 1933, merely interfered with the diving stages, while the necessarily hard, smooth surfaces of the walls and ceiling played havoc with the acoustics.

Not that this put off promoters. Throughout most of the 20th century hundreds of baths staged dances and concerts, among them **St Matthew's Street, Ipswich**, seen here being boarded over for the winter (*right*). Led Zeppelin played there in the 1970s, while one of Cross's own designs, at Epsom – opened in 1939 and almost identical to Bournemouth – hosted the Rolling Stones in 1963.

» competition pools to follow, such as Frankfurt (1925), Bologna (1927), and Amsterdam for the 1928 Olympics.

In 1929 the Piscine Molitor in Paris showed how an indoor and outdoor pool – a *bassin d'hiver* and a *bassin d'été* – could operate within the same complex. Not until the 1960s would something similar appear in Britain (as reported in the next chapter).

Two other characteristics set British pools apart from their Continental counterparts, again until the 1960s.

Firstly, in Britain there was never any likelihood of state funding or support for a long course (or 50m) competition pool, and secondly, while there seemed to be no objection to installing metric diving boards – standard in Britain by the 1930s – pool dimensions remained defiantly Imperial.

As recommended by the ASA the most common standard lengths remained, as before 1914, at either 75' or 100', although in the 1930s some pools did stretch to 120', or even 132' in one instance (at Seymour Place in Marylebone).

As to depths, these increased a great deal during the 1930s.

Until 1914 most deep ends measured 6–7'. During the 1930s this increased to between 9'–10' 6" at most new gala pools.

Where diving boards higher than 3m were fitted however, the recommended minimums set by the Fédération Internationale de Natation (FINA) extended depths further. For example Westminster's Marshall Street, opened 1931 and designed by Alfred and Kenneth Cross, had a 5m board, but a deep end of only 10'. But by the time Kenneth Cross came to design Seymour Place, in 1937, and both

Bournemouth and Ironmonger Row in 1938, the new standard depth was 12'.

But all these pools fell short of international standards for long course events, which had to be 50m in length (or 165'), with a minimum depth of 4.5m (15') in order to accommodate a 10m diving board.

Clearly the absence of such facilities put Britain's swimmers at a disadvantage compared with their European, American and Australian rivals (a complaint that persists until the present day).

It also meant that when the ASA decided at long last to centralise its annual national championships in July 1935, there were only two options; either to hire the new Empire Pool at Wembley (of which more below), which would have been an expensive gamble for an as yet untried event, or to use one of the larger outdoor pools.

It settled on the Open Air Baths at South Shore, Blackpool, which held 3,000 spectators.

With its usual jocularity, the *Swimming Times* dubbed this historic event 'Swimbledon'.

In common with the headquarters of tennis, however, open air pools were vulnerable to the elements. It was therefore clear that only an indoor pool would suffice, and that, not for the first time in British sporting history, in the absence of any public facilities able to meet long course standards, the ASA would have to depend on the private sector.

Three privately financed indoor swimming stadiums appeared during the 1930s.

One was the aforementioned Empire Pool at Wembley (*see page 196*), built initially to stage the swimming events at the 1934 Empire Games, and later host to the 1936 ASA National Championships and the 1948 Olympics. Also in 1934 was opened the SS Brighton (*page 180*), followed in 1937 by the swimming pool at Earl's Court (*page 212*).

Speculative ventures they may well have been. But in terms of their engineering and architectural specifications, they set standards that were genuinely as good, if not superior than any of their counterparts abroad.

They were also designed to stage a form of entertainment that reached new levels of sophistication during the 1930s.

At the highest level these aquatic spectaculars – a blend of mass, synchronised displays accompanied by light shows and music – featured star performers such as Johnny Weissmuller, the US Olympic swimmer who had made his name in Hollywood as Tarzan.

At local level, they featured the likes of 'Daredevil Peggy' and the 'Lucratics', who advertised their services in *Swimming Times* and were very much in the tradition of professional performers going back to the Beckwith family.

Another popular act was diving supremo Pete Desjardins, from Miami. His 1934 tour took in 30 British pools and was seen by over 250,000 spectators, mostly at local public baths. His 1935 tour itinerary read Marshall Street, Woodford Green, Repton, Derby, Darwen, Coventry, Birmingham, Burnley and Bingley.

Meanwhile at international level, Britain may have lost its ranking as a premier swimming nation, but between 1920–32 local clubs still managed to produce several Olympic medallists and world record holders, including Joyce Cooper, Lucy Morton and Elizabeth Davies.   »

SIEBERIZE

- *The* HYG-GARD-ALL CLOTHES HANGER SYSTEM IS SPECIALLY DESIGNED FOR
- **SWIMMING BATHS** *and*
- **OPEN AIR POOLS**

UNRIVALLED and UNIQUE. IT PROVIDES FACILITY for DRYING and AIRING CLOTHES ABSOLUTE HYGIENE at ALL TIMES NEAT PRESERVATION of ALL GARMENTS EASY and SPEEDY CHANGING ELIMINATION of MAINTENANCE CHARGES MAXIMUM SAVING of SPACE LOW COST OF INSTALLATION

YOUR **CLOAKROOM**

- *Free* SERVICE

A scheme showing the most economical and space saving install-ation for your establishment will be submitted, free of charge and without obligation, on receipt of dimensions of the space available.

Minimum Cost!   Maximum Benefit! AN INVESTMENT NOT AN EXPENSE !

JAMES SIEBER · AFRICA HOUSE · KINGSWAY · LONDON

▲ Olders readers will hardly need reminding of the once ubiquitous **Hyg-Gard-All** wire basket system, introduced during the 1930s as a more efficient alternative to the old system of changing cubicles, where bathers left their clothes for the entire duration of their swim.

Although costly to install and to staff, and requiring space which, in existing baths was not easy to create, Kenneth Cross (in whose 1938 book this advert appeared) reckoned that by using baskets four or five bathers could use each cubicle during the average time it would have been occupied by one bather under the old system.

But how to maximise revenue without overcrowding the pools?

One requirement of the basket system was that bathers had to carry or wear numbered keys, tags or rubber wristbands in order to retrieve their clothes. It was therefore a simple step to colour code those items and allocate each colour a time period.

Shown above is a rare indicator light from the 1930s. When one of the four coloured bands lit up, bathers knew that their allotted time was over.

The light, as advertised on an internet auction site, is one of many items of baths memorabilia avidly sought by collectors, one of whom, Joan Gurney, has assembled the superb Bathing Bygones Collection.

This includes a 1934 standard issue **Nottingham Baths** bathing slip (*below*). Such slips cost 4-6d to buy at the time, but could be hired with a towel (similarly embossed) for free. At auction today the price would be nearer £20.

One reason that baths operators preferred bathers to hire costumes rather than bring their own was that they could ensure they had been sterilised, and that the dye would not discolour the water.

» Competitive swimmers were to be found in every sector of the workplace too. There were clubs for the police and for the old boys of public schools. In London's 13 Business House Leagues (four for ladies, nine for men) there were 101 teams in 1935, among them the BBC, GEC and LCC, Harrods, Selfridges, Unilever, Bovril, Peek Frean, WH Smith and Carreras.

Even the 'Nippies' (waitresses at J Lyon's tea houses) had a team, and indeed their own pool at the company's Sudbury sports ground, which had 20,000 members.

These works teams were in addition to hundreds of clubs based at public baths, many with wonderful names such as the Shiverers, Otters, Seals, Penguins and numerous Leanders. No Sharks, Stingrays or Barracudas, it will be noted.

Private pools were almost as widespread. Apart from the growing domestic market amongst the super rich, in central London the YWCA built its own pool in Great Russell Street (now a hotel), while the department store Bourne & Hollingsworth built one for its staff in Gower Street.

Most elaborate of all was the pool designed by Clough Williams-Ellis of Portmeirion fame) for the Ladies' Carlton Club on Grosvenor Place (sadly since demolished).

So the 1930s were, on the whole, golden years for British swimming pools. And they at least ended with two public indoor baths that finally met international standards (both featured later); Blackpool's 165' long Derby Baths and Aberdeen's Bon Accord Baths, which had Scotland's first 10m diving board. (By 1939 several outdoor pools also had 10m boards.)

But as the following case studies illustrate, the legacy of the 1930s is becoming almost as threatened as that of the pre-1914 era.

Including Bon Accord, actually completed in 1940, there are 83 partially or wholly surviving public baths buildings from the inter war period (*see Directory*).

But in March 2008 Bon Accord became the latest of this era to close, and indeed of the 83 surviving buildings, only 56 were actually operating as pools, wholly or partially, or were awaiting re-opening. Moreover, of these 56, seven faced possible or certain closure over the next five years.

What puts their significance, and therefore their plight into even sharper relief is the fact that following the outbreak of war, it would be another 21 years before baths construction restarted.

In design term the historic baths of the 1930s thus represent a high point, but to a large extent, an end point too.

▲ Opened in 1931, the Grade II listed **Bristol South Baths, Bedminster**, was the third of six baths completed between the wars by the city's Baths Committee, whose chairman from 1911–37 was Colonel Henry C Woodcock; stockbroker, sportsman, aviator and one-time Conservative MP.

Only Birmingham, which built seven baths between 1923–40, would surpass this level of activity.

What is also noteworthy about Bristol's baths is that, following the completion of Bristol North in 1922 (*page 168*), the next five were designed by one man, Charles Dening, who was, even more unusually, in private practice.

Dening (1876–1952) is well remembered for his churches, his Elephant House at Bristol Zoo, his 'Wigwam' at the Red Lodge, his seminal books on Bristol's Georgian architecture and its old inns, and for his wartime paintings. Yet for his public baths, hardly at all.

Was this perhaps because, as fellow architect Eustace Button once said of Dening, 'he felt it was bad form to design a building that flaunted its own individuality'?

Before his involvement Bristol already had six indoor and four outdoor baths dating from prior to 1914, two of which survive; the Grade II Hotwells Baths, on Jacob's Wells Road, opened in 1889 and since 1979 serving as a dance studio, and the Grade II* open air Clifton Victoria Pool, built privately in 1850 but taken over by the city in 1897 and re-opened in 2008 after a ten year campaign (*see Liquid Assets*).

But as the city's suburbs extended during the 1920s, Woodock resolved that more baths were necessary in order to meet his target of every home in Bristol coming with one mile of a facility.

Dening's baths, characterised by their extensive use of plain brick and limestone dressings, were at Broad Weir (opened May 1930) and Bristol South (a year later), both of broadly similar design, though Bristol South's pool was larger at 100' x 35'.

These were followed by similarly matching designs, each with 75' x 30' pools, at Shirehampton (1935), Speedwell and Knowle (both 1937).

As Reginald Colwill wrote in *Swimming Times* in February 1936, a Bristolian had boasted to him, 'We have a swimming bath at every street corner now!'

Though not quite true, as a result of Woodcock and Dening's building programme, user numbers more than doubled, from nearly 313,000 in 1925 to 750,000 by 1936.

Following a radical and often controversial series of eight closures from 1995–2005 (which included two 1960s pools, at Henbury and Filwood), only two of Dening's baths remained in use by 2008.

After suffering from budget cuts in the 1980s, and despite repairs in the early 1990s, Bristol South (*shown above and top right*) has needed careful nursing to stave off the effects of its ageing fabric and plant, and its lack of a modern ventilation system. One possible plan, dependent on funding, is for a £6-7m refurbishment, to include improvements to the neighbouring Dame Emily Park.

However the **Jubilee Pool** (*right*) is almost certain to close when a new 50m pool at Hengrove opens in September 2010.

THE SWIMMING POOL

▲ Having hosted the ASA's first centralised championships at its Open Air Baths in 1935, Blackpool Corporation clearly saw that hosting major swimming events could be good business for the resort.

Costing a colossal £270,000 and named after Lord Derby, the **Derby Baths** on the **North Shore, Blackpool**, was the first publicly funded, long course competition pool in Britain.

Designed by Borough Engineer JC Robinson and opened unofficially just before war broke out in 1939, the baths was in fact Blackpool's third major facility completed that year, following the Odeon Cinema and Opera House (both listed).

In addition to a 30' x 30' learner pool its main seawater pool, slightly narrower than the SS Brighton but still with an awesome capacity of 435,000 gallons (three times that of a standard gala pool), was 165' x 55'. This corresponded closely to international metric norms for a 50m pool. In order to accommodate a 10m diving board it also had a 16' deep end, (Only two other British pools were similarly equipped: the Empire Pool and, by 1940, Bon Accord.)

After the war the Derby Baths became a firm favourite in aquatic circles. From 1953–63, from 1965–70 and between 1974–80 it hosted the ASA's annual 'Nationals' week and the 1980 Olympic trials. Its seawater pool hosted several world records. There were plenty of guesthouses in the vicinity, and when not competing swimmers could take in the sea air and enjoy the many pleasures, and temptations, of Blackpool.

But the upkeep of such a large facility proved a heavy burden for the town, and in 1990 it closed. The site, on the corner of Derby Road, is now the Hilton Hotel.

▲ Nautically inspired in both name and decor, the **SS Brighton** (short for Swimming Stadium), was the first of three privately financed indoor swimming stadiums to open during the period 1934–37.

With seats for 1,900 and a pool measuring 165' x 80' the SS Brighton was billed as the world's largest indoor *seawater* pool, whereas Wembley's Empire Pool (*see page 196*), opened four weeks later, advertised itself as the largest indoor *freshwater* pool. Both were then eclipsed by Earl's Court (*page 212*), opened in 1937.

All three were designed to be multi-functional – the SS Brighton and Wembley to serve as ice rinks during the winter, Earls Court to be primarily an arena and exhibition centre – and all ultimately failed

as swimming venues. But the SS Brighton was the most shortlived.

The concept had originally been intended by architects Jackson and Greenen for a site in Bournemouth (where the practice also designed

OPENING JUNE 29 1934

SS BRIGHTON

the Grade II listed Mallard Lane bus garage). But after planners there turned it down, the Brighton politician and wealthy socialist Sir Herbert Carden snapped up the idea and had it built on West Street (not far from the former site of Brill's Baths, *see page 45*).

As a building the £80,000 SS Brighton was much admired.

But as a public pool, despite a series of lavish aquatic displays and prestige water polo matches it lost £25,000 in its first season.

As planned, in October 1935 the pool gave way to the ice rink, and that was how it stayed; the SS Brighton Ice Rink becoming home to the hugely successful **Brighton Tigers** ice hockey team, until its much lamented demolition in 1965. The site is now a hotel.

Not the Empire Pool but the 'Wembley' of English swimmers all the same, Derby Baths were faced in yellow glazed tiles with green faience (as at the SS Brighton), with seats on three sides of its pool. Many of these had obstructed views. Just like the real Wembley Stadium, in fact, and every other British football ground of the era.

▶ This sandstone entrance block is all that survives of the Grade II listed **Kingsway Baths**, **Lancaster**, designed by Frederick Hill and opened by the Minister of Health, Walter Elliot, in June 1939.

Lancaster was one of the last new baths in Britain to be equipped with slipper baths, and one of the first to have no roof skylights. Instead, as seen above in its 'major' pool, there were glazed screens which could be opened by electric motors to create an outdoor effect.

Note also the proscenium arch framing the diving boards, behind which were artistes' dressing rooms.

Since the baths' closure in 2005 the surviving elements have been incorporated into a retail park.

Also opened in 1939 was the **City Baths, Sun Lane, Wakefield** (*right*), designed by Percy Morris and S Hutton, with decorative mouldings in white concrete, alas lost to posterity when the building was demolished in 2007.

Awaiting a similar fate in 2008 was **Chadderton Baths, Middleton Road** (*opposite top*), closed in 2007. On its opening in April 1937 architect JAC Taylor described its exterior as being deliberately 'plain and severe in outline', and yet the interior featured numerous Art Deco details in etched glass and tiling.

Chadderton was the home pool of possibly Britain's greatest ever Olympian, Henry Taylor, to whom a display in the adjoining sports hall is dedicated.

As early as 1936 plans were drawn up for public baths to be used as decontamination centres in the event of gas attacks, but when war finally broke out in 1939 the majority of baths simply closed.

Some were turned into first aid posts or, as at Millwall and Rotherhithe in London, taken over by ARP units. Bootle Baths doubled as a mortuary, while all Liverpool baths and several in London stored water for the Fire Service (having the letters EWS, for Emergency Water Supplies, painted prominently on their exterior).

Hove Marina baths, due to open in late 1939, was immediately requisitioned as a naval training centre, called HMS Alfred, and was opened to the public only in 1946, as the King Alfred Centre. Blackpool's Derby Baths was also used to teach tens of thousands of soldiers and sailors to swim.

As listed below, 22 indoor public baths are known to have suffered war damage. Of these, the most regrettable losses in architectural terms were at Old Kent Road and Whitfield Street (both London), and Old Trafford, Manchester.

Barrow: Abbey Road, b.1915, bombed 1941, interior rebuilt 1958
Birkenhead: Argyle St, b.1882, not reopened after bomb damage, demolished 1969
Birmingham: Green Lane, b.1902, main pool destroyed 1940, rebuilt 1951
Birmingham: Kent Street, b.1933, Gala pool bombed 1940, building remains
Dover: Marine Parade, b. 1878, destroyed by shelling
Exeter: Kings Alley, off High Street, b.1893, destroyed May 1942
Liverpool: Balliol Road, Bootle, b.1888, bombed 1941, one pool rebuilt 1952
London: Whitfield Street, b.1878, destroyed (see page 55)
London: Goulston Square, Whitechapel, 1878 section bombed, rebuilt 1962
London: Lower Road, Rotherhithe, b.1885, bombed 1940/44/45, rebuilt 1963
London: Ealing, Longfield Ave, b.1886, bombed 1940, repaired, demolished 1970s
London: Betts Street, Shadwell, b. 1888, destroyed 1941
London: Hornsey Road, Islington, b.1892, bombed 1941, rebuilt 1962
London: Kennington Road, Lambeth, b.1897, destroyed by V2 rocket January 1945
London: Pitfield Street, Shoreditch, b. 1899, bombed, demolished c.1950s
London: Glengall Road, Millwall, b. 1900, bombed 1941, rebuilt 1963–66
London: Old Kent Road, Camberwell, b.1905, destroyed 1940
London: Birchanger Rd, Sth Norwood, b. as open air 1881, covered 1914, bombed 1941
Manchester: Leaf St, Hulme, b. 1860, bombed 1941, demolished 1976 (see page 43)
Manchester: Northumberland Ave, Old Trafford, b.1904, destroyed 1940
Skegness: Scarborough Avenue, b.1882, demolished after bomb damage
West Bromwich: Lombard Street, b.1875, bombed November 1940, rebuilt 1959

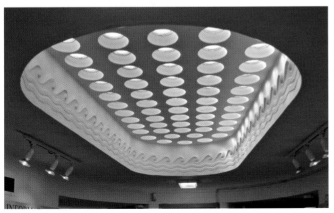

Vitruvian plaster scrolls and circular skylights adorn the entrance hall to the Grade II listed Arnos Pool, London, designed by WT Curtis and HW Burchett for Middlesex County Council and opened in May 1939. Still in use, albeit with a more recent suspended ceiling blocking out its clerestory windows, the pool is adjoined by a public library.

Case Study

Victory Baths, Renfrew

Opened September 22 1921
Address Inchinnan Road, PA4 8ND
Architect TG Abercrombie
Cost not known
Pool 75' x 35'
Owner Renfrewshire Council
Operator Renfrewshire Leisure
Listed Category B (1971)

On the south bank of the River Clyde and barely a mile from Glasgow Airport, the Victory Baths is one of the last to have been gifted by a philanthropist.

As its name suggests, it serves also as a war memorial.

Inside the lobby is displayed a large walnut board on which are recorded the names of 1,300 men from Renfrewshire who served in the armed forces during the First World War, including the 124 who lost their lives.

Above this memorial is a bust of the baths' donor.

Sir Frederick Lobnitz (1863–1932) was born in Renfrew, the son of a Danish immigrant whose shipyard on the Clyde became one of the two largest builders of dredgers in the world. (The other was also based in Renfrew.)

Come 1914, having a name like Lobnitz cannot have been easy. But Frederick worked tirelessly for the war effort, rising to become Director of Munitions in Scotland and receiving a knighthood in return, as well as the Légion d'Honneur from France.

The baths that he and Lady Lobnitz funded – designed by the Paisley architect Thomas Graham Abercrombie – is an appealing blend of styles.

Located in the town centre next to a fortress-like police station dating from 1910 (*on the left, below*), its symmetrical entrance block is dressed in sandstone quarried from Cullaloe in Fife, with crow-stepped gable ends and a central tower topped by an ogee dome.

Over the door (*left*) is a plaque commemorating the Lobnitz's gift, flanked by two coats of arms. That of the Burgh of Renfrew bears the inscription, 'Deus gubernat navem' (God steers the ship).

That there was only one entrance does not signify that mixed bathing had caught on in Renfrew by 1921. That would come after the Second World War. But the net result is that once it did become the norm, unlike at earlier baths – where surplus male or female, first or second class entrances had to be blocked off (for example at Govanhill, six miles to the east) – at Renfrew no such measures were necessary.

Also original are the wrought iron railings and copper lanterns mounted on each gate post.

Similarly the simple redbrick pool hall, though quite different in character to the front, is also remarkably unchanged, save for the ugly but necessary installation of air vents (*right*), albeit softened by artificial greenery.

The baths cannot be considered innovative for its time. Its pool hall was merely a late version of the standard shed-like construction that had been common since the 1890s. But its fully glazed roof is rare, if not unique, and lends the pool a light and airy feel.

The retention of cubicles means also that Renfrew retains many of the qualities of a traditional baths (although there is also a sauna, dance studio and beauty treatment area in the building).

Thus while those in search of flumes and wave machines head off to the Lagoon Leisure Centre in nearby Paisley, the Victory Baths' regulars – of whom there are some 64,000 a year, many travelling in from Glasgow especially – remain happily content to enjoy this intimate swimming experience.

Two other regulars are rather less welcome, however.

Several baths are reputed to have ghosts. But Renfrew has two. One, seen in a basement passage, is a women in a white dress. The other is a boy, said to have broken his neck in the 1920s after diving into the pool wearing a German helmet brought back from the trenches by his father.

In 2007 a tremulous duty manager captured the wee lad on his mobile phone's video camera, floating in and out of walls and above the water.

Internet users will no doubt know where to view this scoop.

Case Study

Paddington Central Baths, London

Opened June 26 1925
Address Queenway, W2 5HS
Architect Herbert Shepherd, plus
HA Thomerson for second phase
Cost £105,000
Pools 100' x 35' and 75' x 30'
Owner City of Westminster Council
Operator Courtneys Leisure
Management
Listed Grade II (1994)

Known today as the Porchester Centre, this is a building of two distinct halves.

Its western half, originally called Paddington Central Baths, opened in 1925 and is accessed from an entrance (*top left*) at the northern end of Queensway, one of the prime thoroughfares of Bayswater.

On its eastern flank, entered from Porchester Road, is an adjoining block opened in 1929 and containing Porchester Hall (a public assembly hall), a public library and a suite of Turkish and Russian baths known as The Spa.

Such multi-functionality within one site is not unique. And yet the Porchester Centre offers that rare blend; public sector accessibility within a building that, in parts, has the feel of a private club.

The Borough of Paddington (which became part of Westminster in 1965, along with the City of Westminster and the Borough of St Marylebone) had not fared well with its first baths. Detailed on page 54, this opened in 1874 on a site two hundred yards further down Queensway (then called Queens Road), and was an expensive, four pool complex, but with a problematic layout. The Borough sold it in 1900, bought it back again in 1906, but finally sold the site to Whiteley's department store in 1910.

A year later Harold Burgess was commissioned to design new baths on the current site, only to be scuppered by the war in 1914. Local architect Herbert Shepherd then took over the scheme, with the foundation stone being laid in November 1923.

First and second class pools, both of which are still in use, were built, at right angles to each other. Also provided were 62 slipper baths and a wash house. Affluent though much of Bayswater is, there were railwaylands, a canal and a former workhouse only a short distance away to the north.

That said, the wash house entrance was hidden away at the back of the building.

All other departments were entered under a portico with gates bearing the gilded initials PB (for Paddington Borough).

Through these visitors entered a double height lobby (*opposite*), topped by a glazed dome and featuring a marble floor and statue of a maiden, teak panelling, glazed terracotta facings and a grand staircase leading up to the boardroom of the Baths and Wash Houses Committee.

Although now somewhat compromised by modern day clutter, all these fittings survive in good order, as does a First World War Memorial and a copper plaque marking the baths' opening.

Also worth noting in the lobby is a water colour showing the building in its original guise.

Since 1925 there have been two major refurbishments, the first of which, in 1986, saw the original teak poolside cubicles removed.

Steel framed and vaulted roofs with recessed skylights such as this at the Porchester Centre's main pool, became a familiar feature of baths during the inter war years. But the use of glazed terracotta panelling and oval windows puts it into a separate class. Note also how discreetly the modern ventilation ducts have been tucked under the gallery. Pevsner dismissed the style of the adjoining Porchester Hall (*left*) as 'flabby Beaux-Arts Baroque'. But its Turkish baths, famously frequented by the smart set and cabbies alike, are revered.

The former second class pool, now called the Small Pool (though it is still a sizeable 75' x 30') has also been fitted with a suspended ceiling.

Because the baths serves one of the wealthiest parts of London it is tempting to consider it in isolation from those Edwardian pools of splendour that we have praised so highly in the previous chapter.

Equally, being hemmed in by surrounding buildings, and having an irregular layout, it appears to lack definition and presence.

Yet in detail and in finish the Porchester Centre is without doubt one of the finest survivors of the first half of the 20th century, and one which, moreover, has been admirably maintained and adapted to the modern era.

Case Study

Northumberland Baths, Newcastle-upon-Tyne

Opened November 7 1928
Address Northumberland Road
NE1 8SE
Architects Nicholas and Dixon-
Spain
Cost not known
Pools Men's 100' x 40' (now 25m)
Women's 75' x 33'
Owner Newcastle City Council
Operator Newcastle Leisure
Listed Grade II (1994)

By the 1920s Newcastle could claim to have the oldest public baths in Britain.

Opened in 1839 on Ridley Place, on land leased from the hospital of St Mary Magdalen, the original Northumberland baths was a private venture, costing £7,300 and designed by Newcastle's most celebrated architect, John Dobson.

For its time it was remarkably advanced, in that it housed two of the largest indoor pools in the country (larger than those at the Pierhead in Liverpool), measuring 90' x 45' and 54' x 17'.

The Council took it over in 1858, which meant that following the demolition of the Pierhead Baths in 1906, Northumberland Baths was the oldest in public ownership.

Come the 1920s, however, there was little desire to conserve

an outdated building. Instead, the site was redeveloped into the baths we see today, also called the Northumberland Baths, but nowadays known as the City Pool.

Planning began in 1921 with a visit by a deputation to the Central Baths in Bradford, as a result of which the Baths Committee opted for a multi-functional building combining baths and a public hall.

Following a design competition adjudicated by Alfred Cross, a London firm, Nicholas and Dixon-Spain, was then appointed in 1924.

Given the size of the scheme and the harsh economic times, it took four years to complete the building – one that has definite parallels with its contemporary in Paddington (*see previous page*).

The western part of the site (running appropriately enough alongside John Dobson Street), housed pools for males and females, a small slipper bath section (six male, three female), and a comparatively large Turkish baths suite in the basement, often described since as the 'best kept secret in town'.

The eastern part of the site consisted of the City Hall – which, with seats for 2,518 became Newcastle's prime concert venue – and a caretaker's flat.

Linking these elements, a two storey frontage on Northumberland Road was designed to offer maximum flexibility. Thus during the swimming season entry to both pools and the City Hall was via the central block. But in winter, when each pool was boarded over for various uses (including as a cinema), separate entrances were opened on either side, through matching colonnades. In this way, and by using a series of interior doors and passages, all three large spaces could be used independently or in tandem.

Being next door to a concert venue has had its advantages and disadvantages. On the plus

side, the heating system on the baths side serves all parts of the building. Thus whenever there has been talk of closing the baths, the cost of having to install a separate system for the City Hall has helped to stave off the threat.

On the down side, during orchestral performances in the hall, members of local clubs training in the adjacent smaller pool have had to refrain from whistling, cheering or even, it is said, using fins, to avoid loud splashing. (Since the opening of a new concert hall at the Sage Gateshead in 2004, that may be less of a problem, however.)

Otherwise, apart from the City Pool's imposing presence and its robust construction, its greatest asset is perhaps its location.

While the likes of Birmingham, Liverpool, Leeds and Bradford have lost their own central baths – leaving daytime workers with nowhere convenient to swim – usage at the City Pool, the self-styled 'Biggest Health Club in the City', suggests that John Dobson in the 1830s and the Baths Committee of the 1920s could hardly have picked a better site.

Now boomed to a length of 25 metres, with a small children's pool at the end, the City Pool's main pool is a typical design of its era. The smaller, former women's pool, is similar but without a spectator gallery. Both originally had demountable poolside cubicles that could be removed when the pools were boarded over for other uses.

Case Study

York Hall, Bethnal Green, London

Opened November 5 1929
Address Old Ford Road, E2 9PL
Architect AE Darby (Borough Engineer)
Cost £190,000
Pools 1929: 90' x 40', 75' x 31'
1967: 33.3m x 12.5m, 12.5m x 6m
Owner Tower Hamlets Borough Council
Operator Greenwich Leisure Ltd
Listed unlisted

Many a public swimming pool has led a double life during the winter, boarded over for dances or badminton, carpet bowls or public meetings.

But in London by far the most popular winter use for pools was boxing, most famously Lime Grove Baths in the west, Hornsey Road in the north and Manor Place in the south.

But the daddy of them all, the venue most revered by boxing afficionados – the amateur fraternity above all – was in the east, at York Hall in Bethnal Green.

So successful, in fact, that there has been no swimming in its first

class pool since the late 1940s, since when the floor has stayed firmly down.

Now part of Tower Hamlets, Bethnal Green was one of the last London boroughs to adopt the 1846 Act when, in 1900, it opened its first baths and wash house in Cheshire Street. This, however, had no swimming pool, the Baths Committee having decided that slipper baths and a laundry were important, given the social and welfare needs of this, one of the poorest parts of the east end.

Besides, there was already a privately run swimming baths in the area. Opened in 1895 on

Mansford Road, the Excelsior Baths had two pools, 102' x 36' and 60' x 20'. In 1898 these were purchased by a charitable institution, Oxford House, well known for its social outreach in the east end. But the upkeep proved too much and so when the Borough of Bethnal Green chose not to buy the baths in 1920 the building was turned into a cinema (eventually demolished in 1968).

Anxious now to plug the gap in local provision, the Borough did not have to look far for the perfect site. Directly behind the Town Hall stood, on Old Ford Road, the Colman's starch factory.

Not only was this ideally located, but within the site was a 360' deep artesian well, sunk by Colman's in 1898 and able to yield 8,000 gallons an hour.

Borough Engineer AE Darby drew up plans for a two pool complex, with 90 slipper baths, Turkish and Russian baths, and a public laundry. But as in Newcastle it took over four years to realise these plans, years blighted by economic hardship, the General Strike and shortage of materials.

Opening day in 1929 was to prove defining in two respects.

Firstly, the honours were performed by the Duke and Duchess of York (the future George VI and Queen Elizabeth, later to be Queen Mother). Hence the name York Hall.

Secondly, this being November, the gala pool was already boarded over, so not until the following April did swimming commence.

Was this an omen?

Over the ensuing years York Hall certainly garnered legendary status. Its Turkish and Russian baths, the cheapest in town, became a favourite haunt of east enders, especially it is said, of course, amongst members of the underworld (the Kray twins included, naturally).

Meanwhile, so popular did the gala pool become for amateur boxing nights that in around 1950, as mentioned earlier, the floor was left down, leaving only the smaller pool in use for swimming.

York Hall's first major upgrade followed in the mid 1960s.

The small pool was demolished to make way for a 33.3m pool (*right*) opened in 1967, while the baths' laundry was replaced by a laundromat incorporated into Mayfield House, a block of council flats built next to the baths. Both new structures, designed by Kenneth Wakeford, Jerram and Harris, are still in use today.

But in the case of the new pool it has been a close run matter.

In 2003, to howls of outrage from the boxing world, Tower Hamlets announced that York Hall would close, having become a £600,000 a year burden.

'Pulling down York Hall would be like tearing down Nelson's Column,' fulminated an American boxing fan. 'Criminal!' reckoned John Stracey, a former world welterweight champion who had boxed there as a schoolboy.

Many were shocked to discover that the building was not even listed (whereas two K6 telephone kiosks in front of it were).

Faced with a now formidable gathering of objectors, Tower Hamlets returned bruised to its corner and in February 2004 announced it had found a

champion. As part of a 15 year deal to run the Borough's leisure centres, Greenwich Leisure Limited had been signed up to take over York Hall's operation and oversee a £4.5m refit.

Fittingly, its final phase was unveiled in January 2008 by George VI's nephew, the Duke of Kent.

And very fine it is too, preserving the best of the building's original

features with a modern fitness centre and a revamped spa.

For regulars of the old Turkish baths this spa was an upgrade too far; to them yet another example of the east end's creeping gentrification. But for boxing fans, York Hall was worth saving at almost any cost.

Oh, and the swimming pool remains pretty popular too.

On boxing nights the seats in the York Hall gallery are said to be better than anything Madison Square Gardens can offer. (For a ring side seat of your own, the GLL's virtual tour of York Hall is recommended.) Next door, the 1967 pool – the first built in Britain at a length of 33.3m, following the switch from the 110' standard – may not have quite the same intimacy but does retain one of the few 'horseshoe' 5m diving boards still in use.

Case Study

Marshall Street, Soho, London

Opened April 17 1931
Address Marshall St, W1V 1LS
Architect AWS and KMB Cross
Cost £173,000
Pools 100' x 35' (being refurbished) and 70' x 35' (demolished 2009)
Owner City of Westminster Council
Listed Grade II (1982)
Closed August 1997
Re-opening 2010

Hemmed in between shops, offices, flats and two multi-storey car parks, 300 yards north of Piccadilly Circus and within hailing distance of Carnaby Street, Marshall Street occupies a site on which public baths have stood longer than any other in London.

For it was on Marshall Street that the Vestry of St James, one of the earliest local authorities to adopt the 1846 Act, opened its first baths in June 1852 (a year before Endell Street, half a mile to the east).

Built next to a workhouse and designed by PP Baly, the St James Baths cost £21,000 and offered a wash house, 120 slipper baths, and a small 40' x 30' plunge pool.

In common with all early baths this soon proved too small, and despite an extension in 1861, the building was substantially remodelled in 1893–95 by Alfred Cross and Henry Spalding. Even then the site still allowed only two comparatively small pools, 60' x 22' and 40' x 36', with greater priority accorded to a 70 stall wash house and 73 slipper baths (facilities that were extremely well used by Soho's many rooming-house dwellers and workers).

Planning for what we may consider the third Marshall Street Baths started in 1925 under Westminster's Borough Engineer LJ Veit. But by the time the old baths were demolished in 1928 and adjoining properties had been purchased to enlarge the site, Alfred Cross once again, together with his son and partner Kenneth, had taken on the job.

Certainly the design bears all the hallmarks of Alfred Cross.

Seen above, its Marshall Street frontage – a narrow, steel-framed structure, described as 'Roman Renaissance' and faced at street level in Portland stone – acts as a screen to the structures behind.

Its northernmost bay, it may be noted, set slightly forward, has a short tower that originally was capped by a belvedere (similar to that of Haggerston, page 126).

This bay gave entry to a Maternity and Child Welfare Centre, hence the matronly figures above the oriel window, flanking the portcullis of the Westminster coat of arms (right). CW Dyson was the sculptor.

On the upper floors of the front block were slipper baths and offices for the rates department, while at ground level, a full length and handsomely fitted entrance hall with a mahogany ticket kiosk served, in the spirit of the age, both the first and second class pools and slipper baths, male and female.

At the rear of the building, entered from Dufour's Place, there was also a public laundry and a large depot for the council's street cleaning vehicles and staff.

The Cross' attention to detail (and Westminster's budget) can be measured by the continuation of the ground floor stone rustication and brick detailing around the side elevation of the second class pool into Dufour's Place, even though it was clearly a back entrance.

The second class pool itself was a plain affair internally, with steel arched roof vaults and recessed skylights and, owing to the lack of space, poolside cubicles.

Between this and the front block, on the same axis, the first class pool was, however, of a quite different order (*see right*).

Firstly, its vaulted roof was constructed in reinforced concrete and had integrated glazed sections, shedding light across the hall. Secondly, its changing facilities were located in separate side rooms (as was the growing trend), and thirdly, Alfred Cross' favoured amphitheatre seating lined both sides of the pool.

But it was the use of materials that really set this pool apart from others of the period. Both the tank and the lower walls were lined in creamy white Sicilian marble, with insets of green Swedish marble. At the shallow end was a fountain (*see opposite*), originally featuring a merchild with two dolphins, sculpted by Walter Gilbert.

For Alfred Cross, Marshall Street would be the last baths of his long career. He died in late

1932, leaving Kenneth to enjoy the baths' instant status as a regular venue for local, national and international swimming and diving events. (The 10' deep end was fitted with a 5m diving stage donated by the Lady Mayoress.)

Hollywood star Johnny Weissmuller swam here in the late 1940s. During the 1950s Judy Grinham and Margaret Edwards set numerous backstroke records.

And yet the pool did have its critics. *Swimming Times* in 1936 complained that turning at both ends was hard because of the positioning of the hand rails and the scum troughs, and because the shallow end was only 3' deep. One competitor complained that the water was as 'heavy as lead'.

Otherwise, Marshall Street became an integral part of Soho, a place where market traders and night owls, pensioners and local schoolchildren, actors and shop workers lent it a diversity to match its decor; sociable yet institutional, glamorous yet bohemian.

Predictably, its closure in 1997 caused an uproar, moreso when a developer annnounced plans to incorporate the main pool into a private club, and it took ten long years of lobbying by the Friends of Marshall Street Baths before a chastened Westminster was finally able to confirm its reopening as a public facility, as part of a £25m redevelopment plan.

Started in August 2008 and to be funded largely by the construction of flats, offices and studios on other parts of the site – overseen by the Marshall Street Regeneration consortium – the baths element of the scheme, by Finch Forman architects, includes restoration of the first class pool and Gilbert fountain (but alas the removal of the seats), the creation of a gym

on the site of the second class pool (also regrettably demolished), the conversion of the entrance hall into a café and the addition of spa facilities and treatment suites.

Played in Britain will therefore eagerly return to Marshall Street in our forthcoming study, *Played in London*. For with over 150 years behind it, this is one West End show that must go on.

'One of the most beautiful indoor pools in this country,' wrote Roger Deakin in his classic *Waterlog* (*see Links*). Deakin, together with actor and TV personality Michael Palin was able to stir up much needed public and media attention to Marshall Street's plight following its closure in 1997. But alas his death in 2006 deprived him of the chance of seeing the pool re-open.

Case Study

Queen Street, Derby

Opened July 30 1932
Address Cathedral Road, DE1 3PA
Architect C H Aslin
Cost £79,250
Pools 100' x 40' (now 25m) and 100' x 32', plus teaching pool
Owner Derby City Council
Listed unlisted

Along with Derby's much lamented Art Deco bus station (b.1933, demolished 2006), Queen Street Baths was one of several civic buildings designed by the respected Borough architect Charles Aslin.

Aslin went on to be elected president of RIBA from 1954-56, coincidentally preceding in office Kenneth Cross, whose father's influence can clearly be seen here,

in the gently vaulted roof form and in the amphitheatre seating.

In 1949 those seats were filled to capacity when Derby hosted the ASA's National Championships. In winter the pool was boarded over to became the 1500 seater King's Hall.

Despite subsequent upgrades, in 1989 the baths closed for three years to undergo a £3.1m refit (by the Gibson Hamilton Partnership).

This included converting the Gala Pool to a 25m deck level pool, revamping the former ladies' pool next door and a children's pool added in 1962, and creating a new entrance on Cathedral Road.

The building was also renamed the Queen's Leisure Centre; not to retain the Queen Street link but because the Queen herself cut the ribbon, in April 1992.

Thimblemill Road, Smethwick

Once in while, along comes a building that perfectly captures the spirit of the age.

In terms of large span public assembly halls, that building was the Royal Horticultural Society's exhibition hall, opened off Vincent Square, London, in 1928.

With its tall, reinforced concrete parabolic arches, supporting a stepped series of flat roofs and glazed clerestories, the RHS Hall had clearly been influenced by the swooping airship hangars built in Orly, France, in the early 1920s.

Given the breathtaking internal space that this structural form creates, it was purely a matter of time before a public baths followed suit. And the first to do so was in Smethwick, just west of Birmingham, in 1933, where the pool hall (*right*) was almost a carbon copy of the RHS Hall.

A similar design at Poplar (*see page 174*) was in mid construction at the time. Others would follow, at Seymour Place (Marylebone), Northampton and Lancaster (all detailed in this chapter).

But Smethwick set the trend.

Designed by Chester Button and Borough Engineer Roland Fletcher, here was Britain's first genuinely Moderne baths.

The building has enjoyed a varied history. During the war its basement was used as an air raid shelter (as surviving signs and graffiti attest). In the late 1950s it hosted swimming matches against France, Sweden and Germany.

Boarded over in winter it was used for dances, boxing and wrestling. In November 1962 a little known band called the Beatles played there, as did the Kinks and the Who, and Tommy Cooper.

Since then a 5m diving board (framed by the blank proscenium arch) has been removed, and the café overlooking the shallow end has become a gym. But the building otherwise rejoices in a wealth of original Art Deco detailing, enhanced in 2008 by a sensitive £1.3m refurbishment.

When you visit, as you should, see also on Thimblemill Road an equally arresting library by Button and Fletcher, opened in 1937 and also listed Grade II.

Together, they represent 1930s civic architecture at its very best.

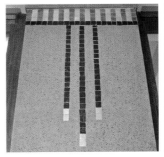

Opened March 30 1933
Address Thimblemill Rd, B67 5QT
Architect Chester Button with Borough Engineer Roland Fletcher
Pools 100' x 35', plus 20m x 9m learner pool added 1968
Owner Sandwell Metropolitan Borough Council
Operator Sandwell Leisure Trust
Listed Grade II (2003)

Case Study

Empire Pool, Wembley

Opened July 25 1934
Address Engineers Way, HA9 0DW
Architect Sir E Owen Williams
Cost £150,000
Pool 200' x 60'
Owner Wembley Stadium Ltd.
Closed (as pool) 1948
Current owner Quintain Estates
Current operator Live Nation
Listed Grade II (1976)

Considering that the last time anyone swam in it was during the 1948 London Olympics, and that it was open to the public for only five summer seasons, the Empire Pool – the largest indoor pool the world had ever seen – could be judged a failure.

But as the sign above its entrance said in 1934, this was the Empire Pool *and* Sports Arena, offering not only aquatic sports, surf bathing and swimming, but also boxing, dancing, ice hockey and ice skating. To which we could add in its later life athletics, Horse of the Year Shows and, of course, many a rock concert.

To put the Empire Pool in context, imagine a building that combines the flexibility of, say, the modern day O2 Arena, with the swimming and diving facilities being provided at the Aquatic Centre for London 2012.

No designer would dream of trying to do such a thing today.

Yet virtually all baths architects of the inter war period faced just such a challenge; to provide a pool hall for swimming from April to October, and for dry sports and other activities the rest of the year.

The difference at Wembley, however, was that this was a commercial venture, with no public funding at all.

Evaluating the Empire Pool purely as a pool is therefore not appropriate. More important is the context in which it was designed.

The British Empire Games, first staged in Hamilton, Ontario, in 1930, had been awarded to

Johannesburg for 1934, only for the offer to be withdrawn over concerns as to how black and Asian athletes would be treated.

London was a late replacement.

For the athletics the former Olympic stadium at White City needed little work to make it ready. But its outdoor pool (*see page 119*) had long been filled in, leaving the capital with no aquatic facility large enough for the Games.

Enter at this point Arthur Elvin, chairman of Wembley Stadium Ltd. For some time Elvin had wanted to increase revenues at the Wembley Park site, much of which had lain empty since the 1924 Empire Exhibition.

He had first considered building an indoor arena after seeing an ice hockey match in 1932. But Elvin also harboured ambitions to build a public pool. This, it was said, stemmed from an experience during the First World War, when his inability to swim had led to him being recaptured after escaping from the Germans.

And now the prospect of the 1934 Empire Games gave Elvin the incentive he needed to satisfy both ambitions within one building.

Incredibly, once the decision had been made, the Empire Pool was designed and built within just ten months. Yet whereas, back in 1923, Wembley Stadium had been famously erected in 300 days – and would suffer the consequences forever after – the Empire Pool was an absolute masterpiece.

For this the credit must lie with its visionary architect, Sir Owen

Williams, who, as described overleaf, fulfilled Elvin's brief with scientific exactitude.

As planned, following its opening by the Duke of Gloucester in July 1934, and the staging of the Empire Games a month later, the building operated as a public pool during the summer.

It also staged the ASA's National Championships in 1936, and the European Championships in 1938.

During the winter it was then boarded over to serve as an ice rink. On Thursday and Saturday nights two resident ice hockey teams, the Lions and the Monarchs, drew huge crowds.

Other events included a circus, a Festival of Youth rally, tennis and even table tennis. In 1936 alone, between the arena and the stadium, Wembley clocked up attendances of over two million.

War interrupted this success, but come 1946 the complex proved more popular than ever. Total attendances that year reached a staggering record of 4.4 million.

But the pool stayed shut. Partly this was because it would have been costly to recommission. But mainly it was because all the other events were proving too lucrative.

Indeed the pool might never have been filled again had it not been for the 1948 Olympics, and even then it suffered so many leaks that throughout the Games it had to be regularly topped up.

Nevertheless it fulfilled its role as the first indoor pool ever to have hosted an Olympiad perfectly (under the supervision,

incidentally, of temporary arena manager, Bert Cummins, editor of *Swimming Times*).

The Empire Pool's last day of swimming was Saturday, August 7. In the afternoon, Cathie Gibson of Motherwell won Britain's only swimming medal of the Games, a bronze in the 400m freestyle. After the final water polo match, there then followed a non-Olympic contest between teams from Europe, the Americas, Australasia and Asia, watched by a crowd of 7,000.

As they departed, workmen started erecting a boxing ring over the pool for the next day's events, and in September the water was drained for the very last time.

A great shame for British swimming, no doubt. But not for Wembley's shareholders.

▲ Photographed shortly before its opening in 1934, and with several buildings from the 1924 Empire Exhibition still standing, the **Empire Pool** stood in stark contrast to the **Empire Stadium**.

For the stadium, on which Owen Williams had worked as an engineer with architect Maxwell Ayrton, concrete had been used to express traditional forms of architecture.

For the pool, Williams harnessed the properties of reinforced concrete so that in effect the structure *was* the architecture. Not a single element was superfluous. (Those blocks on the corner towers, for example, were water tanks.)

Thus while the stadium looked to the past, the pool was a meticulous exercise in modernism, of form following function.

◄ In order to meet Arthur Elvin's brief to create a multi-functional and fully serviceable arena, and to complete the task in time for the Empire Games, Owen Williams based his design on precisely calculated units that were also suited to *in situ* concrete fabrication.

Elvin also insisted that every seat offer unobstructed views with perfect sightlines, whatever the event.

Working from the geometry of each seat, Williams therefore evolved a series of grids 44' wide, each served by identical stairways, exits and buffet bars. (Apparently Elvin needed persuading on the last point, since this meant dispensing with the long bars that were so much a feature of the stadium.)

The upper tier, cantilevered at an angle of 30° from each of the 15 massive concrete frames along both sides, had fixed seats. The mid tier had sections that could be removed to make room for terrace cafés and a restaurant.

At ground level, wide, shallow terraces could be used either by bathers, or, on competition days, for judges and officials, or for temporary seating when the pool was boarded over for other events.

Thus the capacity could vary between 5-7,000, depending on the configuration.

Most impressive of all was the column-free roof, said to have had the largest clear span in the world at the time, measuring 236' 6".

Each of its slender, tapering beams – like 'acrobats leaning against each other' in the centre, wrote one critic – was angled at 15°. This, calculated Williams, was the angle at which concrete could best be poured without shuttering, and was also ideally suited for the fixing of the 56,000 square feet of glazing that bathed the interior in natural light.

SUNBATHING TERRACES, EMPIRE SWIMMING POOL, WEMBLEY

The pool itself, fitted with Britain's first wave machine (an idea copied from Luna Park in Berlin), measured 200' x 60'. For nearly half its length, however, it was shallow, starting at only 3", whereas the deep end reached 16' 6". This was to meet international standards for diving, for which a 10m board was provided (one of few in Britain at the time).

To create a 50m length pool on race days, meanwhile, a wooden pontoon (forerunner of the modern boom) was floated across its width.

For the public, another innovation were the lockers, 1,250 in total, located in changing areas under the mid tier of seats. Each key was fitted with a rubber wristlet containing a waterproof purse, 'large enough to contain half a crown.'

Compared with other London pools, which typically cost 6–8d for adults and 3–4d for children, the Empire Pool was expensive. Entry ranged from 1s to 1s 6d for adults, and from 6d to 9d for children. But, like lidos of the period, it did offer a complete day out. Apart from the wave machine, a paddling pool, a range of cafés and bars, and dance bands playing twice a day, large doors at the east end opened onto a sun terrace and boating lake (part of the 1924 exhibition grounds). Opening hours were long too, from 9am to midnight on six days a week and from 7am to midnight on Sundays. On a busy summer's day, it was said, up to 5,000 people could pass through its doors.

▶ The glazing has been replaced by solid panels, and seats now occupy the east end (where once stood the diving board). Otherwise today's **Wembley Arena** – its maximum capacity now 14,500 – is still recognisable as the Empire Pool.

The current name was formally adopted in 1978. But the fate of the pool itself was sealed four years earlier, when the timber platform erected after the Olympics was finally replaced by a concrete floor (following a mishap during a Horse of the Year Show).

Unbeknown to most concert goers the pool itself remains *in situ*, however, complete with scum trough, depth markers and round, underwater lights (*below right*) that in 1934 seemed so magical.

This, after all, was an all-electric building, with further deep pits around the tank perimeter to house the all important wave and ice making machines, and giant boilers that promised to heat the pool, 'whatever the weather', to a constant 75 degrees.

Much of the tank is now used for storage and access. But note that unlike public baths, it was never tiled. Being a great believer in high quality concrete finishes Williams deemed this unecessary.

Similarly on the walkways around the pool, instead of laying standard non-slip flooring he painted the cement with a retardant (to prevent it from setting too quickly) and then sprayed it with a hose to create a pitted surface.

Alas no pre war colour images of the pool survive. But as described, steel and wooden fixtures were generally painted green, doors for the public were orange and those for emergency exits were vermilion.

Williams being a purist, all else was bare concrete. He left it to the public to provide the real colour.

For those who followed the tortured, ten year gestation and construction of the new Wembley Stadium, two items in the foyer of the neighbouring arena remind us of just how supremely effective was the collaboration between Arthur Elvin and Owen Williams. Above is the Empire Pool's foundation stone, laid by the Earl of Derby. The other commemorates the pool's opening by the Duke of Gloucester... 160 days later.

▲ Since a much needed £35m revamp, completed by its new owners in 2006, Wembley Arena has gained a new lease of life. Apart from a clean up of all its external and internal surfaces, the former west entrance is now the back-of-house business end, for unloading equipment and so on, while the east end (*above and left*) forms a new entrance, fronted by a public piazza.

By doing this, and by clearing the tawdry post war buildings that had risen around its flanks, and by removing years of accumulated signage, at last the arena can now be enjoyed for what it is – one of the greatest, perhaps even *the* greatest of all leisure buildings of 20th century Britain.

Meanwhile, the new stadium next door, completed in 2007, looks pretty fine too.

Case Study

Pioneer Health Centre, Peckham, London

Opened 1935
Address Frobisher Place, St Mary's Road, Peckham SE15
Architect Sir Owen Williams
Cost £38,000 (whole building)
Pool size 75' x 40'
Owner formerly Pioneer Health Centre Ltd., currently private flats
Listed Grade II* (1972)

While in the worlds of sport and entertainment the Empire Pool (*see previous case study*) was considered one of the great wonders of the 1930s, it was another design by Owen Williams that most caught the imagination of intellectuals and Modernists.

Nowadays the notion that prevention is better than cure is axiomatic within professional health circles. But in the 1930s this was still a quite radical idea, and to many observers the two main promoters of the Pioneer Health Centre, the biologists Dr George Scott Williamson and Dr Innes Pearse, were no more than cranks.

Their first centre had been in a house on Queen's Road, Peckham, set up in 1926.

Even though a relatively prosperous working class area, the doctors were shocked at how few individuals seemed to be free of any health concerns.

But instead of simply treating illness, Williamson and Pearse set out to change people's lifestyles.

The response was positive. But the building proved inadequate, so after it closed in 1929 the pair started to solicit donations for a purpose built centre.

Williams himself was no ideologue. But he did know how to bring a building in on budget. His emphasis on functionalist design also dovetailed perfectly with the doctors' holistic approach.

The result of their collaboration was a concrete frame, three storey symmetrical building that appeared to be a smaller version of Williams' iconic Boots factory in Nottingham, opened in 1932.

To create space for gardens and recreation, the building was set back from the road, with the entrance rather oddly tucked away at the back, where visitors had to ascend two flights of stairs to access a reception on the first floor.

On this level, a series of interconnected spaces divided by glass partitions were intended primarily for social activities, the nature of which was left to participants. (Williamson rejected the concept of leadership.) Cork was used for the flooring, to allow children to go barefoot.

On the ground floor was a nursery, gymnasium and lecture room. On the top floor was a library, study areas and doctors' rooms (these being the only private areas within the centre).

Whose idea it was to build a pool in the heart of the building is not known. Heated indoor pools were an expensive luxury, then as now, and the budget was tight.

On the other hand the doctors clearly reasoned that a pool would bring health benefits, while allowing them to observe people at play. (Social research was a key element of their approach.)

At a time when swimming and sun worship were in vogue the pool's presence would also, no doubt, attract more people.

Entry was for members only, and only families, rather than individuals, were allowed to join, at 1s per week. Once enrolled, members were encouraged to use the facilities as they would a club, the sole condition being that everyone would be subject to an occasional medical examination.

Apart from a wide range of social activities, members were also invited to buy organic food, produced by the centre's farm in Bromley. (In 1946 both Williamson and Pearse became founding members of the Soil Association.)

By 1939, 875 families had joined up, and the centre appeared to have fully justified its founders' faith, even if there had been teething problems, particularly that of children running wild.

During the war the centre closed, partly because its large expanses of glass were deemed too hazardous (though later it was used as a factory for aircraft components). Then in March 1946 3,000 people attended a re-opening party, and all seemed rosy until steadily rising costs led Williamson and Pearse

(who were married in 1950) to seek help from the Ministry of Health.

They were refused. The Centre's membership charges, its emphasis on prevention, and its allegedly lax approach to record keeping made it anathema to officials of the new NHS. Thus the dream ended in 1951, and for the next half century the building served various purposes, including as a college, until in recent years it was converted into flats.

But the pool survives, albeit modernised with a much extended shallow end and a roof level air duct. Access to its classic diving board has also been removed.

Despite this, for lovers of 20th century modernism, the building, now listed Grade II*, remains as fresh and as important as ever.

As to the centre's *raison d'être*, some critics argue that the doctors were middle class meddlers bent on social engineering.

But for those who espouse healthy living as an alternative to dependency on intervention and pharmaceuticals, Peckham has long been revered for being a true pioneer, and one, moreover, with a swimming pool at its heart.

Although the four towers were originally chimneys, up on the roof of the former health centre – once used for exercise classes – there are distinct echoes of the Empire Pool (*see page 197*). Also as at Wembley, all the centre's concrete surfaces, originally left bare, have been painted to create a softer, less clinical ambience.

Upper Mounts, Northampton

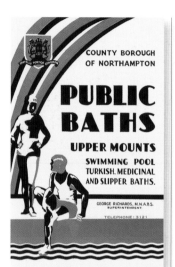

COUNTY BOROUGH OF NORTHAMPTON

PUBLIC BATHS

UPPER MOUNTS

SWIMMING POOL TURKISH, MEDICINAL AND SLIPPER BATHS.

GEORGE RICHARDS, M.N.A.B.S. SUPERINTENDENT.

TELEPHONE: 3121

Opened October 3 1936
Address Upper Mounts, NN1 3DN
Architect Ernest Prestwich
Cost £52,500
Pools 100' x 40', plus 25m teaching pool added 1974
Owner Northampton Borough Council
Operator Northampton Leisure
Listed unlisted

It is no accident that great buildings often come about as the result of close collaboration between architect and client.

In the public baths sector, two of the best examples of this were Alfred Cross' working relationship with EJ Wakeling at Haggerston (see page 126), and the combination of Owen Williams and Arthur Elvin at Wembley, (page 196).

Similarly in Northampton, the outstanding quality of the baths on Upper Mounts may be directly attributed to the pairing of architect Ernest Prestwich with the unlikely chairman of the Baths Committee, WJ Bassett-Lowke.

Based in Leigh, Lancashire, Prestwich (1889–1977) was a partner in his father's practice, one that had already designed three public baths in Leigh, Stockport and Ashton-in-Makerfield.

In the 1920s, Ernest started to make his own name as a planner for the Lever Brothers at Port Sunlight, and as a designer of war memorials for Leigh, Blackpool, Harrogate and Doncaster.

In the 1930s he then worked on major civic centres for Rugby, Portsmouth and, in partnership with the noted Welsh architect Percy Thomas, for Swansea (1934), Swinton and Pendlebury (1938), and Tunbridge Wells (1939). He also designed Armley's Public Baths in Leeds, opened in 1932.

In fact it may well have been at Northampton that Prestwich and Thomas first met, for Thomas was the assessor for the design competition launched by the council in 1932 for its own civic centre; a centre that was to feature a fire station, police headquarters and public baths. (Northampton was, at the time, one of the last large towns in England yet to have built a public indoor pool. Norwich was another.)

The chosen site for this trio of grand, civic statements was a wide thoroughfare that, until cleared in the early 1930s, had been a typical Victorian street lined by terraced houses and shops, but dominated on one side by a sprawling county prison. Indeed the baths site had, until 1922, been the prison recreation yard.

Wenman Joseph Bassett-Lowke, meanwhile, was one of Northampton's most charismatic businessmen, founder of Britain's leading manufacturer of model railways (a market that Hornby would enter in the 1920s).

But Bassett-Lowke was much more than a model maker.

Obsessed with art and design, he was an early member of the Design and Industries Association (motto 'Fitness for Purpose') and a champion of Modernism.

Indeed his house at 78 Derngate, remodelled in 1916–17 by Charles Rennie Mackintosh, is still a place of pilgrimage, as is New Ways, the house that Bassett-Lowke and his wife commissioned in the mid 1920s from the renowned German Modernist, Peter Behrens. Both are now listed Grade II*.

As well as being a patron of the arts – in 1926 he helped form the Northampton Repertory Theatre – Bassett-Lowke was also a diligent town councillor, in particular as chair of the Baths Committee. He also had two talented swimmers in the family; one niece, Vivian, went on to become a national backstroke champion and Empire Games medallist, whilst another,

THIS FOUNDATION STONE WAS LAID BY HIS WORSHIP THE MAYOR ALDERMAN A. BURROWS J.P. THE 12TH DAY OF SEPT. MCMXXXV

J.C. PRESTWICH AND SONS ARCHITECTS · J.A. GLENN AND SONS LTD. CONTRACTORS

THE SWIMMING BATHS AND FIRE STATION, NORTHAMPTON.   G 7995

Janet, became editor of *Swimming Times* during the war.

Now town councillors who like to think they have an eye for design can often turn out to be an architect's worst nightmare.

But in the case of Northampton, a series of fact-finding visits to the best new baths in the country, plus the confluence of Bassett-Lowke's eye for detail and Prestwich's rigorous sense of proportion and massing, resulted in a triumph.

Not that it was all plain sailing.

Prestwich's original plans, presumably in response to the brief, was for a combination of a multi-functional indoor pool hall with an outdoor pool alongside (a juxtaposition that was surprisingly rare before the 1960s).

But the estimated costs of just over £100,000 proved too high, so a simpler plan costing half that was agreed, for a single pool hall (for swimming only), Turkish baths and 22 slipper baths (12 male, 10 female).

Performing the opening ceremony in October 1936 was Lord Burghley, newly appointed as chairman of the British Olympic Association and gold medallist at the 1928 Olympics (whose running feats were celebrated in the film *Chariots of Fire*).

As Bassett-Lowke remarked, how fitting for Lord Burghley to have been present, for during construction of the baths a section of the original town walls had been uncovered; walls that Lord Burghley's ancestor, the Earl of Exeter, had demolished at Charles II's behest in 1662.

The following day the doors were opened to the public, and over 10,000 queued to take a peek.

And who can blame them for their excitement.

Time to turn the page...

Civic dignitaries – the baths and fire station captured shortly after their completion in 1936. Opposite, the finely chiselled foundation stone.

◀ Triumphal arches and an architectural triumph. Goodness, they knew how to design swimming pools in the 1930s, did they not?

'The **Mounts Baths**,' reported the *Northampton and County Independent*. 'offers something of the dignity of a modern cathedral.'

On its tenth anniversary in 1946 a celebratory gala was held.

So efficient had the Bell's filtration system proved to be, noted the brochure, that in ten years the pool's 135,000 gallons of water had never needed changing.

One further factor had been the placing of the changing rooms away from the poolside, forcing swimmers to pass through showers and footbaths in specially designed 'cleansing rooms', as recommended by the Ministry of Health.

From the 1946 brochure we also learn that during the war, when the Mounts was one of few baths to remain open, user numbers reached a record 284,450 in 1941, including 91,000 servicemen and women stationed in nearby bases.

In the aftermath of Dunkirk the baths also served as a place of refuge for returning troops.

Since those heroic days, the diving boards and Zotofoam baths have alas been removed, while more positively, in the 1970s asbestos coating (hailed in 1936 as a revolutionary means of insulation and acoustic dampening) was removed. An extension for a teaching pool was also added (though without compromising the splendid façade). More recently a gym has been installed in the former slipper baths area, and a dance studio in the old laundry.

Finally in 1998 the pool hall was repainted in a modern, but, as can be seen, most sympathetic colour scheme. The Turkish baths (*right*), however, retain their original decor.

Here then is a well tended and – as further celebrations to mark its 70th anniversary in 2006 testified – a much treasured building.

Indeed only one thing is lacking. Incredibly, as of 2008, the Mounts Baths remained unlisted.

Of course its design cannot be considered unique. In common with other architects of the period – at Smethwick (*page 195*), Poplar (*page 174*), Liverpool (*page 175 and cover image*), and in our next case study – Ernest Prestwich's use of reinforced concrete arches, flat roofs and stepped clerestories had clearly been influenced by the RHS Hall in London, opened in 1928. This was the look. This was its time.

Yet with respect, none of those other baths, surely, has quite the drama or poise of the Mounts.

Case Study

Seymour Place, Marylebone, London

Opened April 29 1937
Address Seymour Place, W1H 5TJ
Architect Kenneth Cross
Cost £150,000
Pools 132' x 42' (now boarded over), 100' x 20'
Owner City of Westminster Council
Operator Courtneys Leisure Management
Listed Grade II (1989)

Signage apart, at street level there is no hint of what lies within. But from the rootops, Kenneth Cross' restrained, palazzo-style block can be seen to conceal in its centre an ultra-modern pool hall of the type already seen at Smethwick and Northampton. Presumably Cross chose to conceal it from view in order for the building to merge in with its residential neighbours.

As is often the case, the historic baths of the 1920s and 1930s that we so admire today were themselves erected to replace older, and no doubt cherished buildings from the Victorian and Edwardian periods. Indeed three baths in the City of Westminster, at Porchester Place, Marshall Street and here, at Seymour Place, fit into this category.

Now known as the Seymour Leisure Centre, Seymour Place Baths was built originally by the Borough of St Marylebone to replace Victorian baths located 150 yards north on the corner of Marylebone Road (and converted into magistrates courts in the 1950s, *see Chapter Nine*).

Although its foundation stone, laid in 1935, bears the practice name of AWS & KMB Cross, Seymour Place was designed by Kenneth Cross alone, following the death of his father and partner, Alfred Cross, in 1932.

Technically it was thoroughly modern throughout, with all electric services and plant, and one of the earliest installations of a hanging basket system for clothes storage (*see page 177*), a system much favoured by Cross.

As was now the norm, there were also 'cleansing rooms' for swimmers, featuring showers and footbaths, placed between the changing rooms and the pool.

But as a reminder that the terms of the 1846 Act were still not totally obsolete – and that the area around Seymour Place was not as affluent as it might have seemed – there were also 40 slipper baths and a laundry. This had its own entrance on Shouldham Street, to the rear.

Planned like a courtyard, there were two other street elevations, both in brick with Portland stone dressings under a tiled roof.

On Bryanston Place (the southern elevation), a cupola on the roof denoted beneath it the main entrance for bathers, formed by three arched doorways.

An identical set of doors on Seymour Place, meanwhile, provided entry when the main pool was in use as a public hall (known as Seymour Hall).

Today only the Seymour Place entrance is used, and only the smaller of the two pools remains in use for swimming.

The larger of the two, with its eccentric dimensions of 132' x 42', has been boarded over for dry sports since the 1980s, although the tank remains intact and could theoretically be recommisioned.

Its roof (*right*) is in a form that will now appear familiar; formed by a series of concrete arches and stepped clerestories, although unlike Smethwick and Northampton its central section is lined by square skylights.

Still in place is its stage and proscenium arch at the former deep end, and a gallery able to hold 450 spectators on two sides. Overlooking the shallow end is a gym, originally a café.

The small pool (though still 100' long), runs in parallel with the main hall, and has a simpler, lower concrete vaulted roof (*right*), and a narrow spectator area on its south side only. It also features flush heating panels along the wall.

In swimming circles the baths have a special claim to distinction for it was here that in 1961 Dawn Zajac formed the Seymour Synchro Swim School, the first affiliated synchronised swimming club in Britain. This club dominated the sport in its formative years and had several members who went on to win honours in various European Championships.

Case Study

Central Baths, Rochdale

Opened May 25 1937
Address Entwisle Road, OL16 2HZ
Architects SH Morgan, Borough
Surveyor & Architect, and SG Eldred
Cost £67,131
Pools 100' x 36' and 75' x 30',
plus 15m x 6m learner pool added
in 1970s
Owner Rochdale Metropolitan
Borough Council
Operator Link4Life
Listed unlisted

There are two historic baths buildings in the former mill town of Rochdale, Lancashire.

On Smith Street in the town centre stands Rochdale's original public baths, opened in 1868 and therefore one of the oldest surviving public baths buildings in Britain. This served for 69 years before being replaced in 1937 by the Central Baths (now called the Central Leisure Centre), built 200 yards to the east.

Unusually the original building was not demolished, however, and after being used as a youth centre, in 1990 it was converted into a centre for teaching circus skills; unicycling, juggling, trapeze and all (*see Chapter Nine*).

In this respect the old and new baths buildings share one thing in common. Neither of their street frontages gives any hint of the spectacles that lie within.

For despite its rather austere exterior (*below left*) – faced with Accrington bricks and York stone dressings, little changed since 1937 – inside the Central Baths lies one of the most impressive and well preserved Art Deco pool halls of the period (*opposite*).

One of two original pools in the building, its vaulted, panelled and partially glazed roof may be typical of the period. But the raised viewing balconies on either side, and the balcony overlooking the shallow end, are highly unusual, and a reminder that the pool was designed equally for winter use as a public hall.

For the same reason, two street entrances were provided. The central one (*as seen left*) was originally for spectators and people attending winter events. The one to its left, now unused, was for swimmers and those wishing to use the 25 slipper baths or the Turkish, Russian and foam baths on the first floor.

As was now common, the baths also offered a modern café (*left*), opening out onto the end balcony. (This has since been converted into a dance studio and IT room.)

In common with Seymour Place (*see previous page*) Rochdale was among the first baths to fully comply with the guidelines laid down in 1936 by the Ministry of Health (*page 175*).

For example in the main pool, as can be seen opposite, a barrier

and slight level change divided the 'dry side' seats and balconies from the 'wet' or pool side, with separate entrances to the changing areas under each side balcony.

In those dressing rooms were lockers with numbered metal tokens, and a chute for used towels to be sent down to the basement laundry without needing to be handled by attendants.

Other advanced features included a Royle's filtration system that could turn round the water in both pools and their respective showers and footbaths within a three hour period (compared with an average of 6-8 hours in earlier

systems), and the provision of a car park at the rear and a drop-off area in front of the entrance.

Although not a new idea (it had been first implemented at London baths in the 1890s), the baths also sourced its steam heating from a neighbouring Refuse Destructor Works, thereby avoiding the need for separate boilers and a chimney.

That arrangement has since been superceded. But a measure of how successful the design has proved otherwise is that both the main pool and the adjoining small pool remain in use, and apart from modern colour schemes and new lighting, are little altered.

Elsewhere in the building the Turkish and Russian baths also survive, while the slipper bath areas have been converted into a gym and various fitness studios.

The addition of a learner pool in the 1970s also means that Rochdale is one of the few public facilities to offer three pools.

It is also one of the few town centre baths still in operation.

Over 70 years old it may be therefore, but Rochdale is proof that well designed historic baths can fulfil modern needs, and in this case, do so in a style that is both wonderfully theatrical and yet entirely practical.

'A positively breathtaking picture of loveliness,' declared the *Rochdale Observer* in May 1937, a description that still holds good over 70 years later. Apart from the addition of a blue thermal cover, (seen here rolled up at the shallow end), the only other significant additions have been the modern globe lights and uplighters, which replaced the original ceiling lights. Note also the individual ceiling panels, designed to dampen echo. Another advanced feature was the installation, by the Smethwick firm of Henry Hope & Sons, of electrically operated skylights, for added ventilation.

Case Study

Earls Court, London

Opened September 1 1937
Address Warwick Road, SW5 9TA
Architect C Howard Crane with
consulting engineer RJ Siddall and
LG Mouchel & Partners
Cost £1.5 million
Pool 195' x 95'
Owner EC&O Venues
Listed unlisted

When advance publicity for *Great Lengths* was first displayed by English Heritage at the London Book Fair in 2007, little did any of the thousands of visitors or exhibitors in the main hall realise that they were standing on top of the greatest length of them all; that is, the largest indoor pool ever built in Britain, and quite probably the world too.

Or that this massive pool is still there, capable of being filled and ready for action in a matter of days, using the same equipment as when the hall opened in 1937.

Even more remarkable is that, despite the vast sums invested, throughout the building's life the pool has been used for swimming for only 34 days, in 1948.

(Coincidentally that other great swimming arena of the 1930s, the Empire Pool at Wembley, *see page 196*, was also last used in 1948.)

So why did Earls Court have such a pool, and why now celebrate what appears to have been a monumental folly?

The answer to the second question, of which more later, lies in the pool's hydraulic floor system, a mechanical forerunner of the moving floors that are now so commonplace in modern pools.

But to answer the first question we must go back to 1851.

Ever since the Great Exhibition in Hyde Park, a succession of companies have vied for the capital's potentially lucrative, but also risk laden business of staging exhibitions, trade fairs, indoor sports and mass extravaganzas.

After the Crystal Palace was re-erected at Sydenham in 1854, there followed the Agricultural Hall in Islington (1862), Alexandra Palace (1873), Olympia (1886), the original Earls Court (1887), White City (1908) and Wembley (1924)

Each would have its triumphs. But every one has suffered calamities and bankruptcies too.

Earls Court, as told by John Glanfield in his entertaining history (*see Links*), was originally laid out by a Yorkshire showman, John Whitley, with exhibition halls, gardens and a 20,000 capacity outdoor arena. Its first events, in May 1887, were an American trade exhibition and the first ever appearance in Britain of Buffalo Bill's Wild West Show.

In 1896 a redevelopment saw the opening of the 6,000 seat Empress Hall and a giant ferris wheel.

Earls Court had the advantage of excellent rail connections and a central location. But the site itself was awkwardly split into three sections, and was crossed by four railway lines. It was also in direct competition with Olympia, less than a mile away, and White City, three miles northwards.

Of the three, Earls Court seemed the least likely to survive beyond the 1920s. By then, it had been virtually abandoned, while in 1930 Olympia opened its second exhibition hall (the Empire Hall, now Olympia 2).

But even this was not spacious enough for some exhibitors, and so once White City's fate was sealed by the sale of its exhibition halls for housing in 1935 (leaving the former Olympic stadium to concentrate on greyhound racing), a group of businessmen led by Sir Ralph Glyn, a director of the LMS Railway, decided that the future for London exhibitions lay in a larger facility at Earls Court, on a 12 acre site next to the Empress Hall.

Specifically Glyn's company intended for the new Earls Court to become the permanent home of the annual British Industries Fair. Sponsored by the Department of Overseas Trade, since 1920 the BIF had been spread across three sites; White City, Olympia and Castle Bromwich, Birmingham.

Before its new hall was completed Earls Court also managed to poach both the Ideal

Home exhibition and the Motor Show from Olympia.

Meanwhile it invested in an upgrade of the Empress Hall, now renamed the Empress Stadium.

This, thanks to the acumen of the company's managing director, sports promoter Frank Lewis, now became the new home of the National Sporting Club's Monday night boxing events. Lewis also persuaded promoter Claude Langdon to transfer his popular ice shows and ice hockey matches from the Hammersmith Palais.

By positioning itself in such direct competition with both Olympia and Arthur Elvin's Empire Pool, Earls Court thus brought to a head an extraordinary wave of speculative enterprise, aimed at tapping the public's voracious appetite for what Robert Siddall, Earls Court's consulting engineer, described as 'large-scale spectacle and sensation'.

On the south coast backers of the SS Brighton (see page 180) were equally caught up in this belief that somehow, as American showmen might have hollered, 'build it and they will come'.

In fact just as US interests would drive an arena boom in 1990s Britain, so too did American thinking and expertise play a major part in Earls Court.

Hegeman Harris Ltd of New York (engaged at the time in the construction of the Rockefeller Centre in Manhattan), were the chosen contractors, while the architect was the Detroit based Howard Crane, one of the leading cinema designers of the period.

Even the engineering firm that devised the pool's hydraulically operated moveable floor, Frasers & Chalmers of Erith, in Kent, was an English subsidiary of the US giant, the General Electric Company.

Work on what was to become the largest building in Europe (in terms of volume), started in mid 1936, and presented all manner of engineering challenges.

Apart from the site being split by railway lines and bordered by busy main roads, there were four underground tunnels running at angles either side of the new building, so that piling had to be done with immense care, and much of the load had to be borne by massive concrete slabs bridging the various obstacles. Over 3,000 men were employed in its construction, six of whom died.

With supreme optimism, Ralph Glyn had based his business plan on being able to open the new Earls Court in early 1937. But a series of strikes and steel shortages held up the work, resulting in a major falling out with the American contractors and the humiliating loss of the 1937 BIF and Ideal Homes Exhibition to Earls Court's rivals. And by the time the building finally did open, with the Chocolate and Confectionery Exhibition in September 1937, the total bill had reached a colossal £1.5 million.

Nevertheless a steady stream of well attended events followed; the Business Efficiency Exhibition in late September, the Motor Show, the Bicycle and Motorcycle Show, a commercial vehicles exhibition, a dog show, and in September 1938, the Dairy Show, lured from its traditional home at the Agricultural Hall in Islington (now the Business Design Centre).

Most spectacular of all was Claude Langdon's *Winter Calvalcade*, in December 1938, for which a 100' tall ski slope covered in crushed ice and bordered by artificial trees formed the centrepiece. Some 350,000 people

came to see the show, in which tightly clad girls, expert skiers and a yodeller from Penge thrilled the audience under alpine sunsets.

Yet six months later Earls Court Ltd slid into receivership under an avalanche of debts. One of its last events before war broke out and the building was commandeered for the manufacture of barrage balloons, ironically, was a mass rally by British fascists, addressed by Sir Oswald Mosley, on July 16.

Howard Crane, meanwhile, stayed on in London until his death in 1952, leaving behind one other fine building, the 1938 Gaumont Cinema on Holloway Road (now the Odeon, listed Grade II).

Of course in the post war years Earls Court proved able to survive these growing pains, and remains in business today, having been brought under the same wing as Olympia during the 1970s.

Since then, the Empress Stadium has given way to Earls Court 2, opened in 1991, while in 2012 the main hall will host the volleyball for the London Olympics.

Some might say that it should be staging the swimming instead.

To learn why not, read on.

▲ Although not used for swimming at any time other than in 1948, the **Earls Court** pool attracted much attention from baths engineers and the technical press in its early years. Here we see it with two of its three moveable floor sections (each 65' long), in tilted mode, forming depths of 3' 4" down to 7' 3½", with the third forming a deep end at a maximum depth of 13' 4".

Note the watertight access door on the side of the tank.

With two tiers of fixed seating plus demountable tiers around the pool's edge, Earls Court's maximum capacity in 1937 was 23,000. Today it is 19,100.

The three sections can also be raised to 5' above floor level to form an elevated stage (below).

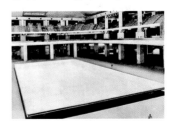

▶ Down in the dimly lit, 20' deep underbelly of **Earls Court**, a forest of plinths, props and girders holds up the three sections of the pool floor. As *Baths and Baths Engineering* put it in 1937, 'one of the most interesting engineering feats accomplished in recent years.'

And what a testament to the precision of **Fraser & Chalmers'** workmanship that after over 70 years the system – which runs on electric motors, high pressure water, oil and liberal daubings of grease – still operates perfectly.

Apparently based on technology developed for aircraft carriers, it works as follows.

In the raised position (as shown here, when an exhibition was in full flow in the hall above), the three 240 ton floor sections are supported on 96 steel props, mounted on concrete plinths.

To lower the floor, six cylindrical hydraulic rams, two per floor section (*shown right, and in the diagram*) raise the floor by a few inches, thereby allowing each of the steel props to be removed. This is a day's work for eight staff.

The floor sections are then lowered on the rams to the desired level, and locked into position by chocks fitted to 12 heavy steel rack and pinion columns (*opposite and below*), attached to the underside of the floor. (The rams themselves are not load bearing.)

These steel columns, linked to a control room where every movement can be monitored (*opposite*), ensure that as each section is raised or lowered it remains exactly horizontal. As a further precaution, guide wheels attached to the outer edges of the floor sections run in channels formed in the side of the pool tank.

Hinges and additional underfloor hydraulic ramps also allow each section to be tilted, with a rubberised canvas section inserted between two of the sections when one is lowered to form a deep end (*as shown on previous page*).

Until 1977 the hydraulic rams were powered from high pressure mains supplied by the London Hydraulic Company, whose five pumping stations on the Thames circulated water at up to 800psi (compared with 60psi for domestic useage), for the use of thousands of hydraulic cranes, fire hydrants and lifts around the capital.

(Its pipe network has since been used to carry telecom cables.)

Also of note is that once the floor is in the desired position and the taps are turned on, the entire pit floods. That is, the pool floor is neither watertight at the edges nor at the joins. After the pool is emptied, therefore, every drop of residual water has to be pumped out from the pit, and all moving parts cleaned, oiled and re-greased.

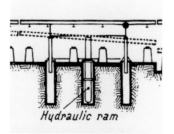

Hydraulic ram

SECTION B

9'-4" LEVEL DO NOT TILT ON BASE →	POSITION 5 DO NOT TILT ← ON BASE
TILTING POSITION 6'-10" LEVEL ON CHOCKS → OFF CHOCKS →	POSITION 4 ← ON CHOCKS ← OFF CHOCKS
4'-10½" LEVEL ON CHOCKS → OFF CHOCKS →	POSITION 3 ← ON CHOCKS ← OFF CHOCKS
PHILBEACH	BROMPTON
GROUND LEVEL ON CHOCKS → OFF CHOCKS →	POSITION 2 ← ON CHOCKS ← OFF CHOCKS
5'-0" ABOVE FLOOR ON CHOCKS → OFF CHOCKS →	POSITION 1 ← ON CHOCKS ← OFF CHOCKS

No computers or hi-tech wizardy, just good old fashioned levers, wheels and a simple control panel allow Earls Court's technical crew to effect and monitor the raising and lowering of each of the three pool floor sections. Two red balls suspended in fluid indicate the exact level and angle of each section. As a visual aide, the words Philbeach and Brompton refer to the two sides of the pool, named after the nearest roads flanking Earls Court. Even closer, only a few feet away from the blue concrete lining wall of the pool tank, are tunnels carrying District Line underground trains between Earls Court and West Brompton. For sure, here lies a subterranean world that might well have been designed for Wallace and Gromit.

Henry Seff's "AQUASHOW"

EARLS COURT · FEB 23 – MAR 27

Health and Holidays Exhibition 1948

Programme 1/-

◀ The Earls Court pool has been filled for several events, for example the Ideal Homes Show and the Boat Show. But the only known occasion it was used for swimming was Henry Sieff's **Aquashow**, staged as part of the Health And Holidays Exhibition in 1948.

Top of the the the bill, making his first appearance in Britain, was Johnny 'Tarzan' Weissmuller (born, as the programme noted, in Winbar, Pennsylvania), and his co-star, Olympic skater turned swimmer, Belita Jepson-Turner (born Nether Wallop, Hampshire).

Joe Loss provided the music, while former US Olympic diver 'Stubby' Kruge performed stunts, along with Marco & Smith (Britain's own 'crazy high-diving act' fresh from Blackpool's Tower Circus).

Yet for many the real attraction was the 'Aqua Lovelies'.

Lovely they may have been, but they had to be tough too. Part of the show's staging required them to swim through underwater tubes so that they could pop up, seemingly out of nowhere. But because Earls Court's electric boilers were unable to heat the massive volume of water without the rest of the building being cold, the water was never warmer than around 45° F.

Apparently Weissmuller was less than amused, while the Aqua Lovelies, it is said, were blue in the face for much of the performance.

▲ Filling up the pool at Earls Court – as seen here for the **2007 Earls Court Boat Show** – takes 82 hours.

This is because its extra large dimensions, plus the fact that the entire tank has to fill above and below the floor level, amounts to 2.25 million gallons, the equivalent of four Olympic-sized pools.

Small wonder that Earls Court has never been able to heat the water to a temperature bearable for most swimmers, let alone hardy Aqua Lovelies or Hollywood stars.

It then takes 24 hours to empty, but only after notifying the water authorities, such is the strain that this outflow has upon the sewers.

Each time the pool is filled and emptied costs around £14,000.

Case Study

Flag Lane, Crewe

Opened November 6 1937
Address Flag Lane, CW2 7QX
Architect Leonard Reeves, Borough Engineer, Surveyor and Architect, and H Knowles
Cost £34,090
Pools 100' x 35' plus 30' x 20' learner pool
Owner/Operator Borough of Crewe and Nantwich (to become Cheshire East Council in April 2009)
Listed unlisted

Flag Lane was Crewe's first council funded baths, but not the first baths in the town. As in that other great railway town of Swindon (*see page 88*), the first baths had been built by Crewe's largest employer, the London and North Western Railway Company.

Opened in 1866 on Mill Street this had a 34' x 24' unheated open air pool and 22 slipper baths.

But it was plainly inadequate, and so in 1934 Crewe Corporation resolved to build its own baths on a site closer to the town centre.

Accessed from Flag Lane, the site was bounded to the west by the bowling green of the Hop Pole pub, and sloped ten feet from north to south down towards the narrow Valley Park and the Valley Brook.

In order to take advantage of this slope Borough Engineer Leonard Reeves was asked to design the

pool so that on its south side it could be opened onto a sun terrace, which in turn was to overlook a paddling pool near to the brook.

A laundry was also located at basement level on the south side, facing the park, to make full use of natural light and ventilation.

As chronicled by Barbara Billups (*see Links*), one part of the brief dropped in the planning stage was for the pool to be convertible into a public hall for the winter. Hence a gallery was built only at one end of the pool, entered via a café above the entrance hall (*above left*).

Although working to a tight budget, Reeves incorporated several of the latest design innovations; electrically operated windows and skylights for added ventilation, underwater viewing windows and a separate learner pool, located within the main hall.

For adults there were dressing rooms flanking each side of the pool, fitted with teak cubicles (since replaced). For schools use Reeves also added separate, open plan dressing rooms for boys and girls, each with their own entrances, explaining that such an arrangement 'from experience, is very desirable' (allowing, as it did, greater supervision by teachers).

Such was the level of interest on the baths' opening day that Flag Lane had to be closed to traffic to cope with the crowds, and only the lucky few made it inside to see the opening ceremony, which included a display by a former diving champion from Egypt.

Interestingly, admission fees were 6d for adults and 3d for children, with towels and bathing costumes or slips costing an extra 1d or 2d, and a slipper bath costing 6d. Comparing these fees with the pre-1914 levels it can be seen just how little prices had risen since those set down in the 1846 Act and its later amendments.

A Zotofoam bath, however, with its promise to rid bathers of '1-3 pounds of superfluous fat with one hour!' was rather more expensive at half a crown.

Since 1937 the Zotofoam has gone, as have the slipper baths. The sun terrace, meanwhile lasted barely a season, once it was realised that swimmers brought in dirt on their feet.

Otherwise, Flag Lane remains pleasingly intact, and popular too. In the period 2006–08 its user numbers increased by 25 per cent, to over 165,000 a year. It also acts as host to eight clubs (with their own club room in the basement). These include the Seahorse SC, which, when formed in 1956, was the first club outside London to teach disabled children (adopting the Halliwick method, established in the early 1950s).

Another mark of Flag Lane's calibre is that in September 2008 the independent Quest Quality Scheme for Sport and Leisure ranked it as one of the top 20 leisure centres in the country (the only pre-war facility to be so highly commended).

Despite this accolade, pending a public consultation launched by the local council in late 2008, its days could be numbered, however.

Three options are up for discussion.

The first is to revamp Flag Lane itself. The second is to replace it with a new £14–15m leisure centre next to the Cumberland Arena (a sports centre and athletics track dating from 1980, just under a mile away on the north eastern side of the town centre). The third is to build a larger aquatic centre in conjunction with the Manchester Metropolitan University on its Crewe campus, a mile to the east.

One of Flag Lane's drawbacks is apparently its poor access for cars. Yet the building itself, and its site – if the landscaping and brookside setting were enhanced – have many advantages too.

The final decision will rest with the new East Cheshire Council, due to take over from the current council in April 2009.

Rather better to look at, than to look from (at least in terms of its sightlines), Flag Lane's unusually curvaceous gallery overhangs the learner pool. To the rear of this is a gym, in what was originally the baths' café.

Case Study

Ironmonger Row, Islington

Opened first phase: June 13 1931,
second phase: October 22 1938
Address Ironmonger Row and
Norman Street, EC1V 3QF
Architect AWS and KMB Cross
Cost £57,000 (second phase only)
Pools 100' x 35' and children's
pool 50' x 21'
Owner Islington Borough Council
Operator Aquaterra Leisure
Listed Grade II (2006)

Nowhere in Britain has there been such a concentration of public and private baths as in the square mile or so surrounding Ironmonger Row.

Between Holborn in the west, Whitechapel in the east, St Paul's to the south and Hackney to the north, no fewer than fourteen baths sites have been identified from the period 1742–1939.

Closest of all to Ironmonger Row, Bath Street, where the Peerless Pool stood until 1850 (*see page 21*), lies 100 yards to the east. Shepherdess Walk, location of the Metropolitan Baths until c.1905 (*page 27*) lies 300 yards to the north, while a similar distance to the north east, Pitfield Street (*page 126*) was in use from 1899-1939.

Before the mid 19th century this concentration can largely be ascribed to the proliferation of streams and wells, hence the area's cluster of breweries and spas (such as Spa Fields, Bagnigge Wells, home of Nell Gynne, and of course Sadler's Wells).

Thereafter baths proliferated more in response to the needs of the spiralling population, or because their backers sniffed a commercial opportunity.

Yet in the heart of this most populous of areas, where once had lain the 'great fen' beyond the City walls, Finsbury was actually the last borough in London to adopt the 1846 Act, and the slowest of all to then implement it.

Before the borough came into being in 1900, none of its former vestries had built baths,

and even after its first Baths and Washhouses Committee was formed, it rejected plans drawn up by Alfred Cross in 1902 for baths on Clerkenwell Road, stating that they were too costly.

Several other proposals met the same fate before the Committee was then wound up in 1905.

Indeed not until 1928 did Finsbury address the issue again, by which time a survey of the borough's households found that only four per cent had baths.

Better late than never, as it were, Ironmonger Row was the response to this damning discovery.

Once again Alfred Cross, by now in partnership with his son Kenneth, was commissioned.

There were two phases.

The first, contemporaneous with the architects' work at Marshall Street, whose design it closely matches (*page 192*), was completed in 1931.

Occupying the southern half of the site (formerly made up of terraced houses), it consisted of a four storey rectangular block housing a public laundry and slipper baths (41 male, 41 female).

Mirroring the provision of the mothers' and children's clinic at Marshall Street, there was a large room set aside for children, and a designated area for storing perambulators.

But funds being limited there was no pool, and so the borough's swimmers had to wait another seven years before the second phase was completed, on the northern half of the site.

This phase was designed by Kenneth Cross alone, Alfred having died in 1932. But it closely conformed with his father's style; being essentially utilitarian, conservative and using high quality, robust materials and finishes throughout.

As such it has withstood the wear and tear of heavy usage extremely well.

Its first major refurbishment in the late 1980s, completed at a cost of £1.5 million, resulted in only minor internal modifications to the slipper bath areas, to the Turkish baths and to the wash house, which was converted into a modern laundry.

Externally, twee canopies were also fitted over alternate windows and doors along the two main street frontages.

Fortunately these have since been removed, and moreover, the baths' future has been further assured by two measures. In 2006 the building was listed, while a year later Islington Borough Council (into which Finsbury was absorbed in 1965) announced plans for modernising both the baths, the neighbouring Finsbury Leisure Centre – a drab brick 1975 shed of a building – and the gardens onto which both faced.

Following a public consultation, as of late 2008 these plans had yet to be formalised, although Islington had certainly committed £12.35m towards the scheme (of which at least £2m was needed simply for basic repairs to the baths' external fabric).

On top of this a further £3.8m had been allocated from the EC1 New Deal for Communities fund, a government backed programme for aiding deprived neighbourhoods.

From this book's perspective what is most encouraging about the proposals is that they acknowledge the contribution, and the sense of continuity, that an historic baths can offer as part of neighbourhood regeneration.

In this respect, although its demographic may be different, Ironmonger Row shares many qualities with Marshall Street, itself undergoing a renaissance.

The people of Finsbury may have waited longer than most to have a swimming pool on their doorstep. But at least they seem set to have this fine one in their midst for a good while longer.

◀ Looking north across St Luke's Gardens – on the south side of which stands the Grade I Church of St Luke's, completed by Nicholas Hawksmoor in 1733 (now used as a concert hall) – the two phases of **Ironmonger Row Baths** can be clearly distinguished.

To the right is the earlier part, immediately identifiable as the work of Alfred and Kenneth Cross with its palazzo-style formality, red brick and stone dressings and hipped roof. Note also the roundels above each ground floor window, features it shares with Marshall Street and Seymour Place.

This block includes the main entrance on Ironmonger Row (*below left*), with its reminder of the building's parent borough and its original purpose.

On the left, linked by a bridging block, is the 1938 swimming pool extension, which has the look of a 19th century non-conformist chapel, yet houses an otherwise fairly standard 1930s pool hall.

Yet it sits comfortably enough in what is now a conservation area; one which, if Islington's plans are realised, will be greatly enhanced by the creation of a new baths entrance facing onto the gardens, together with the replacement of the unloved Finsbury Leisure Centre (on the west side of the square) with a new centre that, likewise, will also turn its face to the gardens.

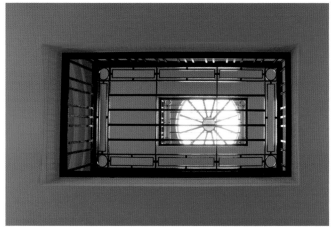

▲ Just what you need after the gym or a Turkish bath – a classic 1930s **Berkel weighing machine** supplied by Wilkie Speak Goss of Essex takes pride of place in the Ironmonger Row entrance hall.

In the days before fizzy drink vending machines colonised the public realm, scales such as these were once a staple offering at public baths.

On the first floor, an even rarer survivor is this cabin, added in 1938, from which an attendant would dispense soap and towels to women using the **slipper baths**. To comply with Ministry of Health guidelines on hygiene a chute inside the cabin led down to the establishment laundry, also added in 1938 in the area originally designated as a children's room.

A few slipper baths remain in place along the corridor, albeit not of any distinction and now used for storage. But the public laundry, modernised in 1960, still functions.

Meanwhile, the view from the ground floor up through the ornate grille of the **internal lightwell** to the circular roof lantern above (*top*), is just one of many handsome features of the 1931 block.

▲ In contrast with its exterior, Ironmonger Row's **main pool** offers a typically bright 1930s interior, with an elliptical plastered ceiling supported on square piers.

Alas two of these considerably obstruct views from the gallery (in direct contradiction of Alfred Cross' own admonition, as voiced in his 1906 treatise on baths design, of other architects who committed similar errors). But the original teak bench seats, which hold 380 spectators, are admittedly splendid, and when packed on gala nights the stadium-like atmosphere is said to have set many a pulse racing.

Best remembered of these were the galas laid on by the illustrious **Highgate Diving Club**, which used Ironmonger Row because its 12' deep end was the deepest in the capital, at least until Crystal Palace opened in 1964.

Among other notable features are the underwater lights and the 'armoured glass' which screens the children's pool from the shallow end. Above that screen is a glass fronted gym. Originally, however, this area was unenclosed, and had an additional terraced viewing gallery that doubled as a café.

Finally we must mention the Turkish baths in the basement, a London institution no less than those at the Porchester Centre and York Hall. Film buffs may know them from a bloody fight scene in David Cronenberg's 2007 film, *Eastern Promises*. But in real life they are said to be the friendliest in town, with an especially loyal clientele amongst women.

Case Study

Bon Accord, Aberdeen

Opened August 30 1940
Address Justice Mill Lane, AB11 6EQ
Architect Alexander McRobbie, City Architect's Department and TF Anderson, City Engineer
Cost £37,000
Pool 120' x 42'
Owner Aberdeen City Council
Listed Category B (1991)
Closed March 31 2008

We conclude our pick of inter war baths with a truly wondrous building whose name and fate could hardly be more intertwined.

'Bon Accord,' which has been the city of Aberdeen's motto for nearly 600 years – and is a name that has been adopted by countless sports clubs, societies and businesses since – means literally 'good agreement'.

And a good agreement is exactly what the baths' fate rested upon as *Great Lengths* went to press.

In swimming circles the name first arose in 1862, when Bon Accord Swimming Club formed on the banks of the River Dee. In 1877 it played a key role in the evolution of water polo (*see page 61*).

Ten years later Aberdeen's first indoor pool, a private venture, opened on Constitution Street. This was followed by the public Bathing Station, built overlooking the sandy expanse of Aberdeen Beach, in 1897. The private baths then closed in 1901, since when its premises have served as a tram depot, and more recently as the Satrosphere Science Centre.

Planning for the more centrally located Bon Accord Baths started in the early 1930s, but although its foundation stone was laid in 1936, it was not until August 1940, at the height of the Battle of Britain, that the building was complete.

Owing to its location Bon Accord soon became known as the 'uptown baths', to distinguish it from the 'downtown baths' on the beach. And in fine 'uptown'

company it was too. Next door was the 1932 Regent Cinema (later an Odeon), while opposite, entered from Union Street, stood the 1933 Capitol Cinema.

Both fine buildings.

Of this trio, Bon Accord had by far the most austere frontage (*see below*), a monolithic granite block, with four vertical mullions (originally topped by flagpoles) tying it to the ground and framing the entrance.

This was a challenging building.

Once inside, however, where rippled sycamore panelling lined the curved walls of the lobby, the baths took on a quite different, softer guise, not unlike that of a cinema in fact, or even, as one stepped into the pool hall (*opposite*), an ocean liner.

Artfully proportioned and bathed in natural light, this was 1930s baths architecture at its very best; the end gallery, all angles and curves, being a particular triumph of Art Deco composition. (For an even better view see inside the back cover.) All it needed was for Johnny Weissmuller himself to appear on the balcony to anoint this temple of aquatic finery.

At the opposite end stood a further delight. Framed by two tall windows (*see opposite*) this was a concrete diving stage, featuring boards of 1m, 3m, 5m, 7m and 10m over the 15' deep end.

To add to the drama, the pool was an unusually lengthy 120'.

For over 60 years the Uptown Baths was enjoyed by divers, swimming clubs, city workers and schoolchildren.

And then in February 2008, only a few weeks after it had reopened following a brief period of repairs, Aberdeen City Council decreed that it would close for good at the end of March. The baths, it had now reckoned, was costing £842,000 per annum to keep open. Each swim was being subsidised to the tune of £11. Instead, if funds could be secured, a new 50m pool planned in conjunction with Aberdeen University, would become the new focus for swimming in the city.

A 13,000 signature petition hastily collected by a 79 year old Bon Accord regular suggested that not everyone agreed with this analysis. Thus eight months after the closure, the newly formed Friends of Bon Accord Baths approached the Council with its own plan to form a community trust to run the baths.

Not only was this a beautiful building in reasonably good order, argued the Friends, but it also had great untapped potential as a health and sporting hub, regardless of whether or not a 50m pool was built elsewhere.

The opening of a hotel on an adjacent site also offered a wider potential market. On the other hand, the Odeon cinema next door was itself now a health club, albeit a private one, with a 20m pool of its own in the former auditorium.

By the time you read this, a decision may well have been made.

Fingers crossed, then, that the outcome will be a good agreement. A Bon Accord for Bon Accord, one of the truly great lengths of 20th century Britain.

Set in parkland with a steel framed hall housing a 110' x 42' pool – complete with a 5m diving board, underwater observation windows, 474 seats and extensive double glazing to let in natural light but also provide thermal insulation – Hornchurch Baths, Essex, opened in 1957 at a cost of £160,000, could be considered an archetypal small town facility of the 1950s.

Yet in one respect it was unique. For remarkably, this was the only public indoor pool built in England throughout the entire decade. In Wales, Cardiff's Empire Pool opened a year later, but not until building restrictions finally eased in 1960 did the floodgates open, releasing a tide of new baths and new ideas. Many of these failed. But Hornchurch lives on.

Chapter Seven

Post War 1945–1970

As Britain's newly elected post war Labour government set about the momentous task of rebuilding the nation's battered infrastructure and restoring its weary morale, there seemed every chance that sport and recreation would play a key role.

As early as 1943 Patrick Abercrombie had stated in the *County of London Plan*, 'Adequate open space for both recreation and rest is a vital factor in maintaining and improving the health of the people,' a sentiment echoed by his fellow town planners in bomb-scarred Hull, Plymouth, Manchester and Coventry. In plan after plan, no less than boulevards, parks, stadiums and recreation grounds, baths and lidos appeared to have secured their place in this shared vision of civic renewal.

Or so members of the National Association of Baths Superintendents (*see right*) must have felt as they convened at Paddington Baths in 1946 for an exhibition held to celebrate the peace and look forward to the future. A future, it seemed, that was ripe with possibilities.

On July 5 1948 the new National Health Service came into being.

Three and half weeks later, the Olympic Games were opened at Wembley Stadium, with the aquatic events scheduled to take place at the Empire Pool next door.

So could this have been the moment to finally square the circle between health and sport? To heed the urgings of those, such as Kenneth Cross, who saw physical culture and health as two sides of the same coin, with sport, exercise and diet at the vanguard of preventative medicine?

Fast forward another decade and we have at least one part of the answer.

In 1958 a book appeared: *Modern Swimming Pools of the World*, by Dr Dietrich Fabian, featuring an array of ultra-modern concrete and steel aquatic centres with vast pool halls, extensive glazing, sweeping saddleback roofs and hydraulically adjustable diving boards.

And where were these modern marvels? They were in Peking (opened in 1955), in Melbourne (built for the 1956 Olympics), and in Tokyo (1958). In West Germany alone there was Wiesbaden (1954), Karlsruhe (1955), Bremerhaven (1956), Wuppertal (1957) and Essen (1958).

By contrast only one British venue was pictured; the Empire Pool, Wembley, built in 1934. A world class structure, no doubt. But its swimming pool had been dry since the 1948 Olympics.

Britain, clearly, was no longer a leading player on the international aquatic scene, either in terms of its facilities or its performance levels. Between the 1948, 1952 and 1956 Olympics combined, British swimmers and divers won just one gold, and three bronze medals.

At local level the situation was similarly under strain.

During the war, and the austerity years that followed, maintenance regimes had been severely cut, leaving many of Britain's indoor and outdoor baths looking tired and shabby.

And yet the pressure on these facilities continued to mount, as user numbers rose to record levels in the late 1940s and early 1950s.

Swimming was a cheap form of relaxation. Working hours were »

Launched in 1949 by NABS, the National Association of Baths Superintendents, *Baths Service* succeeded the pre-war *Baths & Baths Engineering*. Remarkably, throughout the war NABS had kept in touch with its members, many of whom were on active service, with a newsletter, *Baths Bulletin*. From this we learn in 1942 of the death of 40 year old RB Edwards, superintendent of Flag Lane, Crewe, while on mine sweeping duties in the North Sea. In 1962 NAB became the Institute of Baths Management.

▲ Built on the banks of the River Taff, for the British Empire and Commonwealth Games in July 1958 (for which the athletics venue was the adjoining Arms Park), the **Empire Pool, Cardiff,** was the only major pool built in Britain during the 1950s, and at £710,000 was the costliest on record.

It was also only the second public indoor pool, after Blackpool's Derby Baths, to be built to Olympic standards for length and depth, albeit still using Imperial measurements (which meant that at 55 yards long it was actually 11.5 inches, or 29.2cm, over the 50m mark, until being resized to the metric standard in 1970).

Although clearly influenced by the Festival of Britain, one critic called the Empire Pool 'exceptionally dull', noting that its tubular steel diving stage could have come from a 1930s lido.

A little harsh perhaps, but certainly the building's form, if not its styling, was deeply rooted in pre-war thinking.

But in the end it was the Empire Pool's prime city centre location, not its design, that, despite widespread protestations from users and from the 20th Century Society, saw it demolished in 1998, after just 40 years use, to make way for the redevelopment of Cardiff Arms Park into the Millennium Stadium.

The bulk of the site was then further redeveloped into a multiplex cinema.

Described by one critic as 'the most interesting covered pool yet completed in Britain,' Wythenshawe Baths, opened in 1961 at a cost of £250,000, was designed by Leonard Howitt, the City of Manchester architect, and featured double-glazed screens, underfloor heating and a parabolic roof with no skylights. It was demolished in 1989.

» falling, and mixed bathing had now become the norm, so that it was not just a question of nursing existing facilities through the hard times – there would be very few closures of Victorian and Edwardian baths until at least the 1960s – but of needing more.

According to the Wolfenden Report (of which more later), the majority of towns with populations of 20,000 or less still had no public baths by 1960.

Just about the only work that did take place in the immediate post war years was to finish off those baths whose completion had been interrupted by the war.

The Hove Marina, requisitioned by the Navy in September 1939, was finally opened to the public in 1948 as the King Alfred baths (incidentally the first known baths with its own underground car park). Even more belatedly, the official opening of Derby Baths, Blackpool, took place in 1960. Lord Derby performed the honours, 21 years after his grandfather had laid the foundation stone.

Meanwhile war damaged baths, such as at Abbey Road, Barrow and Lombard Street, West Bromwich, had to wait until the late 1950s before materials and funds were released for their restoration.

As for new construction, the period 1945–60 saw only two public indoor pools completed in the whole of Britain; the aforementioned Hornchurch in 1957 and Cardiff (see left) the year after. Elsewhere, architects and planners played a waiting game. Planning for Southampton's new baths, for example, began in 1954, but would not be completed for eight years, while in Portsmouth, the Victoria Baths, whose site had been readied in the late 1930s, was not completed until 1967.

But there was activity in other sectors of pool provision.

At least four outdoor pools were built in the 1950s, while as the result of a Ministry of Education recommendation that pools should be incorporated into new school designs and ideally opened to the public out of school hours (an idea that has in recent years been widely revived), by 1960 the number of school pools had risen to around 600. Many were pre-fabricated outdoor pools of a basic standard. But at least they helped ease the pressure on public baths, as did lidos during the summer months, especially the hot summer of 1959, when several lidos clocked up record numbers.

By then the block on public baths construction had just started to ease. A year earlier, amongst the first tranche of loans sanctioned by the Ministry of Housing and Local Government were schemes for Connah's Quay, Consett, Ebbw Vale, Filwood and Kingswood (Bristol), Norwich, Southampton, Stechford (Birmingham), Walsall and Wythenshawe (*see opposite*), all opened in 1961 and 1962.

And from then on there appeared to be no holding back.

Indeed during the decade from 1960–70, 197 public indoor baths are recorded as having been built, more than in any other decade since the 1846 Act, and more than twice as many as in the 1930s.

Far from being viewed as yet another golden era, however, the 1960s is chiefly remembered as an era of poorly designed and often malfunctioning pools, in the same way that most civic architecture of the period is also written off.

As with all blanket judgements, that is unfair. As our case studies show, some 1960s designs were fresh and innovative.   »

BUTLIN'S BOGNOR REGIS
Indoor Heated Pool

▲ Never mind knobbly knees and glamorous grannies – in the late 1950s Britain's newest and most colourful swimming pools were to be found at **Butlin's holiday camps**.

Bognor Regis, opened in 1960, was the seventh of nine indoor Butlin's pools built between the early 1950s and 1966 (more than any local authority). The others were at Skegness, Clacton, Filey, Minehead, Pwllehli, Barry Island, Ayr and Mosney (Ireland).

Each 100' pool was built to a standard blueprint, with multi-coloured tiled surrounds, glazed roofs and side screens opening onto an outdoor pool or garden, and with a children's area in the shallow end, enclosed by walled barriers which proved ideal for swimmers to perch and pose upon.

To add a splash of excitement, water jets would periodically spurt up from the sides, or oxygen bubbles rise up from the floor. Most camps also featured 'Oasis' lounges, from which swimmers could be viewed through display windows. As at Filey (*below*), these were fronted by fish tanks for added effect.

But perhaps the abiding memory of Butlin's pools – recorded so vibrantly by John Hinde's postcard company (*see Links*) – was of the plastic foliage and vines hanging from the roof, interspersed with

imitation parrots and monkeys, swinging on perches. As the 1958 brochure waxed, these lent 'an exotic touch to a scene of incomparable beauty'.

At their peak in the 1960s over a million campers per year stayed at Butlin's. But none of the original pools survive, having either been demolished along with the whole camp or, as at Bognor, Ayr and Skegness, replaced in the late 1980s by free-form leisure pools.

▶ There had been public baths on Southampton's Western Esplanade since 1853, each incarnation combining outdoor and indoor pools with slipper baths. And for all its concrete, steel and glass modernity, the **Central Baths, Southampton,** was planned along similar lines. Designed by City Architect Leon Berger and opened in March 1962, the baths followed a familiar layout for the 1960s; with a single pool hall housing a 110' x 48' main pool and a learner pool of 60' x 25', flanked on both sides by seating for 902 spectators.

In common with its Victorian predecessors, there were also 30 slipper baths and a pumping system which diverted water from the nearby estuary. The brackish water was then stored in basement settling tanks before being filtered in readiness for the two pools.

A second phase envisaged a 50m outdoor pool and diving pool alongside, with sun terraces and a stand for 2,000 spectators.

But having spent £472,000 on phase one the Borough Council quietly shelved these plans (as did most other local authorities who harboured similar ambitions of an indoor-outdoor complex).

Crosby Baths (*right*) just north of Liverpool (facing the beach where Anthony Gormley's iron men now stand watch) was also filled from an estuary (the Mersey), using a similar system of settling tanks.

Opened in November 1963 it was one of the first baths to have a completely flat roof, which in the corrosive air of the waterfront proved less than ideal.

In the late 1990s both these distinctive baths were replaced; by the Crosby Leisure Centre (*see Played in Liverpool*) and in Southampton by The Quays 'Eddie Read' Swimming & Diving Complex.

CENTRAL BATHS, SOUTHAMPTON

THE BATHS, CROSBY   M 6575

» Nevertheless, it cannot be denied that whereas the lifespan of late Victorian and Edwardian baths has frequently ranged from 70–100 years, those from the 1960s have proved much less enduring.

Or that the main reason for this is that so many of them have proved to be uneconomical to run.

Of the 197 baths recorded from the period, 55 had closed by 2008 (some of them lasting barely 30 years), and a further 20 at least are expected to have closed by 2015.

Moreover, of the 142 still in use by late 2008, the majority have been refurbished to a degree that has rarely proved necessary for pre-war baths. Several, in fact, are virtually unrecognisable from how they appeared when first opened.

There are numerous reasons why so many 1960s baths have proved problematic. Not least, after a hiatus of two decades, by 1960 there was an understandable shortage of architects or engineers with experience in the field.

In addition, their adoption of large expanses of glazing was not only let down by the inadequacies of the systems themselves (particularly with regard to double glazing), but also resulted in many pools suffering from glare, which made it hard for pool attendants to monitor activity in the water, and even harder for spectators at galas to keep track of the action.

(On the other hand, designers of the 1960s could hardly have anticipated that a design ethos aimed at making baths ever more transparent – of bringing the outdoors indoors, as it were – would one day be discredited on the grounds that extensive glazing encouraged voyeurism.)

Other common faults were the use of flat roofs with a short life span, the inadequate planning

of changing rooms (particularly when located at basement levels, requiring swimmers to go up and down stairs to and from poolside), and the positioning of diving boards so as to make them a hazard to other swimmers, or to make it difficult for spectators to watch divers in action (for example against fully glazed backgrounds).

Another serious flaw, albeit one committed unwittingly, was the widespread use of asbestos based coatings on internal walls and ceilings. Known by such trade names as Limpet, Pyrok and Kenspray, these spray-on renders were hailed at the time for their ability to combat condensation, absorb sound and offer fire resistance. Needless to add, their removal in later years would cost local authorities dearly.

But perhaps the most fundamental problem afflicting public baths of the 1960s was that they were caught in the midst of much wider social and political debate as to what their primary functions should be.

Of course this was hardly a new debate. Ever since 1846 the role of public baths had been continually adjusted to take »

▲ Opened in 1962 and located a short walk from the nation's first ever pedestrianised town centre – opened by the Queen three years earlier and now a conservation area – **Stevenage Baths** was one of several civic amenities to emerge from the office of Leonard Vincent, Chief Architect and Planner of the Hertfordshire new town.

Since its designation under the 1946 New Towns Act, Stevenage's population had risen from 6,000 to 30,000 by the time the baths opened. Also completed around that time had been a college, dance hall, bowling alley and library.

Although now crowded in by neighbouring developments, the baths' basic form survives, and is notable for its clean geometry and simplicity. Indeed, coming from a period when over elaboration was rife, this simplicity may well have been its saving grace.

But nor can it be denied that since a £2.5m revamp in 2000, which yielded such gains as a new 25m deck level pool, the recladding of the building has obscured or replaced much of the varied range of original external finishes – that wonderfully concise 'swimming' sign included – and most of its

characteristic cedar ceiling strips and glazed screens (replaced partly because it is now deemed preferable for passers by not to be able to see the swimmers within).

Still, the wonderfully angled diving board (*below*), where at least three Olympic divers have learnt their craft, does still stand, albeit without its top board.

Stevenage is thus a welcome 1960s survivor, but one that, having been stripped of its original purity and lightness would, in an ideal world – like much else in the town's now historic centre – be a worthy candidate for rather more sensitive conservation.

▶ Designed by Sir Basil Spence, Bonnington and Collins, and opened by the Queen in November 1964, **Swiss Cottage Sports Centre** (its very title a badge of modernity) and its adjoining library, costing £977,000 overall, were planned as the first phase of a Civic Centre for the London Borough of Hampstead.

Once it became known that Hampstead was to be absorbed into the new borough of Camden in 1965, however, the Civic Centre idea was dropped, leaving Sir Basil reportedly so frustrated that he never visited the site again.

Certainly the two buildings, linked by a walkway, formed an odd couple. Both faced in Portland stone, the rectilinear baths block, square in plan, was characterised by horizontal glazing, while the long slender library had curved ends and vertical glazing. The glazing on both buildings was further emphasised by projecting louvres, designed to reduce glare and solar heat gain.

Inside was a prototype multi-functional sports centre – possibly the first in Britain to be fully accessible to disabled users – dominated by two 110' pools. These were serviced in the centre by an A-shaped structure which, as at Crystal Palace (*see page 236*), supported the building's 230' span reinforced concrete flat roof.

Alongside these pools lay a 75' teaching pool, a gymnasium, café,

squash courts (another sign of the times) and, perhaps surprisingly given the locality, slipper baths. These cost 6d a time, plus 6d for a towel from the centre's automated dispenser (*centre*), which less surprisingly did not survive for long.

On the south side of the block there was also a sun terrace (*top*), screened by abstract panels designed by William Mitchell.

Almost inevitably for the period, there were flaws. The 5m diving stage in the major pool (*lower right*) faced the seats, whereas diving is best viewed from the side. And as the major pool was 12' 6" at its deepest, there was no real need for an 11' 6" deep end in the minor pool (one reason why, in later years, it remained boarded over). At the same time the teaching pool had a diving pit that was too shallow. Nor did the sun terrace catch on, backing as it did onto a main road.

These issues, compounded by its poor energy efficiency and high running costs persuaded Camden to build a new sports centre on the site, opened in 2006, while saving, and refurbishing the library.

Ironically Camden then also opted to invest heavily in the refurbishment of one of its other properties, a mile to the east. This was Kentish Town Baths (*see page 102*), opened in 1901.

Such is the lottery of baths design.

» into account shifting social and economic trends. For example, by the 1960s the advent of coin operated laundrettes had severely reduced demand for wash houses, yet in certain areas there clearly remained a need for slipper baths.

But with the publication of the Wolfenden Report in September 1960, the debate took on a new direction, and one that would lead inexorably to public baths becoming focused not only on swimming and diving, but on sport and fitness more generally.

Published by the Central Council for Physical Recreation and officially entitled *Sport and the Community*, the report set out to investigate how Britain might catch up with its European rivals, but without sacrificing the finer aspects of its sporting scene; its emphasis on volunteerism and on sportsmanship in particular.

Wolfenden's main contribution was to pave the way towards the formation of the Sports Council in 1965, an idea, based on the Arts Council (formed in 1946), that had received all party support in the run up to the 1959 election.

Taking an advisory role at first, before gaining executive powers in 1972, ultimately the Sports Council, and its counterparts in Scotland and Wales, would have a profound influence on the funding, design and management of all public sporting facilities, swimming pools included.

But Wolfenden also had much to say on swimming pools *per se*.

There were, it reported in 1960, 792 public pools in Britain, of which 238 were open air, and only two were of Olympic standard (Blackpool and Cardiff). What was needed therefore, first and foremost, was more pools, in the right locations and of the

right dimensions. The report further recommended that these new pools should be indoor (a statement that still rankles with the lido lobby half a century later).

Wolfenden was particularly keen on the concept of what it termed the 'large barn', a multi-functional building in which 'wet' and 'dry' sports co-existed under the same roof. The earliest of these

were at Crystal Palace (*see page 236*) and Swiss Cottage (*see left*), both 1964, and Port Talbot, opened as the Afan Lido in 1965 (even though its pool was actually indoors).

Most ambitious of all, in 1967, was the £1m Billingham Forum on Teeside, by Alan Ward, Elder, Lester & Partners, and now Grade II listed. This colossal development – described by »

◄ Opened in 1963 and due to be replaced in 2010, **Felling Pool, Gateshead**, by JH Napper & Partners, dominates the west side of Fewster Square, a typical 1960s shopping precinct.

Although clearly influenced by the 1956 Melbourne Olympic Pool, in common with so many pools of the period it suffered numerous design flaws, not least having an entrance accessed only by stairs, a learner pool located behind the main pool's deep end (whereas convention dictates that it should have been at the shallow end), and an absurdly over generous provision of seating for 1,000 spectators.

By comparison, the pool at **Walton-on-Thames** (*left*), opened in 1965 with an identically-sized 110' x 42' pool, offered only limited poolside seating.

As would be expected of a design by Arup Associates, Walton was an exceptional building, consisting of a podium at first floor level (owing to the low lying ground conditions) and roofed by a series of tapered, pre-cast concrete beams and strengthened glass (shades of Wembley, undoubtedly). Though it suffered from acoustic problems and draughts, Walton was otherwise one of the great pool halls of the decade.

But sadly not good enough for modern tastes, and in 2006 it was closed and demolished.

▶ During the 1960s the *Swimming Pool Review* often bemoaned what it called the 'Olympic pool mania' spreading amongst local authorities.

Opened in September 1967 as a replacement for Cookridge Street, the £1.2m **Leeds International Pool** on Westgate represented the high point of this mania.

Designed by John Poulson in association with City Architect, EW Stanley, it was Britain's first 50m pool, but as at Coventry this was supplemented by a diving pool to create a T-shape overall, the central section being 33.3m long.

Apart from the vast cost of heating this volume of water (there was also a 58' x 24' learner pool) and the sheer scale of the building (96,500 square feet), its main quirk was the placing of the pool. The building's essentially square plan was turned 45° within the site (like a diamond), with the diving pool pointing north to the top of the diamond and the 50m tank placed on the east-west axis.

Although aesthetically stunning – it won a Civic Trust award in 1969 – the effect of this internal layout was said to be disconcerting, particularly as anyone doing the back stroke was prone to lose their sense of direction if they looked up at cross angles of the ceiling.

Note also the blocks of seating either side of the 10m diving board (similar to the one at Crystal Palace, *see page 236*). Overall there were 1,100 seats.

As a competition venue the Leeds pool never quite lived up to its billing, although it was not true, as often claimed, that it was too narrow and an inch too short.

In 1988 it hosted Olympic trials, and in 1993 was used a subsidiary to Ponds Forge in Sheffield for the 1993 European Championships. The pool was also well used by the

City of Leeds SC (of which 1988 Olympic gold medallist Adrian Moorhouse was a member).

Its technical flaws were legion, however. Within four years of opening Leeds City Council issued a claim for £278,000 worth of repairs against Poulson, whose firm also designed pools at Newburn and Eston (though Poulson had rather more serious worries at the time, being jailed for corruption in 1974). In 1978 the Council even considered demolishing it entirely.

But they demurred, until the axe finally fell in October 2007. As an iconic 1960s design its loss was greatly felt, but even more so because its central location made it a great boon to city centre workers.

» Pevsner as 'the grandfather of all leisure centres' – combined a theatre, ice rink, swimming pool and sports hall, and was funded by Billingham Urban District Council in a deliberate rush of spending before its absorption by Teeside County Borough in April 1968 (a scenario that would see many other lavish pools and sports centres completed during the late 1960s and early 1970s by outgoing councils in anticipation of local government reorganisation).

Indeed as the 1960s progressed and across the nation public coffers were steadily replenished, an almost Edwardian spirit of civic one upmanship returned.

In 1961, according to the *Swimming Pool Review* (launched the year before), of 1,400 local authorities in England and Wales, excluding London and County Councils, 946 were unable to fund even a minimum sized public pool. Yet by the end of decade, a record number of pools had been completed.

There was an even greater boom in schools provision, with an estimated 4–5,000 pools being built by education authorities during the decade.

Which brings us finally to one of the other great issues of the period, that of pool dimensions.

After decades of pools being built mainly to lengths of 75' or 100' (though with several eccentric deviations along the way), the early 1960s saw the adoption of yet another new standard.

It was not yet metric, despite the opening in December 1960, of Britain's first metric pool in London, on the site of the former Endell Street Baths, Holborn. This was a 25m indoor pool, built alongside a pre-existing outdoor pool known as the Oasis (which has a fascinating story of its own, as featured in *Liquid Assets*).

Rather, the new standard for the 1960s was to be 110 feet.

This was chosen because, for competition purposes, three lengths of a 110' pool came close to matching the minimum international race distance of 100m. (In fact it was a tad longer, 330' being 584mms, or 23" over the 100m mark.) The standard width, meanwhile was set at 42', this being sufficient for six lanes.

These standards formed part of several recommendations laid down in a design bulletin issued in 1962 by the Ministry of Housing and Local Government (*see Links*).

Yet five years later it was all change yet again, when in April 1967 the ASA finally bowed to pressure to conform with the rest of Europe by reducing the standard length by just nine inches, from 110' to 33.3m, thereby ending once and for all British swimming's adherence to Imperial measures.

'A commendable and far seeing decision,' as reported in the *Swimming Times*.

Britain's first 33.3m pool opened that same year at York Hall, London (*page 191*), as did the first 50m pool, in Leeds (*opposite*). There then followed a hectic nine year period in which a hundred or so 33.3m pools were built.

But that was not the end of the matter. Following a decision by the international swimming body, FINA, in 1969, that only metric records would be recognised thenceforth, in 1976 the Sports Council finally decreed that all future smaller pools be not 110', and not 33.3m, but the new short course standard of 25m.

How foreigners must have smiled at those crazy Brits.

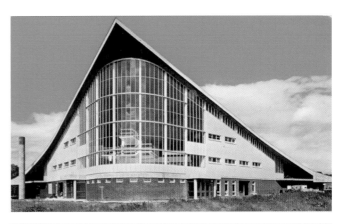

▲ Described at its opening in May 1970 as 'hyperbolic, parabolic and diabolic', **Wrexham Baths** (*top*), designed by Williams Bros, was a bold experiment that would end up requiring a £4.1m overhaul by S&P Architects in 1997. Known today as the Waterworld Leisure and Activity Centre its reclad roof is now a much admired landmark.

Keeping a rather lower profile, but much of its original character, is **Broughton Pool, Salford** (*above*) by Brownrigg & Turner, opened in 1967. Both buildings originally cost in the region of £400,000.

Case Study

National Recreation Centre, Crystal Palace

Opened July 13 1964
Address Ledrington Rd, SE19 2BB
Architects L Martin, H Bennett, N Engleback and ER Hayes
Cost £1.75m (whole complex)
Pools main: 165' x 66' (now 50m); diving: 52' x 66'; teaching 24' x 61'; plus 25m pool added 1975
Owner LCC (1951–65), GLC (1965–86), Bromley Borough Council (1986–2006), London Development Agency (2006–)
Operator CCPR (1964-69), Sports Council (1969-2004), Greenwich Leisure Ltd (2004–)
Listed Grade II* (1997)

Since it was coined by *Punch* magazine in 1851 as a barbed epithet for Joseph Paxton's iron and glass Great Exhibition hall in Hyde Park, the name Crystal Palace has taken on a variety of associations.

After Paxton's structures had been re-erected in Sydenham, south London, in 1854, Crystal Palace became synonymous with perhaps the grandest ever amusement park of the Victorian era. This was where FA Cup Finals were staged from 1895–1914, and where, at the 1911 Festival of Empire Sports (a forerunner of the Commonwealth Games), swimming races took place in one of the park's artificial lakes.

Crystal Palace has special resonance amongst historians of athletics, bowls, cricket, cycling and motor racing, and of course is also the name of a football club based a mile or so south of Sydenham, but which formed originally amongst workers at the park in 1905.

But for all its rich sporting heritage, Crystal Palace has long suffered from an identity crisis.

On one hand the park itself is an important open space and local amenity, protected by three Acts of Parliament and a raft of planning restrictions. It is also listed Grade II* on English Heritage's Register of Historic Parks and Gardens and contains six listed structures or sets of structures, of which the National Recreation Centre is the most prized, having been listed Grade II* in 1997.

Yet equally, ever since Paxton's halls were tragically destroyed by fire in 1936, Crystal Palace Park has been seen as an unresolved opportunity, and one that, as a result, has invited a succession of planning initiatives designed to restore the site's sense of purpose.

So where does swimming fit into all this?

A year after the fire, architect Horace Parnacott drew up plans for the Crystal Palace Trust to turn the palace site into a sports, arts and exhibition complex, featuring a 25,000 capacity stadium, an ice rink and a large swimming pool.

Then in 1945, as the park lay virtually derelict following its military occupation during the war, the Trust launched a design competition with an astonishingly ambitious brief. This called for two theatres, two concert halls, a dance hall, an 8,000 capacity amphitheatre and a stadium for 100,000 spectators, no less.

Given not only the hardships of the period but also the park's extremely limited transport links, there was never any chance of the winning scheme being implemented. But one other part of the brief did appeal, and that was for the provision of multi-purpose halls for swimming, ice skating and indoor sports.

Unable to cope with the scale of Crystal Palace's problems, in 1951 the Trust handed over the site to the London County Council, which then hired Sir Gerald Barry, Director of the Festival of Britain, to draw up fresh plans.

It was at this point, curiously, that the Duke of Edinburgh – tasked with the role of creating a sports-related memorial for his recently deceased father-in-law, George VI – showed Barry some sketches of how a single building might provide for swimming and indoor sports under one roof. (Whether this was the Duke's idea or was based on a centre he had seen abroad is not known. But if the latter, its identity has not been traced, at least not in Europe.)

In 1953 the LCC's Architects Department under Leslie Martin took over the project, although by the time funds were released and work finally started on site in 1960, Hubert Bennett at the LCC had assumed overall control.

By then five other national sports centres had opened, at Bisham Abbey (1947), Lilleshall (1951), Snowdonia (1955), Largs (1958) and the Cairngorms (1959). Then in 1960 the new town of Harlow became the first local authority to open its own municipal sports centre.

None of these had swimming facilities, however, nor spectator accommodation, whereas Crystal Palace was to have a 12,400 capacity athletics stadium and an Olympic sized pool with 1700 seats, adjoined by a sports hall fitted with 1270 retractable seats.

Alongside this was a 12 storey athletes' hostel, plus outdoor areas for football, tennis and hockey.

In total, these facilities occupied 40 acres in the centre of the park's near 200 acre expanse.

Apart from the fact that the National Recreation Centre was Britain's first purpose-built, publicly funded national centre – a concept that had previously seemed quite alien, or at least distinctly Continental to British sport's factionalised leadership – the most radical aspect of the scheme was the sharing of wet and dry sports within one building.

As such, the NRC was a genuine pioneer of the multi-functional approach championed by the Wolfenden Report in 1960, and a building that would prove highly influential in the years to follow.

It was therefore appropriate that the NRC should have been opened by the man who may have played a role its design, the Duke of Edinburgh, in July 1964.

Over the next three decades, at least until the opening of Ponds Forge in Sheffield in 1990 (*see next chapter*) the NRC (more recently known as the National Sports Centre) took centre stage in British swimming, staging Olympic trials, internationals, national and district championships, and in 1969, the centenary gala of the Amateur Swimming Association.

Several world records were broken, and many a world star performed there, including Mark Spitz and Shane Gould.

Yet as the *Architects Journal* noted in April 1967, despite it being designed specifically for elite swimmers, divers and water polo players, around 70 per cent of its users were actually local residents.

Even at that early stage the building's shortcomings were apparent, and although in 1975 a a more energy efficient 25m pool was added to the south of the main centre, by 2004 the Sports Council reckoned it was losing £2 million a year.

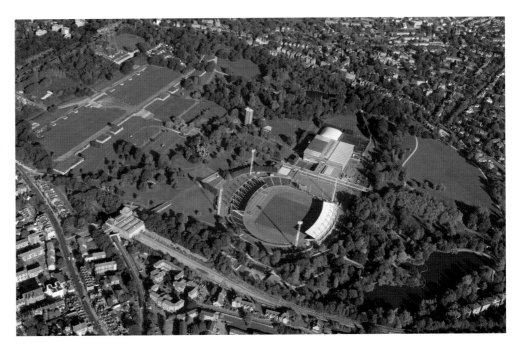

For a period it seemed as if the centre was doomed, until in 2007 it was agreed that in the run up to the Olympics the NSC would be refurbished and kept in action until at least 2012. Described overleaf, this work is costing an estimated £14m and is scheduled to end in April 2009.

After 2012, it is then expected that the NSC's main pool hall will be converted into a dry sports area and the centre's main activities transferred to the Olympic site at Stratford, nine miles away.

Meanwhile a masterplan, drawn up by Latz & Partners for the site's latest owners, the London Development Agency, proposed the construction of a new 50m pool within the park, aimed more at community and regional usage.

The plans partly depend, however, on cross funding from residential developments on the park's perimeter.

▲ Viewed from the south, the **National Sports Centre** sits in the centre of Crystal Palace Park.

Top left are the upper terraces on which Paxton's halls stood until 1936. Also visible is the base of the TV transmitter tower, completed in 1956. To the left of the NSC is the 12 storey athletes' hostel, while to the right is the cricket ground where WG Grace was briefly in harness between 1900–04.

The 16,500 seat stadium, to which the Jubilee Stand (with the white roof) was added in 1977, occupies the area where Cup Finals were staged between 1895–1914.

The sports centre itself is on an area previously called the Northern Ground, used for football, cycling and motorsports. Both areas had originally been fountain basins, laid out by Paxton in the 1850s.

Another sport staged within the park was motor racing. At its peak between 1953–72,

almost unbelievably some of world's leading drivers, such as Mike Hailwood, Graham Hill and Emerson Fittipaldi, roared around the 1.4 mile tarmac circuit at speeds of up to 103mph. Traces of the track can still be seen today.

Under the LDA's masterplan approved in 2008 the two grandstands will be demolished, as will the athletes' hostel and the ramp running between the stadium and sports centre. The white air filled bubble behind the sports centre will also go, so that the sports centre will stand alone, with its sunken access roads infilled to ground level.

The new 50m pool, meanwhile, will be built on the west side of the athletics track, closer to the station (seen straddling the railway line, lower left).

It is also planned to restore the park's central pedestrian axis leading from the upper terrace.

▶ Viewed from the south at ramp level, the striking geometry of the **National Recreation Centre** at **Crystal Palace** is clear to see.

As is evident, the oversailing roof structure, originally engineered by Ove Arup & Partners, is supported by a reinforced concrete A frame running through the central axis. From this the upper seating tier of the pool is cantilevered, while in the void below are squash courts.

But for all its structural genius, the NRC's inherent faults cannot be denied. For example the ramp (built partly to straddle the motor racing track) has been used only rarely as an entry point, whereas everyday users of the pool have to enter via an uninspiring basement door.

Siting the changing rooms at basement level was a further basic error, while the extensive use of glazed curtain walling – a feature common in 1960s pools but nowhere styled with such conviction as here – creates considerable specular reflection.

But perhaps the most serious design flaw was the lack of any sealed barrier between the wet and dry areas at the upper level. This not only created acoustic problems, but more seriously made it impossible to control temperature levels. For whereas the air in a pool hall needs to be maintained at around 28-31° C, a sports hall should not be higher than 12-16°.

These faults, combined with the volume of space to be heated, and the complexities of the building services – hidden away so as not to compromise either the interior or exterior elevations – have made the NRC a costly place to run and a tricky one to maintain.

Thus the NRC's pool hall is scheduled to be converted into a dry sports area some time after 2012, at which point the basement

will be closed off, the squash courts converted into dressing rooms, and the magnificent diving board left as a sculptural reminder of the building's aquatic past.

An even greater change is due for the exterior, where the infilling of the sunken roadways and the removal of the ramp and the later 25m pool (whose pyramid skylights can be seen top right), will turn the NRC into a free standing pavilion.

There are of course parallels here with the Empire Pool at Wembley.

By losing the water, the building may live on, while by removing the external clutter, it may look better than ever.

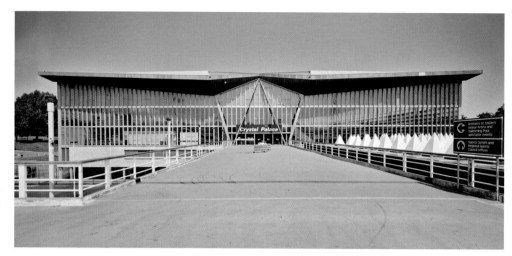

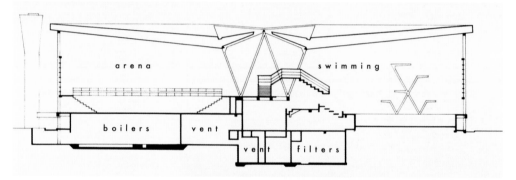

▲ A board level view shows why **Crystal Palace** is so highly prized. The 50m pool in the centre has an even depth of 6' 9" to create faster swimming conditions, to enable starts and turns to be practiced at both ends and to conform with water polo requirements.

Underwater observation windows run the full length of the pool, while Crystal Palace was Britain's first pool to have a permanent electronic timing system, still in place (on the left), and operated from the cabin seen opposite in the right.

As common in the 1960s, the roof is lined with teak slats. When Arup Associates started on the latest refurbishment in 2007 asbestos was detected above the slats, thereby delaying its re-opening by several months.

Although destined to close after 2012, one element of the revamp has been to extend the 50m pool by just 10mm to fit electronic touch pads. In this way Olympic swimmers can train here until the Aquatic Centre at Stratford is ready. Thereafter this magnificent space will be covered.

Apparently there is room for seven 5-a-side football pitches.

Case Study

Coventry Central Baths, Coventry

Opened April 23 1966
Address Fairfax Street, CV1 5RY
Architects Arthur Ling and Terence Gregory (City Architects), Michael McLellan and Paul Beney
Cost £1.04m
Pools main: 165' x 56' (now 50m), training: 110' x 42' (now leisure pool); learner: 42' x 27'
Owner Coventry City Council
Operator Coventry Sports Trust
Listed Grade II (1997)

For the citizens of Coventry the 1960s were indeed swinging. Its factories had full order books. Its newly pedestrianised shopping precincts were bustling. Even its modest football club was on the up, eventually reaching the First Division in 1967.

Coventry could even claim to have become a tourist destination, as thousands of visitors flocked to see the city's iconic modern cathedral, designed by Sir Basil Spence and consecrated in 1962.

Had they ventured just around the corner, however, they would have seen one further example of the city's resurrection.

Both of Coventry's public baths had been hit during the Blitz of 1940. Foleshill Baths, completed only in 1937, was able to be patched up and re-opened in 1946, though it had to be extensively

rebuilt in 1960. But the Central Baths on Priory Street (designed in the 1890s by Spalding and Cross, with Harold Burgess), 200 yards from the cathedral, was damaged beyond repair, and was eventually demolished in 1966.

(Not entirely though. In the centre of the car park which now occupies the site, directly opposite the current baths, is a small brick block which apparently housed the old baths' filtration tanks.)

Planning for its replacement, meanwhile, began in 1954 under the direction of City Architect, Arthur Ling. Michael McLellan, at the time working on the Belgrade Theatre, completed in 1958, then became lead designer.

As occurred elsewhere, funds for the scheme took time to be released, and even then, such was the building's scale that it took four years to complete.

But it was well worth the wait. As one observer put it, the new Central Baths was 'modern, as only Coventry can be'.

As at Swiss Cottage (*see page 232*), where coincidentally Sir Basil Spence had been involved, there were three pools, together with a small slipper bath section, a café, restaurant, sun terrace and an area called a games deck.

But the star of the show was its Olympic sized main pool, the fourth in Britain after Blackpool, Cardiff and Crystal Palace.

At Coventry there was a difference, however, because extending from its main axis was a diving pit, thereby forming a T-

shaped tank (a configuration that Leeds would also later adopt).

Facing each other across this pit were 10m and 5m diving stages, each formed by a central stem clad in brickwork, with projecting slab-like concrete boards.

On the opposite side was a spectator gallery, fitted with 1,174 upholstered seats.

Certainly Sports Minister Denis Howell was impressed. Back in harness after Labour had returned to power in the March 1966 elections (three weeks prior to the baths' opening), Howell declared that the Central Baths would become a training centre and venue for international events.

It did not work out quite like that, largely because the main pool was too narrow and because both ends were only 3' 3" deep, with the deeper section in the centre, aligned with the diving pit.

This was to allow the maximum number of schoolchildren to be taught at the same time. But it was hardly suitable for diving and turning in competitive events.

Other aspects of the baths have also proved problematic.

Apart from the usual issues of glare associated with large expanses of glazing, the pool can be overly hot in summer and, owing to its air conditioning, too cold in winter.

Rather more successful has been the provision of a gravity sand filtration system, said to be unique in Britain. (All other sand systems work under pressure). This was able to turn over the

660,000 gallon main pool in three hours, and remains in use today, apparently with excellent results.

The building's structural form has proved equally enduring. Most eye catching of all is the bird's wing cantilevered roof, supported on four stanchions set outside the building and seen to great effect from both the main frontage on Fairfax Street and from the rear on Cope Street (*see opposite*).

Since 1966 there have been two significant changes. In 1977 a sports centre was built on its eastern flank. Known locally as the Elephant (because of its hulking appearance) it is linked to the baths by a footbridge. Then in the 1990s the intermediate pool was converted into a leisure pool.

Combined, and now known as the Coventry Sports and Leisure Centre, the complex attracts around one million users per year.

But it is costly to operate, and is in acute need of a major overhaul, particularly the double glazing and the main pool's roof, which leaks. It can also be seen that netting hangs from the ceiling (*above right*), after one of the aluminium slats fell off during the 1990s.

That should be remedied in 2009, when it is also planned to turn the former sun terrace facing Cope Street (now shaded by mature trees) into a garden and skateboard park.

Otherwise, the building's future is assured only until 2012, thanks to its designation as an Olympics training venue.

In its favour is its robust structural state, its Grade II listing, and its convenient location, next to the bus station.

But will that suffice? Some have called the Coventry Sports Centre 'a cathedral of swimming'. Yet faith alone may not be enough.

Three in a row – at the far end of the T-shaped main pool (*top*) lies a teaching pool, above which is a fitness studio in the former restaurant. Beyond that is the intermediate pool, originally a standard rectangle (*above*) but now a leisure pool (*above right*). The depressing nets under the main pool roof should hopefully be gone by the end of 2009.

Case Study

Richmond Baths, Richmond-upon-Thames

Opened June 25 1966
Address Old Deer Park, TW9 2SF
Architect Lesley Gooday
Cost £478,000
Pools indoor: 110' x 42' and 42' x 24'; outdoor: 110' x 42'
Owner Richmond Borough Council
Operator SpringHealth Leisure
Listed Grade II (1996)

For a period during the 1960s it looked as if the idea, seemingly an obvious one, of building indoor and outdoor pools on the same site, might just catch on. After all, it worked in Paris, where the legendary Piscine Molitor had been in business since 1929.

Early examples on these shores included those at Loughborough College in 1939 and at various Butlin's holiday camps, starting at Skegness in the early 1950s.

These were followed in the public sector by two London examples that remain in operation today, the Oasis, Holborn, and Park Road, Hornsey. In both cases, however, the indoor pools were built alongside pre-existing outdoor pools, as an afterthought.

As regards purpose built indoor/outdoor combinations, several were planned, notably at Southampton (*see page 230*), but only two appear to have been built.

The first, opened in 1962, was at Stechford, Birmingham (where the outdoor pool was built over in 1991). The second, and seemingly the last, was at Richmond.

Opened shortly before the 1966 World Cup, Richmond Baths stood out for two reasons.

Firstly its indoor and outdoor pools (both heated) were built to the same competition dimensions of 110' x 42' (making them amongst the last in Britain to be built to Imperial dimensions).

Secondly, the baths was built within an historic park.

The Old Deer Park is a 363 acre, mostly flat expanse of grassland, owned by the Crown Estate and lying on the banks of the Thames next to Kew Gardens. Within it stands the 1769 Grade I Kew Observatory, and the 1886 Grade II pavilion of the Richmond Athletic Club (now a rugby ground).

Indeed the Pools on the Park – as the baths have since been rebranded – form only one element within an intriguing cluster of sporting sites (including also golf, cricket and bowls) to which *Played in Britain* will return for *Played in London* in 2011.

Given this setting, were it not for the busy Twickenham Road which flanks the site, the Pools could be considered almost idyllic. On the other hand, the road and the proximity of Richmond station do make it readily accessible, and the landscaping around the outdoor pool does provide privacy.

But the main reason why Richmond is such an outstanding facility, and why it was worthy of a Civic Trust award in 1967, is the sheer quality of its architecture.

This is a building both simple and logical in plan, interesting yet not too fussy in elevation, and with a clarity of space and light that lends genuine pleasure to the swimming experience.

Of especial note is the raised walkway which acts as a bridge between the indoor and outdoor sections, thereby unifying the two visually, and at the same time providing an elevated viewpoint and sun terrace (*above on the left*).

On the south side of this bridge, the teaching pool is also of interest. This has a lower ceiling to absorb noise, plus wide, non slip steps for easier entry, and heated benches for pupils to stay warm when not in the water.

It is a great shame that, as is the modern way, the building's once elegant full height entrance hall has been filled with clutter, and further compromised by the insertion of a first floor dance studio. The loss of both the main pools' diving boards is similarly to be regretted, if only because they were themselves so artfully designed (as at Coventry).

The building has also needed a major overhaul in the 1990s, and continues to require careful attention and regular investment.

One future plan is to investigate the idea of a retractable roof over the outdoor pool. But even in its current state the Pools on the Park are proof positive that at its best, 1960s baths architecture did move the genre on to new heights. And also – as its many devoted users would testify – that the indoor/ outdoor combination is one that surely merits a revival.

Case Study

Aquarena, Worthing

Opened January 27 1968
Address Brighton Road, BN11 2EN
Architect Attenborough & Jones
Cost £376,522
Pool sizes main: 33.3m x 42' and
Learner: 12.5m x 30'
Owner Worthing Borough Council
Operator Worthing Leisure
Listed unlisted

If the Pools on the Park represent one of the high points of 1960s baths architecture, the Aquarena is considered by many as one of the lows.

Described variously as a power station, a swimming factory, and most critically of all as a crematorium – that 90 foot chimney was apparently forced upon the designers in order for it to comply with the Clean Air Act – the Aquarena might have gained a better press had it been designed for a large city, or even a parkland setting. But on the seafront of sleepy old Worthing, between terraced boarding houses and a garden promenade? Small wonder the town was up in arms.

But not necessarily Worthing's swimmers, and certainly not the town's youth. They welcomed the Aquarena as a long overdue replacement for the Heene Baths, which dated back to 1866 and had been considered obsolete even in the 1930s.

As one of the first baths of the period (after the Oasis in Holborn in 1960) to have adopted a brand name, rather than being called Worthing Baths, the Aquarena was undoubtedly a trendsetter. It had a two storey car park, green plastic seats, red brickwork, and rubberised pool surrounds.

It also had only the second 33.3m pool in Britain (after York Hall). Thus when the Worthing SC hosted the ASA's inaugural short course national championships in 1971, which should really have been staged over 25m, jokers were quick to dub the event 'the intercourse championships'.

The building had its quirks too. A slightly recessed diving pit (*seen below right in the foreground*) was neither here nor there. A series of sliding doors opening out onto the large boating lake which lay between the building and the beach (*right*) were unsuccessful too and were later bricked up.

But worst of all were the building's structural faults.

In December 1977 the Aquarena was closed for repairs which, in the end, led to an almost complete rebuild costing £3m (ten times the original building costs) and took nearly five years to complete.

For their losses Worthing Council accepted a £1.2m out-of-court settlement, though the pool itself was much improved.

Indeed it has served Worthing well ever since, has remained popular with swimmers, and there will undoubtedly be a many a wistful sigh when, as now seems likely, it is demolished in 2013.

In the meantime, work on its £20m replacement, to be built on the adjacent paddling pool and playground area, is planned to start in 2010. This, it should be noted, will have a separate diving pit, and a 25m eight lane pool so that Worthing can once again attract championships to their seaside resort – but without the risk of saucy comments.

Case Study

Putney Pool and Dryburgh Halls, Wandsworth

Opened March 1968
Address Dryburgh Rd, SW15 1BL
Architect Powell and Moya
Cost £535,000
Pools main: L shaped 33.3m x 42'
plus diving bay 42' 6" x 34' 6";
teaching pool 42' x 24'
Owner Wandsworth Borough
Council
Operator DC Leisure
Listed unlisted

Now here is a rare treat; a 1960s pool designed by one of the great architectural partnerships of the post war era, Powell and Moya (who were responsible for the famed Skylon at the 1951 Festival of Britain), and, moreover, one of the few pools in London still to have its diving boards in use.

Located within a residential area and set back from Richmond Road by a sunken car park and garden in front (*above*) – so as to preserve a number of mature plane trees on the site – Powell and Moya's original design consisted of five linked, mainly white rendered concrete and glazed blocks.

Entry is from Dryburgh Road, which, because of its slope, brings visitors onto the first floor of the complex. From here, to the left a corridor leads to a function suite and meeting rooms, known as Dryburgh Halls, raised on stilts above the car park (*above left*).

A second block to the left contains a teaching pool at ground level, while at the rear of the site is another block for the plant and boilers, backing onto a railway line linking Clapham Junction with Richmond. (Pools on the Park, *see page 242*, is three miles westwards.)

But the largest and most interesting of the blocks at Putney

is that of the main pool, also at ground floor level but with a first floor gallery running along two sides, one of which has its original laminated seats for 368 spectators.

As can be seen opposite, the pool itself is L-shaped, thought to have been the first of several of this type built during the 1960s. Cheaper to construct and operate than a separate diving pool (as existed at Crystal Palace), such an arrangement made it possible for diving to take place while the main 33.3m axis of the pool was in use.

(Note that such was the British ambivalence towards metrication that although the pool's length was metric, its width and depths were still in Imperial measures.)

Also of interest is the ceiling of the pool hall, formed by a series of reinforced concrete V beams. Not only do they look fine, as they appear to float above the glazed infills above the side walls, but they conceal within them various lighting and ventilation services that can be easily serviced from the flat roof above.

Had Powell and Moya's original design been left intact, the Putney Leisure Centre, as it is now called, may well have been listed. But in the 1980s the corner of the L-shaped pool hall was infilled by a clumsy, glazed extension which houses a jacuzzi at pool level and a fitness suite above.

No doubt the extra facilities are much appreciated. But the extension has undoubtedly

compromised the clean lines and almost ethereal transparency of Powell and Moya's original design, both from within and without, and meant the sacrifice of a courtyard and several trees, around which the whole composition of five blocks was centred.

A second courtyard and a roof terrace have been similarly covered by other extensions over the teaching pool and entrance block.

In the groove – Putney's 5m diving board sits neatly under the apex of the one of the roof's V beams. One 3m and two 1m springboards complete the set. To shed extra natural light but without creating glare, the V beam on the far right is glazed on its outer edge, so that the roof appears to float. Before the 1980s infill on the left, glazed screens looked out onto the garden beyond.

Case Study

Dollan Baths, East Kilbride

Opened May 27 1968
Address Brouster Hill, G74 1AF
Architect Alexander Buchanan
Campbell
Cost £600,000
Pool 165' x 48' (now 50m), learner
pool 16' x 32' (now splash pool)
Owner South Lanarkshire Council
Operator South Lanarkshire Leisure
Listed Category A (2002)

Every new town needs a focal point, a landmark, a prestige building or a piece of public art to capture the imagination of its newly arrived residents and give them pride in their adopted home.

For East Kilbride, the first of five new towns designated in Scotland during the post war period, Dollan Baths ticked all those boxes, and more. Indeed, over 60 years since East Kilbride's development began in 1947 the building continues to be emblematic of the town today.

Labour politician George Brown had cut the first sod in September 1964, while the structure itself, to borrow Harold Wilson's phrase during the election campaign the following month, appeared to have been 'forged in the white heat' of the technological revolution.

Even its name evoked the spirit of revolution, for before he became chair of the East Kilbride Development Corporation, Sir Patrick Dollan (who died in 1963) had been a rebel rousing socialist agitator on Clydeside.

And what better way to demonstrate the egalitarian spirit of 1960s Britain than to build daringly modern public utilities for the enjoyment and benefit of ordinary working people?

East Kilbride may never have gained for itself a senior football club, unlike the new towns of Cumbernauld and Livingston. But in the Dollan Aqua Centre, as it is now known, it could boast Scotland's first ever long course pool and, furthermore, one unlike any other pool ever seen in Britain.

It is often said that its architect, Alexander Buchanan Campbell, was inspired by Kenzo Tange's National Gymnasium for the 1964 Tokyo Olympics.

Inspired perhaps. But the Aqua Centre is defiantly a building in its own right.

Hugging the windswept contours of Brouster Hill – which overlooks the town centre – it has often been likened to a billowing marquee, because its roof is formed by four concrete and vaulted parabolic segments, 342 feet in span, tied down at each end by splayed buttresses and anchored to the hilltop by massive concrete footings.

If just one strut were to break its moorings, it seems, the whole building might just float away.

In truth there have been times since the pool opened in 1968 when those in charge of budgets in East Kilbride might have wished exactly that to happen.

For a start, despite its 600 seats and the provision of cabling routes and camera positions for future media coverage – there was even an observation window to the diving area intended for broadcasters' use, which greeted visitors as they arrived – Dollan's dimensions were not, after all, sufficient for international events.

For some reason the architect went for 165' rather than 50m (even though Leeds, opened a year earlier, had already adopted the metric length). At six lanes wide Dollan was also too narrow, and was thus soon eclipsed as

Scotland's major swimming venue by the Royal Commonwealth Pool, Edinburgh. opened two years later (*see next page*).

On the other hand, so popular was the new centre with local users that these oversights hardly mattered. They loved it. It was an inspiring community asset, a wonderful place to swim, and it did put East Kilbride on the map (not least bringing a flock of architects and engineers to see it).

Nor was there much controversy when in 1994 the baths required a £4.5m overhaul by pool specialists FaulknerBrowns and Ove Arup engineers. After all, it had been heavily used for nearly 30 years.

As part of those works the 165' pool was shortened to 50m, a moveable pool floor inserted, and a glazed-in entrance area with a cantilevered canopy was introduced at the east end, to free up extra space inside and also to deter youths from climbing up the concrete struts (which are admittedly, sorely tempting).

But when South Lanarkshire Council was told in February 2008 that the building would have to be closed yet again for a further £4.7m worth of repairs, this time relating more to repairs of the concrete fabric and the upgrading of its mechanical and electrical services, there were real fears that this 1960s icon might yet be doomed, at least as a swimming venue (since its Category A listing precluded demolition).

By the time the work started in October 2008 the estimated bill had risen to £6.4m.

Yet remarkably little dissent has been heard in East Kilbride about this second extended closure in fifteen years, even amongst the town's swimmers. On the contrary, they say that

this building is their cathedral of swimming, and that, like all cathedrals, its upkeep is a long term commitment.

All being well Dollan will re-open in January 2010, and the following year will play host, at last, to a major international event, the 2011 International Children's Games, otherwise known as the 'mini-Olympics'. Lucky kids.

On the crest of Brouster Hill, with the town centre just behind, the Dollan Aqua Centre manages to be both handy and aloof. Since its mid 1990s refit the teaching pool has been replaced by a splash pool with a flume, seen snaking out of the north side (where the original glazing has been covered). But as seen from the interior (*left*), on the south side the upper glazing survives. A first floor gym overlooks the far end, while at the entrance behind this (*below left*) the new canopy provides an uplifting welcome.

Case Study

Royal Commonwealth Pool, Edinburgh

Opened January 16 1970
Address Dalkeith Road, EH16 5BB
Architects John Richards and Euan Colam at Robert Matthew, Johnson-Marshall & Partners, with Tom Ridley at Ove Arup & Partners
Cost £1.6m
Pools main: 50m x 21m; diving: 20m x 15.75m; teaching: 66' x 35' (all to be reconfigured by 2011)
Owner City of Edinburgh Council
Operator Edinburgh Leisure
Listed Category A (1996)

According to Finnish architect Alvar Aalto, a building should not be properly judged until it is at least 30 years old.

Yet such are the qualities of the Royal Commonwealth Pool (or RCP) that it was listed Category A by Historic Scotland a mere 26 years after its opening – a rare accolade, since only five other post 1970 buildings in Scotland are ranked this highly.

As the most modern pool in Britain to have been listed the RCP is therefore our final case study (in a city, moreover, that has eight other listed baths buildings, and more Victorian pools in operation than any other). It is also an apposite building on which to finish this section.

In earlier examples from the post war period, such as Crystal Palace, Coventry and Leeds, we have seen how the desire to make architectural statements did not always result in technical or operational efficiency.

By contrast, even as it prepares for a £37m refurbishment in 2009, the RCP has been refreshingly immune from such accusations.

Perfect it may not be. But a truly historic and groundbreaking design, of that there can be no doubt.

The RCP has four key assets: a wonderful setting (*as seen above in 1970, and opposite*), just south of the city centre; a striking architectural form, quite different from any of its predecessors in the 1960s;

an internal spatial arrangement that combines transparency with an astute configuration of engineering and building services, and last, but by no means least, aquatic facilities that have made it popular both as a centre for elite training and for community use.

Indeed in many respects the RCP may be considered the most intelligently planned and executed of all post war pools; a building designed from the inside out in a way that challenged established notions of pool architecture and redressed many of the flaws so often found in its contemporaries.

As often the case with major baths projects, its story begins with a fact finding mission. It was in 1962 that architect John

Richards (of the much respected practice Robert Matthew, Johnson-Marshall & Partners), together with two engineers, Jack Black (Superintendent of the city's Baths and Wash Houses), and two Edinburgh councillors, set off to visit Crystal Palace, Coventry, Cardiff and Southampton, and the best modern pools they could find in Denmark, Holland, Germany and Sweden.

Originally their project was titled the Central Swimming Pool, which, despite the name, was envisaged as a Wolfenden era wet and dry sports centre, to be sited at Meadowbank, east of the city centre, where there were plans also for an athletics stadium and velodrome. Combined, these facilities were to form the basis for Edinburgh's bid for the 1970 Commonwealth Games.

However by the time the bid was won, in August 1966, planners had realised that Meadowbank was too small, and so the pool was moved to a new site, which had the advantage of being closer to the University of Edinburgh.

For its actual construction, John Richards used his favoured method of pre-fabricating as much as possible off site, so that once the concrete foundations and the three in-situ pool tanks were ready, the rest of it, said Richards, could ideally be erected 'by people in clean overalls'.

Strikes delayed its progress by three months, and from an original estimate of £1m the final cost was nearer £1.6m. Even so, compared with other major pools of the period, this was relatively speedy and by no means extravagant.

Besides, the RCP proved its credentials almost instantly.

Opened by Princess Anne in January 1970, in May of that ››

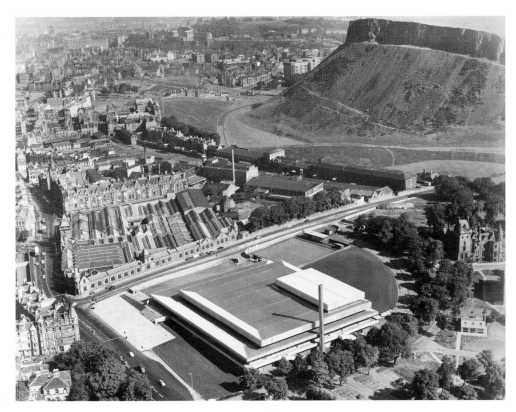

▲ Viewed from the south in 1970, the slab-like minimalism of the **Royal Commonwealth Pool** maintains a low profile amid its turreted and gabled sandstone neighbours. Over its shoulder looms the Salisbury Craigs (top right), while eastwards, out of the frame to the right, rises Arthur's Seat.

On the north side of Holyrood Park Road, facing the pool (centre left) can be seen the sprawling printworks of Thomas Nelson & Sons, the largest of some sixty printers that once rattled Auld Reekie's pavements with the clatter of hot metal. Indeed the land on which the pool was built was formerly Nelson's sportsground, one part of which, the Parkside Bowling Club (formed in 1902 as a printers'

club) sits on the northern corner of the pool (and is still there today).

On the far right, amid the trees, stands St Leonard's Hall, built for Thomas Nelson in 1870 and by 1970 forming part of the Pollock Halls of Residence (though from 1925–39 it was a girls' school called St Trinnean's, said to have been partly the inspiration behind Ronald Searle's St Trinian's novels).

Several of the blocks of student halls built around St Leonard's Hall served as the athletes village for the Commonwealth Games.

As can be imagined, the RCP's impact on its environs invited some startled reactions in 1970, rather as if a Terence Conran coffee table had been dropped into a chintzy Morningside parlour.

And yet from Dalkeith Road (*as seen opposite*), the building did its best to appear understated. Apart from the avoidance of any extraneous detailing, only in the rear western corner did the building extend to a third storey, to accommodate the diving pool. The designers also studiously ensured that the roof surfaces were kept free of clutter in order not to mar the view from the heights beyond.

As it transpired, arguably a more shocking modern building was soon to rise up on the printworks site. Opened in 1976, the brassy, glassy and sassy offices of Scottish Widows, designed by Sir Basil Spence, Glover and Ferguson (also Category A listed) made the RCP look like a model of sober restraint.

▶ Having identified common faults at other pools (namely glare, noise, heat loss, condensation and the cost of heating and ventilating large pool halls), the design team for the **Royal Commonweath Pool** adopted an innovative, engineering-led solution based on a series of overlapping planes which also took advantage of the site's drop of around 4–5m from Dalkeith Road.

Thus the three pool tanks were excavated, allowing all wet areas to be at ground level, and all dry (or access) areas to be at first floor level, entered from Dalkeith Road. This allowed the tallest section, the diving pool, to be located at the lowest point of the site, at the rear.

To minimise glare but still admit natural light, each flat roof had a deep overhang, while all external surfaces in between were glazed, using stylish Iroko (or African teak) framing. Inside this outer skin, each of the two pool halls were similarly sealed within an inner screen of glazing, to form a thermal break between the wet warmth of the pools and the cold air outside. The architects called this 'inhabited double glazing'.

It had the added benefit of creating transparency, so that visitors could see right through the building, across the pools, to the heights of Arthur's Seat beyond.

Spacious circulation routes were further enhanced by white terrazzo flooring (to reflect daylight), wood panelled solid walls, and extensive use of Iroko slats on the ceilings, to assist with acoustic damping.

A further design feature was to hide the ventilation system within the roof voids, and to heat the roof in order to avoid condensation. Although not sustainable by modern standards, this top down approach created a noticeably comfortable and dry environment.

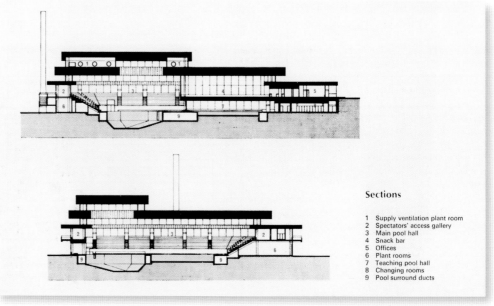

Sections

1. Supply ventilation plant room
2. Spectators' access gallery
3. Main pool hall
4. Snack bar
5. Offices
6. Plant rooms
7. Teaching pool hall
8. Changing rooms
9. Pool surround ducts

» year the pool staged its first international, Britain v. the Soviet Union (which was also, incidentally, the first all-metric aquatic event in Britain). In July came the Commonwealth Games, a great success apart perhaps from Scotland managing only one bronze medal in the pool, courtesy of David Wilkie, whose home pool at Warrender Baths (*see page 80*), lies barely a mile to the west.

The RCP was itself a winner. In 1970 it received a Structural Steel Design award, followed by a RIBA regional award a year later and a Civic Trust Award in 1972.

But the building's highest compliment came from the public.

According to the *Architects Journal* user numbers reached an average of 15,000 per week in its first year, with an astonishing 8,000 visitors recorded on individual days.

Admittedly this included many who simply came in to wander around, eat in the snack bar and enjoy the public areas.

For Scottish divers, meanwhile, the RCP was the only pool in the country to offer international level training facilities.

Since 1970 there have been a number of changes. The snack bar has been turned into a children's play area. The creation of a health club and extra offices have interrupted the transparency of the upper level, as has the installation, behind one spectator gallery, of an electronic scoreboard (bought second hand from Los Angeles after the 1984 Olympics and used when the RCP staged its second Commonwealth Games in 1986).

At the rear of the site a sauna suite was built in 1975 and, most intrusively of all, in 1992 a flume added, only to be closed in 1999.

None of these changes are irreversible however, and when the building's future came under scrutiny in 2004 it was apparent that although trends in usage had changed – for example there was no longer the need for so much

spectator seating – its basic fabric remained sufficiently sound for it to be both modernised, and to a large extent for much of its original legibility and lightness to be restored.

These works, to be funded jointly by the City of Edinburgh (£32m) and sportscotland (£5m), are to be carried out by S&P Architects and started in August 2009, so that by 2011 the revamped pools will be available for training prior to the 2012 Olympics. The RCP will then host the main diving events at the 2014 Commonwealth Games, which are otherwise to be staged in Glasgow.

Thus the building will have well and truly lived up to its title, becoming the first swimming pool ever to have staged events in three Commonwealth Games.

Proof positive that however problematic the 1960s were in terms of pool design, the decade ended, in Edinburgh at least, in triumph.

▲ 'Economy of expression was our aim,' John Richards later stated of the RCP, a design ethos that extended even to the 108' tall steel chimney, seen here with Arthur's Seat in the distance.

Note the external walkway which invited the public to promenade around the exterior, as well as serving as an escape route.

The relationship of the three pools (*left*) shows how the diving pool was set at angle to save space and to improve sightlines from the spectator galleries.

Under the southern gallery (numbered 32 on the key) was a training tank for rowers.

Plan at Pool Level

1 Men's changing room
2 Laundry
3 Women's changing room
4 Changing room for boys and clubs
5 Changing room for girls and clubs
6 Paraplegics' changing rooms
7 Lavatories
8 Quick-dry room
9 Showers
10 Main pool
11 Diving pool
12 1 m and 3 m springboards
13 5 m, 7·5 m and 10 m platforms
14 Teaching pool
15 Spectators' seating
16 Heated benches
17 Staff common room
18 First aid room
19 Laboratory
20 Store
21 Pool staff changing room
22 Engineering staff changing room
23 Oil tanks
24 Extract ventilation plant room
25 Boiler plant room
26 Main switchboard
27 Transformer substation
28 Workshop
29 Engineer's office
30 Water treatment plant room
31 Supply ventilation plant room
32 Rowing training tank
33 Telephone exchange

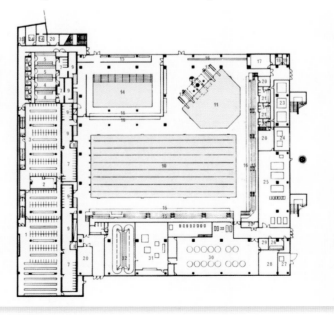

▲ No glare but plenty of flare – the **Royal Commonwealth Pool** attracts 550,000 users per year, but is now set to become even more popular, largely by being more flexible.

The 50m pool is to be rebuilt to 51.5m, to allow for two 25m deck level pools with a traversable boom in the centre. (When moved to one end this will restore its length to 50m.) One of the 25m lengths will be deepened to the international minimum of 2m, with the other similarly deepened but fitted with a moveable floor.

Meanwhile both the diving pool and the teaching pool (seen under the welcome sign) will also be rebuilt, to form two further 25m pools, each fitted with moveable floors allowing depths of up to 5m (for diving) and 1.8m (for learners and disabled users) respectively. Thus in its various configurations the RCP will be able to stage long or short course races, plus water polo and synchronised swimming, while at the same time answering the needs of everyday swimmers of all ability ranges.

To restore transparency, the scoreboard (right) will be replaced by a more compact model, while in public circulation areas solid partitions will be removed. To create space and to improve sightlines the gallery seating will also be reduced from 1,600 to 900.

Other works include demolition of the sauna suite, modernisation of the changing rooms, restoration of the Iroko ceiling slats and the addition of solar thermal roofing and grey water recycling systems.

◄ Rather than extend the entire pool hall roof to accommodate a 10m board, as at all other British pools, at the RCP only the section above the diving pool is raised.

The fixed boards (of 10m, 7.5m and 5m) are also bespoke, each stem formed by concrete-filled stainless steel tubes and served by flights of steps on self supporting columns so that, as divers ascend them, the boards do not vibrate.

As is the norm, the pool surface is agitated so divers can 'spot' the surface. Also standard are the underwater observation windows for training and broadcast purposes.

When the diving pool is rebuilt in 2009–10 its depth will increase from 4.5m to 5m (though with a moveable floor), and the existing boards replaced with new models, based on the originals.

Together with the building's dry dive training areas this will make the RCP Scotland's designated centre of excellence for diving.

Amid the widespread culls of the 1970s and '80s, few local authorities saw fit to commemorate the central role that historic baths had played in community life. The London Borough of Islington did though, re-erecting in 1988 a section of ironwork from Greenman Street Baths (known as 'The Tib', as it bordered Tibberton Square) within a small park, named Tibby Place, laid out on the site of the baths. Designed by AH Tiltman and opened in 1895, with three pools, 93 slipper baths and a 65 stall wash house, the baths had closed in 1984. The ironwork is thought to have formed the roof either to the ladies' pool or the wash house. Laundry Lane runs alongside the park, which is opposite a listed Peabody Estate.

Chapter Eight
Post 1970

During the formative years of Britain's conservation movement in the 1960s, there were too many high profile battles – for the likes of St Pancras Station, plus numerous churches and country houses – for humble historic baths to gain much attention.

Besides which, in local government circles the case against old baths was becoming increasingly difficult to counter.

Historic baths, went the argument, no longer appealed to a public intent on seeking out modernity (a public that in their own homes were doing their best to rip out or cover up every vestige of Victoriana they could find).

They were located in declining inner city areas. Their slipper baths and public laundries were now anachronistic. They were having to be subsidised to the detriment of other public services. Modern standards of hygiene were harder to maintain, as were higher water temperatures, especially now that modern pools were open all year round, rendering as untenable the tradition of old pools being boarded over in winter. (Led Zeppelin's gig at St Matthew's Street Baths, Ipswich, in 1971, would therefore be amongst the last of its kind.)

The charge sheet was a lengthy one, and as councils diverted funds to newer facilities and thereby allowed older baths to decline more rapidly, the criticisms became self fulfilling.

But three other crucial factors were equally at play.

Firstly, local government reorganisation in the early 1970s created a window of opportunity during which outgoing councils indulged in one last spending spree, while, in an attempt to prove their worth, incoming authorities equally pressed ahead with their own prestige works.

The result was a sudden rush of sports and leisure centres, most of which replaced older facilities.

Secondly, for the first time in British political history, sport now had an entrée to government, in the form of the Sports Council.

With its own Technical Unit for Sport set up to offer guidance on facility design and management, not surprisingly the Sports Council was geared more towards new build than to conservation.

Indeed in 1972 it predicted that all baths dating from before 1914 would close within a decade.

But the Council was hardly alone in believing this. For the third factor to arise during the 1970s was the emergence of 'leisure' as a central tenet of policy makers. Increasingly, argued sociologists and economists, the British public would have shorter working hours and greater leisure time to fill.

Sport, patently, would be a major beneficiary of this trend.

Then along came the 'leisure pool', making its first appearance at Bletchley in 1974.

Once local authorities saw how popular this and subsequent freeform pools could be, they all wanted one (despite various unpublished studies showing that

their higher running costs, when added to loan charges on their capital costs, actually made most leisure pools more expensive than existing subsidies to older ones).

This tension between the needs of serious lane swimmers and those more interested in leisure (the very antithesis of sport, of exertion and of competition) continues to have a bearing on pool provision today.

Taken together, these factors – local government reorganisation, the modernising drive of the Sports Council and the rise of the leisure pool – were to have a devastating impact on historic baths during the latter decades of the 20th century.

In the previous chapter we noted that a record number of 197 public indoor baths are known to have been built in the 1960s. Many, however, were in areas hitherto without facilities, particularly in new towns and suburbs.

Regarding the number of new pools built during the 1970s, precise figures are surprisingly difficult to pin down, perhaps because there were so many.

One Sports Council source, for example, estimated in 1981 that an astonishing 450 indoor pools had opened between 1970 and 1977 (when an economic downturn slowed the rate considerably). Yet another estimated 240–250.

But whichever figure one takes, the numbers far outstrip any previous decade since the passing of the 1846 Act.

In short, spanking new swimming pools, leisure pools ⟩⟩

Reflecting the changes – no longer *Baths Service* but *Baths Service and Recreation Management*, the magazine of the Institute of Baths Management shows one of the new generation of leisure pools, at the Wester Hailes Education Centre, Edinburgh (still in use today). The magazine was rebranded again in 1990 as *Recreation*, while the organisation itself finally dropped the word 'baths' from its title to become the Institute of Sport and Recreation Management in November 1993.

▶ Opened for swimming in February 1974, two months before Bletchley Urban District Council was absorbed by Milton Keynes, the £2.5m **Bletchley Leisure Centre** was Britain's first local authority leisure pool.

Linked by carpeted concourses to a sports hall, indoor bowling green, squash courts, theatre and youth club, the complex's trademark feature was its pyramid spaceframe, glazed with tinted GRP panels. Under this lay a freeform pool with connecting lagoons, water slide, sandy beach and palm trees transplanted from Portugal. Another innovation was its 'changing village', designed for family use.

Traditionalists were horrified. But 500,000 people visited in its first year (more than twice than might have been expected for a larger traditional pool).

Bletchley was the work of Faulkner–Brown Hendy Watkinson Stonor, who as FaulknerBrowns went on to become one of Britain's leading pool architects. Apparently they had developed the concept after noticing how few people at the Royal Commonwealth Pool in Edinburgh actually swam rather than splashed around for fun.

But they were not alone in their thinking. A month after Bletchley another leisure pool opened at Whitley Bay, followed by a third at Herringthorpe, Rotherham, both by Gillinson Barnett, a practice from which Peter Sargent and Mark Potiriadis later emerged to form S & P Architects.

Whitley Bay closed for a revamp in 2007. Herringthorpe was replaced in 2008, and despite attempts to have it listed, Bletchley is to be superceded in late 2009.

Regretting its demise, CABE described it as 'a beautiful and intelligent building'.

» and sports centres were as emblematic of 1970s Britain as kipper ties, chopper bikes, glam rock and Morecambe and Wise.

As to how many Victorian and Edwardian baths were demolished during this period, again accurate figures are elusive. But a figure of 140–150 would not be far off.

Meanwhile, of those that did survive the 1970s, if not always as working pools, around 20 had, by 1980, gained some protection from having been amongst the first tranche of baths listed by the Department of the Environment.

This process started in Scotland, with the Drumsheugh and Western baths clubs listed in 1970, followed in the public sector by the Victory Baths, Renfrew, in 1971, and Alloa in 1972.

In England the first public baths to be listed were Chester and Nechells, Birmingham, in 1972.

By 1990 the nationwide total had grown to 30.

Although it proved impossible to retain swimming at nearly half of these baths, listing saved all but two of the total from demolition.

The two were at Silchester Road, Kensington (by Thomas Verity, opened in 1888) and Fairmeadow, Maidstone (by Ashpitel and Whichcord, opened in 1852).

Kensington's demise prompted what may well have been Britain's first concerted baths campaign.

As an operational baths its fate had already been sealed by the opening of the new Kensington Pools in 1969. But when the Royal Borough of Kensington and Chelsea then decided in 1974 to demolish the old baths, local groups combined to argue that Verity's building should be preserved for community use.

Such was their case that even Nikolaus Pevsner voiced his   »

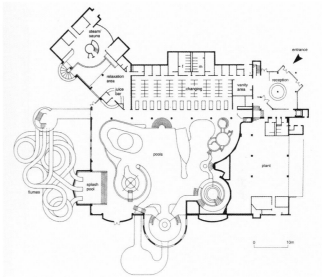

▲ The Berkshire new town of **Bracknell** already had a three pool leisure centre (dating from 1967) when it decided to commission the **Coral Reef**, a £7.5m extravaganza, designed by Sargent & Potiriadis and opened in October 1987.

Coral Reef took the theming of leisure pools to new levels, with its Blue Lagoon and Atlantis sections, a galleon (*left*), three flumes that extended beyond the main hall and a Lazy River which flows in and out of the building (and is therefore open only in the summer).

In structural terms its most interesting feature is its timber beamed and bolted roof, springing from timber columns. On the down side, the bolts require annual x-ray inspection, while the ceiling lights require platforms for maintenance.

But otherwise, for a facility so predicated on a theme, Coral Reef has proved remarkably enduring, and still attracts around 400,000 people a year, 80 per cent of whom travel from outside the area.

Even more unusually, both this and the leisure centre (which attracts 215,000 annual users) are both still operated by the local Bracknell Forest Borough Council, rather than by a leisure operator.

In 1989 the Doncaster Dome, by FaulknerBrowns, eclipsed all other leisure centres in Europe, in size and in sheer flamboyance. Costing £26m and attracting over a million users per annum, the centre's facilities include leisure pools, a heated outdoor pool, two ice rinks and a sports hall. The *Architects' Journal* praised it as 'outrageous', like 'an architectural nougat'.

Campaign literature – Silchester Baths in 1976 and below, an impromptu poster issued by the Pool Users Association at the Infirmary Street Baths, Edinburgh, in September 1987.

support, while John Betjeman declared, 'The baths are on a human scale in an inhuman area. Silchester Baths are as important to the area as the Royal Exchange is to the City of London.'

Following the baths listing in March 1975 the case went to a public enquiry, as a result of which the Environment Minister rejected the Council's application.

But after a second enquiry was forced in April 1979, to widespread outrage the minister responsible in Margaret Thatcher's recently elected Conservative government, Michael Heseltine, reversed the decision, leading to Silchester Road's demolition in 1985.

This needless destruction – the site has remained a car park ever since – proved no less of a wake up call to supporters of Victorian and Edwardian baths than the rather higher profile demolition of the Art Deco Firestone building, also in west London, had been in 1980 to members of the recently formed Thirties Society (since renamed the 20th Century Society).

Meanwhile in the Lancashire mill town of Bacup a second baths campaign was brewing. There, the council sought to demolish the 1893 Maden Baths, a measure described by Bacup's vicar in 1981 'as sacrilegious as ripping up gravestones in a public cemetery'.

On that occasion the protestors won, although after years of under investment the baths did finally close in 1995. (It has since been converted into a childcare centre.)

A third campaign, in Battersea, south London, failed to save the 1889 Latchmere Baths in 1981.

But by far the stormiest of all the early baths campaigns was back in west London.

Set against a background of swingeing cuts in public

services and growing militancy amongst public sector workers, on September 30 1979 hundreds of protestors occupied the 1902 Fulham Baths on North End Road (see page 111), following an announcement that the building was to be closed.

A march and 14,000 signature petition failed to reverse the decision, and for the next thirteen months the occupation continued – the longest ever recorded by any baths campaign – before the last protestor, 76 year old Alice Davies, finally left the building on the arm of the Deputy Sheriff of London in November 1980.

It had been an epic, and often bitter struggle, during which, for the first few months, the 'Save Our Baths' activists managed to keep the baths and laundry open through donations and by sourcing supplies of oil to fuel the boilers.

Ultimately, however, the protest failed, and once a new pool was opened nearby in 1982, the rear half of the old baths was demolished, leaving the remaining front section to be later converted into a dance centre.

But Fulham Baths lives on at least on celluloid, having acted as the main location for the 1971 cult movie Deep End, starring Jane Asher and Diana Dors.

Aside from its surreal plot, the film perfectly evokes the chlorine-soaked atmosphere of a run down Edwardian baths during the 1970s; its scrubbed corridors and creaking infrastructure, its time serving attendants, but also the warm fug of the slipper baths and the rich sense of community amongst its regulars.

A rather stronger evocation of this spirit followed in 1987 in the form of Tony Roper's stage play, The Steamie, set in a Glasgow wash

house in the early 1950s, but to its audiences a reminder too of how the public realm appeared to be on the retreat in modern Britain.

As noted in Taking the Plunge, a booklet compiled to accompany an exhibition of bathing heritage at RIBA in 1982 (see Links), 'Most local authorities now seem to see public baths as an embarrassing legacy from the past.'

Organised by SAVE Britain's Heritage (a conservation lobby group set up in 1975), Taking the Plunge was a significant milestone in the battle for historic baths.

Not only was it a passionate call to arms for conservationists, but it was also the first time since the late 19th century that anyone had attempted to place the story of public baths within a historical and social context.

At the time of its publication, the outlook for historic baths appeared exceptionally gloomy.

For if slipper baths and steamies had had their day, then in the new Thatcherite way of thinking, swimming pools, old and new, now had to prove their worth in the marketplace. And if local authorities could not rise to the challenge, that left plenty of opportunity for private operators.

Amongst the earliest to test this market were David Lloyd and Holmes Place, each of whom established their first health and fitness clubs in 1980, to be followed in later years by such chains as Esporta, Virgin Active and Fitness First.

In consequence, as shown in Table 2 (page 13), since the 1980s the number of private locations with pools (if not the number of pools overall) has overtaken the total in public ownership.

And so, in the 1980s the die was cast. »

Built on the site of an old steel mill, initially for the World Student Games in 1991, **Ponds Forge, Sheffield**, designed by FaulknerBrowns, is now England's leading competition pool.

Both its 50m pool (which has 2,600 seats) and diving pool meet Olympic standards, although in order to remain viable it also features a leisure pool, two fitness suites and a multi-functional sports hall and events arena. Although the 50m pool admits only limited natural light, the building as a whole (*as seen below*) is encased in a curvaceous glazed screen.

Also by FaulknersBrowns, and designed initially for the 2002 Commonwealth Games, the **Manchester Aquatic Centre** (*below left*) houses two 50m pools (one being at basement level), and at one end features a shallow children's pool and two somewhat token palm trees. As seen here, its main pool (which at 21m wide is narrower than Olympic standards) can be divided into two or even three sections by the use of booms.

▲ While Ponds Forge and the Manchester Aquatic Centre feature steel roofs, laminated timber roofs have returned to popularity in recent years, not least because they are easy to maintain in the chemically hostile environment of a pool hall, are not affected by condensation, and are said to be more sustainable than steel or concrete.

Shown here is the **Littledown Centre, Bournemouth** (*top*) designed by Saunders Architects and opened in March 1989 with a 25m pool. Exceptionally popular with users and still looking as good as new after 20 years, it has won several awards, including for energy efficiency and for its use of wood.

Another award winning 25m pool, voted Cambridge's Building of the Century after it opened in August 1999, is the **Parkside Pool, Cambridge** (*above*), designed by S&P Architects. This has a graceful wave form timber-framed roof supported between two V-shaped steel struts on each side of the pool.

With its turfed terrace facing out onto Cambridge's famous Parker's Piece, Parkside attracted 650,000 users in its first year, four times the numbers recorded at the 1960s pool which it replaced.

》 Determined to cut public spending and curtail the powers of the trade unions, the government introduced a system whereby local authority services were to be subject to Compulsory Competitive Tendering (CCT).

Thus arose a new form of management at swimming pools, one in which outside companies (forming the Leisure Management Contractors Association in 1989) started to take on the role that local councils had served exclusively since the 1846 Act.

Not every local council took this route, in some cases because their own in-house teams proved more competitive than outside bidders, or in a few instances because leisure companies proved reticent to take on ageing buildings.

As a result, as of 2008 around half of all public pools remain under public management.

Of the rest, approximately a quarter of all public pools, including many featured in *Great Lengths*, are now operated by private companies. These include DC Leisure, which in 2008 had 118 sites, Leisure Connection (over 80 sites), Serco Leisure (65 sites), Parkwood Leisure (65 sites) and SLM (over 50 sites).

However a second form of outside contracting has seen a similar number of pools taken over by not-for-profit trusts, also called social enterprises. These range from trusts set up to run a single facility (for example the Jesmond Swimming Project in Newcastle, which took over a 1938 pool from the local council in 1992), up to the likes of Greenwich Leisure Limited, which started in Greenwich in 1993 and now runs over 70 sites within the M25 area.

As of 2008, 120 leisure trusts and social enterprises were members of the umbrella organisation, sporta, set up in 1997. More recently these have included a number of trusts set up by some of the larger urban authorities, such as in Edinburgh, Glasgow, Kirklees, Leeds and Sheffield, although almost certainly more cities will follow.

Meanwhile, defenders of historic baths (which it has to be said includes many of the leisure trusts), have, as we have noted in earlier chapters, themselves become more vocal and organised in their efforts.

Among the most inspirational of these has been Manchester's Victoria Baths Trust, set up in 1993, plus numerous Friends groups in places such as Marshall Street (1997), Haggerston (1999), and Govanhill (2000).

Their combined efforts helped to get the plight of historic baths aired at a hearing of the Culture, Media and Sport Committee of the House of Commons in 2001, which looked at swimming and pool provision generally, and culminated in a report entitled *Testing the Waters* in January 2002.

The formation in 2002 of the London Pools Campaign represented a further boost to campaigners, ensuring that overall, since the start of the 21st century, historic baths have been accorded greater coverage in the media than ever before.

Indeed even as *Great Lengths* was in preparation in 2008, the issue of protecting historic baths gained unprecedented national attention thanks to the director of the Victorian Society, Dr Ian Dungavell, who undertook a mammoth tour of fourteen pre-1914 baths, swimming 1,543 lengths in total (one for each year the baths had been open).

Writing in *Swimming Pool Review* in 1961, TE Bett and John Smith expressed the view that 'the probable life of a public baths establishment is at least 100 years'.

In fact the average age of the baths visited by Ian Dungavell was 110 years.

But will many of them survive much longer?

Of course it falls naturally to the architects and engineers of every generation to confidently declare that they have found solutions that eluded their predecessors.

For example water management systems have improved beyond recognition. Similarly, deck level pools, which obviate the need for scum troughs (by skimming off residues more efficiently from the water's surface), together with the use of moveable floors, have transformed the quality and flexible usage of pool tanks.

Nor can there be any doubt that the introduction of various advanced materials, protective coatings and such building services as heat recovery systems have made today's pools, old and new, more energy efficient and pleasant to swim in than has ever been the case before.

All these advances, where possible, can also be applied to historic baths.

A further development to raise hopes for the survival of historic baths has been the emergence since the 1980s of specialist pool architects, experienced not only in designing modern facilities but also in the conservation and upgrading of older ones. In that respect the classic solidity of many older baths can stand them in good stead when compared with the seemingly lightweight, more warehouse-like nature of some of their modern counterparts.

Whatever their age, pools today must not only justify their existence by being popular with the public but also by being energy efficient and sustainable.

Inevitably there are reasons why some historic baths may not be able to meet those testing criteria.

Yet many of them will, if only they are given the chance.

But of one thing we can be sure.

However clever the designer, and however sophisticated the technology, placing a large volume of heated water inside a building, and then inviting in the public to do their worst on a daily basis is, as it has been since 1846, an act of supreme faith.

The design of indoor pools will therefore never cease to evolve, and never cease to be a challenge.

◀ One of the joys of modern pools is their use of angles and curves, and of lighting to enhance these effects. The **Darlaston Leisure Centre, Walsall**, designed by Hodder Associates and opened in November 2000, has a folded timber semi-monocoque structure forming its roof, with controllable louvres on the exterior to minimise glare and solar gain.

Cardiff International Pool (*centre*) opened in 2007 as the centrepiece of Cardiff Bay's International Sports Village (and as a replacement for the 1958 Empire Pool), is ovoid in plan, split into two sections: an Olympic sized 50m pool with 900 seats on one side, and on the other a leisure pool which can be adapted to form a 25m warm up pool for international events.

Finally (*below*) a tantalising impression of the interior of the **London Olympic Aquatic Centre** for 2012, by Zaha Hadid, S&P Architects and Arup Associates, shows how it might look in post Games mode, with its banks of seating reduced from 17,500 to 2,500. By far the most expensive pool ever planned in Britain, the centre will have an Olympic sized main pool, a second 50m x 20m pool and a 25m x 21m diving pool, and will replace Ponds Forge as England's main events venue and Crystal Palace as a training centre for London and the South East.

Going to waste – opened in 1898, the Grade II listed Manor Place Baths, Southwark, closed in 1978 but has been successfully recycled; its front block as a Buddhist Centre (*see page 267*) and its first class pool as a waste depot. As it happens there has been a depot on part of the site since 1873, which is partly why the baths was sited next door, so that the refuse incinerator could be used to fuel the boilers. (Shoreditch Baths, opened in 1899, was similar). The window at the far end features the arms of the Vestry of St Mary Newington. Apart from swimming, the Manor Place pool hall was a well known boxing venue during the winter months. For another view of the pool, see page 116.

Chapter Nine
Adaptive re-use

Government thinking on the use of historic buildings is best summed up in a document first issued in 1994, called Planning Policy Guidance Note 15: Planning and the Historic Environment (or PPG15). This states that 'the best way of securing the upkeep of historic buildings and areas is to keep them in active use...' and that 'the best use will very often be the use for which the building was originally designed...'

But PPG15 also recognises that for the majority of historic buildings to survive, they must also be economically viable, and that in order to be so, some degree of adaptation may be necessary.

Amongst swimmers, opinion on this most delicate of subjects is often divided, usually based on whether the pool being closed is to be replaced by another that is equally as convenient to reach, is a similar or larger size, and is affordable. But equally there exists a strong belief that whatever their future use, public baths buildings should always remain within the public realm, rather than being sold to the highest bidder.

With or without water, goes the argument, a baths building can still perform a capacity building role within a local community.

Certainly the re-use of indoor pools for other purposes is nothing new, perhaps the earliest known example being Michelangelo's conversion of the ancient Roman Baths of Diocletian into a church in the 1560s.

More recently, and rather more mundanely, Collier Street Baths in Salford (see page 46) stayed open for barely 25 years, and has since 1880 spent most of its life as a warehouse and factory.

As PPG15 goes on to state, it is deciding what the 'second life' of a historic building might be that is often the most sensitive judgement planners have to make.

In the Directory (see page 278) are listed 288 indoor baths built before 1945 that still stand, wholly or partially, of which exactly half are no longer in use for swimming.

Of these 144 survivors, as of late 2008, a quarter remained either unoccupied or at least unused for any purpose. Of the remainder, the most common forms of

adaptive re-use have been either for educational purposes or for residential accommodation.

The next main categories of usage are for specific sports (such as climbing, boxing, badminton or gymnastics); as arts venues or rehearsal spaces; as centres of prayer by different faith groups, and as multi-functional community centres.

For all these uses the height, width and layout of former baths can prove ideal, if sometimes costly in terms of upkeep, heating and security.

There are known to be four former baths that have been converted to pubs, three that have become museums, two that are now libraries, and two that have become nurseries or childcare centres. Other uses include offices, shops or salerooms, a bingo hall and, most recently, at the Infirmary Street Baths, Edinburgh, a tapestry studio and gallery.

Here then is what has happened in some of the more interesting cases when finally the plug has been pulled, the water has drained away, and a new life begins.

The Grade II listed Hotwell Baths, opened in 1889, has served as the Bristol Dance Centre since 1979, the single pool hall being ideal as a rehearsal studio and performance space. Coincidentally, during rebuilding work it was discovered that an Elizabethan theatre – reputedly where Shakespeare's *Merchant of Venice* was first staged – had once occupied the site. Other performance and dance centres at former public baths are to be found at Smith Street, Rochdale, and North End Road, Fulham (scene of the famous occupation of 1979–80).

▲ Built in three phases between 1849–96, **Marylebone Baths** – the first in London built under the 1846 Act to feature plunge pools – has enjoyed a chequered existence since being superceded by Seymour Place Baths in 1937 (*see page 208*).

The following year the buildings were converted into a dispensary, diptheria clinic and children's library. During World War Two they served as a Red Cross hospital, then, after several failed attempts to sell the site, in 1954 the London Standing Joint Committee took it over for two years, until in the early 1960s the baths was converted into the Marylebone Police Court.

Whether John Profumo (in 1963) or John Lennon (in 1968) noticed or not, the court in which they appeared had been slotted into the former 1896 Ladies' Pool, recognisable only by the surviving ironwork of its spectator gallery.

Certainly none of the many defendants who occupied the cells underneath (*right*) would have had any inkling that they were sitting in a former pool, unless, that is, they happened to have scratched their names on the rear wall and uncovered patches of the original poolside frieze. This aquarium style tilework, painted by WB Simpson & Sons of St Martin's Lane, was more fully revealed after the courts were closed in 2007 (*left*).

Meanwhile, earlier examples of Simpsons' tilework had remained exposed to view at the rear of the site, where a first class pool known as The Pompeiian Bath was erected in 1874. Above right is one of three surviving panels.

Alas, despite efforts to save them, it is thought that all these wonderful tiles will be lost when the buildings are demolished in 2009.

▲ Although the clock tower of the Grade II listed **Small Heath Library and Baths, Birmingham**, opened in 1902, could be mistaken for a minaret, it is not used as one by the Markazi Jamiat Ahl-e-Hadith charity, which has run the building as a community centre since 1979.

Prayers take place in the former first class pool (*left*), while other parts of this splendid building are used as a library, residential accommodation and, in the former boiler house, as a mortuary.

Rebirth being a key tenet of Buddhism, it is fitting that **Manor Place Baths, Southwark** (*left*) was restored in 2007 to become the Kagyu Samye Dzong Tibetan Buddhist Centre, thereby enabling English Heritage to remove it from their Buildings at Risk register.

▲ Patients' files have occupied the cubicles at the Grade II listed former **Cheltenham College Baths** (*see also page 57*) since it was converted into the records office of the Gloucestershire Hospitals NHS Foundation Trust in 2000. Having opened in 1880, the pool had served the college for 109 years.

As part of the £900,000 conversion, carried out by the Heath Avery Partnership, various conditions had to be met. For example the tank was spanned by concrete beams, rather than filled, while the steel framework that forms the upper level of open plan offices (*above right*) is free standing, leaving a small gap between its outer edges and the baths' external walls. Similarly, all drilling and fixing was kept to a minimum, so that in theory all the additions can be dismantled in the future.

The only other significant intervention necessary was the installation of thermostatically controlled skylights to ensure that the mostly paper records of some 600,000 patients are stored in the appropriate atmospheric conditions.

Leamington's public baths (*left*), opened as an extension to the Georgian Royal Pump Rooms in 1890, were converted into a public library in 1999 as part of a £7m restoration of the buildings.

▲ There have to be exceptional reasons for *Played in Britain* to stray overseas, but **La Piscine Musée D'Art et L'Industrie**, housed in former public baths at **Roubaix**, just outside Lille, is one such case.

Designed by Albert Baert and opened in 1932, the baths had a 50m pool (*right*) lined at pool level by showers, with changing cubicles on the upper two storeys (*above*), an arrangement common in France.

The detail throughout is exquisite, notably the extensive use of cream and green tiling, while fan shaped windows at each end depict the rising and setting of the sun.

After the baths' closure in 1985, Jean-Paul Philippon, known for his conversion of the Quai d'Orsay station in Paris into a museum, performed a similar task here in 2001, providing a superb space for the town's collection of fine art, textiles and *objets*, assembled since 1835 by local industrialists.

Easily reached via Eurostar, as both a museum and as an historic baths (with slipper baths, gardens and an excellent restaurant), Roubaix is simply inspirational.

Lister Drive Baths, Liverpool, opened 1904 and closed 1987, is now a quirky pet centre, with the former first class pool (*left*) serving as fisheries. It is worth visiting for its Pilkington tilework alone.

▲ There have been several scene changes at the **Montepellier Baths, Cheltenham**, since it opened in the fashionable spa town in 1806.

As noted on page 23 the baths was taken over by the council in 1898 and a pool added. But at only 64' x 23' in size and with curved ends it was never adequate, and so in 1945, at the suggestion of the town clerk, the pool was converted into what it is now called the **Playhouse Theatre**.

Run by volunteers as an arts and theatre club for the use of amateur companies, the stage sits above the old deep end (traces of which can be seen under the trap door), while under the seats (bought from the Theatre Royal, Bath) the tank area, still tiled, is used for storage. The pool's layout is also still evident from the iron columns, decorative arches and galleries seen here.

A fire in 1950 nearly brought down the curtain on this intimate auditorium, since when it has also suffered from subsidence, and in 2007, shortly after this photograph was taken, from serious flooding.

But the show goes on, making this a double delight to visit for all theatre loving swimmers.

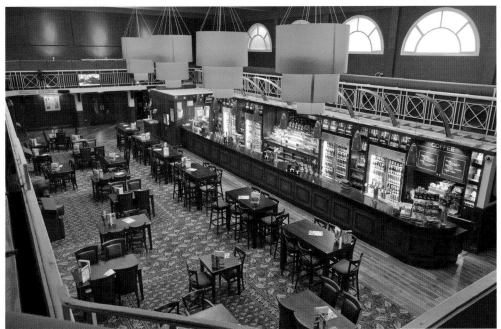

▲ Former baths are ideal for pubs, as the JD Wetherspoon chain has found. The Sir Titus Salt (*above and above left*) was originally the **Bradford Central Baths** (also called Windsor Baths), designed by the City Architect FEP Edwards, with AH Tiltman. Opened in 1905, it was converted into a pub in 1998.

Also by Edwards, **Hillsborough Baths**, **Sheffield**, opened in 1926 and closed in 1990, is now the Rawson Spring pub (*left*). If that balcony steelwork looks familiar, that is because we have already seen it featured on page 2.

Still in Sheffield, Glossop Road Baths (opened 1898) is now the Swim Inn pub (with Spa 1877, a beautifully restored Turkish baths from 1877 next door), while in Kendal, Wetherspoon has converted the Allhallows Lane Baths into the Sir Miles Thompson pub.

▲ Tokens or totems of two Grade II listed baths, now performing supporting roles at award winnng regeneration projects.

Harpurhey Baths, **Manchester** (*left*), opened in 1910 and closed in 2001, now forms part of the campus of Manchester College, where in 2008 the baths' entrance block and one of three surviving pool halls (designed by City Architect Henry Price) was about to be turned into an exhibition and meeting area by Walker Simpson Architects, to complement their first phase development of new, much lauded college and library buildings.

The baths' chimney forms the focal point of a public garden in the centre of the development.

A similar synthesis of old and new, horizontal and vertical, in north London, has seen the chimney of **Tottenham Baths** (*right*), which opened in 1905 and closed in 1991, preserved as part of the Bernie Grant Arts Centre, designed by David Adjaye on the site of the original pool hall and completed in 2007. The bath's Edwardian Baroque entrance block now serves as the entrance to the striking arts centre behind.

▲ Also from 1910 and Grade II listed, **Nechells Baths, Birmingham** was found to have serious structural problems when it closed in 1995, but has since been re-invented as a training and enterprise centre, converted by Christopher Thomas Architects and managed by the Birmingham Foundation (which purchased the building from the City Council for £5).

Externally, contrasting materials and entrances cut into the side elevation shift the emphasis from the former twin towered entrance on the west. Internally the baths' character is retained by such devices as the use of tiled compartments from the slipper bath area to form meeting rooms, and the addition of a mezzanine floor, looking out over the pool hall.

Rolfe Street Baths, dating from 1888 and closed in 1989, used to be in **Smethwick** but now resides at the Black Country Living Museum in Dudley, where its distinctive perforated arched girders – seen also at Nechells and Small Heath (*see page 267*) and several other baths in the region – have been re-erected to form the roof of one of the exhibition galleries.

▶ Several former public baths have been converted into residential accommodation, such as York Street (Barnsley), Grove Lane, Handsworth (Birmingham) and Lime Grove (Hammersmith). But in most cases it is the entrance block that has been turned into flats, with the pool shed behind making way for further residential units.

Not so at Penarth, where the former sea water public baths – opened in 1885 at the height of the town's popularity as a seaside resort, and listed Grade II in 1984 – has recently been converted into four town houses by John Wotton Architects, two pool halls and all.

After the baths closed in 1985 the building was for a while turned into a pub, called the 'Inn at the Deep End', then into a country and western club, before developers bought the site in 2004. They went into liquidation, as did a second company, until the conversion was finally completed in 2008 under the name Balmoral Quay.

Last seen as on the market for £550,000, the largest of the four houses has a loft style open plan space within the roof of one of the pool halls (*right*), and its own luxurious spa. Handily enough it would also appear to have a bus stop right outside the door. Penarth Pier and Cardiff Bay lie just across the road. A great location for a local swimming pool in fact.

After 40 years of neglect as a warehouse, the Grade II listed Blackfriars Road Baths, Salford (*left and above*), built in 1880 next door to the Manchester Tennis and Racquet Club, was renovated and converted at a cost of £450,000 by OMI Architects, who now occupy one of four office studios there. The scheme gained a RIBA regional award in 2005.

▲ We conclude this section with an intriguing example of adaptive re-use, in Runcorn, on the southern banks of the River Mersey.

Earlier we stated that the oldest operational indoor swimming pool in Britain is at Crossley Heath School, dating back to 1864 (*see page 49*). Strictly speaking, we should have said the oldest known *purpose built* indoor pool.

Because the building in which we now find **Runcorn Swimming Pool** was actually built as a market hall, and was opened in September 1856. Designed by a surveyor called Barker it housed 14 shops around the perimeter and was one of the first buildings in the town to have gas lighting.

Perhaps because the town's needs outgrew the building, but also because increasing numbers were drowning in the recently opened Manchester Ship Canal, in September 1908 the market hall was converted into a pool.

A century later the pool is still there, 23m x 10m in size, albeit with few original features following an extensive revamp in 1973.

But it is not alone. In Hexham, in 1974, a pool was built within an 1885 warehouse (closed in 2008), while in Frome an ironworks was converted in 1899, and stayed in use as a pool until 1975.

We therefore wonder, where else might there be redundant buildings – churches, warehouses or whatever – that might also suit conversion into a pool?

After all, adaptive re-use is not a one way street and never has been.

Chapter Ten

Conclusions

Writing on the wall – the Grade II listed Haggerston Baths is one of over 20 historic baths whose future currently hangs in the balance, the uncomfortable irony being its proximity to Stratford, where the costliest pool in Britain is currently under construction for the 2012 Olympics. As cutbacks in local government threaten to bite deeper, supporters of historic baths face an ever harder task of defending their corner.

Having gone on at such great length to tell the story of Britain's historic indoor pools our first conclusion is that, in order to fit in all the material we have amassed, this book might easily have doubled in size.

This truly is a mammoth subject area, and your authors are only too aware that there are many worthy baths around Britain that we have not had room to feature, and that there are specialist areas of pool design and management, and of the history of bathing (such as of slipper baths and Turkish baths) that we have hardly touched upon in any great depth.

Thus while we hope that *Great Lengths* forms a useful background, the book should not be regarded as an end in itself. Rather, our study has raised a number of issues that relate not only to historic baths, but which are of relevance to the heritage of swimming as a whole.

Many of these issues are too complex to be summed up in a few sentences. Nevertheless, it is hoped that the brief points which follow will prompt discussion amongst interested parties.

Pooling resources
There already exists an informal network of swimming- and pools-related campaigners who share news and information via various websites and forums.

In London this role is fulfilled admirably by the London Pools Campaign, whose efforts since 2002 have not only brought attention to the plight of historic baths, but whose Golden Goggles awards have generated tremendous interest and healthy rivalry within the capital's swimming community.

However, there is a case for the setting up of a national organisation focused not only on user groups but on the issues of conserving and managing historic baths themselves, with a central point of contact and a website.

One such model for this is the Historic Houses Association.

Moreover, much of the expertise required to make this succeed already exists amongst campaigners, conservation architects and members of sporta (the umbrella organisation for Britain's leisure trusts).

These range from small social enterprises such as the Victoria Baths Trust and the Jesmond Swimming Project, up to major trusts such as Edinburgh Leisure, which has arguably the most experience of running and renovating historic baths.

Marketing heritage
Whether it be denoted by a golden goggle, a silver slipper bath or a bronze bathing cap, membership of an association of historic baths should become a badge of honour, and enable operators to market their wares more widely.

After all, if the Coral Reef in Bracknell or Waterworld in Stoke can be sold as destinations, why not historic baths too?

They already have marketable assets. Heritage alone is a selling point. But as certain outdoor pools have shown, for example with

No flumes, no slides, no muzak, no fizzy drink machines, no clutter, no fuss – how might the historic baths of the early 21st century send a positive message to the public?

midnight sessions or by targeting specific interest groups or by laying on appropriate lighting, music and refreshments at set times, historic baths have much to offer swimmers that modern pools cannot match.

There may even be potential for considering historic baths as *bona fide* tourist attractions. Again, it works for the Gellert Baths in Budapest, so why not for Marshall Street in Soho?

Listings

As stated in Chapter One, there are 116 listed baths buildings in Britain, of which 52 are currently either operational or are in the process of being refurbished.

There are, however, several more buildings featured on these pages which may well merit consideration for listing.

Three firm candidates are the baths at Westbury (*see page 82*), Glossop (*page 84*) and Upper Mounts, Northampton (*page 204*).

It would be interesting to learn from readers whether any others not featured in *Great Lengths* should also be considered.

Heritage at Risk

The fates of four sites on the *Heritage at Risk* Register raise particular concern, not only as buildings *per se* but as exemplars within the wider context of bathing and swimming history.

These buildings are Collier Street, Salford (*page 46*), Ashton-under-Lyne (*page 64*), Haggerston, Hackney (*page 126*) and Moseley Road, Birmingham (*page 154*).

As the nation's stock of historic baths diminishes with every year, these are buildings whose significance transcends local boundaries, and as such require attention at the highest levels.

The heritage of swimming

During the Euro '96 tournament, English stadiums reverberated with the words of a song entitled 'Football's Coming Home'.

At the 2012 Olympics, it could be said, so is water polo.

But will this be acknowledged, and if so, by whom?

There are museums in Britain for football, cricket, rugby union, tennis, golf, horse racing and rowing. Yet not for aquatic sports.

For an area in which the British have historically played a key role, not only in terms of competition but in administration and (lest we forget) in swimming pool design, this is surely a serious omission.

There is a further need to initiate the process of gathering and archiving all known publications, records and documents relating to the history of British swimming on a formal basis.

Of course it is understood that swimming, diving and water polo are not wealthy sports, and that a museum or any heritage or archive-related initiative will need financial assistance.

On the plus side, we know of numerous handsome buildings that might house such a museum.

Nor is there any shortage of interesting artefacts, images or material, thanks largely to the efforts of a coterie of individuals who have set out over the last few decades to safeguard Britain's aquatic treasures, entirely at their own expense.

If exhibited with sensitivity, as seen for example at Roubaix (*page 269*) – and combined with the chance of visitors being able to swim in an historic pool or take an old fashioned slipper or Turkish bath – a working, living and breathing swimming museum could offer tremendous allure.

Finally, consideration needs to be given to the commemoration of some of the past heroes of British swimming – the David Wilkies and Rebecca Adlingtons of their time – the likes of Captain Matthew Webb, Jack Jarvis, Rob Derbyshire, Henry Taylor, Paul Radmilovic, Jennie Fletcher, Judy Grinham and Anita Lonsbrough.

They too were responsible for some truly great lengths, and deserve to be celebrated.

Boarded up for 20 years, the Grade II listed Stirchley Baths in Birmingham wears its laurels like a wreath, and is one of a growing number of former baths whose future needs urgent consideration before further damage to its fabric sets in. No such danger for the 1884 Forest Hill Baths, however (*left*). London's oldest operating pool at the time of its closure in 2006, it is to be replaced, despite protests, by 2010.

Directory of indoor pools 1800–1970

Part One 1800–1945

This part of the directory lists all baths-related buildings that have incorporated swimming pools, extant as of October 2008. Because their numbers are so few, private and institutional pools built *before* 1918 are included. For 1918–45, *only* public pools are included. Listed buildings are Grade II or II* in England and Wales, Category A, B or C(S) in Scotland.

HAR denotes listing on English Heritage's *Heritage at Risk* register
BAR denotes listing on Historic Scotland's *Buildings at Risk* register, or in Wales, listed as at risk by the local authority

● denotes building currently in use for swimming or in the process of being refurbished for swimming
○ denotes swimming facilities closed, and building either empty or converted to other use

Played in Britain welcomes additions and amendments. Please contact us via www.playedinbritain.co.uk

opened	location	address	listing	notes
1806	Cheltenham	Montpellier Baths, Bath Road GL53 7HG	II	○ built as spa, swimming pool added 1896, converted into Playhouse Theatre 1945
1820	London	Royal York Baths, York Terrace East NW1	II	○ baths area now occupied by Royal College of Music
1827	Huddersfield	Lockwood Spa Baths, Bath Street HD1	II	○ closed 1936, now light industrial use
1847	Bolton	Lower Bridgeman Street BL2 1DG	II	○ closed 1976, front section in use as business centre
1850	Hereford	Bath Street HR1		○ closed c.1930, building in use as masonic hall
1856	Kings Lynn	Common Staith Quay PE30 1LL	II	○ now Conservancy Board offices and leisure/boxing club
1856	Salford	Greengate, Collier St M3	II* HAR	○ converted into factory 1880, unoccupied since early 1990s
1859	Barnstaple	Queen Annes Walk EX31 1EU	II	○ converted into masonic hall 1868, since 1998 Barnstaple Heritage Centre
1859	Halifax	Park Road HX1 2TS	II	○ closed 1990, since 2001 Calderdale Community Church
1859	Scarborough	The Seawater Baths, Bland's Cliff YO11		○ closed 1904, building remains as amusement arcade
1862	Epsom	Epsom College KT17 4JQ		○ closed 1977, building converted into technology centre early 1990s
1863	Cambridge	former Roman Bath Co., Jesus Lane CB5 8BA		○ pool failed, building became the Pitt Club, since converted to restaurant
1864	Halifax	Crossley Heath School HX3 0HG		● oldest functioning pool in Britain
1866	Warrington	Legh Street WA1 1UQ		○ closed 2003, future plans uncertain
1868	Rochdale	Smith Street OL16 1HE		○ closed 1937, now Broadwater Centre for teaching circus skills
1870	Harrogate	Starbeck Baths, Spa Lane HG2 7JF		●
1870	Ashton under Lyne	Henry Square Baths OL6	II* HAR	○ closed 1975, future plans uncertain
1871	Southport	Victoria Baths, Promenade PR9 0DS	II	● renamed Victoria Leisure Southport, private members club, 3 of 6 pools in use
1871	Glasgow	Arlington Baths Club, Arlington Street G3 6DT	B	● private members club
1872	Barrow-in-Furness	Abbey Road LA14 5QW	II	○ closed c.1874, converted into Ramsden Hall
1874	Barnsley	York Street S70	II	○ closed 1980s, converted 1996 into supported housing scheme
1874	London	Seymour Place, Marylebone NW1		○ Pompeiian Baths, closed 1937 (adjoined Marylebone Baths, *see 1897 below*)
1874	Liverpool	Steble Street L8 6QH		● renamed Lifestyles Park Road
1876	Wolverhampton	Tettenhall College, Wood Rd WV6 8QX		●
1876	Cheadle Hulme	Cheadle Hulme School SK8 6EF		○ converted into gymnasium c.1912, then art room, now drama studio (*see 1911 below*)
1877	Bradford	Wapping Road School BD3	II	○ closed c.2000, planning permission for residential conversion
1878	Hastings	White Rock Baths, The Promenade TN34		○ closed 1911, re-opened 1931, closed early 1970s, 1980–97 ice rink, now derelict
1878	Glasgow	Victoria Baths Co., West Nile St G1 2QH	B	○ closed early 1900s, building since used as offices
1878	Glasgow	Western Baths Club, Cranworth St G12 8BZ	B	● private members club
1879	Sowerby Bridge	Hollins Mill Lane HX6 2QG		● scheduled for closure
1880	Cheltenham	Cheltenham College, College Baths Road GL53	II	○ closed 1989, now records office for Gloucestershire Hospitals NHS Foundation Trust
1880	Malvern	Imperial Baths, Avenue Road WR14 3BA		● now used as Malvern St James school pool

opened	location	address	listing	notes
1880	Nottingham	Boden Street, Radford NG7		○ closed 1970s, building unoccupied
1880	Salford	Blackfriars Road M3 7AQ	II	○ closed 1960, used as warehouse, converted 2001 into architects offices
1881	Greenock	West End Baths, Campbell Street PA16 8AP		○ closed 1940s, became Arts Guild Theatre 1955
1881	Eccles	Cromwell Road M30 0GT		○ closed c.1990, converted into centre for people with learning and physical disabilities
1882	Glasgow	North Woodside, Braid Square G4 9YQ	B	● renamed North Woodside Leisure Centre
1882	Redditch	Hewell Road B97 6BA		● originally outdoor, covered 1932
1883	Uppingham	Uppingham School LE15 9QE		● incorporated within new sports centre 1970
1883	Matlock Bath	Matlock Bath, North Parade DE4 3NS		○ former thermal pool, now Koi carp pool within Matlock Bath Aquarium
1884	Kendal	Allhallows Lane LA9 4JH	II	○ as washhouse b.1864, pool added 1884, closed 1980s, now Miles Thompson pub
1884	Blaby	Cottage Homes, Countesthorpe LE8		○ converted into housing c.1970s
1884	Carlisle	James Street CA2 5AH		● renamed the Pools Swimming & Health Centre
1884	Glasgow	Dennistoun Baths Club, Craigpark G31 2HE	B	○ private members club, closed 1993, now snooker club
1884	Ipswich	Ipswich School IP1 3SG		●
1884	Lancaster	Lancaster Royal Grammar School LA1 3EF		●
1884	Whitehaven	Duke Street CA28		○ closed 1986, nightclub 1989–c.2006, plans to redevelop site include demolition
1885	London	Forest Hill, Dartmouth Road SE23		○ closed 2006, site to be redeveloped into leisure centre
1885	London	Ladywell Road, Lewisham SE13	II HAR	○ closed, converted into youth centre, then gym and crèche 1985, currently unoccupied
1885	Penarth	The Esplanade CF64	II	○ closed 1985, converted into pub 1991, converted into residential 2004
1886	Newcastle	Shipley Street (now Place), Byker NE6 2DQ		○ closed c.2000, partly converted into gym, re-opened as Climb Newcastle 2008
1887	Beverley	Ladygate HU17		○ closed 1973, junk shop 1976-2006, sold for redevelopment and part demolition
1887	Edinburgh	Infirmary Street EH1 1LT	B	○ closed 1995, converted into gallery and centre for contemporary weaving 2008
1887	Edinburgh	Warrender Baths, Thurlestane Road EH9 1AP	B	● renamed Warrender Swim Centre
1887	London	Peoples Palace, Mile End Rd E1 4NS		○ closed, building now part of Queen Mary College
1887	Aberdeen	Constitution Street AB24 5TU		○ closed 1901, converted into tram then bus depot, now Satrosphere Science Centre
1888	Westbury	Church Street BA13 3BY		●
1889	Glossop	Howard Park, Dinting Road SK13 7DS		●
1888	Bootle	Balliol Road L20	II	○ demolished 2004, façade retained
1889	Bristol	Jacobs Wells Road, Hotwells BS8 1DX	II	○ closed 1977, Bristol Community Dance Centre since 1979
1889	Liverpool	Newhall L10 1LD		● renamed Lifestyles Newhall, closed 2008, plans for refurbishment
1889	Bradford	Station Rd, Queensbury BD13 1AB	II	● future under discussion
1890	Tunstall	Greengates Street ST6 6BL	II	●
1890	Leamington Spa	Royal Pump Rooms, The Parade CV32 4AA	II	○ closed c.1990, now public library
1890	Manchester	Whitworth, Ashton Old Rd M11 2HB		○ closed 1980s, building derelict
1890	St Helens	Boundary Road WA10 2LT		● renamed Queens Park Leisure Centre, plans for refurbishment
1891	Heywood	Grundy Baths, Fox Street OL10 1EF		○ closed 1975, now Kingdom Hall for Jehovah's Witnesses
1891	Whitchurch	Brownlow Street SY13		○ closed 1974, building unoccupied
1892	London	Dulwich, East Dulwich Road SE22 9AN	II	● renamed Dulwich Leisure Centre, plans for refurbishment
1892	Berkhamsted	Berkhamsted Collegiate School HP4		○ closed c.2000, plans for development
1892	Ilkley	Victoria Hall, Little Lane LS29 8EA		○ closed 1937, now antiques and fine art salerooms
1892	Edinburgh	Drumsheugh Baths, Belford Road EH4 3BL	B	● private members club
1892	London	Camberwell Baths, Artichoke Place SE5 8TS	II	● renamed Camberwell Leisure Centre, future under discussion
1892	London	Hornsey Road, Islington N7 6RZ	II HAR	○ closed 1991, redeveloped into residential 2008, neon sign to be restored
1892	Malvern	Malvern College WR14 3DF		● open, to be replaced by new sports centre 2009–10
1892	Swindon	Milton Road SN1 5JA	II	● renamed Health Hydro
1892	Wellingborough	Dulley's Baths, Castle Way NN8 1XB		○ closed 1918, factory 1920–1995, now Wellingborough Museum
1893	Batley	Cambridge Street WF17 5JH	II	● renamed Batley Baths & Recreation Centre
1893	Bacup	Maden Baths, Rochdale Road OL13 9NZ		○ closed 1990s, converted into children's and community centre 2002
1893	Egham	Royal Holloway College, London Rd TW20 0EX	II	○ closed 1980s, converted into lecture theatre
1893	Liverpool	Quarry Street, Woolton L25 6HD		●
1893	London	Great Smith Street, Westminster SW1P 3BU		○ pools demolished 1970s, front section Abbey Centre and Wash House Café since 1991
1894	Hove	Medina Baths, King's Esplanade B3 2WA		○ 1918-46 Hove Baths, part demolished, surviving section (Medina House) derelict
1894	Glasgow	St Bride's Primary School, Craigie St G42 8NB	B	● former Strathbungo Public School pool
1894	Ipswich	Fore Street IP4 1JZ		●
1894	London	Bathway, Woolwich SE18 6QX		○ closed c.1982, now student union for University of Greenwich

opened	location	address	listing	notes
1894	Port Glasgow	Bay Street PA14 5EB		● closed 2000–04 but re-opened after campaign
1895	Bishops Stortford	Bishops Stortford College CM23 2PJ		○ closed 2001, converted into lecture theatre
1895	Dundee	Lochee Baths, St Mary's Lane DD2 3AQ	B	● renamed Lochee Swim Centre
1895	London	Manor Place, Southwark SE17 3BD	II	○ closed 1978, pool now recycling centre, front block Buddhist Centre 2007
1895	London	Essex Rd / Greenman St / Tibberton Sq. N1		○ closed 1984, part of ironwork structure stands in Tibby Place park
1895	Edinburgh	Dalry Baths, Caledonian Crescent EH11 2AL	B	● renamed Dalry Swim Centre
1895	Nottingham	Stanley Road School NG7 6HW		○ converted into adult education centre 1990s
1896	Barnard Castle	Barnard Castle School DL12 8UN	II	●
1896	Dewsbury	Old Westgate WF13		○ closed 1975, currently unoccupied
1896	Nottingham	Victoria Baths, Gedling St NG1 1DB		● renamed Victoria Leisure Centre, future status uncertain
1896	London	Brentford Baths, Clifden Road TW8	II HAR	○ closed 1990, part converted into residential, remainder future uncertain
1896	Retford	Albert Road DN22 7AW		○ closed c.1976, converted into squash club
1896	Sheffield	Upperthorpe S6 3NA		● now Zest healthy living centre, pool run as part of trust with adjoining library
1896	Sheffield	Glossop Road, S10 2GW		○ closed 1991, now Swim Inn pub, plus restored Spa 1877 Turkish baths
1896	London	City University London, Islington EC1V 0HB	II HAR	○ closed c.1995, converted into School of Arts resource centre 2008
1896	Edinburgh	Dr Bell's Swimming Pool, Junction Place EH6	B	● schools and adult swimming lessons only
1897	Halifax	Warley Road Primary School HX1 3TG		●
1897	Leicester	Cossington Street LE4 6JD		● renamed Cossington Street Sports Centre
1897	London	Marylebone Road NW1		○ closed 1937, converted into Magistrates Court 1960s, to be demolished 2009
1897	London	St John Hackney Central Baths E5 0NU	II	● renamed King's Hall Leisure Centre
1898	Alloa	Primrose Street FK10 1JJ	B	○ closed 1986, gym and museum 1998, plans for conversion to library and dance centre
1898	Glasgow	Maryhill, Burnhouse Street G20 8BG	B BAR	● closed 1980s, currently being restored as leisure centre
1898	Hull	East Hull, Holderness Road HU9 1EA		●
1898	London	Laurie Grove, Deptford SE14 2NH	II	○ closed 1991, now part of Goldsmiths College
1898	Edinburgh	Junction Place, Leith EH6 5JA	B	● renamed Leith Victoria Swim Centre
1898	Loughborough	Memorial Baths, Granby Street LE11 3DU		○ closed c.1975, converted into Charnwood Museum 1999
1898	Rotherham	Moor Road, Wath upon Dearne S63 7RT		●
1898	Pontypool	West Monmouth School NP4 5YG	II	○ built with gym above, pool covered c.2000, converted into arts and music centre
1899	Crompton	Farrow Street, Shaw OL2 8NW		●
1900	Bristol	Muller Homes, Ashley Down BS7 9BU	II	○ former orphanage, pool closed, now refectory for City of Bristol College
1900	Aldershot	Command Swimming Pool, Queens Ave GU11	II	○ closed 1984, future of building uncertain
1900	Edinburgh	Glenogle Road EH3 5JB	B	● renamed Glenogle Swim Centre, closed 2008 for refurbishment
1900	Liverpool	Seamen's Orphanage, Newsham Park L6		○ orphanage and pool closed 1949, hospital 1951–88, currently derelict
1900	Skibo	Skibo Castle, Dornoch IV25 3RQ	B	● private members club
1901	Chester	Union Street CH1 1UA	II	● operated by community trust
1901	Edinburgh	Portobello, The Promenade EH15 2BS	B	● renamed Portobello Swim Centre
1901	London	St Pancras Baths, Prince of Wales Rd NW5	II HAR	● renamed Kentish Town Sports Centre, closed 2007–10 for refurbishment
1902	Birmingham	Woodcock Street B4 7ET	II	● renamed Woodcock Sports Centre, Aston University
1902	Atherton	Mayfield Street M46		○ closed 2005, building to be demolished and site redeveloped
1902	Birmingham	Green Lane, Small Heath B9 5DB	II	○ closed c.1977, in use as mosque
1902	Burnley	Gannow Baths, Sycamore Avenue BB12 6QP		○ closed 2004, in use as church
1902	Elland	Victoria Baths, Town Hall Street HX5 0EB		● renamed Elland Swimming Pool
1902	Glasgow	Whitevale Baths, Whitevale Street G31	B BAR	○ closed c.1978, tenants hall 1986-2004, future uncertain
1902	London	North End Road, Fulham SW6 1LY	II	○ closed 1981, rear pools demolished, front section converted to Dance Attic Studios
1902	Sidcup	The Hollies Childrens Home DA15 8WW		● childrens home closed 1989, pool remains as private members club
1902	Weston super Mare	Knightstone Island BS23 2BG	II	○ closed 1992, developed for residential
1902	Gillingham	North Road, Pembroke ME4 4TB	II	○ closed c.1984, building part of Universities of Medway, future uncertain
1903	Brighton	St Lukes Terrace BN2 9ZE	II	●
1903	Glasgow	Church Street Primary School G11	C(S)	○ closed c.1997, pool block in poor condition, future uncertain
1903	Halifax	Mount Pellon School HX1 4RG		○ closed 2003, building converted into classrooms
1903	Wigton	Wigton, Cumbria CA7 9AT		●
1903	Warrington	Culcheth Cottage Homes WA3		○ homes closed 1936, pool building converted into residential
1904	Birmingham	Cadbury's Girls' Baths, Bournville Lane B30	II	○ closed 1982, possible future as occupational health dept and gym by 2012
1904	Bradford	Manningham Pool, Drummond Road BD8 8DA	II	● future under discussion

opened	location	address	listing	notes
1904	Derby	Reginald Street DE23	II	○ closed 1983, front block converted to residential home for the elderly
1904	London	Acton, Salisbury Street W3 8NW		● future uncertain, chimney listed separately, Grade II
1904	London	Haggerston Baths, Whiston Road, Hackney E2	II HAR	○ closed 2000, building unoccupied awaiting decision
1904	Leeds	York Road LS9	II	○ closed 1968, former library and baths entrance block in poor state
1904	Leeds	Broad Lane, Bramley LS13 3DF	II	●
1904	Liverpool	Lister Drive L13 7HH		○ closed c.1987 now in use as pet centre and fisheries
1905	Ripon	Spa Baths, Park Street HG4 2BD	II	● pool added in 1936, future uncertain
1904	Portsmouth	Eastney Barracks, Melville Road PO4 9TB		● renamed Eastney Swimming Pool, run by city council since 1973
1904	Sheffield	Park Baths, Duke Street S2		○ closed 1991, converted into community youth centre
1904	Glasgow	Balshagray Public School, Broomhill Av G11	C(S)	○ school building became annexe of Anniesland College, pool derelict
1905	Bradford	Windsor Baths, Morley Street BD7 1AQ		○ closed c.1983, now Sir Titus Salt pub
1905	Bradford	Leeds Road BD3 9LY		○ closed c.1962, now Muslim community centre
1905	Bradford	Undercliffe Baths, Otley Road BD3		○ closed 1977, snooker centre 1979–90, now community centre
1905	Cambridge	The Leys School, Trumpington Rd CB2 7AD		●
1905	Dumfermline	Carnegie Centre, Pilmuir Street KY12 0QE	B	● renamed Carnegie Leisure Centre, closing for refurbishment 2009–10
1905	Eastbourne	Motcombe Road, Old Town BN21 1PU		●
1905	Hull	Beverley Road HU5 1AN	II	●
1905	London	Town Hall Approach Road, Tottenham N15	II	○ closed c.1988, converted to community hall, demolished 2007, chimney stands
1905	London	Ashby Mill School, Lyham Road, Brixton SW2		○ pool demolished, buildings converted into residential, boiler house and chimney stand
1905	Rhyl	Huxley Baths, Sussex Street LL18		○ closed late 1930s, converted to indoor market 1951, now shops
1906	Blackburn	Belper Baths, Daisy Lane BB1 5HB		● renamed Daisyfield Swimming Pools
1906	Devonport	Royal Naval Barracks HMS Drake PL2 2BG		●
1906	Lancing	Lancing College BN15 0RW		○ closed 1982, converted to theatre
1906	Liverpool	Picton Road, Wavertree L15 4LP	II	○ closed 1994, entrance block converted into One Stop Shop
1906	Manchester	Victoria Baths, Hathersage Road M13 0FE	II* HAR	○ closed 1993, partial renovation of buildings completed 2008, pools remain closed
1906	Birmingham	Tiverton Road, Selly Oak B29 6BU		● renamed Tiverton Pool and Fitness Centre
1907	London	Chelsea Manor Street, Chelsea SW3 5PL	II	● renamed Chelsea Sports Centre
1907	Birmingham	Moseley Road, Balsall Heath B12 9BX	II* HAR	● main pool closed, smaller pool open, future uncertain
1907	Birmingham	Grove Lane, Handsworth B21		○ pool sheds demolished c.1985, front block retained, Turkish bath area intact
1907	Newcastle	Gibson Street NE1 2LF	II	○ pool closed c.1965, now sports centre with badminton hall
1907	Shipley	Manor Lane BD18 3EA		○ closed 1977, used by furnishers business since 1984
1907	Bradford	Green Lane Primary School BD8 8HT	II	○ closed, building derelict for many years, being converted into gym
1908	Nottingham	Northern Baths, Vernon Road NG6 0BD		○ closed 1998, planning application for change of use to church
1908	Wallasey	Guinea Gap, Riverview Road CH44 6PX		● original frontage survives, new pools built mid 1980s, future uncertain
1908	Stockport	Gorton Road, Reddish SK6 5UG		○ closed 2005, building's future uncertain but likely conversion for other use
1909	York	Yearsley Swimming Pool, Haxby Road YO31 8SB		● originally outdoor, covered 1965
1909	Bath	Kingswood School, Lansdown Road BA1 5RG		●
1909	Forfar	Forfar Swimming Pool, The Vennel DD8 2AN		●
1909	Sheffield	Heeley Baths, Broadfield Road S8 0XQ		●
1909	Dover	Duke of York's Royal Military School CT15 5EQ	II	●
1909	Hamilton	Saffronhall Crescent ML3 6LE	B	○ closed 1995, front block retained as part of residential redevelopment 2006
1910	Belper	Gibfield Lane DE56 1WA	II	○ closed 1983, golf centre, night club, children's nursery since 2003
1910	Birmingham	Nechells Park Road B7 5PD	II	○ closed 1995, converted into community resource centre 2006
1910	Carshalton	Carshalton House, Pound Street SM5 3PS		● part of St Philomena's School
1910	London	Univ of Westminster, Regent Street W1B 2UW		○ former Polytechnic pool, closed c.1982, converted to bar
1910	Manchester	Harpurhey Baths, Rochdale Road M9 4AF	II	○ closed 2001, partially demolished 2004, converted to sixth form college
1910	Rochdale	Castleton Baths, Manchester Road OL11 3AF		○ closed 2005, re-opened 2007 for limited swimming sessions
1910	Oldham	Park Street, Royton OL2 6QW		●
1911	Birmingham	Bournville Lane, Stirchley B30	II	○ closed 1988, building derelict, future uncertain
1911	London	Royal Automobile Club, Pall Mall SW1Y 5HS	II*	● private members club
1911	London	Weston Road, Wood Green N22 6UH		○ closed 1980s, re-opened as the Decorium function suite 1997
1911	Cheadle Hulme	Cheadle Hulme School SK8 6EF		● (see also 1876 above)
1911	Reading	Arthur Hill, Kings Road RG1 4LS		●
1911	Chorley	Brinscall Swimming Pool, Lodge Bank PR6 8QU		●

opened	location	address	listing	notes
1912	Blackburn	Blakey Moor Ladies Bath, Northgate BB2		○ closed 1998, building now part of Blackburn College
1912	London	Barking Road, East Ham E6 2RT		○ closed 1990, front block only retained as part of East Ham Leisure Centre
1912	Wallsend	Lawson Street NE28 6PF	II	○ closed 2004, future of building uncertain
1913	Brighouse	Mill Royd Street HD6 1EY		○ closed 2006, to be demolished as part of site redevelopment
1913	Hawick	Bath Street TD9		○ closed 1982, building in use as sports hall
1913	Manchester	Burton Road, Withington M20 3EB		● renamed Withington Leisure Centre
1913	York	Bootham School YO30 7BU		●
1914	Barnsley	Hough Lane, Wombwell S73 0DP		●
1915	London	Elmfield Road, Balham SW17 8AN		● renamed Balham Leisure Centre
1915	Glasgow	Calder Street, Govanhill G42 7RA	B BAR	○ closed 2001, community trust planning to re-open pools by 2011
1915	Kirkham	Station Road PR4 2HA		● renamed Kirkham Pool
1916	Nottingham	Portland Baths, Muskham Street NG2 2HB		● renamed Portland Leisure Centre
1921	Manchester	Barlow Road, Levenshulme M19 3HE		● renamed Levenshulme Swimming Pools
1921	Buxton	Natural Mineral Baths, The Crescent SK17	II	● closed 1972, pools retained, being refurbished to re-open 2012
1921	Renfrew	Victory Baths, Inchinnan Road PA4 8ND	B	●
1922	Bristol	Bristol North Baths, Gloucester Road BS7 8AT	II	○ closed 2005, possible conversion into medical centre
1922	Gosport	St Vincent College, Mill Lane PO12 4QA		● renamed St Vincent Leisure Centre, shared between college and public
1922	Bloxwich	Field Close, Walsall WS3		○ originally outdoor, covered 1932-34, closed 1991, converted to function room
1923	Birmingham	Harborne Baths, Lordswood Road B17 9QS		● future uncertain
1923	Glasgow	Whiteinch Baths, Medwyn Street G14	B	○ closed 1998, most of building demolished, section of façade retained as feature
1923	Glasgow	Christian Street, Pollokshaws G43		○ closed 1980s, sports centre 1999, then boxing gym, currently unoccupied
1923	Esh Winning	Brandon Road DH7		○ pool, part of Memorial Hall, closed 1920s, building in poor condition
1924	Houghton le Spring	Lambton Lane DH4 6HP		○ closed, building in use by scrap metal dealer
1924	Bolsover	Duke Street, Creswell S80 4AS		● renamed Creswell Leisure Centre
1924	Sutton in Ashfield	Brook Street NG17 1ES		● smaller of two pools open as part of Sutton Pools Complex
1925	London	Porchester Baths, Queensway W2 5HS	II	● renamed the Porchester Centre
1925	Birmingham	Erdington Baths, Mason Road B24 9EJ		● renamed Erdington Leisure Centre
1926	Sheffield	Langsett Road, Hillsborough S6 2LN		○ closed 1990, now Rawson Spring pub
1927	Bingley	Myrtle Place BD16 2LF		● future uncertain
1928	Buckley	Mold Road CH7		○ closed 2005, future uncertain
1928	London	Trafalgar Road, Greenwich SE10 9UX		● renamed Arches Leisure Centre
1928	London	Streatham Baths, High Road SW16 6HX		● renamed Streatham Leisure Centre, due to close for redevelopment
1928	Newcastle	City Pool, Northumberland Road NE1 8SE	II	●
1928	Huddersfield	Scissett Baths, Wakefield Road HD8 9HU		●
1929	London	York Hall Baths, Old Ford Road E2 9PL		● main pool sports hall since c.1950, small pool replaced 1967
1929	Manchester	Manchester Road, Chorlton M21 9PQ		● renamed Chorlton Leisure Centre
1929	Nottingham	Noel Street NG7 6AT		● renamed Noel Street Leisure Centre, scheduled to close 2010
1929	Pudsey	Market Place LS28 7BE		● renamed Pudsey Leisure Centre
1929	Taunton	St James Street TA11JH		●
1930	Bournemouth	Stokewood Road BH3 7ND		● renamed Stokewood Leisure Centre
1931	Ashington	Institute Road NE63 8HP		● renamed Ashington Leisure Centre
1931	Birmingham	Sparkhill Baths, Stratford Road B11 4EA		● closed late 2008 for repairs, re-opening 2009
1931	Bristol	Bristol South, Dean Lane BS3 1BS	II	●
1931	London	Marshall Street, Westminster W1V 1LS	II HAR	○ closed 1997, main pool re-opening 2009 after major refurbishment
1932	Derby	Queen Street DE1 3PA		● renamed Queen's Leisure Centre, entrance now on Cathedral Road
1932	Doncaster	Central Baths, St James Street DN1 3BU		● renamed St James Pool and Everybody's Health Club
1932	Durham	Elvet Waterside DH1 3BW		○ closed 2008, future uncertain but likely to be demolished
1932	Kidderminster	Castle Road DY11 6TH		○ closed 1993, nightclub 1995–2005, demolished 2007 for flats, frontage retained
1932	Leeds	Armley Baths, Carr Croft LS12 3HB		● renamed Armley Leisure Centre
1932	London	Mile End Road Baths, Whitechapel E1 4AQ		○ closed 1981, frontage converted into centre for people affected by HIV and AIDS
1932	London	Clapham Manor Street, Clapham SW4 6DB		● closing 2009, to be replaced by new sports centre by 2011
1932	Manchester	Broadway, New Moston M40 0LN		● renamed Broadway Leisure Centre
1932	Wolverhampton	Heath Town, Tudor Rd WV10 0LT	II	○ closed 2002, future uncertain
1933	Birkenhead	Byrne Avenue, Rock Ferry L42 4PQ		● operated by community trust since 1996

opened	location	address	listing	notes
1933	Birmingham	Kent Street B5		○ closed 1977, converted to warehouse, currently unoccupied
1933	Darwen	Green Street BB3 1AA		○ closed 2006, portico only retained for new leisure centre
1933	Hull	Albert Avenue HU3 6QE		● renamed Albert Avenue Pools
1933	Sheffield	King Edward VII, Clarkehouse Rd S10 2LB		● renamed King Edwards Pool, run by charitable trust since 1993
1933	Smethwick	Thimblemill Road, Smethwick B67 5QT	II	● renamed Smethwick Swimming Centre
1933	Tipton	Queens Road DY4 8ND		● renamed Tipton Swimming Centre
1934	Bathgate	Mid Street EH48 1QD		●
1934	London	Poplar Baths, East India Dock Road E14 0EH	II HAR	○ closed 1988, used as industrial training centre, currently unoccupied
1934	London	Empire Pool, Empire Way, Wembley HA9 0DW	II	○ closed as pool 1948, in use as Wembley Arena
1934	London	Romford Road, West Ham E15 4JF		● renamed Atherton Leisure Centre
1934	Mansfield	Sherwood Baths, Westdale Road NG19 7BZ		● Sherwood Colliery baths, run by council since 1966, being refurbished 2009
1935	Sale	Washway Road M33 7RA		○ closed 1954, converted to ballroom, then bingo hall
1936	Airdrie	Stirling Street ML6 0AH		● renamed John Smith Pool, redeveloped 1995, original façade retained
1936	Rossendale	East Bank Avenue, Haslingden BB4 6NX		●
1936	Northampton	Mounts Baths, Upper Mounts NN1 3DN		● renamed Mounts Baths Leisure Centre
1936	Sunderland	Newcastle Road SR5 1JJ		○ closed 2008, to be marketed for alternative use
1937	Chadderton	Middleton Road OL9 0HG		○ closed 2007, to be replaced by new pool late 2009
1937	London	Seymour Place, Westminster W1H 5TH	II	● main pool converted to sports hall 1980s, renamed Seymour Leisure Centre
1937	Birmingham	Bristol Road South, Northfield B31 2PD		● renamed Northfield Pool and Fitness Centre
1937	Bristol	Speedwell, Whitefield Road BS5 7TJ		○ closed 2005, site to be redeveloped
1937	Bristol	Jubilee, Jubilee Road BS4 2LP		● due to close September 2010
1937	Crewe	Flag Lane CW2 7QX		● future under discussion
1937	Rochdale	Entwisle Road OL16 2HZ		● renamed Central Leisure Centre
1937	Salford	Bridgewater Road, Walkden M28 3AB		● renamed Fit City Worsley Pool
1938	Bridgend	Alfred Street, Maesteg CF34 9YW		● originally outdoor, covered 1969, refurbished 1993
1938	Rothesay	Battery Place PA20		○ closed mid 1980s, converted into residential
1938	Coventry	Livingstone Road, Foleshill CV6 5AR		● renamed Foleshill Leisure Centre
1938	London	New Heston Road, Heston TW5 0LW		●
1938	Newport	Victoria Avenue, Maindee N19 8GF	II BAR	○ closed 2005, future of building uncertain
1938	London	Ironmonger Row, Islington EC1V 3QF	II	●
1938	Newcastle	Jesmond Pool, St George's Terrace NE2 2DL		● closed 1991, re-opened 1992 under community trust management
1938	Newcastle	Fenham Pool, Fenham Hall Drive NE4 9XD		● closed 2003, re-opened 2005 under commmunity trust management
1938	Sutton	Malden Road, North Cheam SM3 8EP		● renamed Cheam Leisure Centre
1939	London	Arnos Pool, Bowes Road, Enfield N11 1BD	II	●
1939	Hove	King Alfred Baths, Kingsway BN3 2WW		○ pool now sports hall, leisure centre added c.1981, future of complex uncertain
1939	London	Twickenham Road, Isleworth TW7 7EU		● renamed Isleworth Recreation Centre
1939	Lancaster	Kingsway LA1	II	○ closed 1997, demolished 2005, elements of façade retained
1939	London	Sherard Road, Eltham SE9		○ closed 2008, site sold for development, future of building uncertain
1939	Willenhall	Bath Street, Walsall WV13 2EY		○ pool closed, building remains in use as Willenhall Leisure Centre
1940	Aberdeen	Bon Accord, Justice Mill Lane AB11 6EQ	B	○ closed 2008, future of building uncertain
1941	Gateshead	Shipcote Pool, Alexandra Rd NE8 4JA		● part of Gateshead Leisure Centre

Part Two 1945 – 1970

These are post war pools that are listed and either in operation or in the process of being refurbished as of late 2008. (Note: there are no indoor pool buildings from this period that are listed but that have been converted to other uses.)

opened	location	address	listing	notes
1962	London	Golden Lane Estate, Fann Street EC1Y 0SH	II	● renamed Golden Lane Leisure Centre
1964	London	Crystal Palace National Sports Centre SE19 2BB	II*	● closed 2007 for refurbishment, re-opening 2009
1965	East Kilbride	Dollan Aqua Centre G74 1AF	A	● closed Oct 2008 for refurbishment, re-opening 2010
1966	Coventry	Fairfax Street CV1 5RY	II	● renamed Coventry Sports & Leisure Centre, refurbishment being considered
1966	Richmond	Pools on the Park, Twickenham Rd TW9 2SF	II	● also outdoor pool
1970	Edinburgh	Royal Commonwealth Pool, Dalkeith Rd EH16	A	● scheduled for refurbishment 2009–11

Links

Where no publisher listed assume self-published by organisation or author

Where no publication date listed assume published on final date within title, ie. 1860–1960 means published 1960

Abbreviations:
UP University Press

Books

Allsop RO *Public Baths and Wash-houses* Spon & Chamberlain (1894)

Amateur Swimming Association Year Books ASA (from 1869)

Ashpitel A & Whichcord J *Baths and Wash-houses – their history* Richards (1853)

Baker WK *Acton* (1912)

Beauchampé S & Inglis S *Played in Birmingham* English Heritage (2006)

Beer G *A village called Starbeck* (1983)

Besford P *Encyclopaedia of Swimming* Hale (1971)

Billups B *Crewe Swimming Baths* (1984)

Bilsborough P *100 Years of Scottish Swimming* SASA (1988)

Binney M et al *Taking the Plunge: The Architecture of Bathing* Save Britain's Heritage (1982)

Bird P *Making a splash: the history of Dulwich Baths* (1993)

Brendon P *The Motoring Century: the story of the Royal Automobile Club* Bloomsbury (1997)

Brooke R *Liverpool as it was in the last quarter of the 18th century 1775-1800* Mawdsley (1853)

Campbell A *Report on Public Baths and Wash-houses* Carnegie United Kingdom Trust (1918)

Cape GA *Baths and Wash-houses* Simpkin, Marshall (1854)

Cottam D *Sir Owen Williams* Architectural Association (1986)

Cross AWS *Public Baths and Wash-houses* Batsford (1906)

Cross AWS and Cross KMB *Modern Public Baths and Wash Houses* Simpkin Marshall (1930)

Cross KMB *Modern Public Baths* Simpkin Marshall (1938)

Darwin B *A Century of Medical Service – the story of the GWR Medical Fund Society 1847-1947*

Deakin R *Waterlog* Chatto & Windus (1999)

Dickens C *Dictionary of London 1879* Howard Baker (1972)

Dudgeon RE *The Swimming Baths of London* (1870)

Ellison P & Howe P *Talk of the Wash House* Picton (1997)

Fabian D *Modern Swimming Pools of the World* National Pool Equipment Co (1958)

Gilmour J (ed) *100 Years of Warrender Baths Club* (1990)

Glanfield J *Earls Court and Olympia* Sutton (2003)

Glendinning M *Rebuilding Scotland: The Postwar Vision 1945-75* Tuckwell Press (1997)

Gomme AH, Walker D (eds) *Architecture of Glasgow* Lund Humphries (1987)

Harper RH *Victorian Architectural Competitions: An Index to The Builder 1843-1900* Mansell (1983)

Hibbert C & Weinreb B *The London Encyclopedia* MacMillan (2008)

Hubbard E *The Work of John Douglas* Victorian Society (1991)

Inglis S *Played in Manchester* English Heritage (2004)

John G & Heard H (eds) *Handbook of Sports & Recreational Design – Vol 3 Ice Rinks & Swimming Pools* Butterworth Architecture (1996)

Jones DL *History of Swimming in Ipswich 1329–1984* Ipswich Borough Council

Juba K *TSB Bank Swimming & Swimming Pool Guide* (1989)

Juba K *A Short History of Water Polo* HNI & LEN (2007)

Juba K *The Story of LEN* HNI & LEN (2008)

Kelly M *Life and Times of Kitty Wilkinson* Countyvise (2007)

Langdon C *Earls Court* Stanley Paul & Co (1953)

Love C (ed) *A Social History of Swimming in England 1800-1918* Routledge (2008)

Loxton S *Loxton's Bristol* Redcliffe Press (1992)

McLeod N *Tales of the Arlington* Hyndland Press (1997)

Mann WM *The Baths: the story of the Western Baths, Hillhead 1876-1990* Western Baths Club

Modern Baths and Laundries National Association of Bath Superintendents (1961)

Nasaw D *Andrew Carnegie* Penguin 2006

Newbold EB *Portrait of Coventry* Robert Hale (1972)

Orme N *Early British Swimming 55BC-AD1719* Exeter UP (1983)

Parr M (intro) *Our True Intent is All for Your Delight – The John Hinde Butlin's Photographs* Chris Boot (2002)

Pass AJ *Thomas Worthington: Victorian Architecture and Social Purpose* Manchester Lit & Phil Society (1988)

Pearson L *Tile Gazetteer: a guide to British tile and architectural ceramics locations* Richard Dennis (2005)

Physick R *Played in Liverpool* English Heritage (2007)

Sachs F *The Complete Swimmer* Methuen (1912)

Scadding A *Benevolence and Excellence: 150 Years of The Royal Medical Foundation of Epsom College* (2004)

Sinclair A & Henry W *The Badminton Library – Swimming* Longman Green & Co (1916)

Smith J *Liquid Assets* English Heritage (2005)

Wilkie D, Besford P & Wilkie TL *Wilkie* Kemps (1976)

Wilkins R *Turrets, towels and taps* Birmingham Museums & Art Gallery (1984)

Williams IA *Cadbury, 1831–1931* Constable (1931)

Williams MT *Washing the Great Unwashed: public baths in urban America 1840–1920* Ohio State UP (1991)

Williams P *Victoria Baths: Manchester's Water Palace* Spire Books (2004)

Williamson E, Riches A & Higgs M *The Buildings of Scotland: Glasgow* Penguin (1990)

Willis P *New Architecture in Scotland* Lund Humphries 1977

Wimmer M *Olympic Buildings* Edition Leipzig (1976)

Winstone R *Bristol in the 1920's* (1971)

Reports

Baly PP *A Statement of the Proceedings of the Committee Appointed to Promote the Establishment of Baths and Wash-houses* (1852)
Ebsworth A *Facts and Inferences from inspection of the public baths in this metropolis* (1853)
Newlands J *Report on the establishment and condition of public baths in Liverpool* (1857)
Payne EH *Suggestions on General Arrangements of Public Swimming Baths* (1912)
Smith W *Swimming Club Directory for the UK* (1885)
Thomson W *Glasgow Corporation Baths and Wash-houses* (1892)
Turner E *Paris Exhibition: Report on Public Baths and Wash-houses* (1889)
Provision for Sport The Sports Council (1971)
Purification of the Water at Swimming Baths HMSO (1929)
Testing the Waters: The Sport of Swimming Select Cttee on Culture, Media and Sport, Second Report HC418 (2001)

Conservation plans and statements

Conservation Statement on Ironmonger Row Baths Architectural History Practice (2007)
Forest Hill Pools, Historic Buildings Report Doug Insall Associates (2008)
Govanhill Baths Statement of Significance Historic Scotland (2005)
Haggerston Baths, Hackney – Conservation Statement Architectural History Practice (2005)
Ironmonger Row – Conservation Statement Architectural History Practice (2007)
Kentish Town Sports Centre: PPG15 Assessment Alan Baxter Associates (2008)
Marylebone Road Baths and Courts – Historic Buildings Report Doug Insall Associates (2006)
Moseley Road Library and Baths Conservation Plan Rodney Melville & Partners (2007)
Royal Commonwealth Pool, Edinburgh Conservation Plan LDN Architects (2007)
Victoria Baths Conservation Plan Architectural History Practice & Lloyd Evans Prichard (2004)

Unpublished dissertations

Ablitt P *The Development of Swimming Pools in the 19th century, with specific regard to Hull* University of Hull (2005)
Campbell D *Scottish Baths 1868–1914 and their Conservation* Heriott-Watt University (1993)
Copeman M *The Public Baths and Wash-Houses of London: 1840-1914* Heriot-Watt Univ MSc dissertation (1994)
Harbar V A *Holy and endangered activity? Birmingham's Edwardian baths* Birmingham University (2007)
Illingworth M *Newcastle City Hall – an architectural history* Univ of Newcastle (1985)
Ramsden S *Baths, Wash-houses, swimming pools and social history: a case for conservation* York University (2001)

Skoski JR *Public Baths & Washhouses in Victorian Britain 1842-1914* Indiana University (2000)

Articles

Bird P *The Origins of Victorian Public Baths* Local Historian Vol 25 (1995)
Bromhead J *George Cadbury's Contribution to Sport* The Sports Historian Vol 20, 1 (2000)
Cross KMB *Public Baths and Their Future Development* Journal of Royal Society for the Promotion of Health (1927)
Grierson AMM *Observations on the Hygiene Conditions of Public Swimming Baths* Journal of Hygiene (1930)
Horwood C *Girls who arouse dangerous passions: women and bathing 1900-1939* Women's History Review Vol 9, 4 (2000)
Parker C *Improving the 'Condition' of the People: the Health of Britain and the Provision of Public Baths 1840–1870* The Sports Historian Vol 20, 2 (2000)
Tiltman AH *Public Baths and Wash-houses* RIBA Journal (1899)

Journals

Architects' Journal; Architect & Building News; Architectural Design and Construction; Architectural Review; Baths and Baths Engineering; Baths Bulletin; Baths Service; Baths Service and Recreation Management; The Builder; Building Conservation Journal; Building News; Building Renewal; Concrete and Constructional Engineering; Design; Design and Construction; Glazed Expressions; Municipal and Public Services Journal; Recreation; Scottish Country Life; Sporting Life; Swimming Pool News; Swimming Pool Review, Swimming Times; Twentieth Century Society newsletters; Victorian Society newsletters

Newspapers & magazines

Aberdeen Evening Express; Aberdeen Press & Journal; Acton Gazette; Alloa Advertiser; Alloa Journal; Birmingham Evening Mail; Birmingham Post; Bolton Journal; Bournville Works Magazine; Bradford Telegraph & Argus; Camden Gazette; Crewe Chronicle; Dunfermline Journal; Dunfermline Press; Eastern Morning News; East Kilbride News; Edinburgh Evening News; Express & Star; Fulham Chronicle; Glasgow Herald; Glossop Chronicle; The Guardian; Hackney & Kingsland Gazette; Halifax Evening Courier; Halifax Guardian; Highbury & Islington Express; Hull Daily Mail; Illustrated London News; Kensington & Bayswater Chronicle; The Lady's Newspaper and Pictorial Times; London; Manchester Evening News; Middlesex Chronicle; Newcastle Chronicle; New Society; Northampton & County Independent; Paisley & Renfrewshire Gazette; Pictorial Bolton News; Pictorial Times; Rochdale Observer; Rossendale Free Press; Salford Advertiser; Scottish Country Life; South London Press; Southport Daily News; South Wales Echo; Sporting Life; Sunday Times; Swindon Evening Advertiser; The Scotsman; The Times; The Times Online Digital Archive 1785-1985; Variant (Glasgow); Western Mail; Wiltshire Times; Yorkshire Post

Websites – heritage

www.english-heritage.org.uk
www.historic-scotland.gov.uk
www.cadw.wales.gov.uk
www.c20society.org.uk
www.victorian-society.org.uk
www.cabe.org.uk
www.savebritainsheritage.org
www.imagesofengland.org.uk
www.rcahms.gov.uk

Websites – historic baths

www.camberwellbathscampaign.org
www.govanhillbaths.com
www.haggerstonpool.com
www.londonpoolscampaign.com
www.moseleyroadbaths.co.uk
www.poplarbaths.org.uk
www.saveladywellpool.com
www.saveourspa.co.uk
www.savevictoriabaths.org.uk
www.victoriabaths.org.uk
www.victorianturkishbath.org

Websites – swimming and pools

www.britishswimming.org
www.scottishswimming.com
www.welshasa.co.uk
www.diving-gbdf.com
www.british-waterpolo.org.uk
www.isrm.co.uk
www.sporta.org
www.lmca.info
www.swimmersguide.com
http://groups.yahoo.com/group/poolingresources

Websites – general

www.architecture.com
www.riba.org
www.scottisharchitects.org.uk
www.british-history.ac.uk
www.oxforddnb.com
www.wellcomecollection.org
www.sportengland.org
www.activeplaces.com
www.sportscotland.org.uk
www.sports-council-wales.org.uk
www.london2012.com
www.butlinsmemories.com
www.abandoned-britain.com

Credits

Photographs and images

Please note that where more than one photograph appears on a page, each photograph is identified by a letter, starting with 'a' in the top left hand corner of the page, or at the top, and continuing thereafter in a *clockwise* direction.

All English Heritage and National Monument Record photographs listed are either © English Heritage or © Crown Copyright. NMR. Application for the reproduction of these images should be made to the National Monuments Record, at Kemble Drive, Swindon SN2 2GZ. Tel. 01793 414600.

English Heritage/National Monuments Record photographs

Steve Cole: 93, 204b, 206, 207ab; Nigel Corrie: 64a, 65, 186abc, 187a, 200b, 201b, 209ab, 220, 221a, 222ac, 223, 264, 267c; James O Davies: 57bd, 68ab, 69b, 82ab, 83, 113c, 114a, 122, 123ab, 168, 173b, 174c, 178, 179abc, 265, 277a; Damian Grady: 143, 237, 246a; Paul McDonald: 147, 150a; Bob Skingle: 4, 10, 17, 30, 31, 46b, 48, 49bc, 57a, 58cd, 92a, 108, 113b, 131abc, 138, 139, 140abc, 141, 142, 144abcd, 145, 146ac, 148, 150b, 182c, 188b, 189, 261c; Peter Williams: 84, 85ab; NMR: 88ab, 89, 129, 198, 236, 238ac, 239

Ian Gordon archive

inside front cover, 7, 28, 34, 39b, 62, 63, 64b, 72b, 76, 77b, 113a, 114b, 116, 118, 119, 120ab, 153b, 169, 172, 174d, 177b, 181ab, 182a, 205, 213ab, 214c, 216, 229a, 230ab, 235a, 262a

Photographers

Mark Allan: 201a; Steve Beauchampé: 109, 111b, 121d, 151b, 154, 155, 157, 158, 159ab, 161abc, 195ab, 267a, 273ac; Tony Bowyer: 110; David Brearley: 112; Jon Burgerman: 94a; Colin Gray: 1; Nick Hanna: 77c; Ellie Harrison: back cover d, 94b, 95c; Keith Hunter: 184ab; Laura Hughes: 224ab, 225bcd; Simon Inglis: back cover abc; 12, 13, 14, 15, 21b, 23abcd, 33a, 51, 57c, 58abe, 60ab, 70, 71abc, 72a, 73, 74, 75abcd, 78ab, 79, 80ab, 81, 86, 87, 90abc, 91ac, 97bcde, 100, 101ab, 102, 103, 107ab, 111ac, 121abc, 124, 125abc, 126, 127ab, 151a, 152, 156, 160, 164, 165, 166abc, 167ab, 174b, 183ab, 187b, 190, 192b, 193a, 201c, 202, 203abc, 208, 214ab, 215abc, 218abc, 219, 221b, 222b, 241abd, 242, 243, 246b, 247, 254, 255abc, 256, 266abcd, 267b, 268abc, 269abc, 270, 271ab, 272b, 273b, 275a, 276ab, 277b; Geraint John: 66, 258b; Alison Kershaw: front flap; Xtina Lamb: 174a; Jon Parker Lee: 149abcdef; Lynn Pearson: 188a; Teri Pengilley: 192a; Ian Segar: 20; Derek Trillo: 235b; Mark Watson: 47, 67ab, 146b, 151c; Bob Wheat 275b; Jason Wood: 182b; Anne Worthington 275ac

Archives and agencies

Aberdeen City Council: inside back cover; AP Archive / RIBA Library Photographs Collection: 231ab, 232ab, 233ab, 234b, 240, 245a, © Joseph McKenzie 248; Bath in Time, Bath Central Library: 26; Birmingham Central Library: 39ac, 171, 176b; Blom Aerofilms: 104; © Bolton Council, Bolton Museum & Archive Service: 29b; Bracknell Forest Council: 259a; © British Library Board. All rights reserved: 53a (EVAN.1882), 95a (CC.2.h.5); Butlin's Archives: 229b; Camberwell Baths Campaign: 91b; Camden Local Studies & Archives Centre: 35, 105ab, 106abc, 232c; Cannons Health & Fitness/Alex Orrow: 153a; City of London, London Metropolitan Archives: 55b; Coventry Heritage & Arts Trust: 241c; Crossley Heath School: 49a; Davlan: 258a; Derby City Council: 194; © Dundee Central Library. Licensor www.scran.ac.uk: 56b; Dunfermline Carnegie Library: 133ab, 134ab, 135ab; Durham Mining Museum: 173a; EC&O Venues: 212; EC&O Venues/Adrian Bray: 217abc; East Anglian Daily Times: 176c; FaulknerBrowns Architects 249bc, 259c, 261ab; Fife Sports & Leisure Trust: 136ab, 137; Walter Gardiner Photography Collection www.westsussexpast.org.uk: 244, 245b; Getty Images: 196, 197; Greenwich Leisure Ltd/Andrew Baker 191ab; Guildhall Library, City of London: 21a, 27b; Joan Gurney: 11, 16b, 56a, 61, 177c; Guthrie Aerial Photography: 249a; Hastings Reference Library: 77a; Hodder Associates: 263a; Institute of Sport & Recreation Management: 227, 257, 292; Islington Library & Cultural Services: 59; Lambeth Borough Council Archives Dept: 53b; Leeds Library & Information Services www.leodis.net: 44, 130, 234a; Link4Life/i2C Photography: 211; Arthur Little: 42, 46a; Liverpool Record Office, Liverpool Libraries: front cover, 24, 25, 29a, 33b, 36, 37, 175; Local Studies, Kensington Central Library: 260a; London 2012: 9, 263c; Manchester Archives & Local Studies: 228b; Manchester College of Arts & Technology/ David Snelson: 272a; Robbie Macgregor: 252b, 253b; Media Wales Ltd: 228a; Mounts Baths Leisure Centre: 204a; © Museum of London: 27a; © National Museums Scotland. Licensor www.scran.ac.uk: 132; National Portrait Gallery, London: 32; Nottingham City Council www.picturethepast.org.uk: 22; Nottingham Evening Post: 6; ©Perth Museum and Art Gallery. Licensor www.scran.ac.uk: 52; Picture Sheffield Collection, Sheffield Local Studies Library: 2; Renfrewshire Leisure: 185; RIBA Library Photographs Collection: 54, 55a, 69a, 199b, 238b; Pat Roberts: 95b; RMJM Architects: 250, 251, 252a, 253a; Rochdale Local Studies Library: 210abc ; © Royal Commission on the Ancient and Historical Monuments of Scotland, Bedford Lemere Collection: 50, 96, 97a; © Royal Commission on the Ancient and Historical Monuments of

Scotland. Licensor www.scran.ac.uk: 99ab; S&P Architects: 8, 262b, 263b; Savills: 274ab; Smethwick Heritage Centre Trust/Victor Bryant: 195c; Sports Stadium Brighton Archive: 180ab; Steele Images: 200a; Tees Active Leisure: 16a; The Carnegie Club at Skibo Castle: 98ab; The Roman Baths, Bath & North East Somerset Council: 18; The Royal Automobile Club: 162ab, 163; ©The Scotsman Publications Ltd. Licensor www.scran.ac.uk: 260b; University of St Andrews Library: 225a; Wellcome Library, London: 19, 38, 40, 43, 45; Wembley Arena: 199a; Westminster City Council: 193b; JD Wetherspoon: 271c; Jo Wilcox: 170; www.everyoneactive.com/Chris Spencer: 226

Books

Campbell A *Report on Public Baths and Wash-houses* Carnegie UK Trust (1918): 117; Cross AWS *Public Baths and Wash-houses* Batsford (1906): 115, 128ab; Cross KMB *Modern Public Baths* Simpkin Marshall (1938): 176a, 177a; Ewart & Son catalogue: 4; John G & Campbell K (eds) *Handbook of Sports & Recreational Building Design Vol 3 Ice Rinks & Swimming Pools* Butterworth Architecture 1996: 259b

Acknowledgements

English Heritage, Played in Britain and the authors would like to thank the many individuals and organisations who have assisted with information, support and access to the nation's historic swimming pools.

They are especially grateful to S&P Architects for their generous sponsorship, and to Keith Ashton, Rob Guy, Mike Lee and Ben Slater at S&P in particular.

Played in Britain is further grateful for the support received from English Heritage's Historic Environment Enablement Programme, and from a number of English Heritage personnel, especially Barney Sloane, Allan Brodie and Gary Winter, and also Elain Harwood, John Hudson, Clare Blick and June Warrington.

Historic Scotland and Cadw have been extremely supportive, as have the Victorian Society and the 20th Century Society.

Special thanks go to Gill Wright and all the team at the Victoria Baths Trust in Manchester, and to Liz Hughes of the London Pools Campaign.

For their support, technical expertise, statistical data and access to documents we are grateful to Noel Winter, Wendy Coles and Tom Neale at the Amateur Swimming Association; to Ralph Riley and Christian Anderson at the Institute of Sport and Recreation Management; to Andrew St Ledger at Sport England, Karen McCall at sportscotland and John Hinton at the Sports Council for Wales.

A number of architectural practices and architectural historians have been tremendously helpful, including Bill Stonor and Jackie Gardner at FaulknerBrowns, Alan Baxter Associates and the Architectural History Practice.

We are also grateful to Played in Britain authors Steve Beauchampé, Lynn Pearson and Ray Physick for additional research, and to the following individuals:

John Anderson (Friends of Bon Accord), Trevor Chepstow (Sports Stadium Brighton Archive), Ian Dungavell (Victorian Society), Peter Fewing (Wembley Arena), Dave Flora (Moseley Road), Terry Gallagher (Kentish Town), Joan and Gerald Gurney, Geoff Hollis (Shaws of Darwen), Sue Hudson (Marshall Street), Geraint John, Andrew Johnson (Govanhill Baths Trust), Vernon Jones (Coal Industry Social Welfare Organisation), Paul Kenny (Fulham), Robbie Macgregor (Royal Commonwealth Pool, Edinburgh), Fred Morris (Chester Swimming Association), James Seymour (Northampton), Malcolm Shifrin (Victorian Turkish Baths wesbite), Ray Simpson (Earls Court), Anne Steer (Arlington Baths Club), Rose Taylor (Crossley Heath School), Sally Wainman (Pooling Resources Yahoo forum), Professor Roger White (Institute of Archaeology & Antiquity, Birmingham University) and Martyn Woodruffe.

Additional thanks go to the dozens of librarians and archivists in local studies and school libraries all over Britain, too many to mention but all so helpful, friendly and a pleasure to deal with.

We are also particularly grateful to the staff at the RIBA Library and photographic archive, and to their counterparts at the Wellcome Library.

Ian Gordon and Simon Inglis wish to express further personal thanks to all the many pool managers, attendants and members of staff who gave up valuable time to show them around their facilities; too many to name individually, but without exception all great enthusiasts and dedicated professionals.

There are no greater supporters of historic baths than the staff who run them.

Ian Gordon wishes to add his own personal thanks to two groups of people.

Firstly, to the many swimmers whose company and friendship he has enjoyed whilst training in different pools around Britain over the last thirty years, and in particular the coaches at Worthing SC and Bournemouth Dolphins SC, especially Laurie Dormer, and to all his friends at the Littledown Masters.

Secondly, to his wife Judy and daughters Sarah and Emma, for putting up with so many impromptu detours over the years to visit baths and swimming pools around Britain with only nominal complaint.

Finally, Played in Britain thanks Beth Macdougall, Bethan Jones and Stephen Clousard at MGA for all their support for the Played in Britain series.

Index